オールドボーイ

ルーズ戦記

OLDBOY

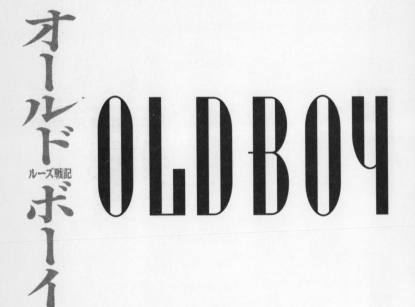

publisher
MIKE RICHARDSON

editor
CHRIS WARNER

collection designer
DARIN FABRICK

art director
LIA RIBACCHI

English-language version produced by DARK HORSE MANGA.

Dark Horse Manga
A division of Dark Horse Comics, Inc.
10956 S.E. Main Street
Milwaukie OR 97222

darkhorse.com

To find a comics shop in your area, call the Comic Shop Locator Service toll-free at 1-888-266-4226

First edition: November 2006
ISBN-10: 1-59307-569-3
ISBN-13: 978-1-59307-569-9

1 3 5 7 9 10 8 6 4 2
Printed in Canada

OLDBOY

volume 2

story by
GARON TSUCHIYA

art by
NOBUAKI MINEGISHI

translation
KUMAR SIVASUBRAMANIAN

lettering and retouch
MICHAEL DAVID THOMAS

DARK HORSE MANGA™

CONTENTS

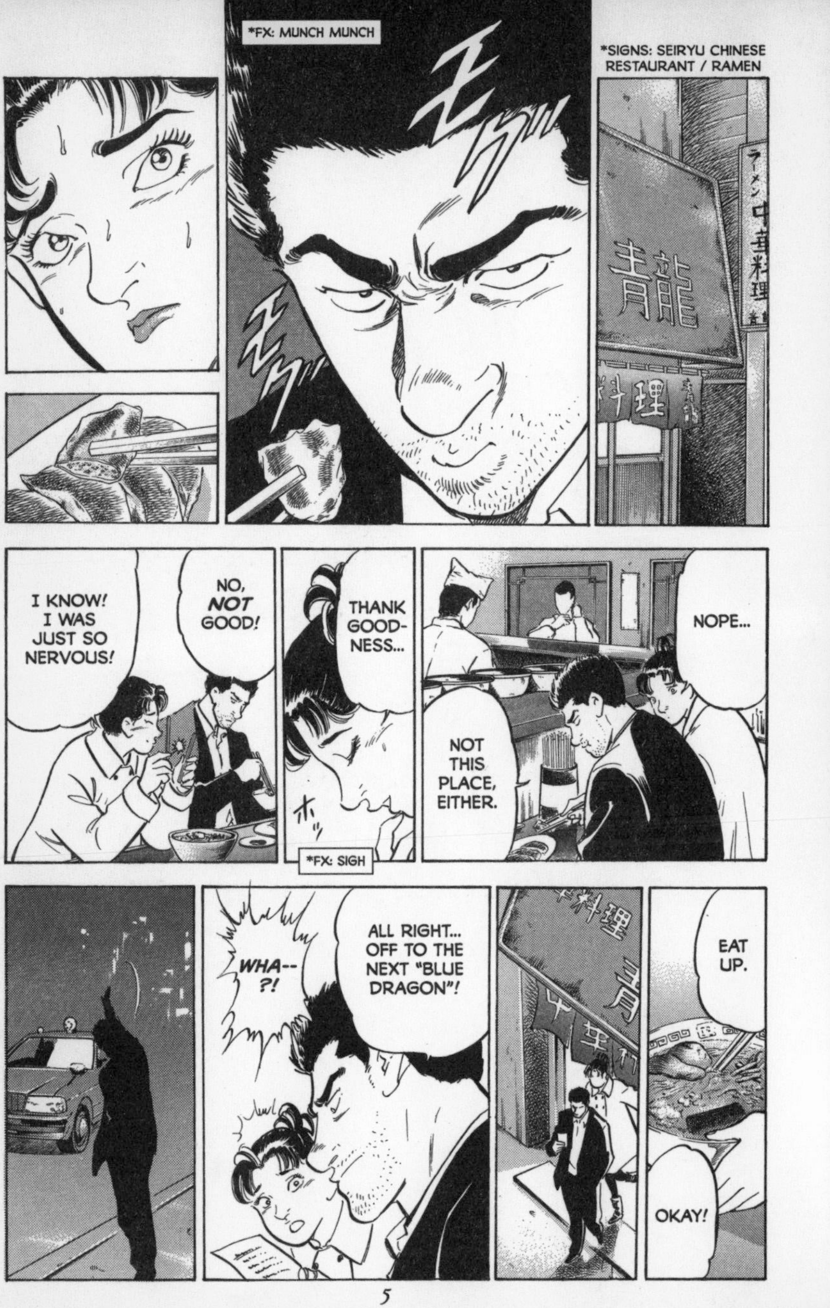
*SIGNS: SEIRYU CHINESE RESTAURANT / RAMEN
*FX: MUNCH MUNCH
NOPE...
NOT THIS PLACE, EITHER.
THANK GOODNESS...
*FX: SIGH
NO, **NOT** GOOD!
I KNOW! I WAS JUST SO NERVOUS!
EAT UP.
OKAY!
ALL RIGHT... OFF TO THE NEXT "BLUE DRAGON"!
WHA-- ?!

第10話◎龍を探せ

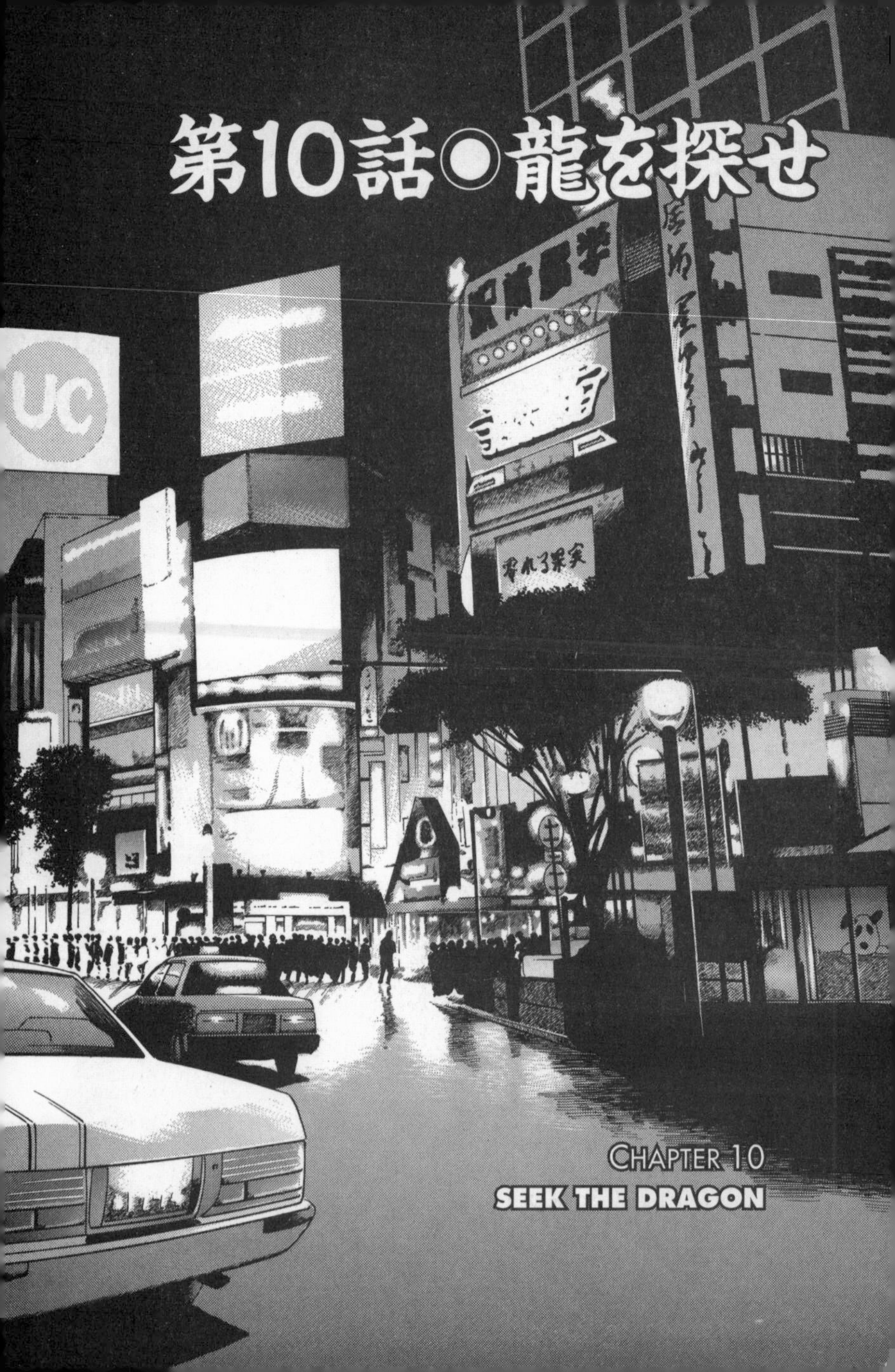

CHAPTER 10
SEEK THE DRAGON

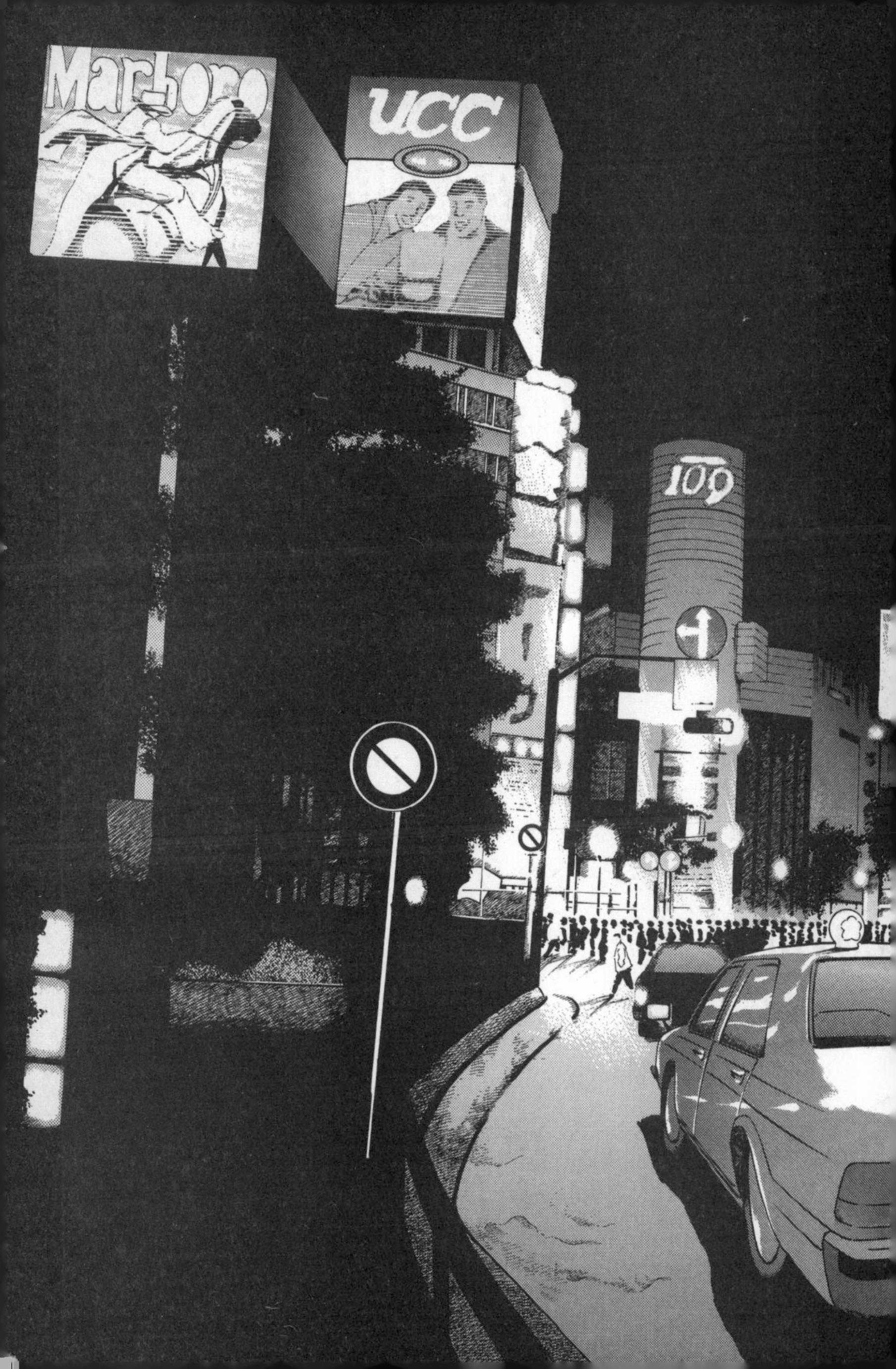

Marlboro
UCC
109

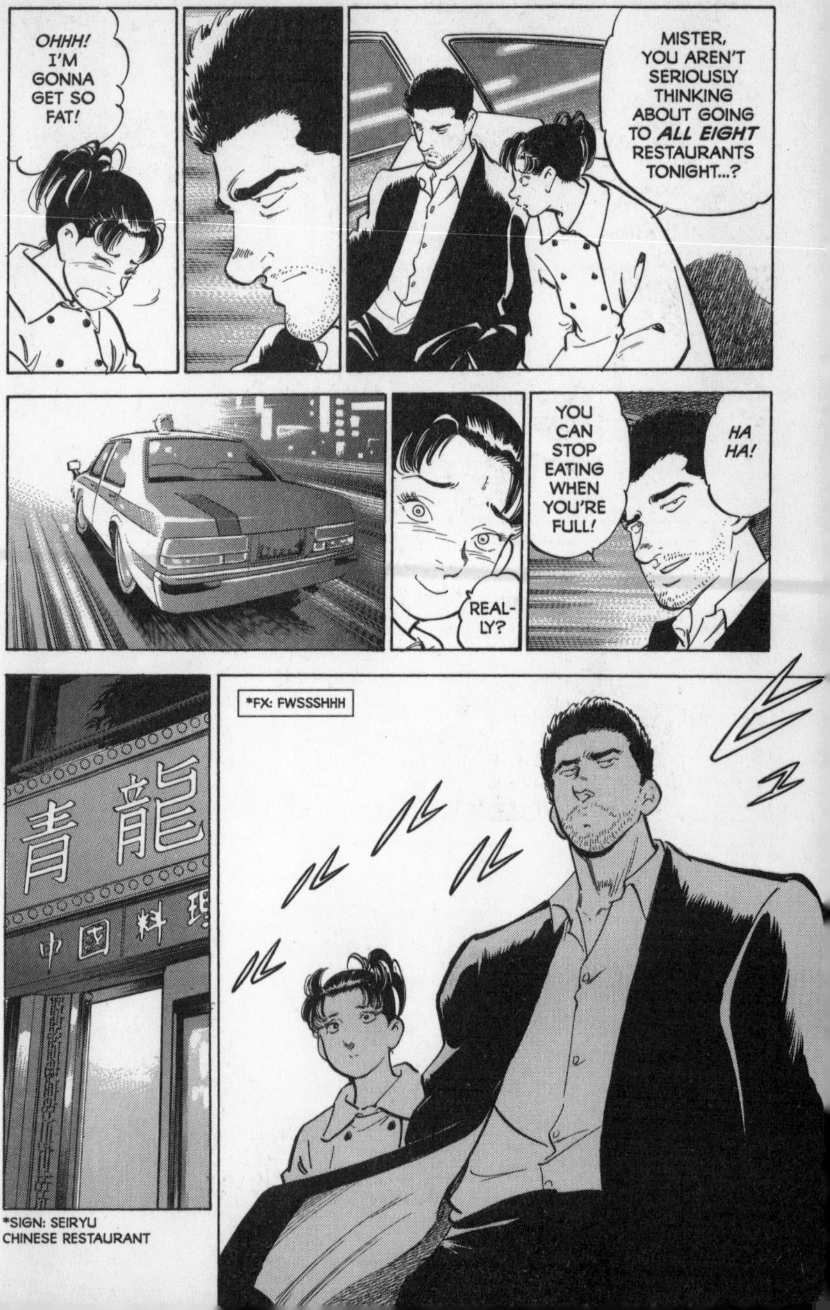
MISTER, YOU AREN'T SERIOUSLY THINKING ABOUT GOING TO ALL EIGHT RESTAURANTS TONIGHT...?
OHHH! I'M GONNA GET SO FAT!
HA HA!
YOU CAN STOP EATING WHEN YOU'RE FULL!
REAL-LY?
*FX: FWSSSHHH
青龍
中国料理
*SIGN: SEIRYU CHINESE RESTAURANT

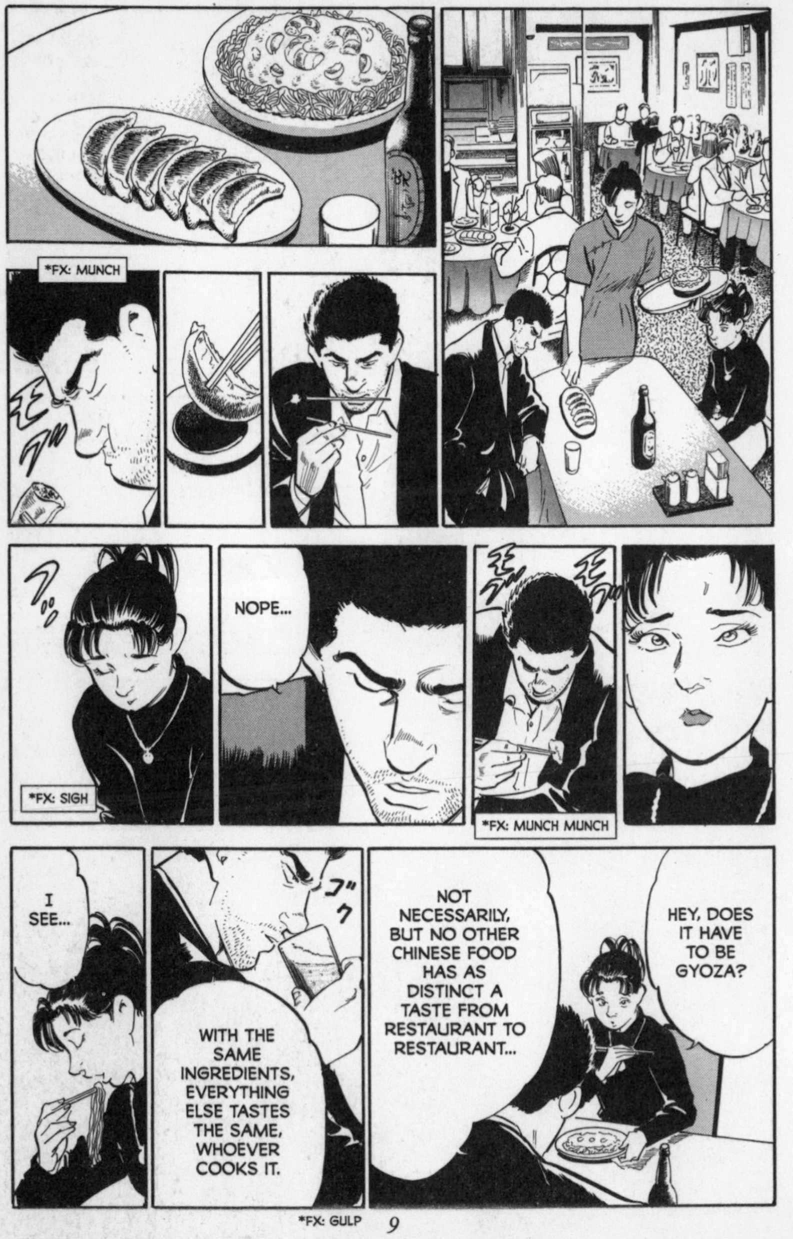
*FX: MUNCH
*FX: MUNCH MUNCH
NOPE...
*FX: SIGH
HEY, DOES IT HAVE TO BE GYOZA?
NOT NECESSARILY, BUT NO OTHER CHINESE FOOD HAS AS DISTINCT A TASTE FROM RESTAURANT TO RESTAURANT...
WITH THE SAME INGREDIENTS, EVERYTHING ELSE TASTES THE SAME, WHOEVER COOKS IT.
I SEE...

*FX: GULP

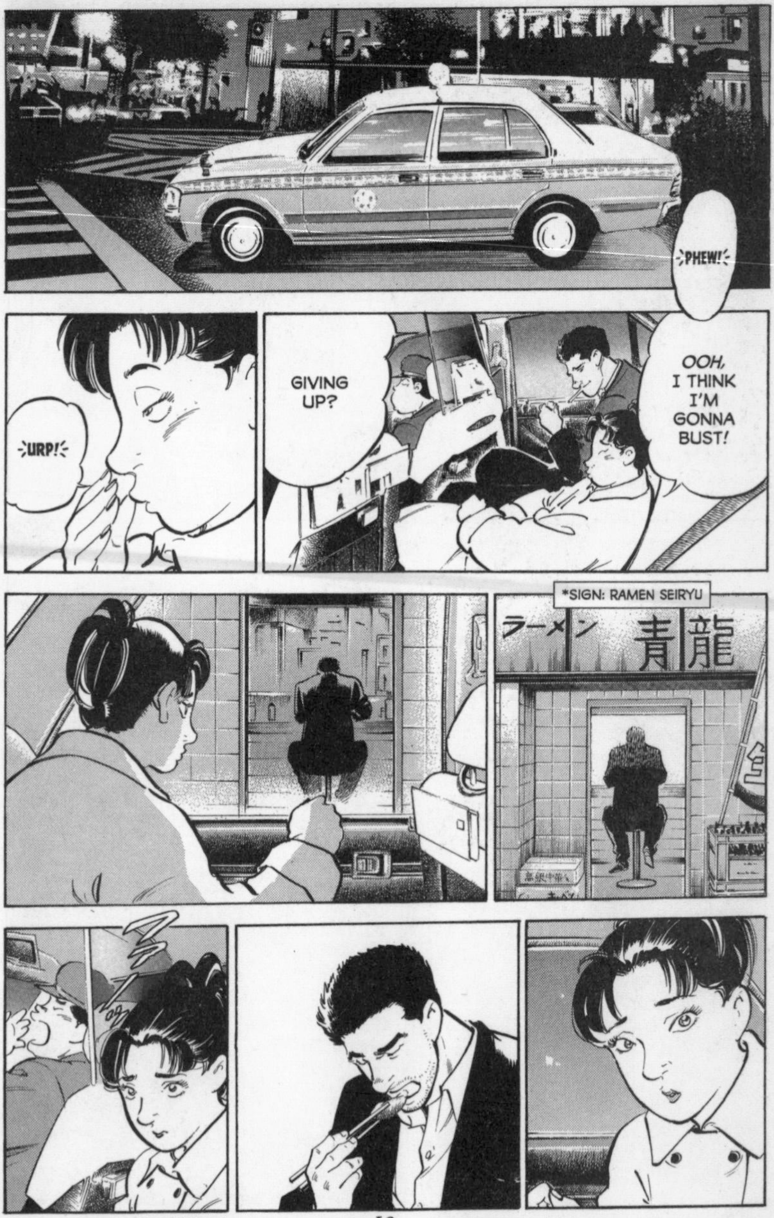
PHEW!
OOH, I THINK I'M GONNA BUST!
GIVING UP?
URP!
*SIGN: RAMEN SEIRYU
ラーメン 青龍

*FX: YAWWWN

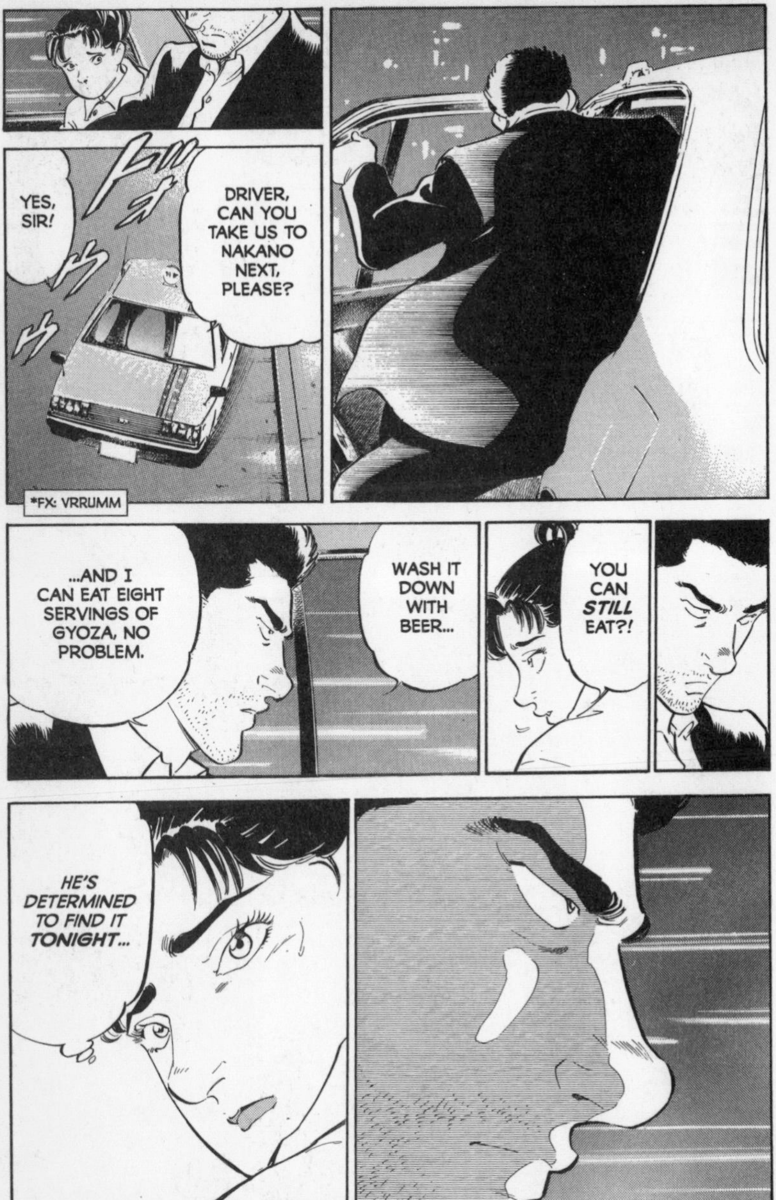
DRIVER, CAN YOU TAKE US TO NAKANO NEXT, PLEASE?
YES, SIR!
*FX: VRRUMM
YOU CAN STILL EAT?!
WASH IT DOWN WITH BEER...
...AND I CAN EAT EIGHT SERVINGS OF GYOZA, NO PROBLEM.
HE'S DETERMINED TO FIND IT TONIGHT...

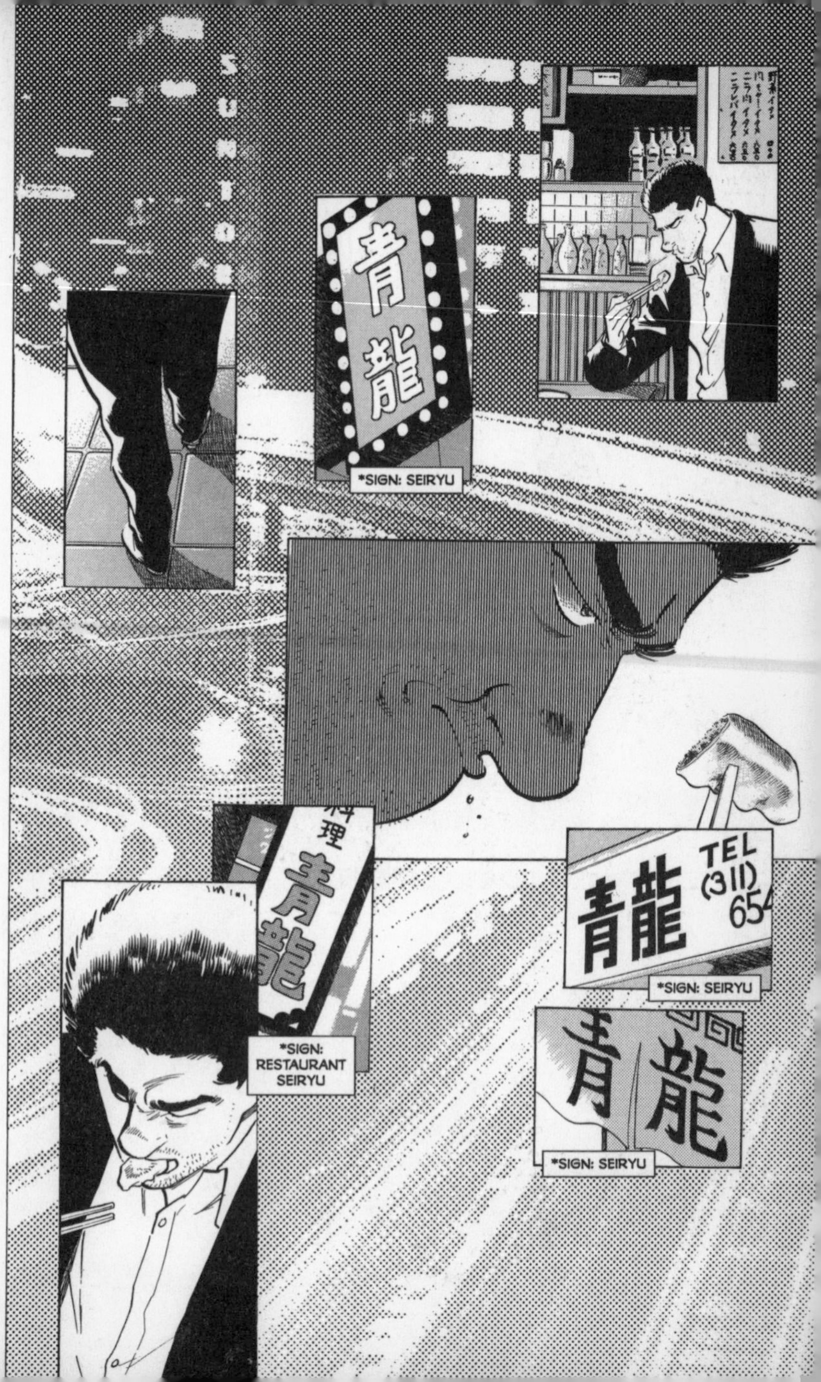
青龍
*SIGN: SEIRYU
青龍
TEL
(311)
654
*SIGN: SEIRYU
青龍
*SIGN: SEIRYU
料理
青龍
*SIGN:
RESTAURANT
SEIRYU

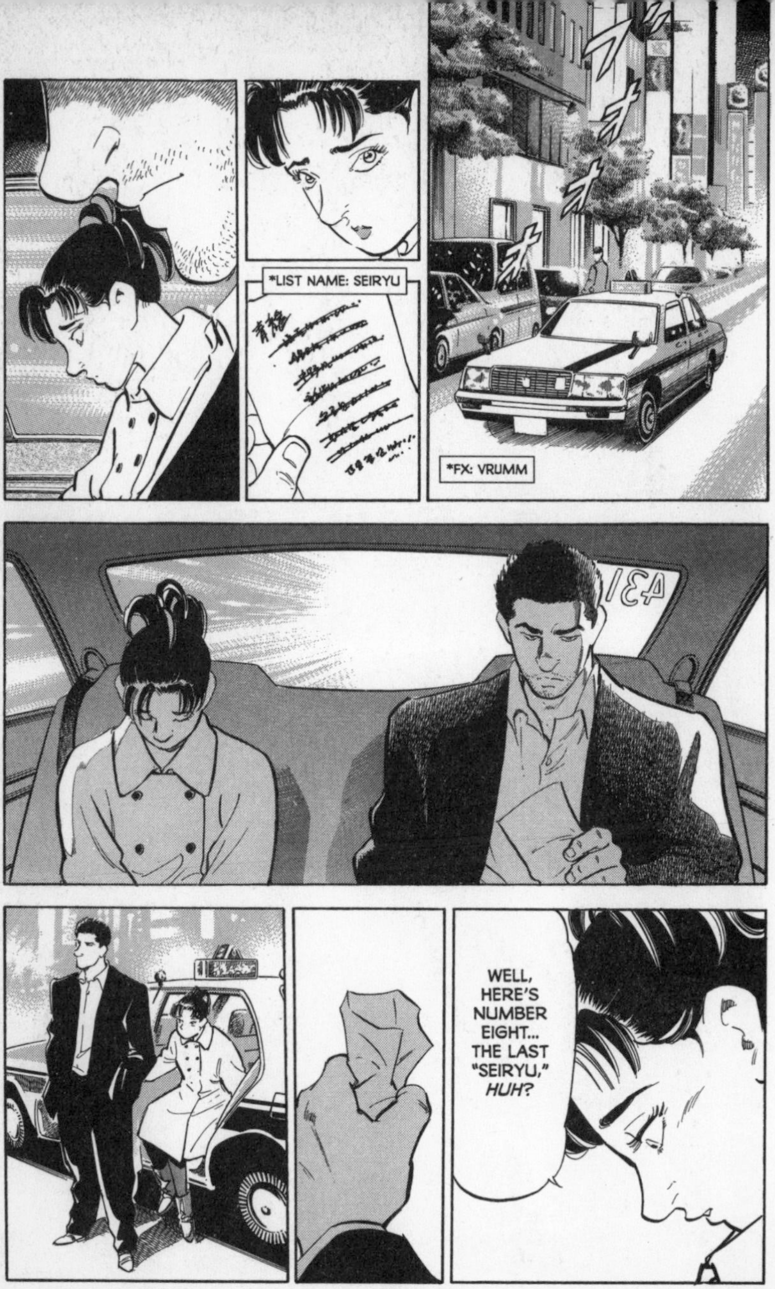
*FX: VRUMM
*LIST NAME: SEIRYU
WELL, HERE'S NUMBER EIGHT... THE LAST "SEIRYU," *HUH*?

*SIGN: RAMEN / SEIRYU / GYOZA

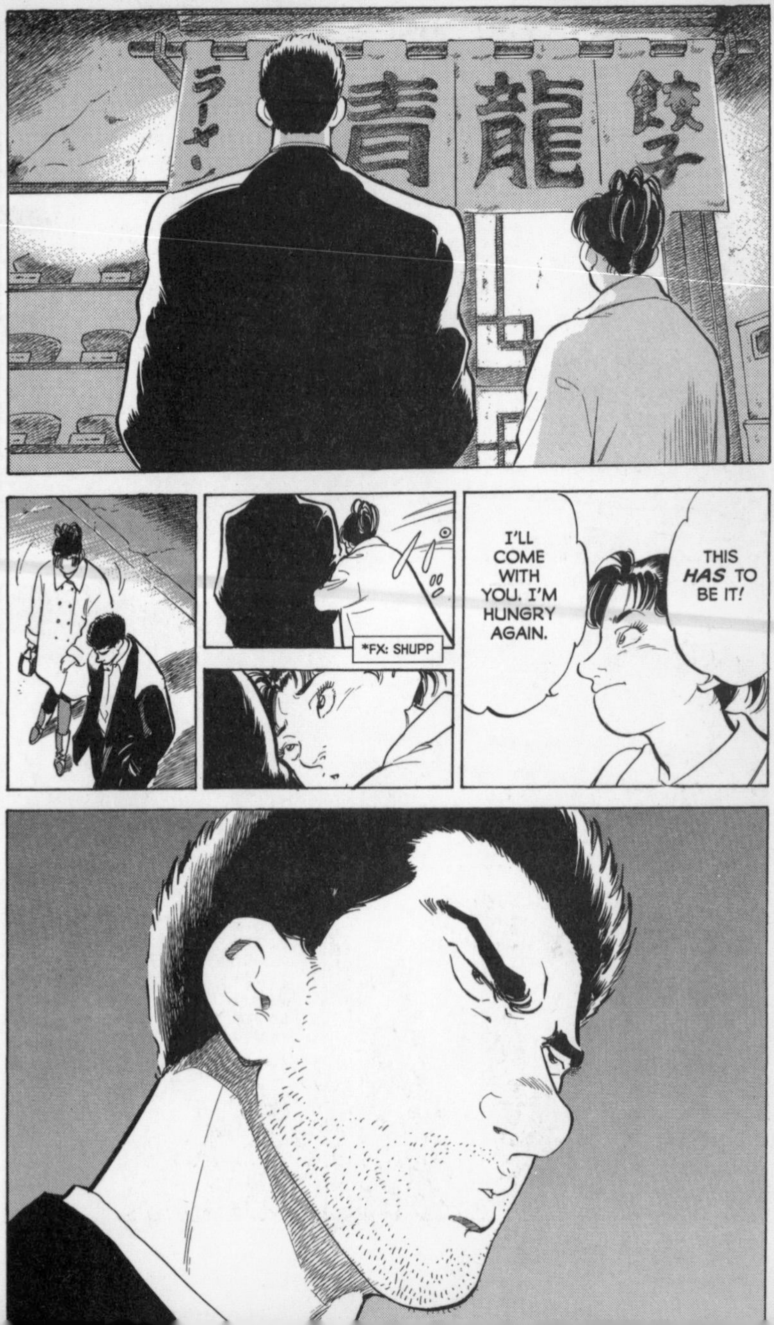
青龍
餃子
THIS *HAS* TO BE IT!
I'LL COME WITH YOU. I'M HUNGRY AGAIN.
*FX: SHUPP

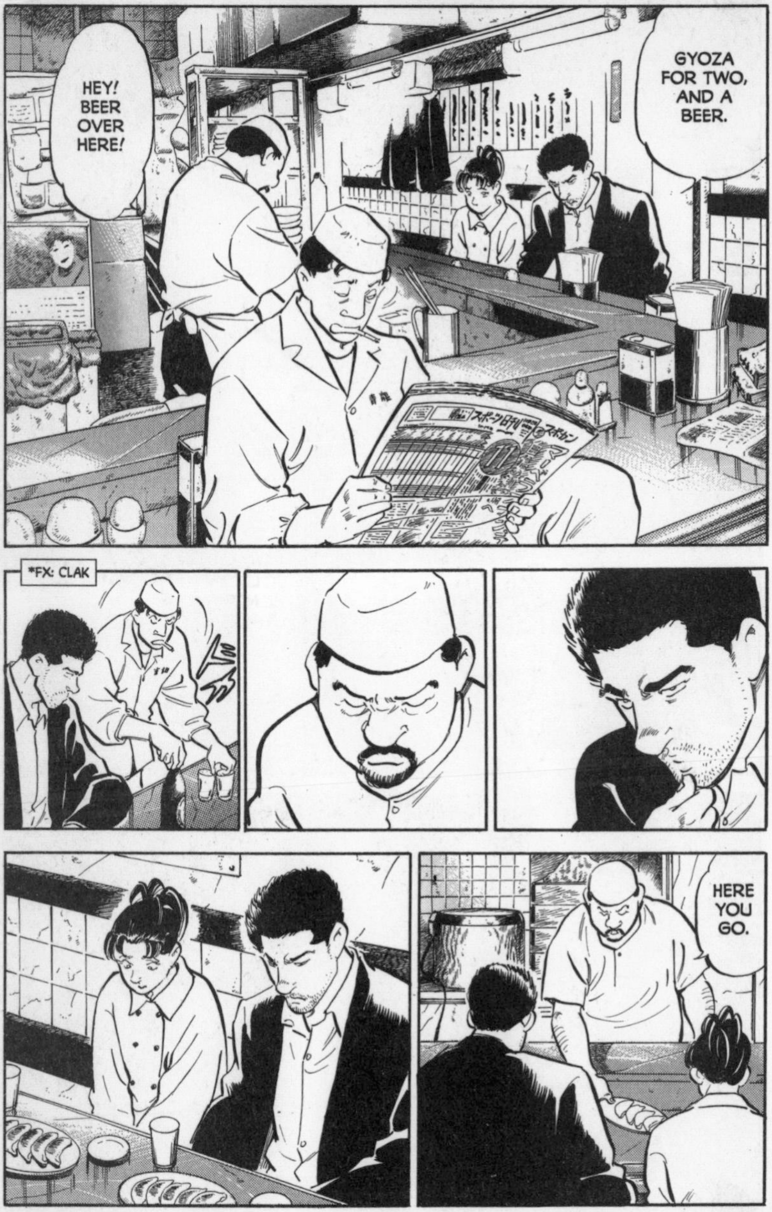
GYOZA FOR TWO, AND A BEER.
HEY! BEER OVER HERE!
*FX: CLAK
HERE YOU GO.

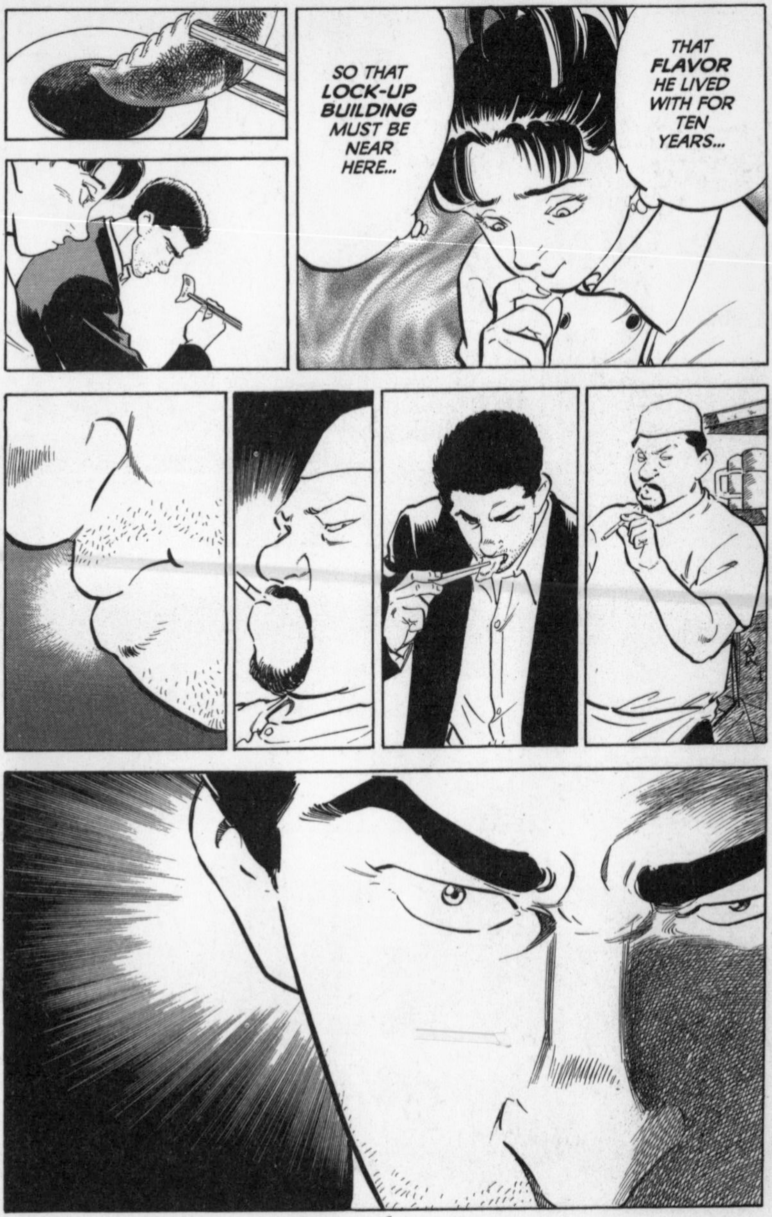
THAT FLAVOR HE LIVED WITH FOR TEN YEARS...
SO THAT LOCK-UP BUILDING MUST BE NEAR HERE...

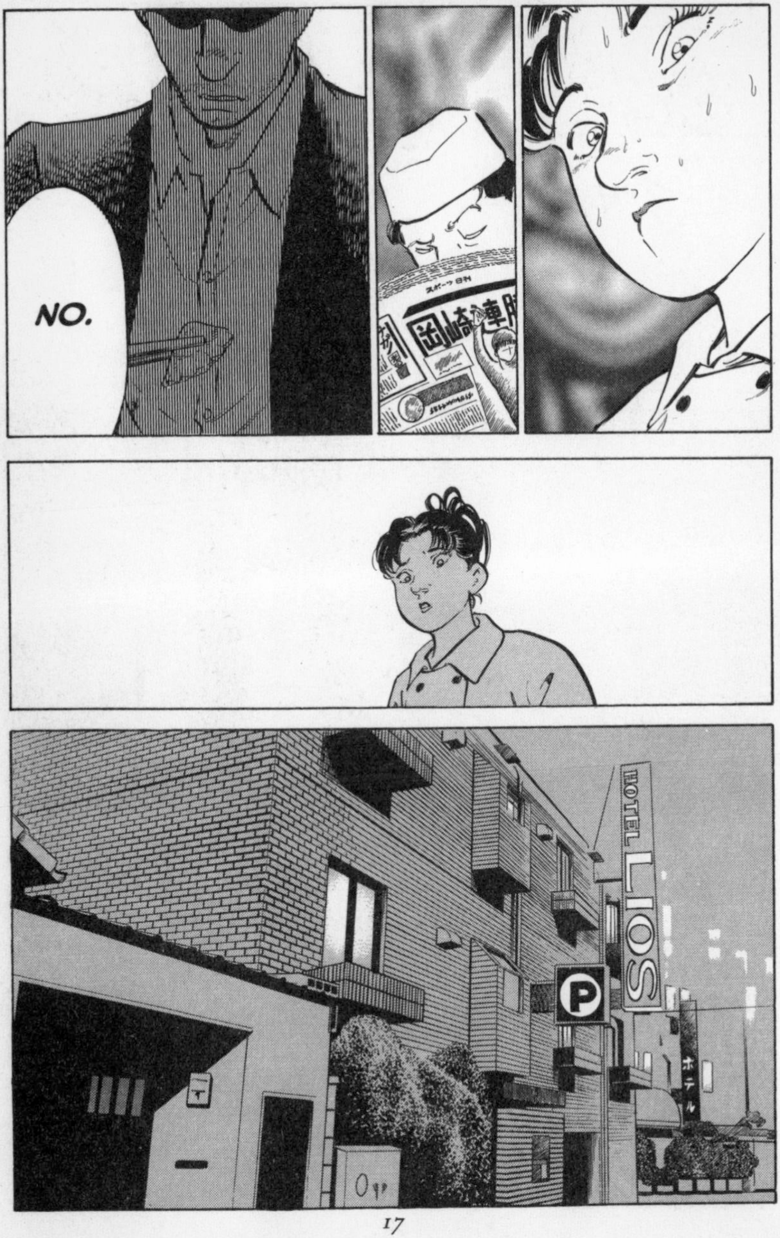
NO.
HOTEL LIOS
P
ホテル

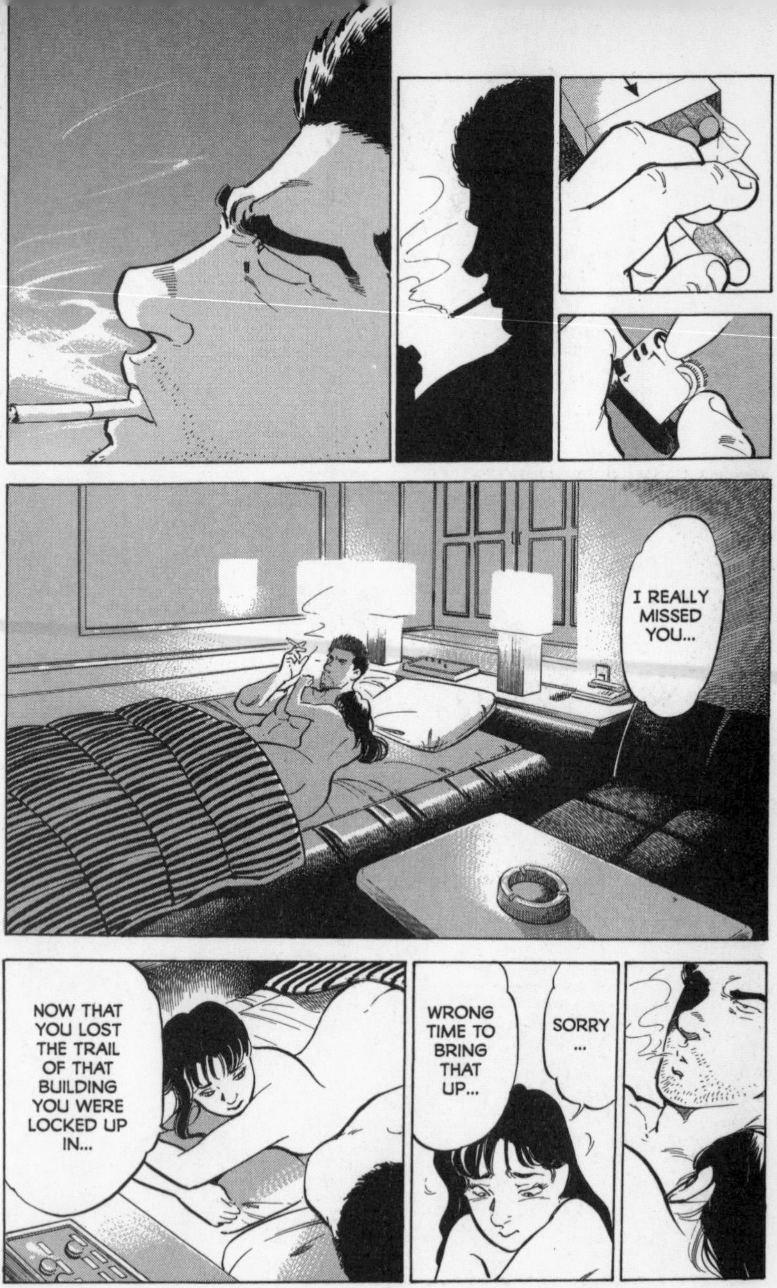
I REALLY MISSED YOU...
SORRY ...
WRONG TIME TO BRING THAT UP...
NOW THAT YOU LOST THE TRAIL OF THAT BUILDING YOU WERE LOCKED UP IN...

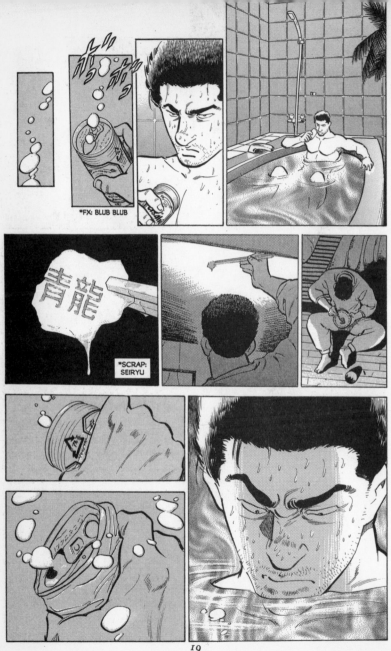

*FX: BLUB BLUB

*SCRAP: SEIRYU

19

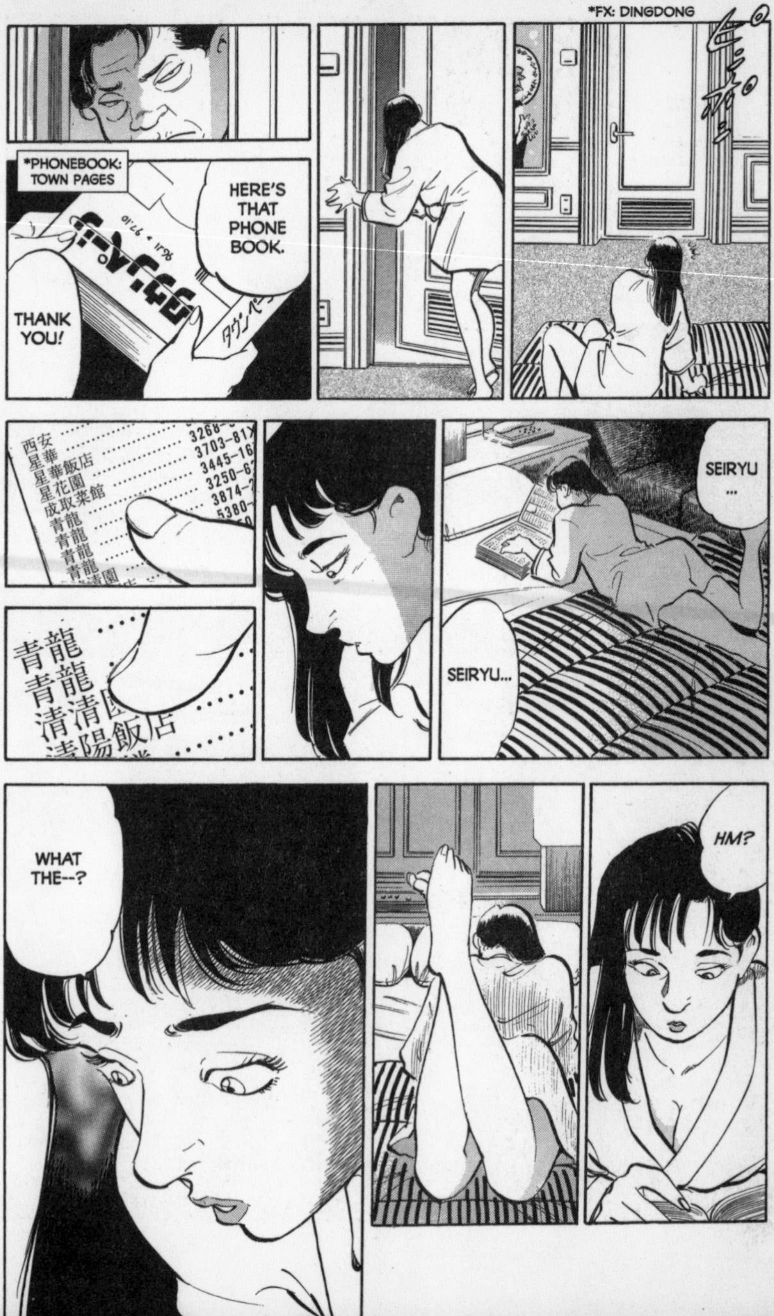
*FX: DINGDONG
*PHONEBOOK: TOWN PAGES
HERE'S THAT PHONE BOOK.
THANK YOU!
SEIRYU ...
SEIRYU...
HM?
WHAT THE--?

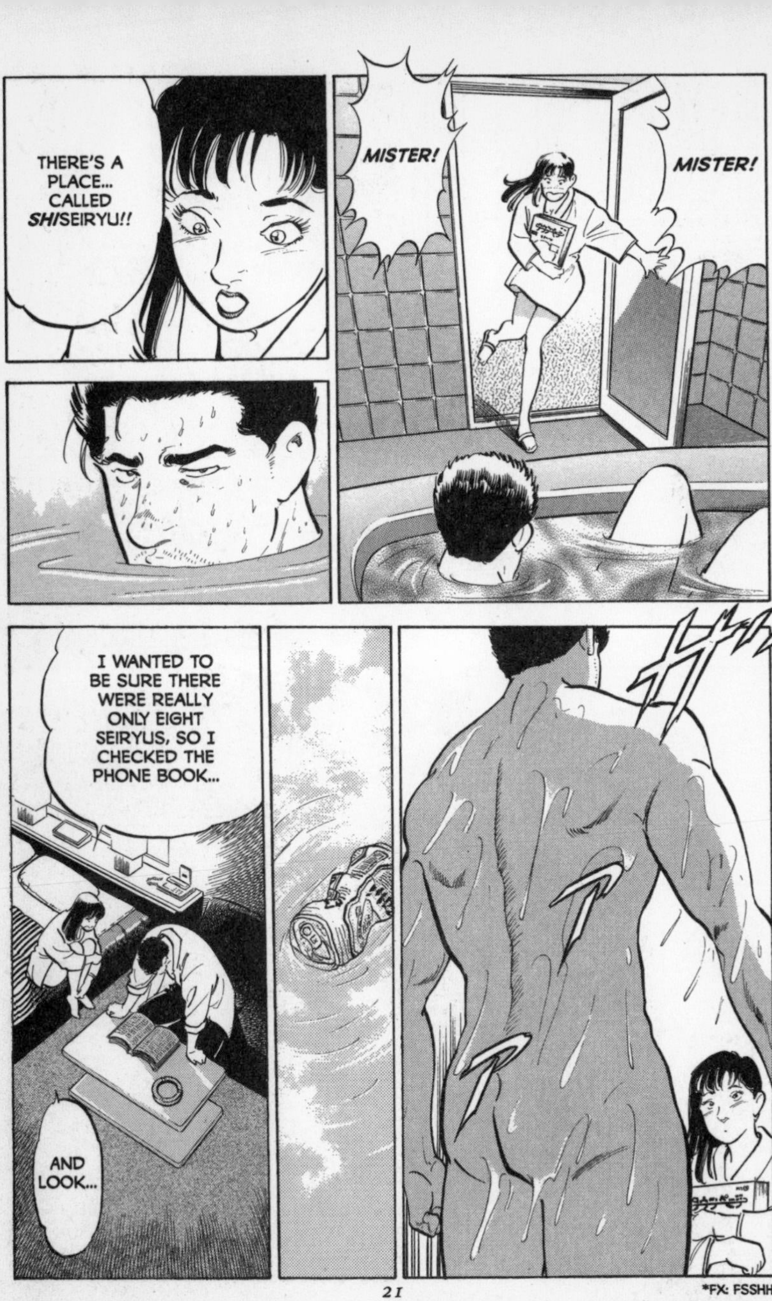
MISTER!
MISTER!
THERE'S A PLACE... CALLED SHISEIRYU!!
I WANTED TO BE SURE THERE WERE REALLY ONLY EIGHT SEIRYUS, SO I CHECKED THE PHONE BOOK...
AND LOOK...

*FX: FSSHH

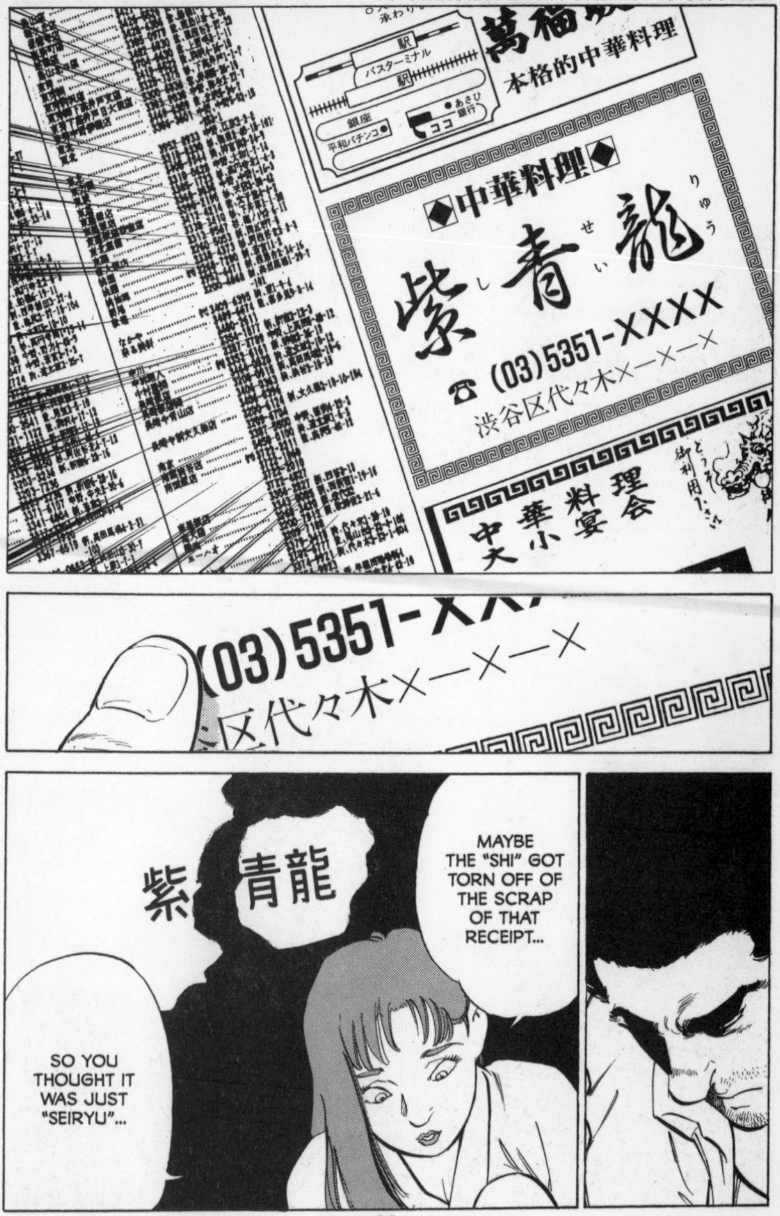

萬福
本格的中華料理
駅
バスターミナル
駅
銀座
平和パチンコ
ココ
あさひ銀行
中華料理
紫青龍
しせいりゅう
☎ (03)5351-XXXX
渋谷区代々木×ー×ー×
中華料理
大小宴会
どうぞ御利用下さい
(03)5351-
区代々木×ー×ー×
MAYBE THE "SHI" GOT TORN OFF OF THE SCRAP OF THAT RECEIPT...
紫 青龍
SO YOU THOUGHT IT WAS JUST "SEIRYU"...

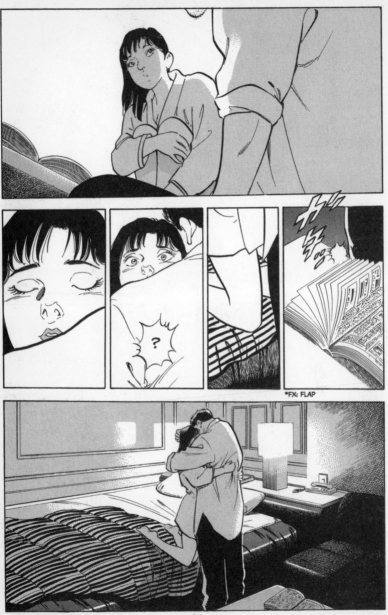

*FX: FLAP

23

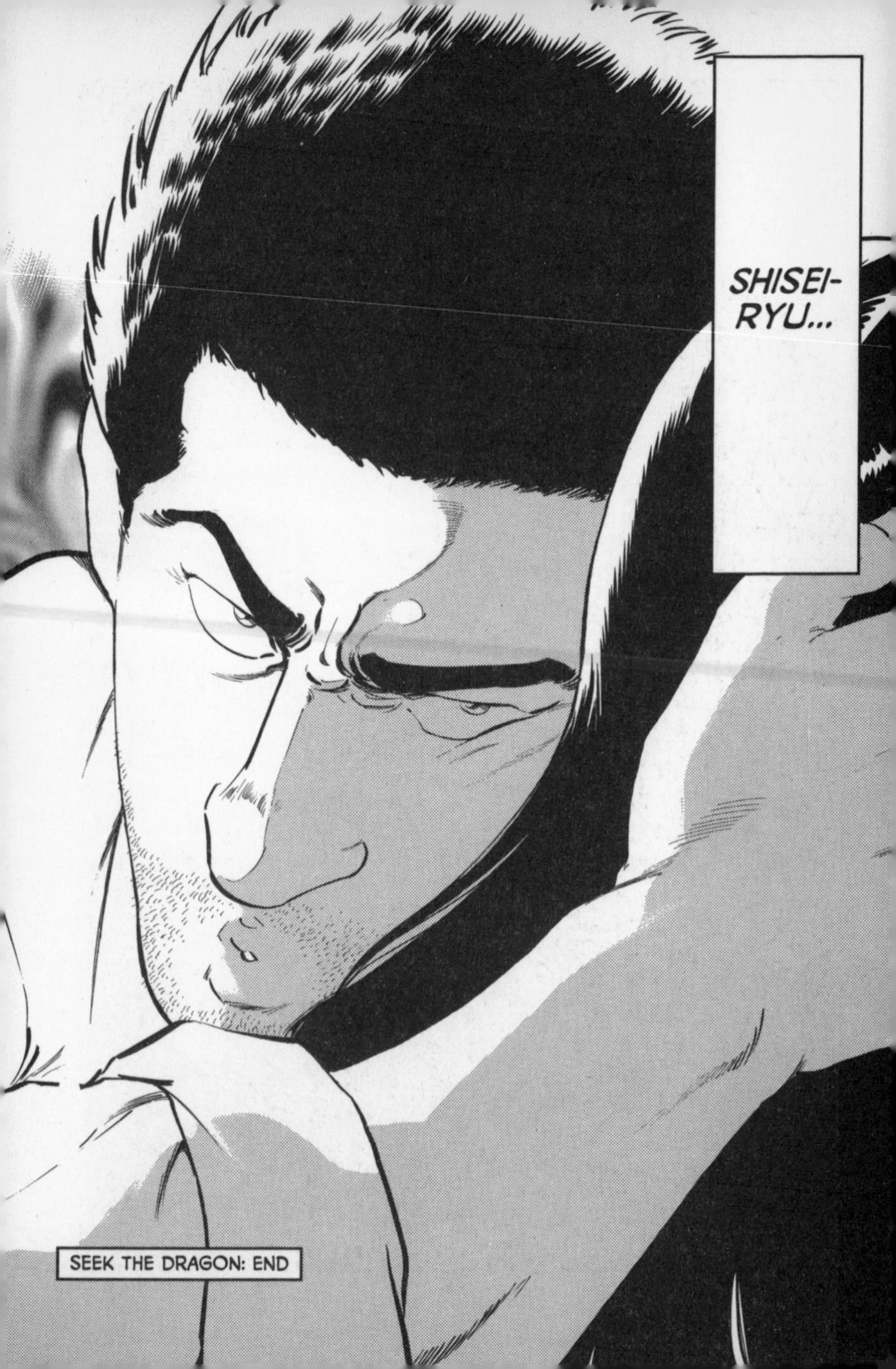
SHISEI-RYU...
SEEK THE DRAGON: END

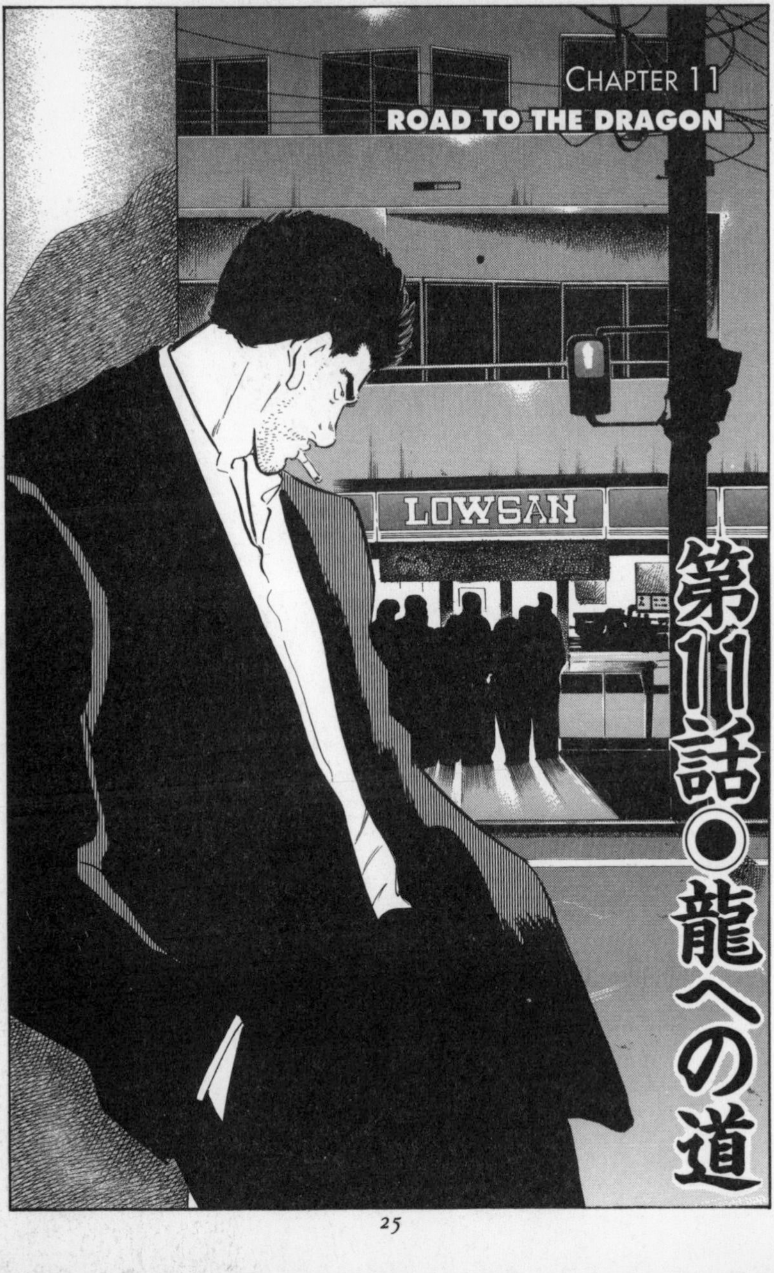
CHAPTER 11
ROAD TO THE DRAGON
LOWSAN
第11話○龍への道

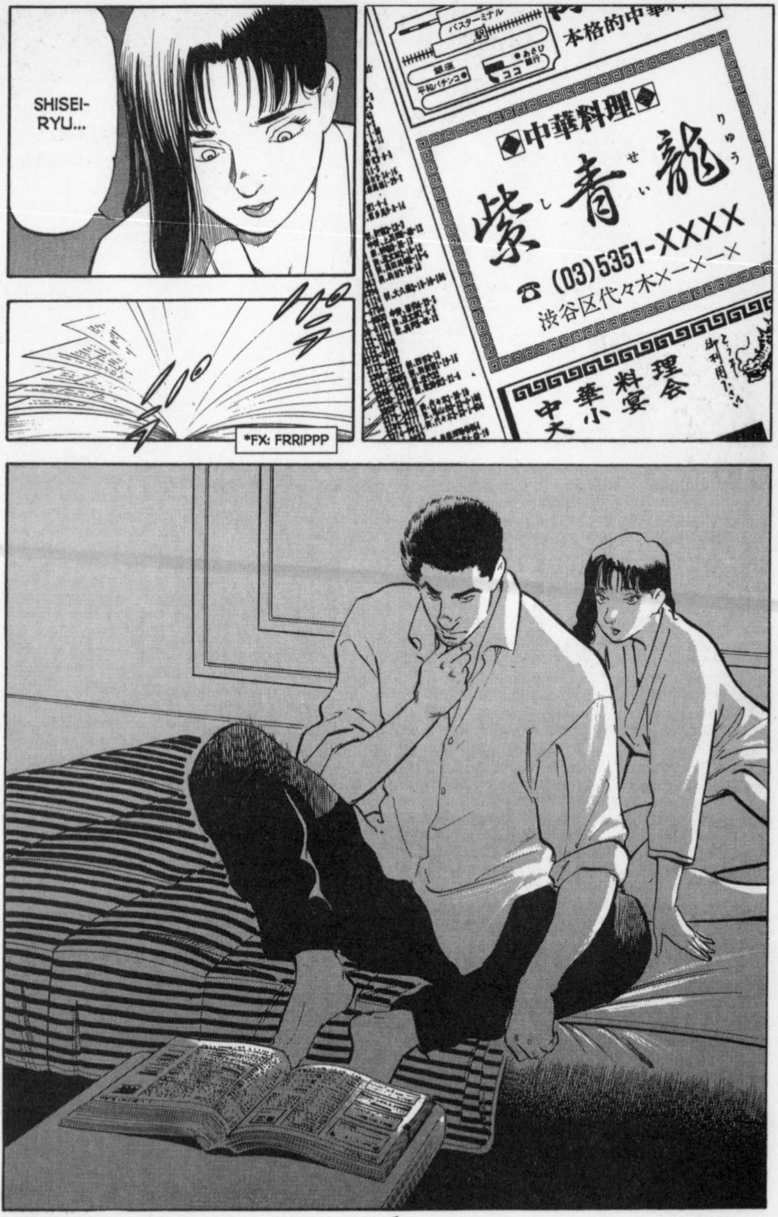

中華料理
紫青龍
(03)5351-XXXX
渋谷区代々木×ー×ー×
SHISEI-RYU...
*FX: FRRIPPP

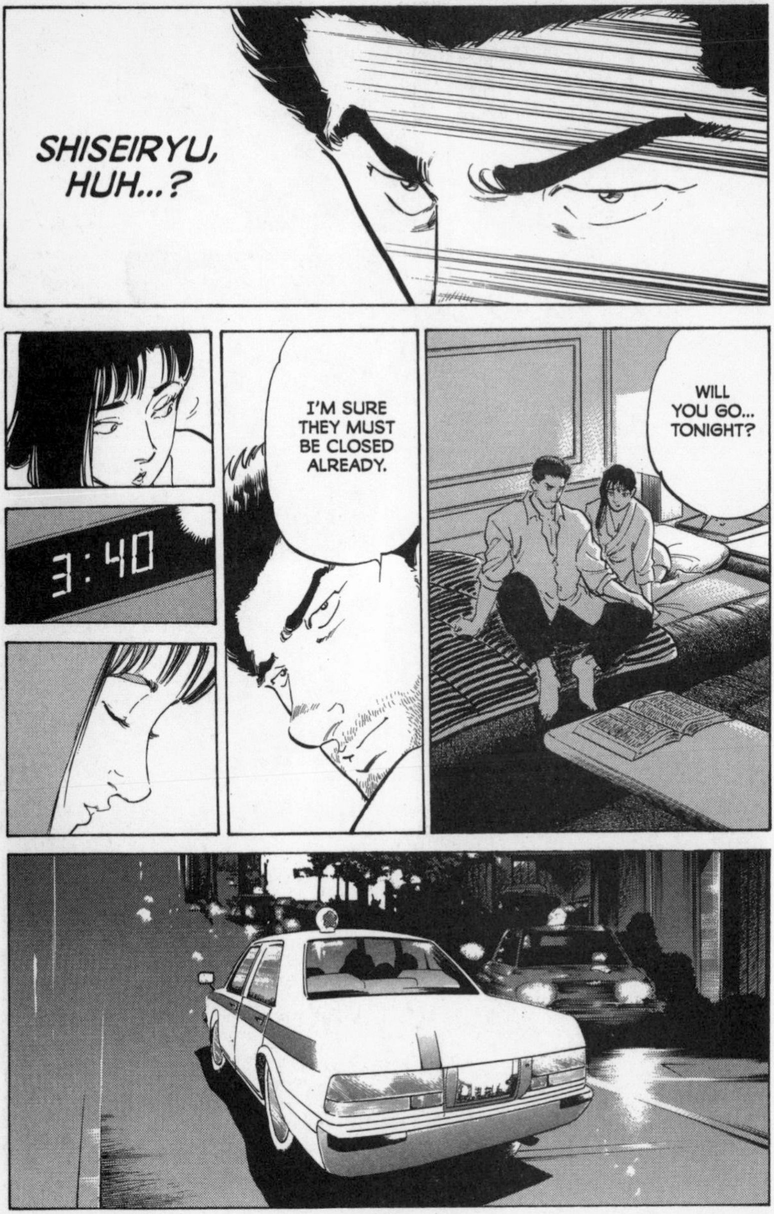

SHISEIRYU, HUH...?
WILL YOU GO... TONIGHT?
I'M SURE THEY MUST BE CLOSED ALREADY.
3:40

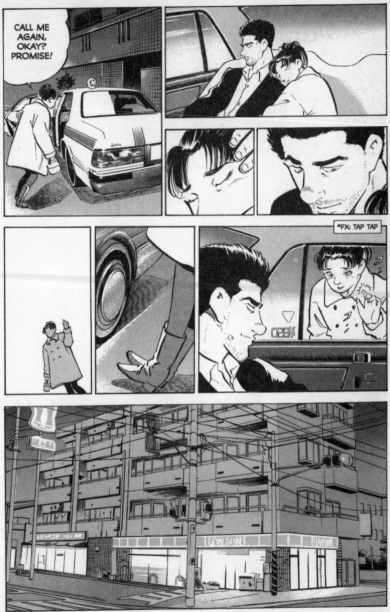

CALL ME AGAIN, OKAY? PROMISE!

*FX: TAP TAP

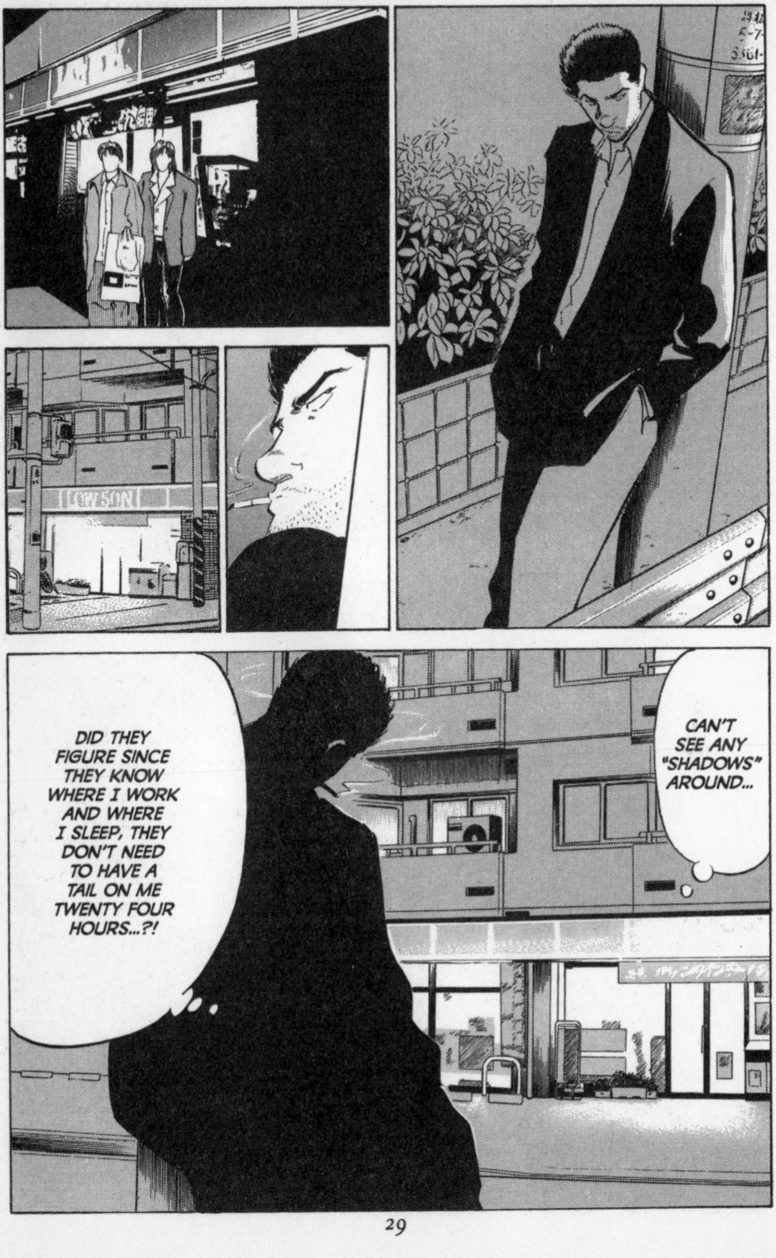
CAN'T SEE ANY "SHADOWS" AROUND...
DID THEY FIGURE SINCE THEY KNOW WHERE I WORK AND WHERE I SLEEP, THEY DON'T NEED TO HAVE A TAIL ON ME TWENTY FOUR HOURS...?!

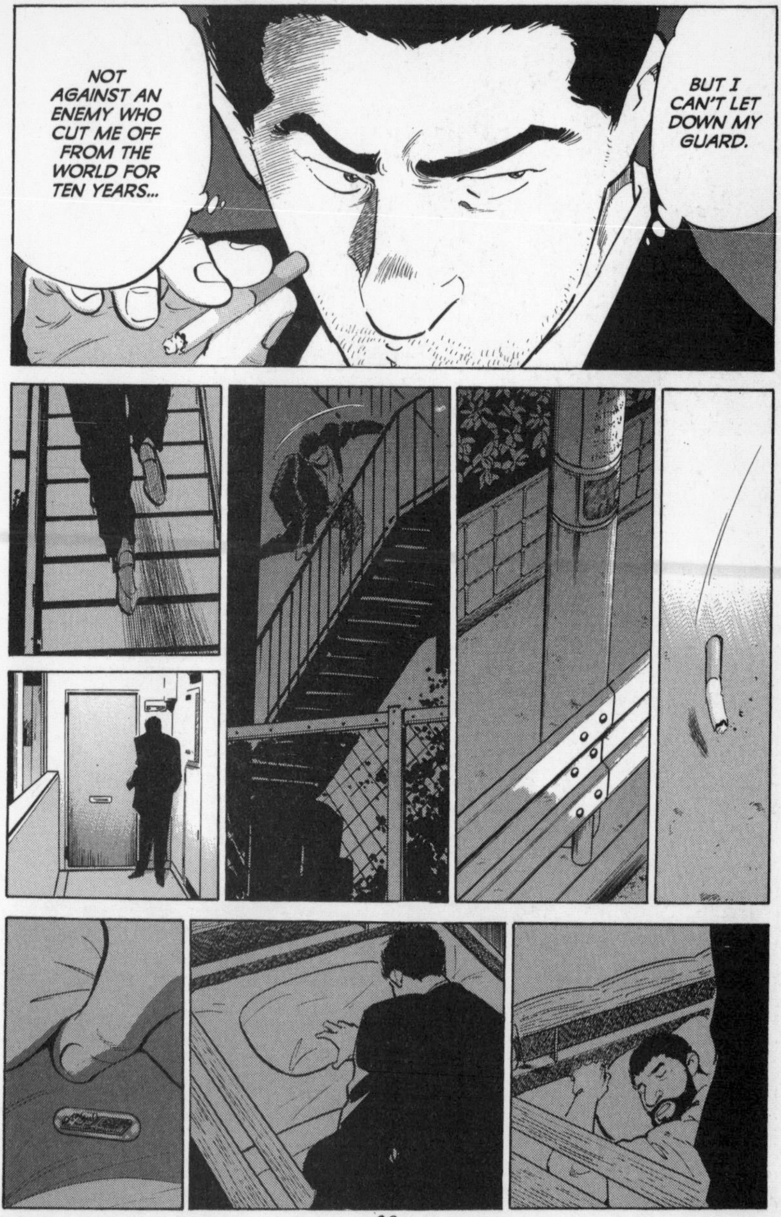
BUT I CAN'T LET DOWN MY GUARD.
NOT AGAINST AN ENEMY WHO CUT ME OFF FROM THE WORLD FOR TEN YEARS...

*FX: CLANGCLANGCLANG GONGGONGGONGONGGONG

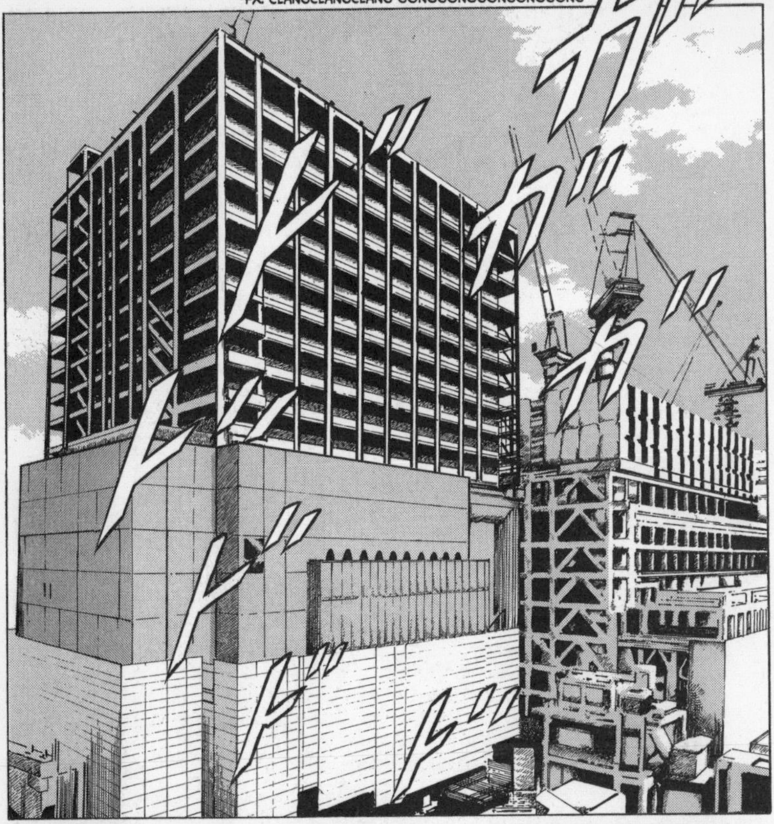

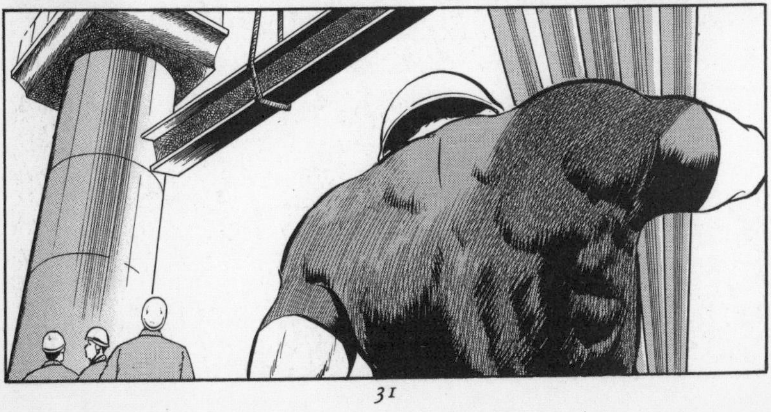

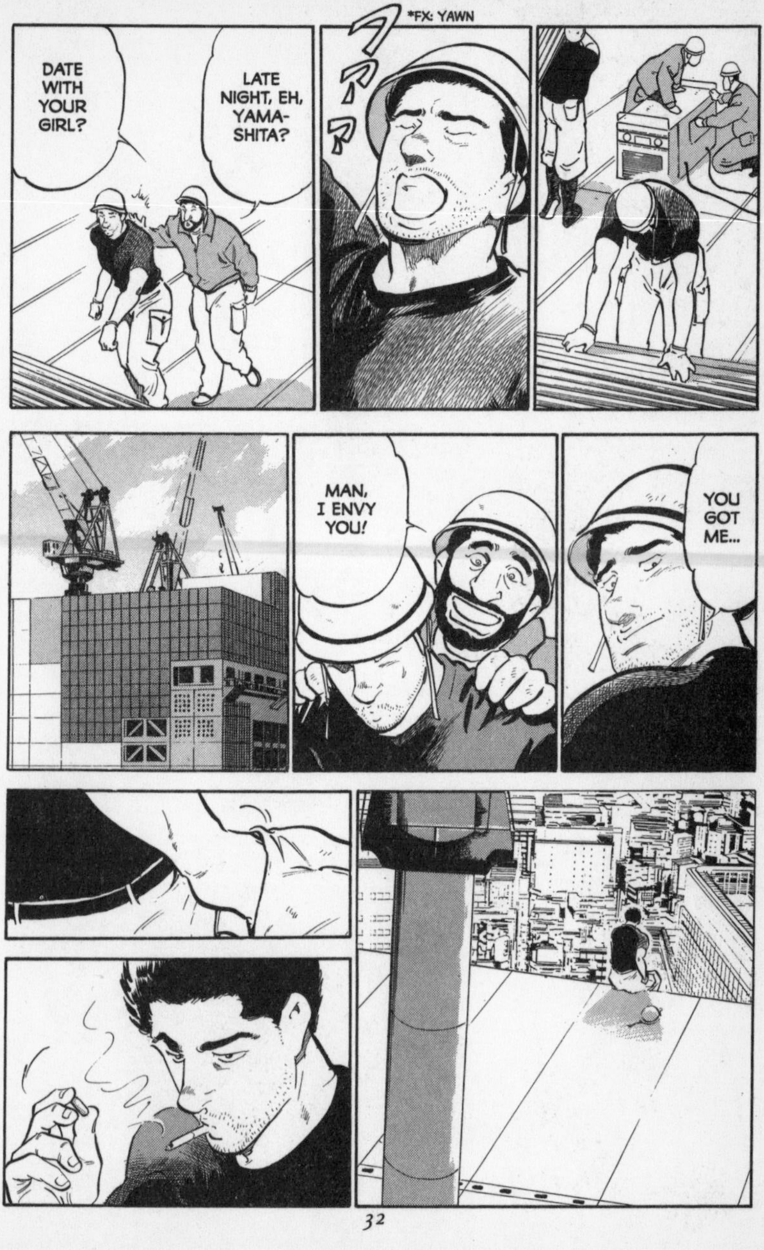
*FX: YAWN
LATE NIGHT, EH, YAMA-SHITA?
DATE WITH YOUR GIRL?
YOU GOT ME...
MAN, I ENVY YOU!

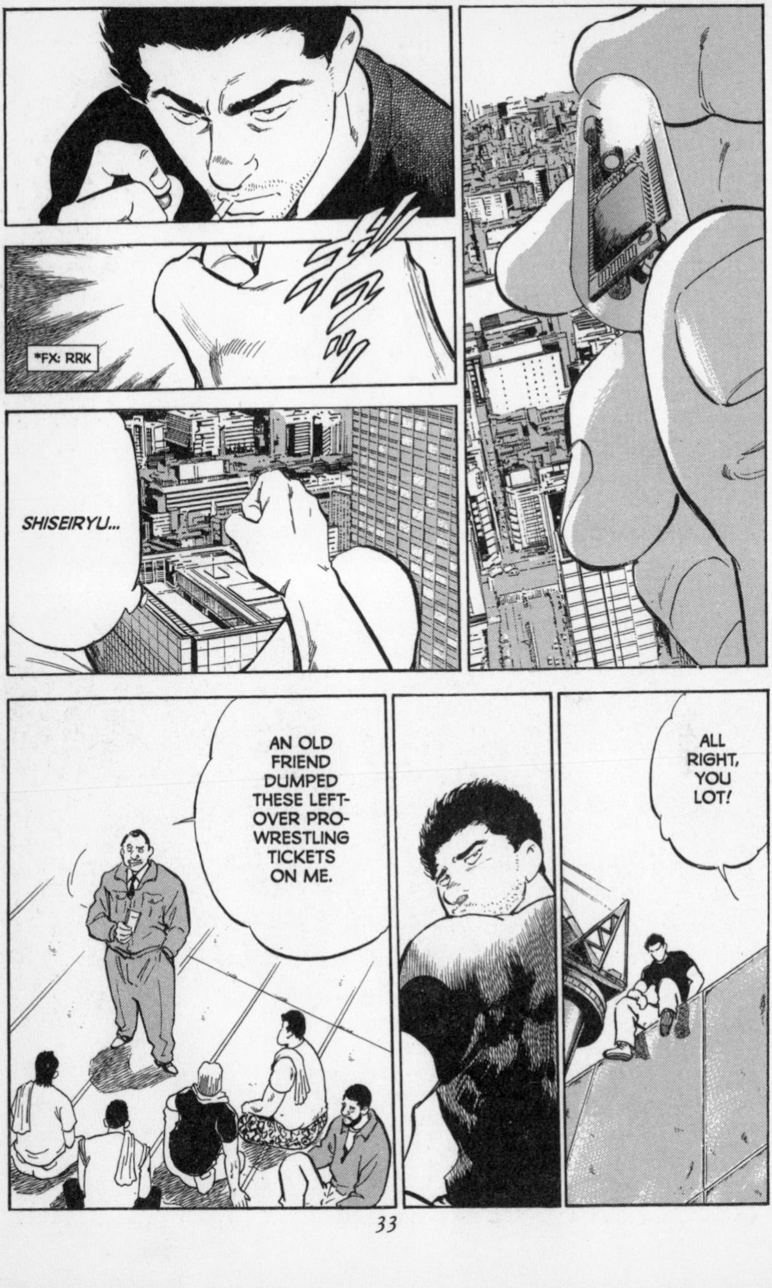

*FX: RRK
SHISEIRYU...
ALL RIGHT, YOU LOT!
AN OLD FRIEND DUMPED THESE LEFT-OVER PRO-WRESTLING TICKETS ON ME.

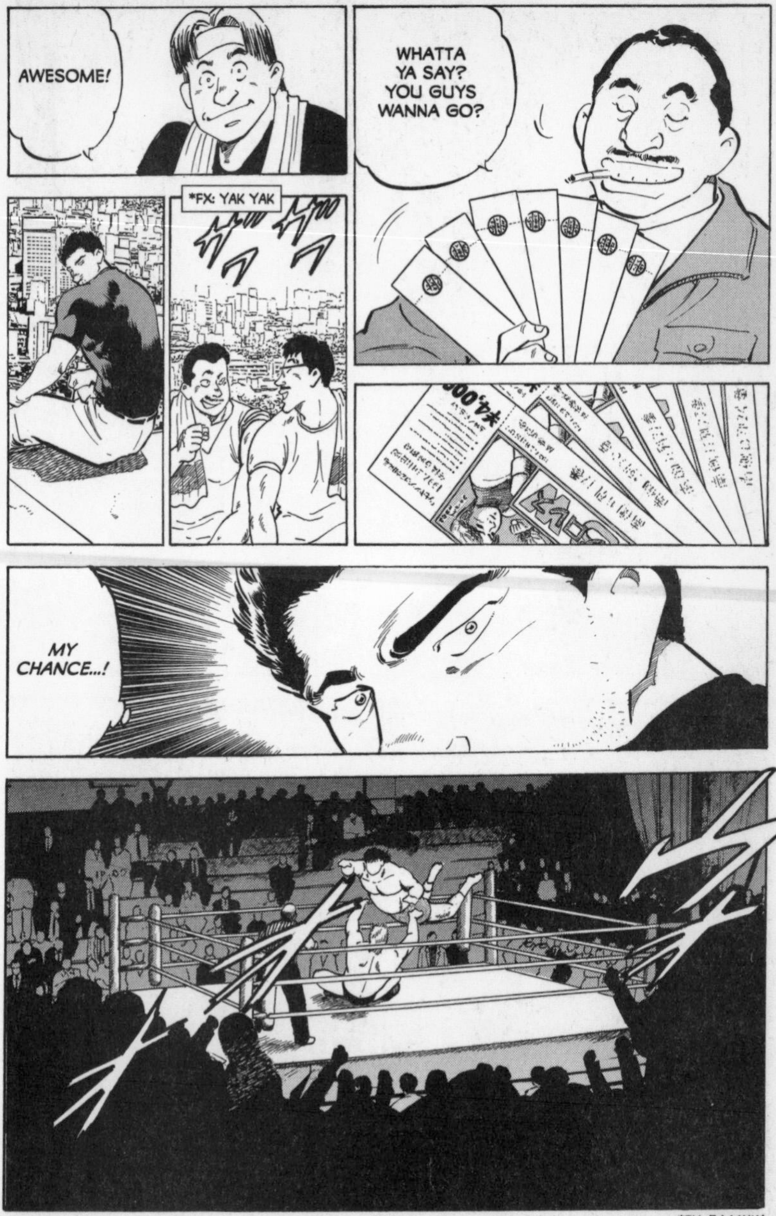
WHATTA YA SAY? YOU GUYS WANNA GO?
AWESOME!
*FX: YAK YAK
MY CHANCE...!

*FX: RAAAHH!

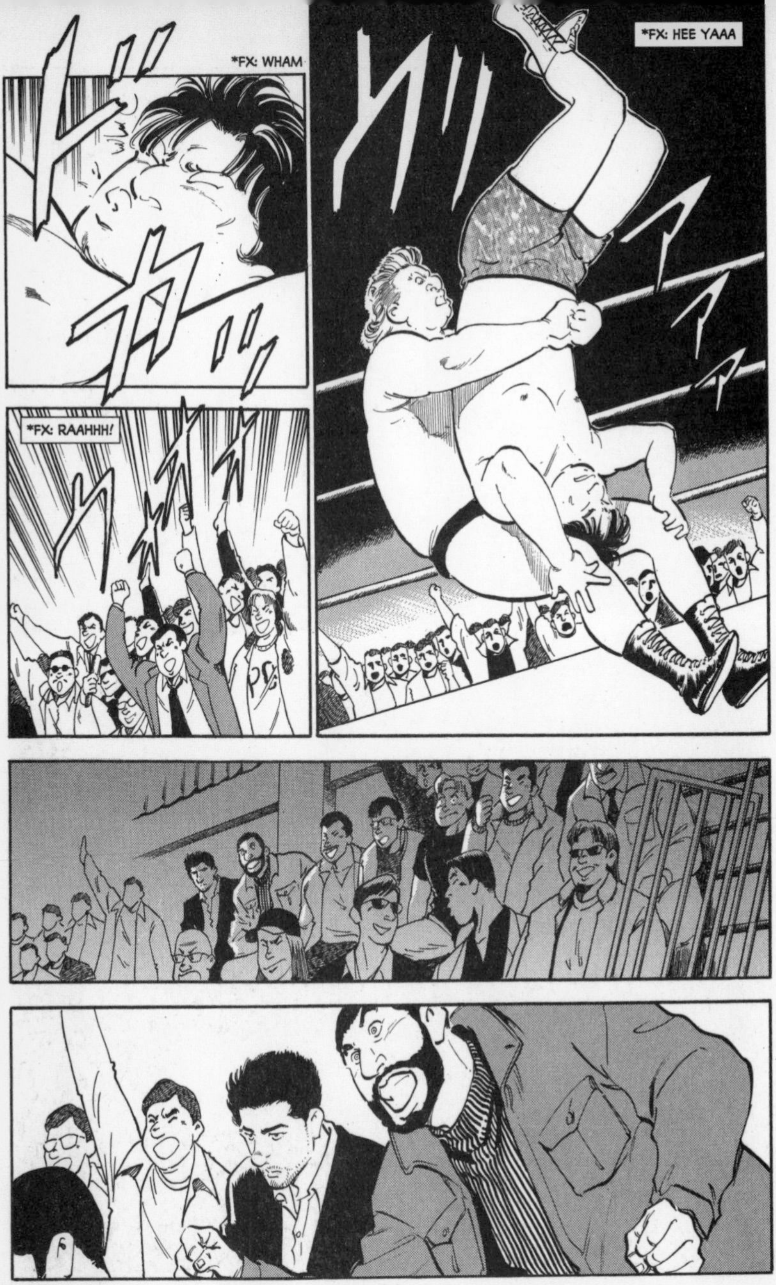
*FX: HEE YAAA
*FX: WHAM
*FX: RAAHHH!

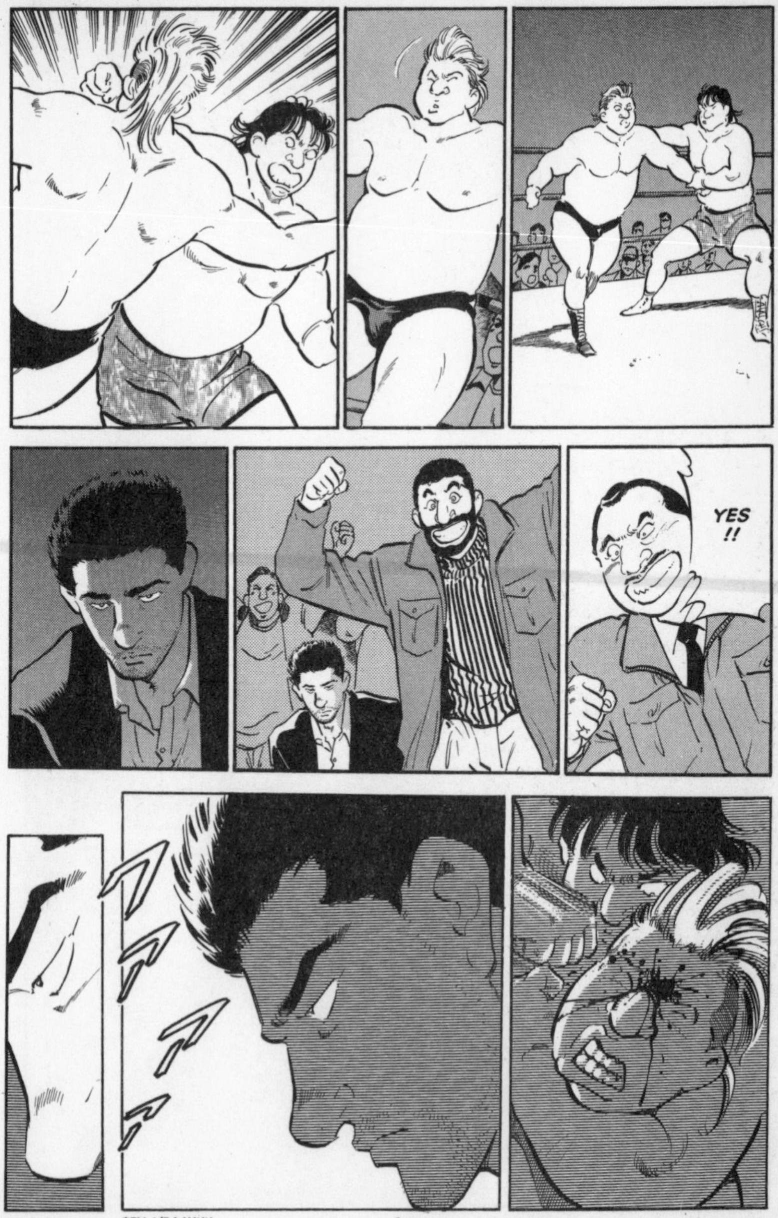
YES !!

*FX: YEAAHHH

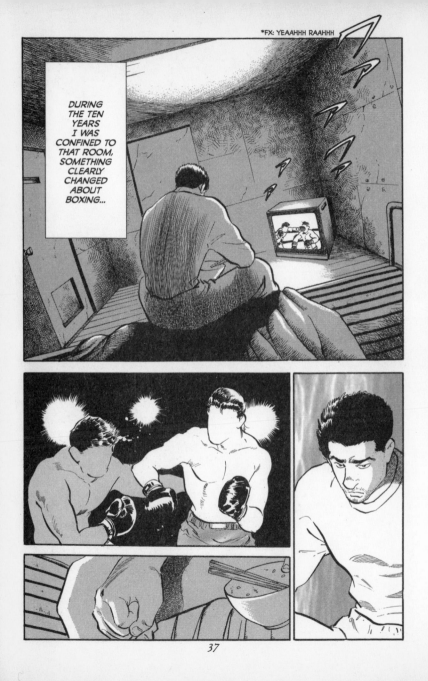

DURING THE TEN YEARS I WAS CONFINED TO THAT ROOM, SOMETHING CLEARLY CHANGED ABOUT BOXING...

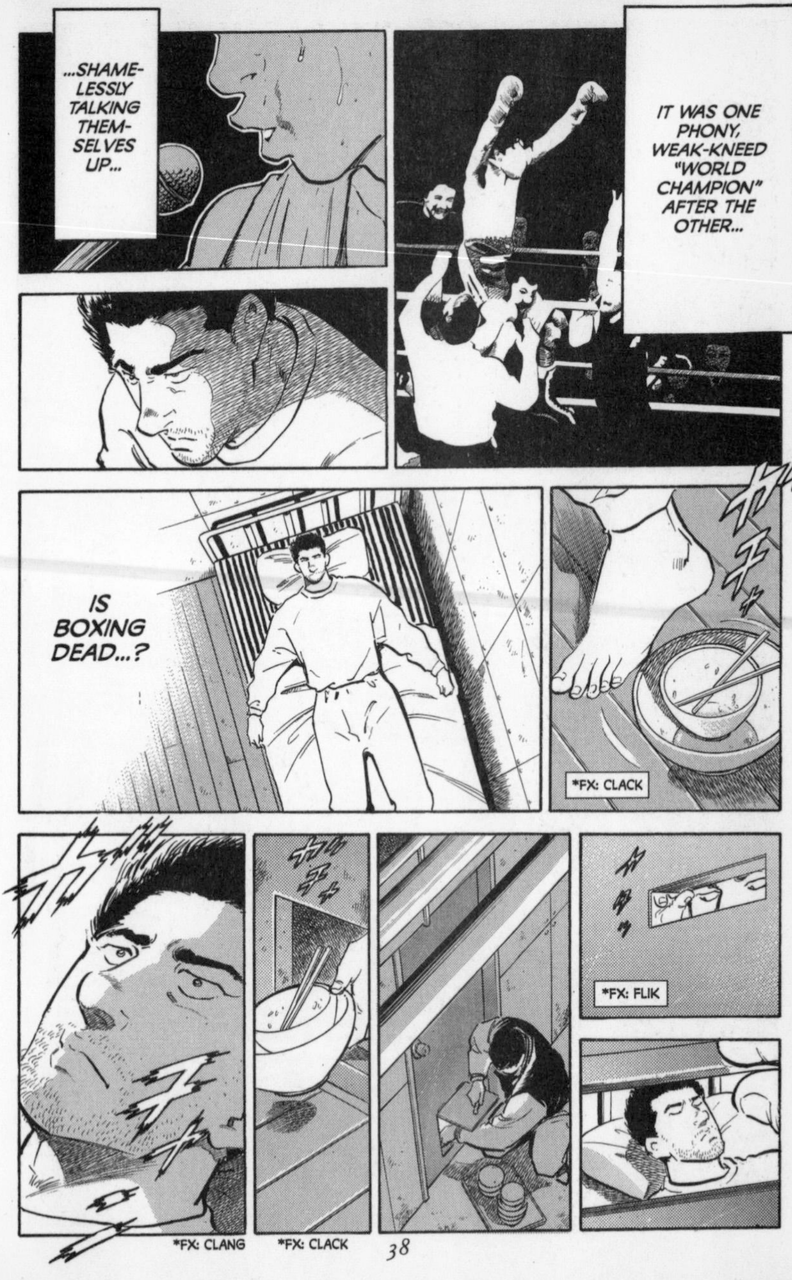
IT WAS ONE PHONY, WEAK-KNEED "WORLD CHAMPION" AFTER THE OTHER...
...SHAME-LESSLY TALKING THEM-SELVES UP...
*FX: CLACK
IS BOXING DEAD...?
*FX: FLIK
*FX: CLACK
*FX: CLANG

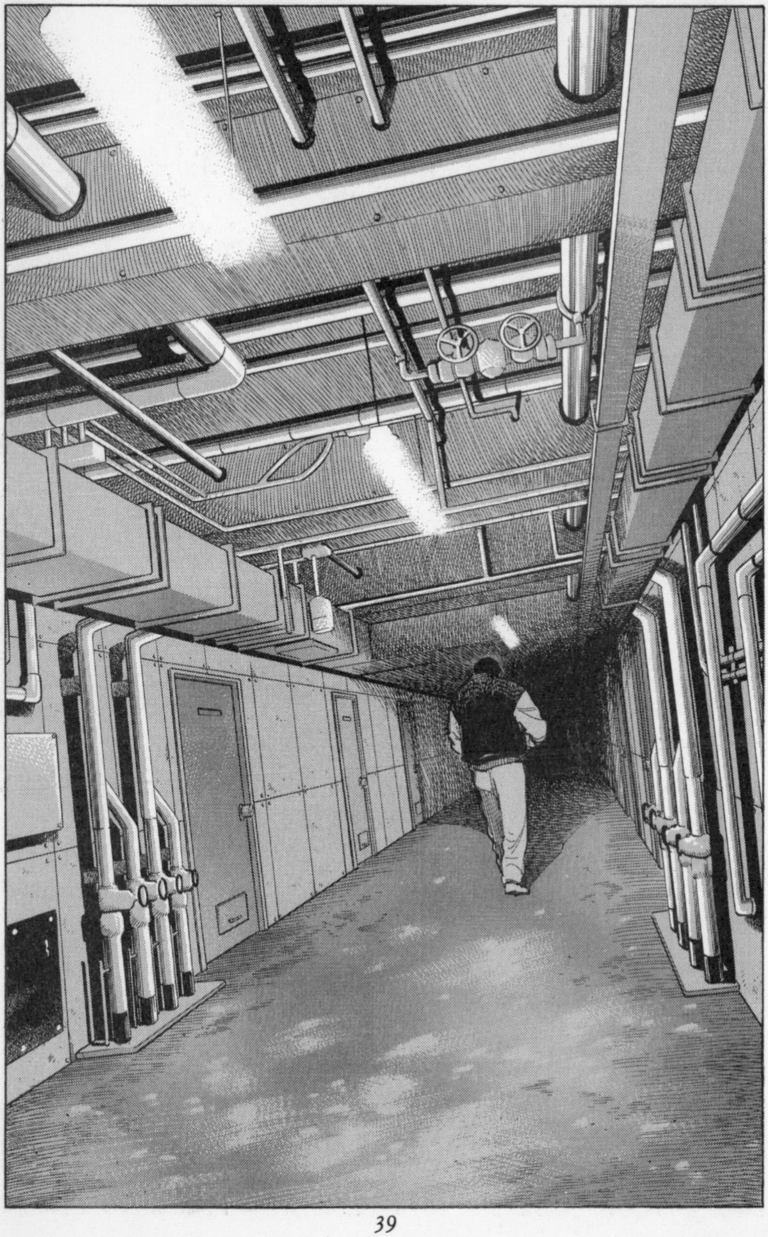

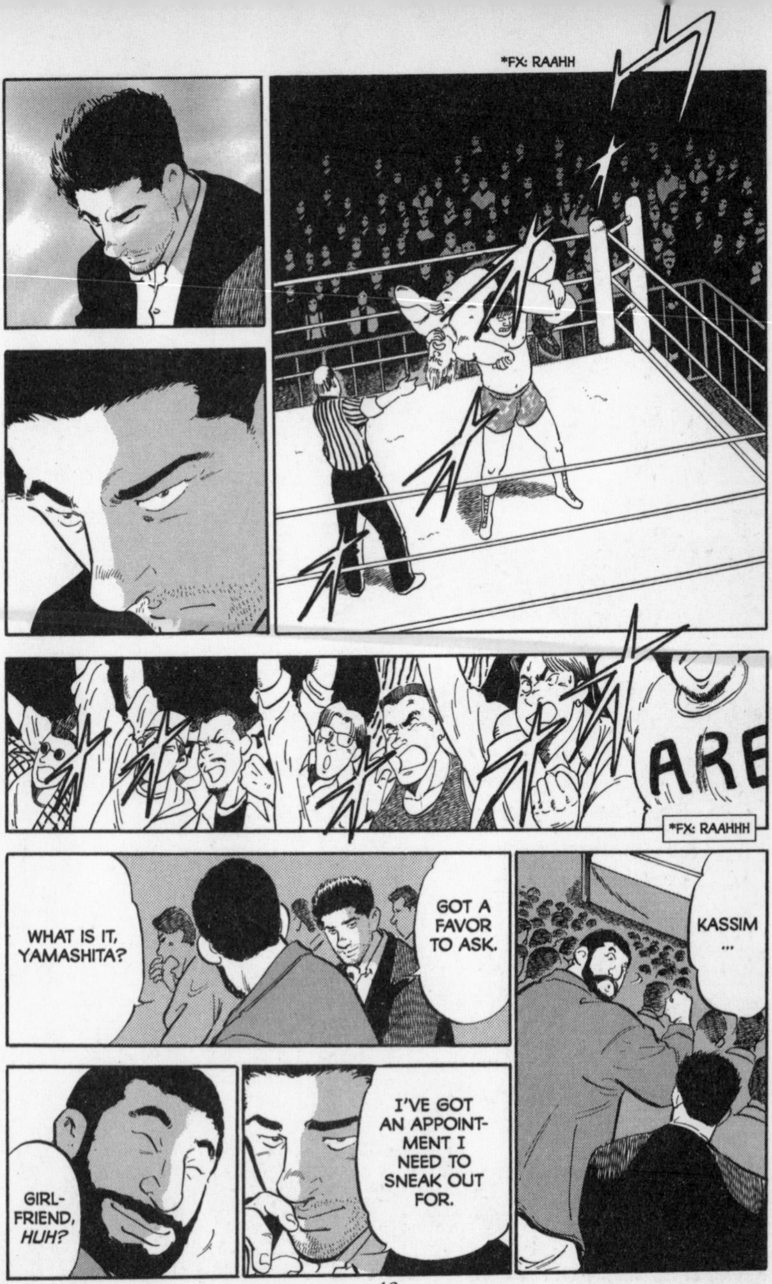
*FX: RAAHH
ARE
*FX: RAAHHH
KASSIM ...
GOT A FAVOR TO ASK.
WHAT IS IT, YAMASHITA?
I'VE GOT AN APPOINTMENT I NEED TO SNEAK OUT FOR.
GIRL-FRIEND, *HUH?*

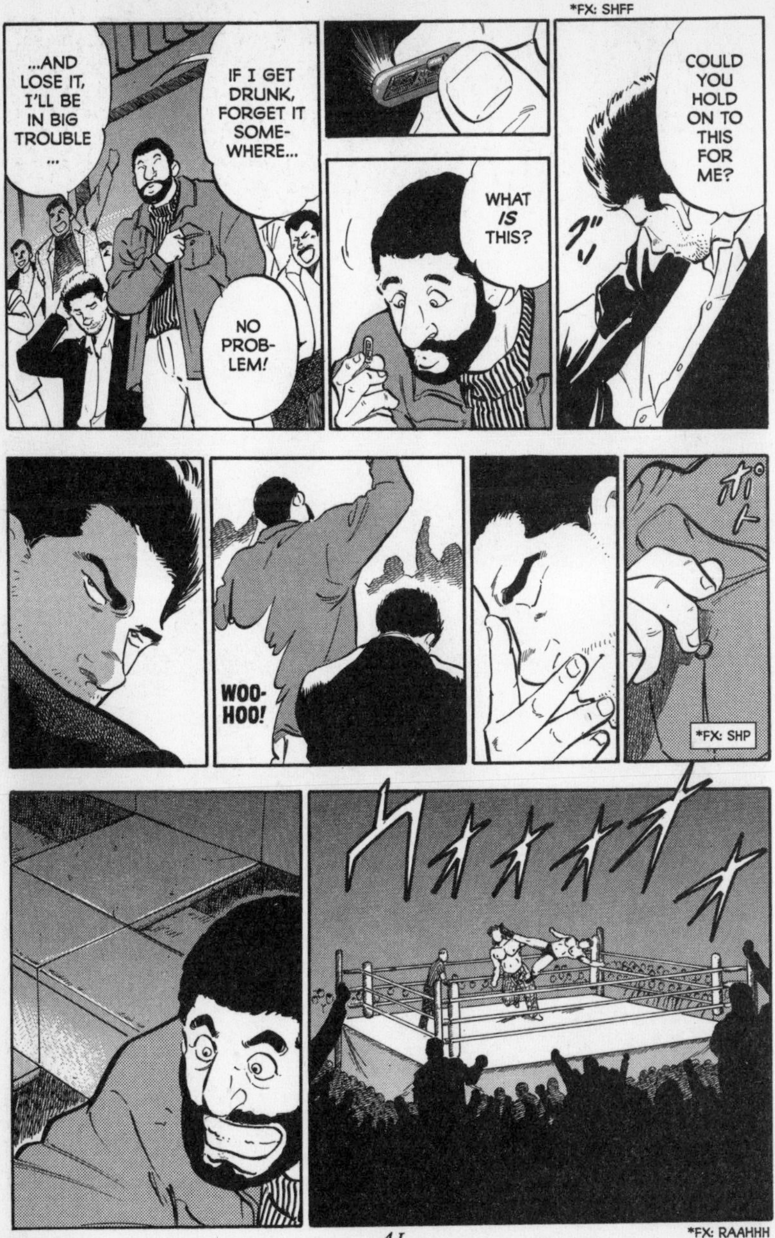
*FX: SHFF
COULD YOU HOLD ON TO THIS FOR ME?
WHAT *IS* THIS?
IF I GET DRUNK, FORGET IT SOME-WHERE...
...AND LOSE IT, I'LL BE IN BIG TROUBLE ...
NO PROB-LEM!
*FX: SHP
WOO-HOO!
*FX: RAAHHH

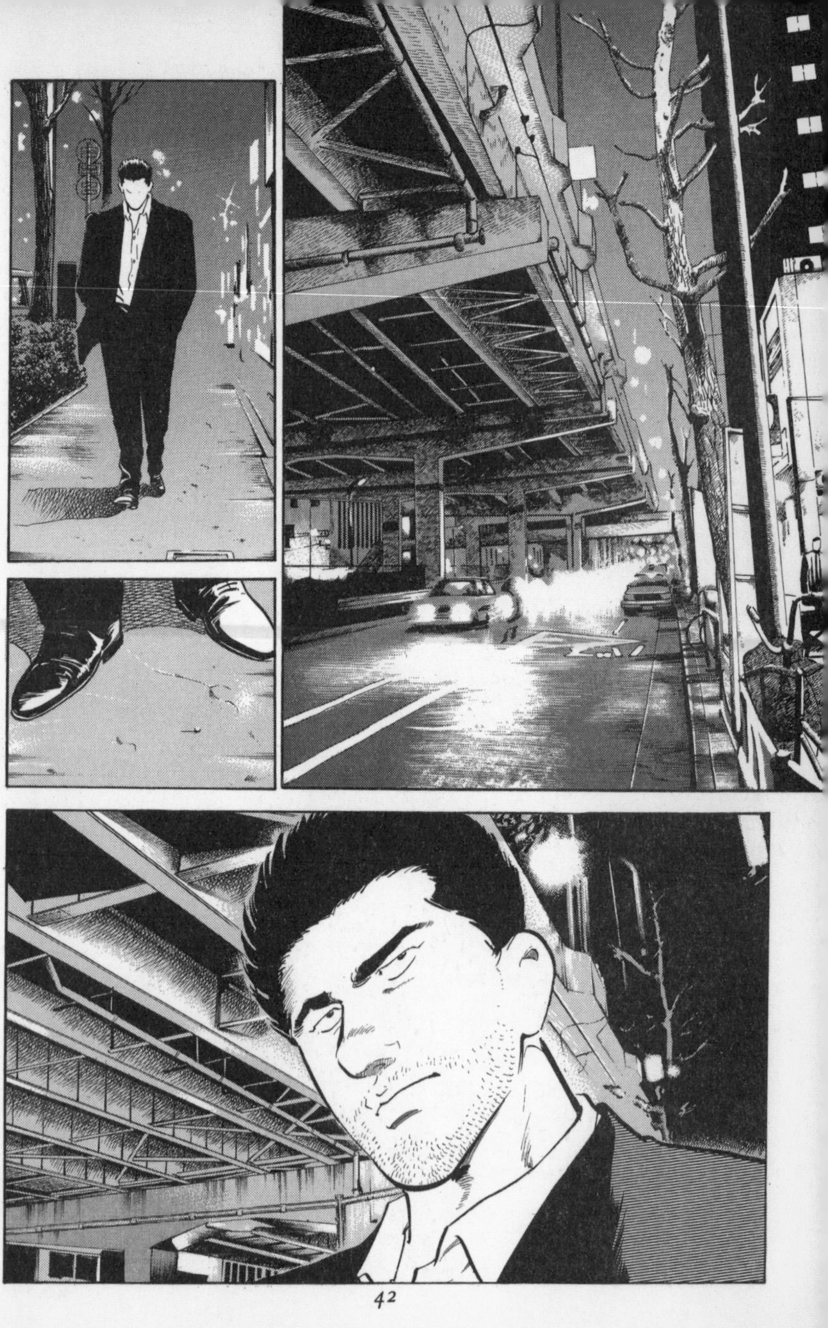

*SIGNS: RAMEN

*SIGN: CHINESE RESTAURANT SHISEIRYU

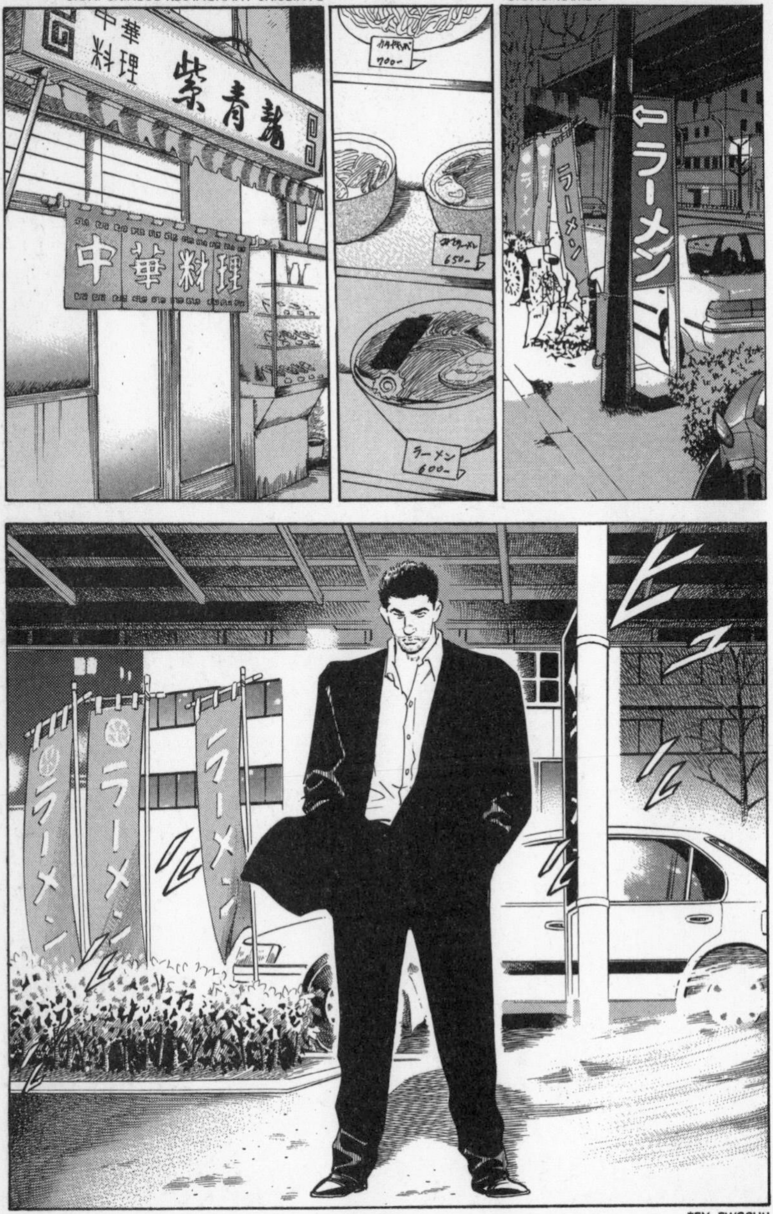
ラーメン
ラーメン
ラーメン
600
650
700
中華料理
紫青龍
中華料理
ヒュ
ラーメン
ラーメン
ラーメン

*FX: FWSSHH

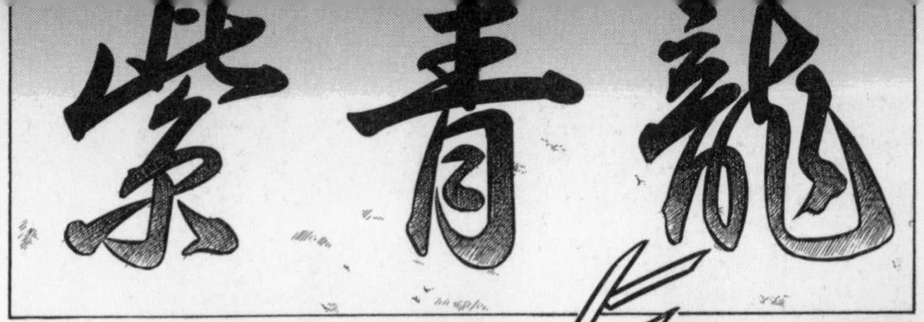
紫青龍

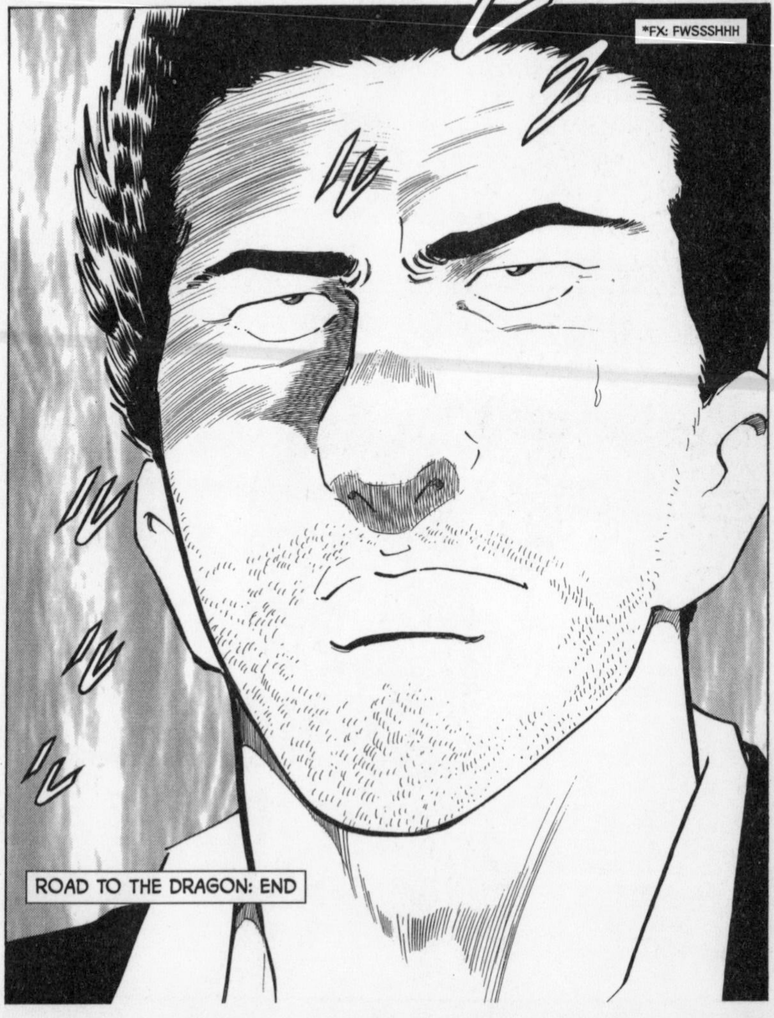
*FX: FWSSSHHH
ROAD TO THE DRAGON: END

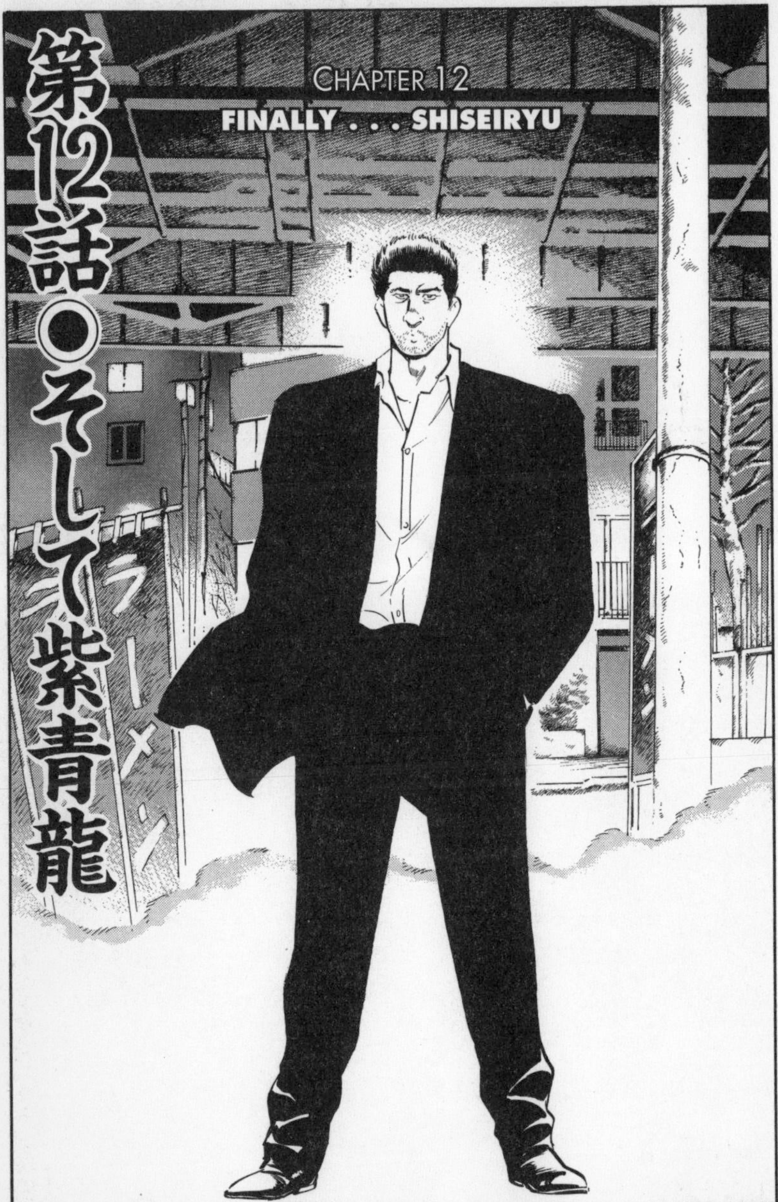
CHAPTER 12
FINALLY . . . SHISEIRYU
第12話○そして紫青龍
ラーメン

*SHOP SIGN: SHISEIRYU

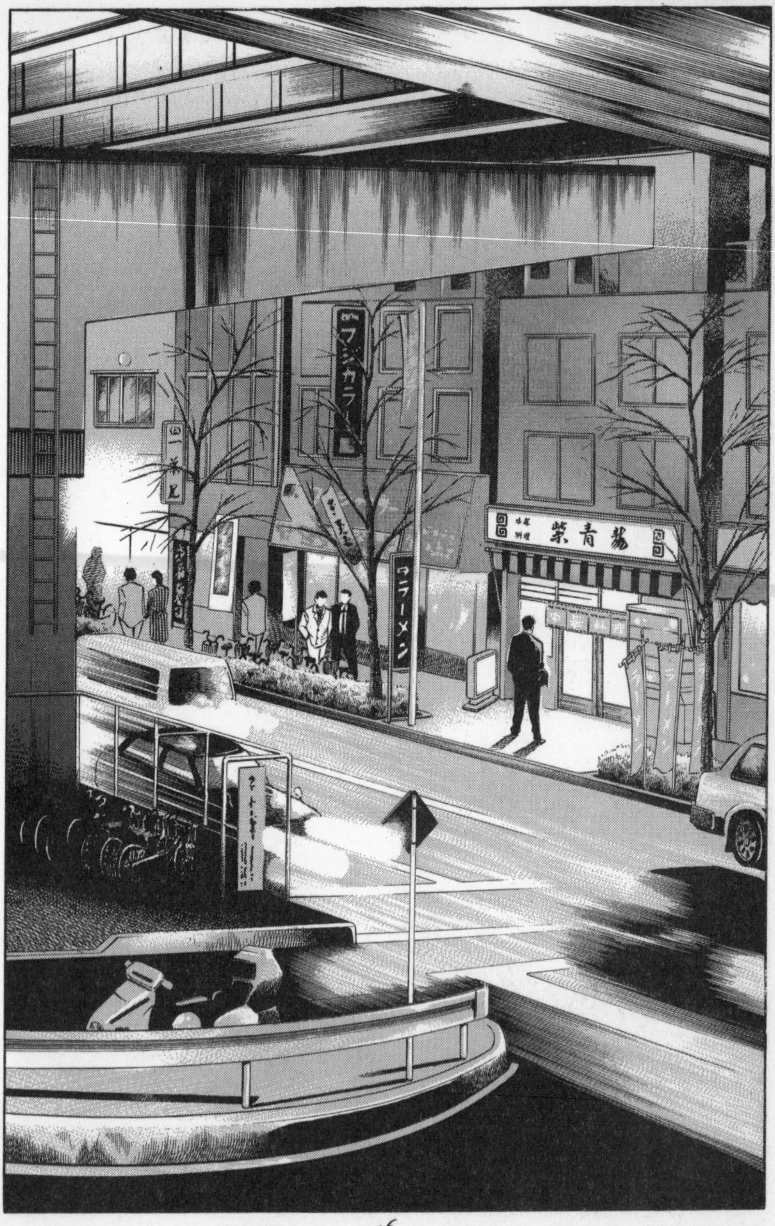
フジカラー
ラーメン

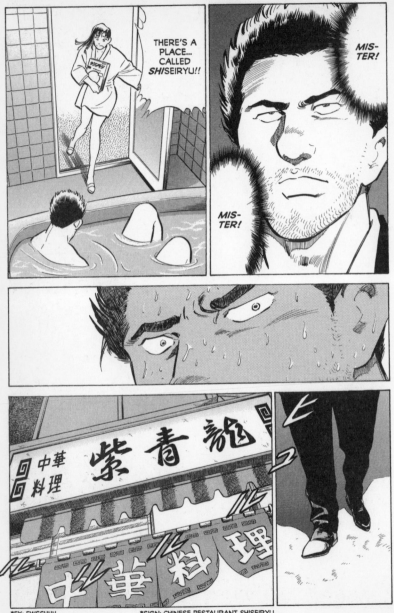

THERE'S A PLACE... CALLED *SHI*SEIRYU!!

MIS-TER!

MIS-TER!

中華
料理 紫青龍

中華料理

*FX: FWSSHHH   *SIGN: CHINESE RESTAURANT SHISEIRYU

*FX: KSZZ KSZZ

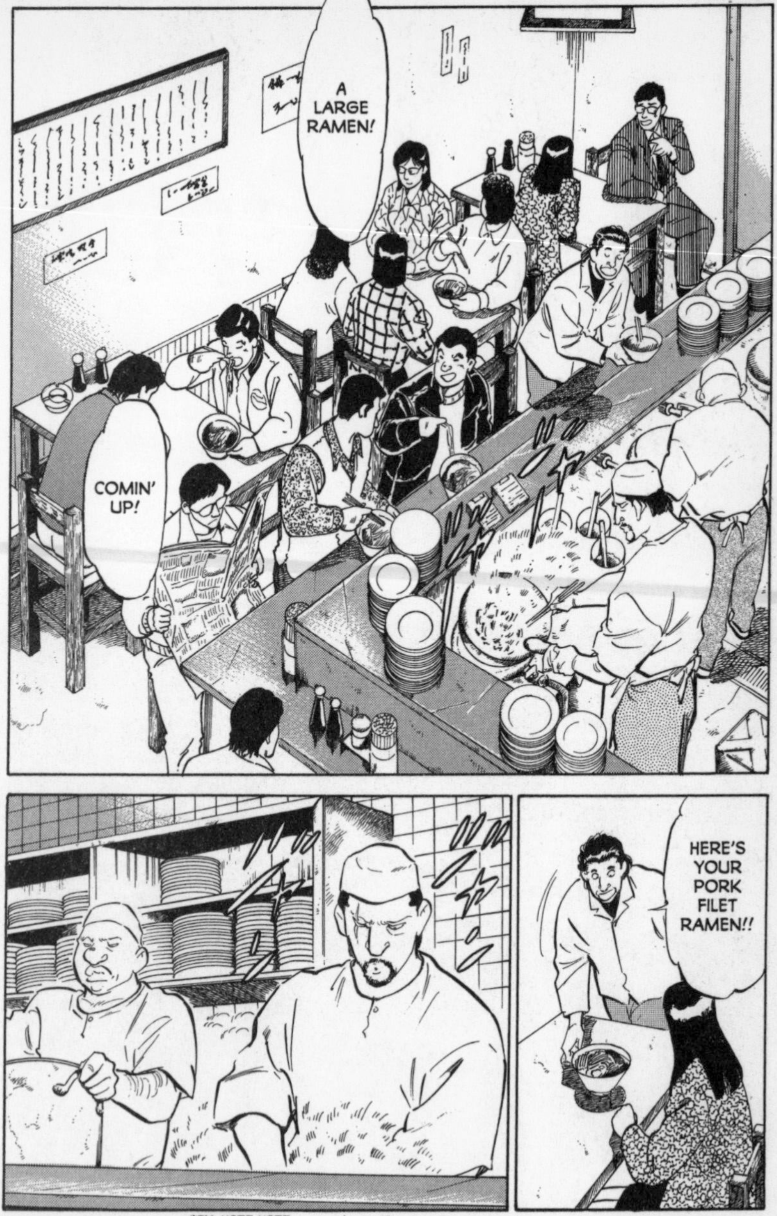
A LARGE RAMEN!
COMIN' UP!
HERE'S YOUR PORK FILET RAMEN!!

*FX: KSZZ KSZZ

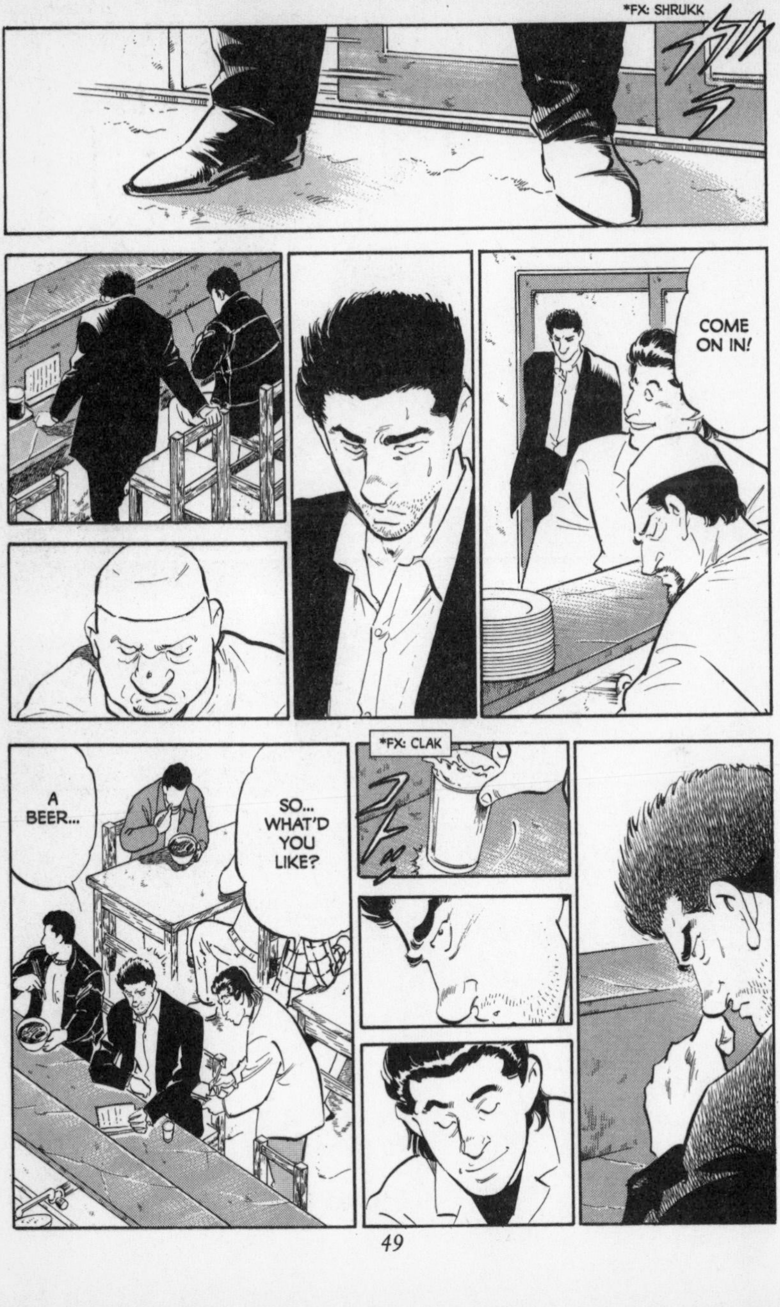
*FX: SHRUKK
COME ON IN!
*FX: CLAK
SO... WHAT'D YOU LIKE?
A BEER...

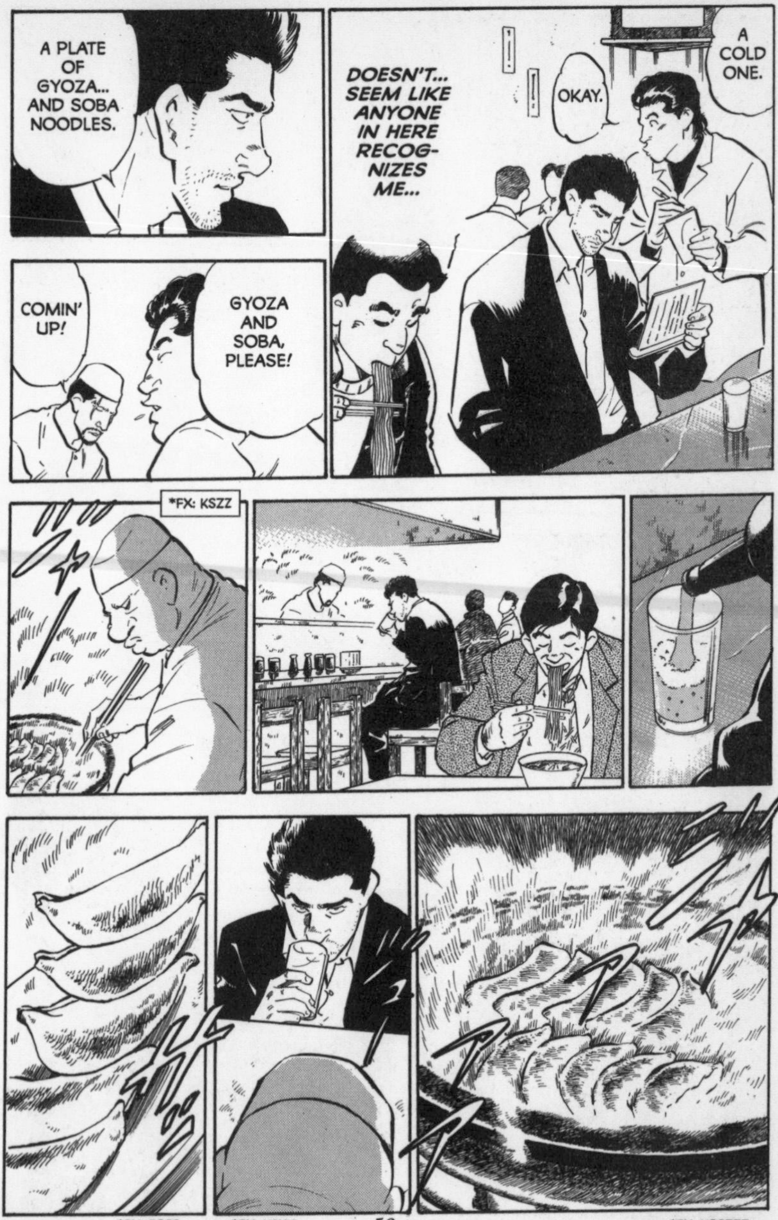
A COLD ONE.
OKAY.
!
!
DOESN'T... SEEM LIKE ANYONE IN HERE RECOG-NIZES ME...
A PLATE OF GYOZA... AND SOBA NOODLES.
GYOZA AND SOBA, PLEASE!
COMIN' UP!
*FX: KSZZ
*FX: KSSZZZ
*FX: KSHH
*FX: FSSS

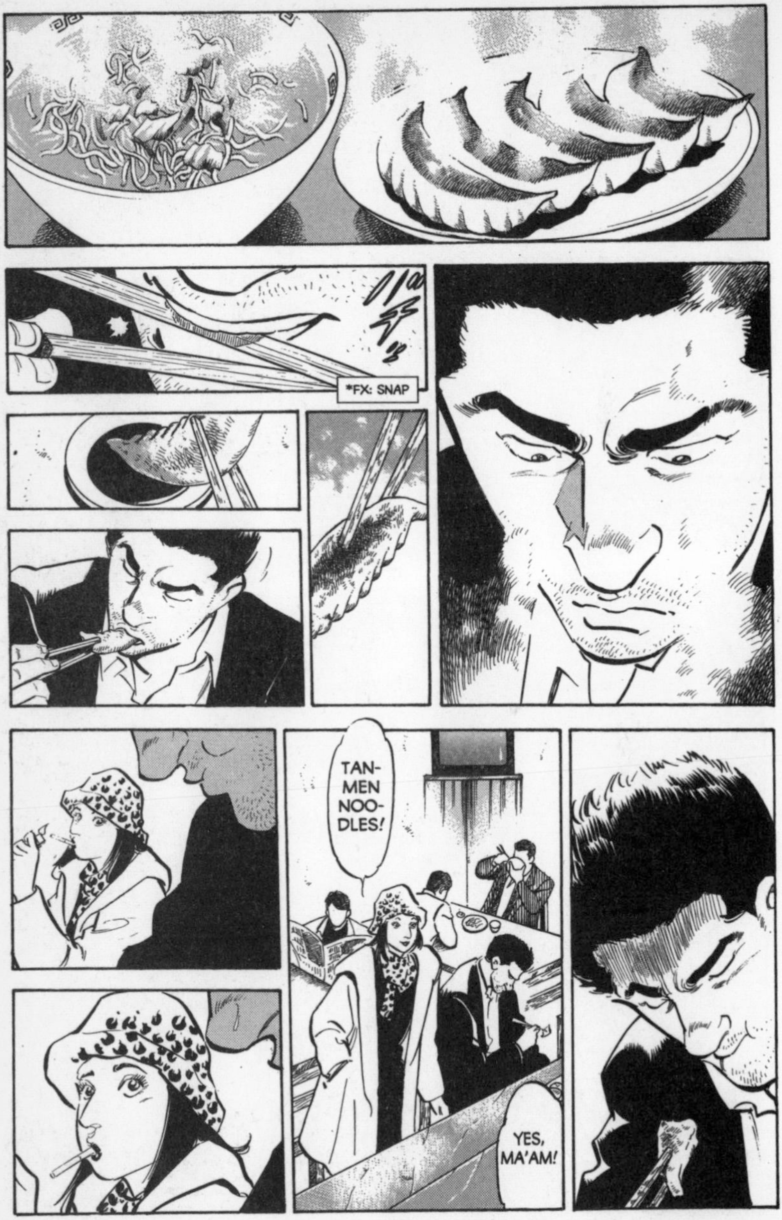
*FX: SNAP
YES, MA'AM!
TAN-MEN NOO-DLES!

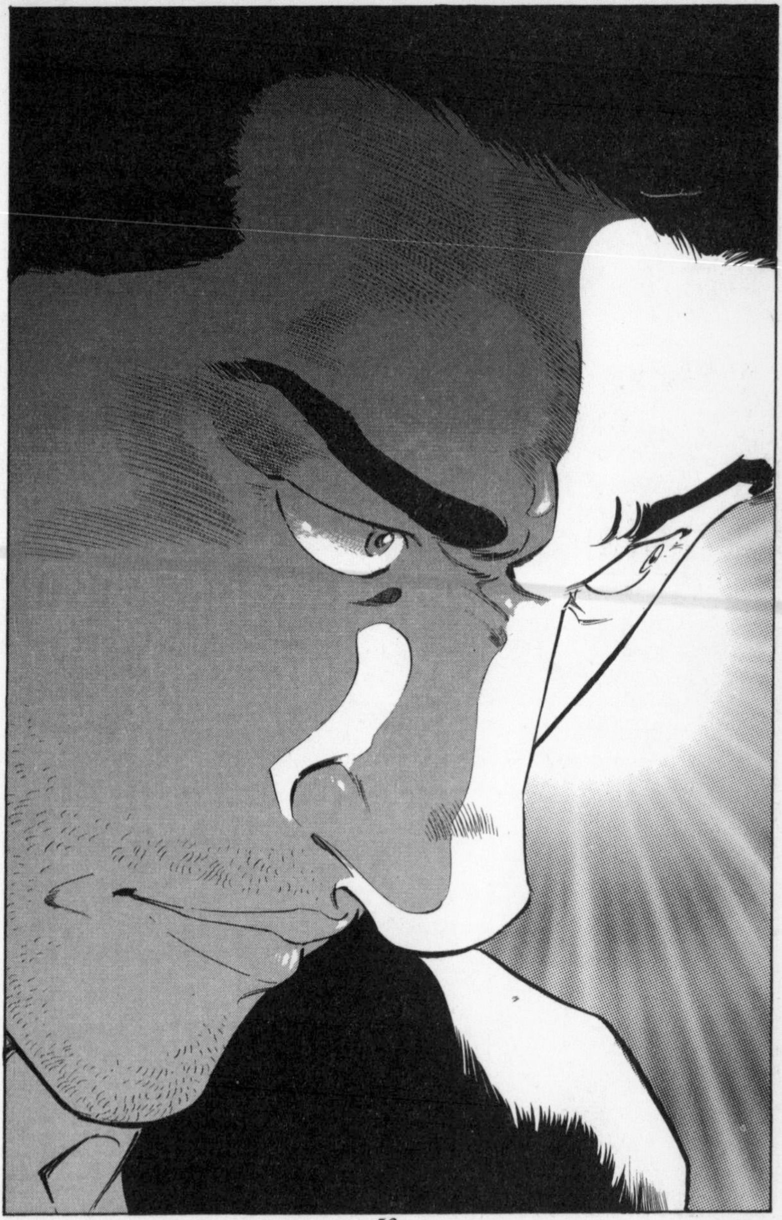

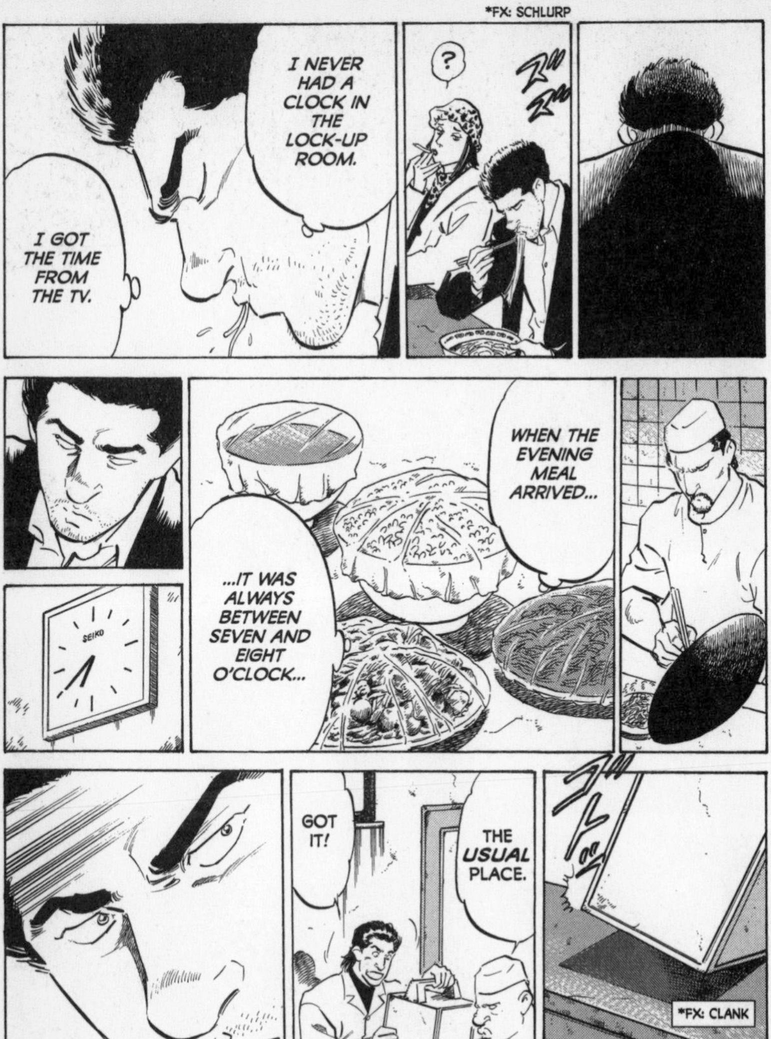
*FX: SCHLURP
?
I NEVER HAD A CLOCK IN THE LOCK-UP ROOM.
I GOT THE TIME FROM THE TV.
WHEN THE EVENING MEAL ARRIVED...
...IT WAS ALWAYS BETWEEN SEVEN AND EIGHT O'CLOCK...
SEIKO
*FX: CLANK
THE *USUAL* PLACE.
GOT IT!
!!

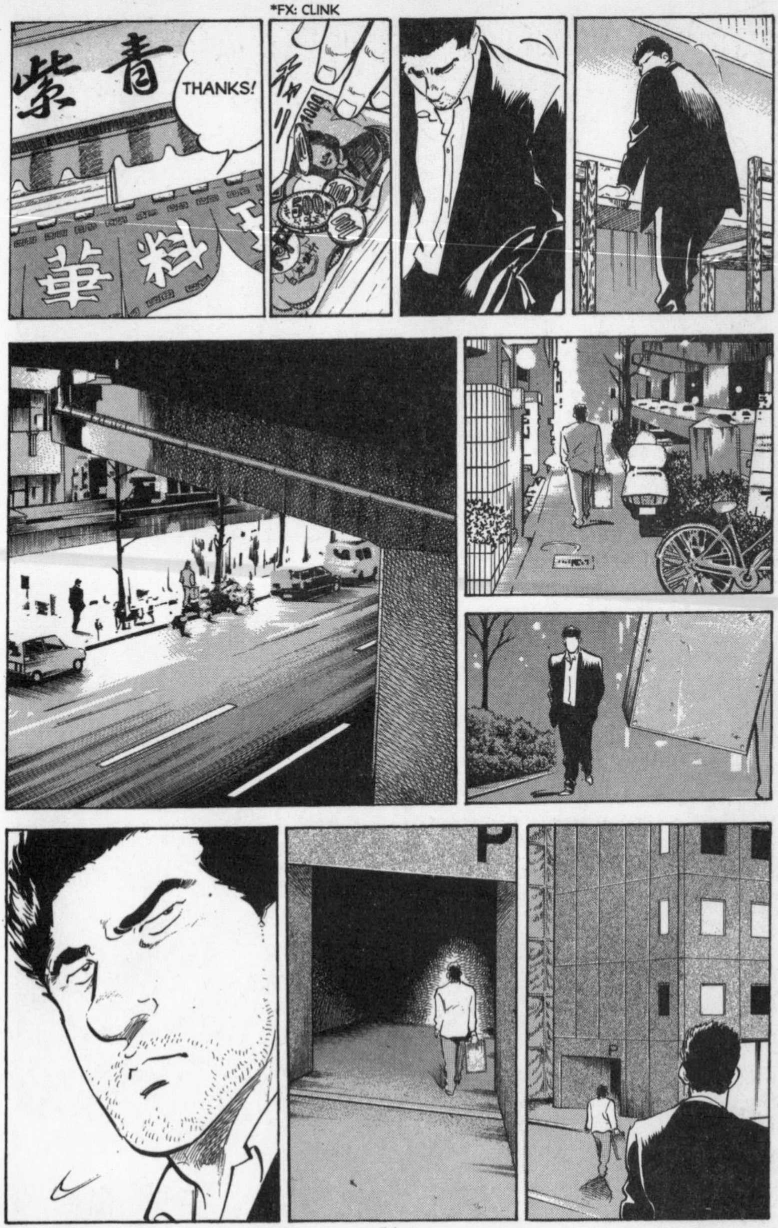
*FX: CLINK
THANKS!

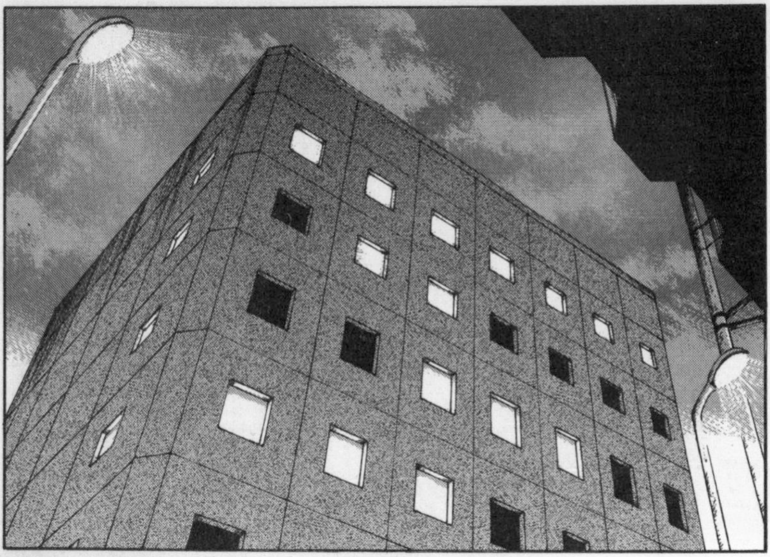

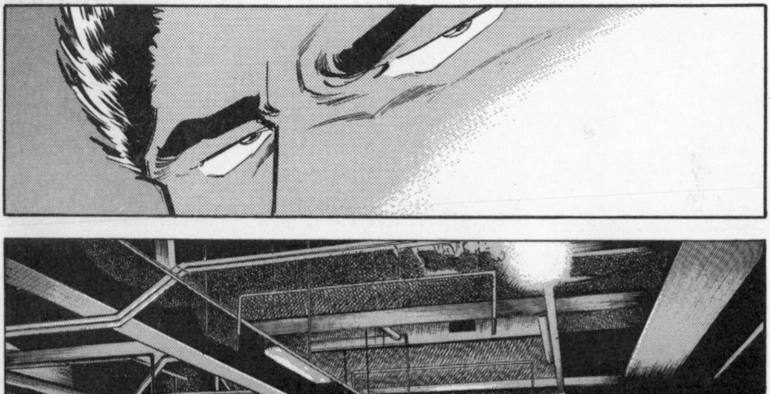

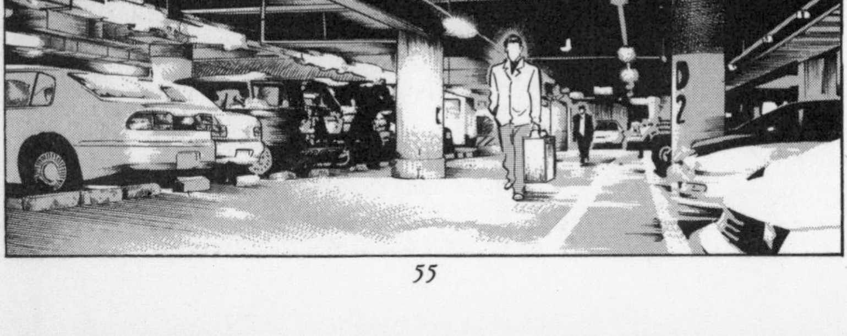
D2

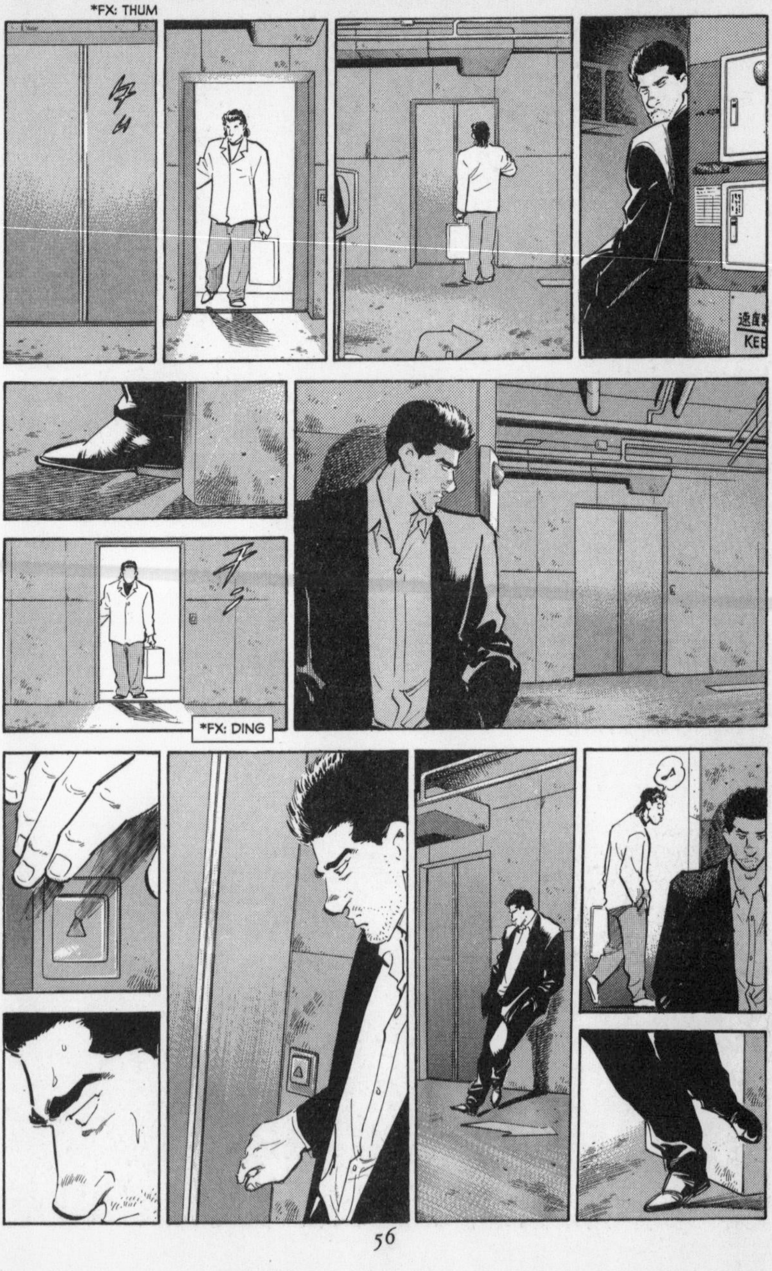
*FX: THUM
KEE
*FX: DING

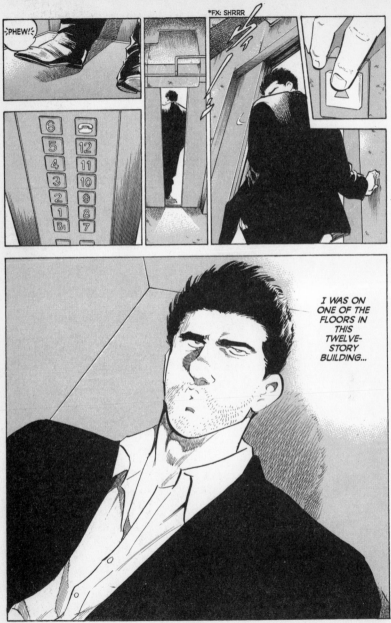

*FX: SHRRR

PHEW!

I WAS ON ONE OF THE FLOORS IN THIS TWELVE-STORY BUILDING...

57

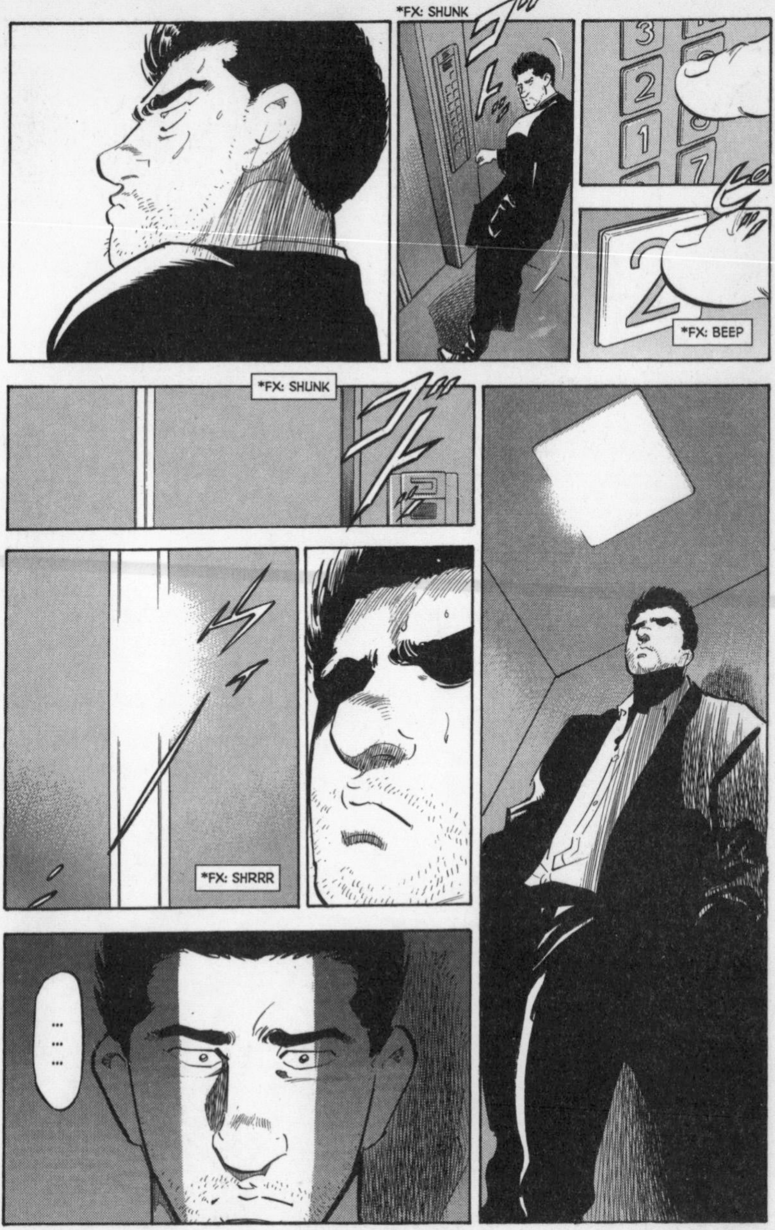
*FX: BEEP
*FX: SHUNK
*FX: SHUNK
*FX: SHRRR
... ...

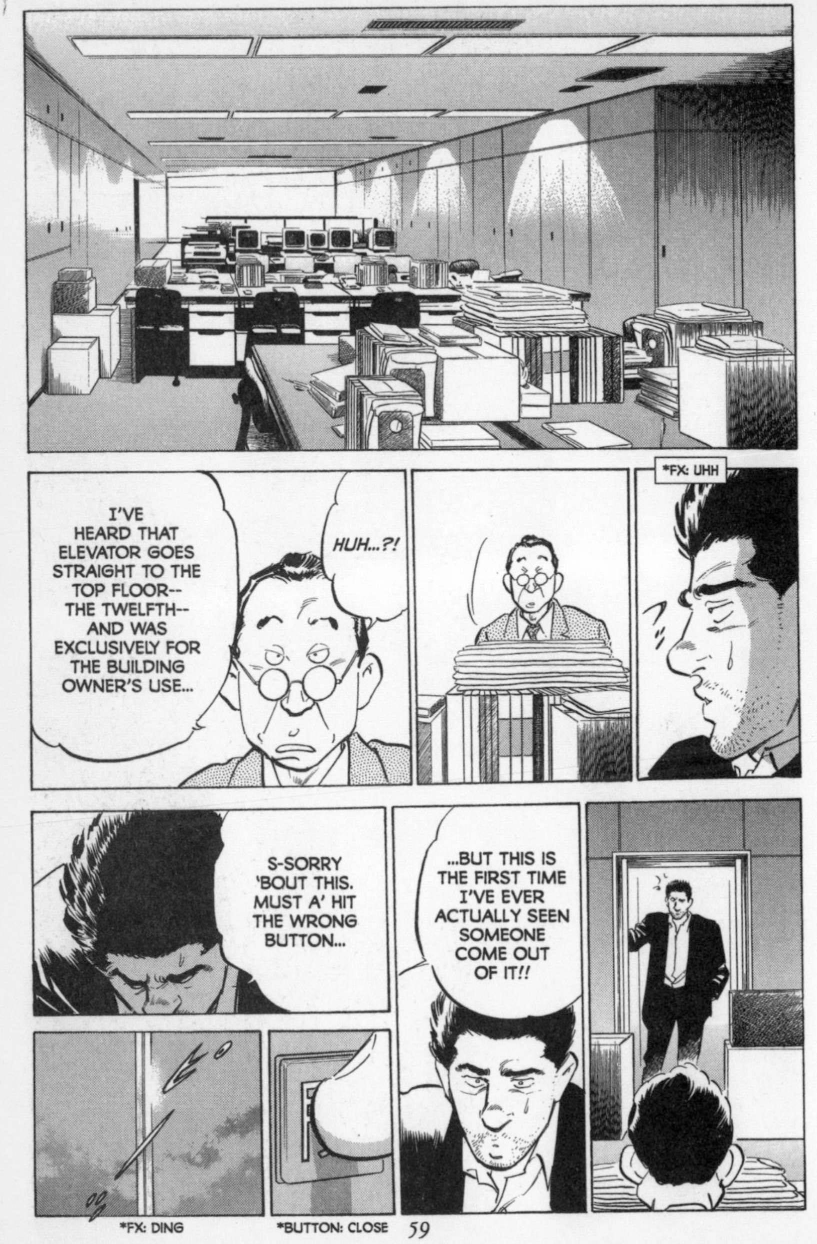
*FX: UHH
HUH...?!
I'VE HEARD THAT ELEVATOR GOES STRAIGHT TO THE TOP FLOOR-- THE TWELFTH-- AND WAS EXCLUSIVELY FOR THE BUILDING OWNER'S USE...
...BUT THIS IS THE FIRST TIME I'VE EVER ACTUALLY SEEN SOMEONE COME OUT OF IT!!
S-SORRY 'BOUT THIS. MUST A' HIT THE WRONG BUTTON...
*BUTTON: CLOSE
*FX: DING

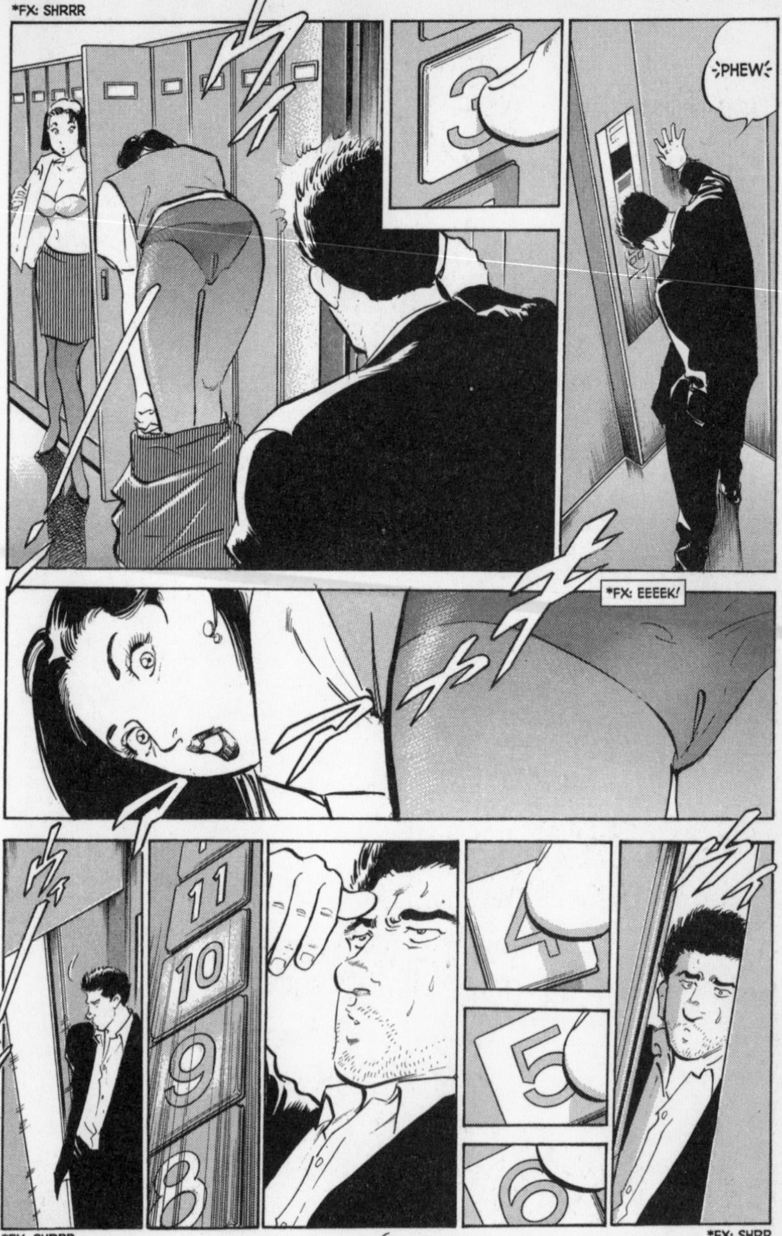
PHEW
*FX: SHRRR
*FX: EEEEK!
*FX: SHRR
*FX: SHRRR

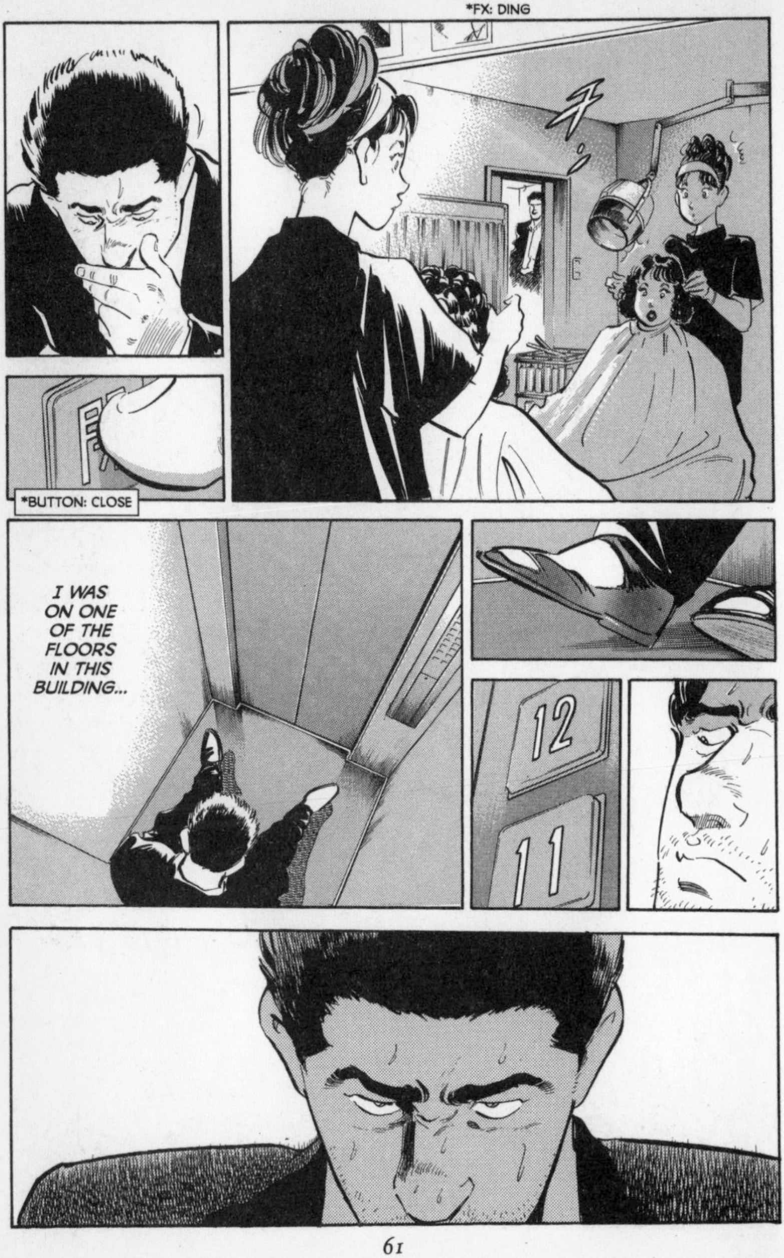
*FX: DING
*BUTTON: CLOSE
12
11
I WAS ON ONE OF THE FLOORS IN THIS BUILDING...

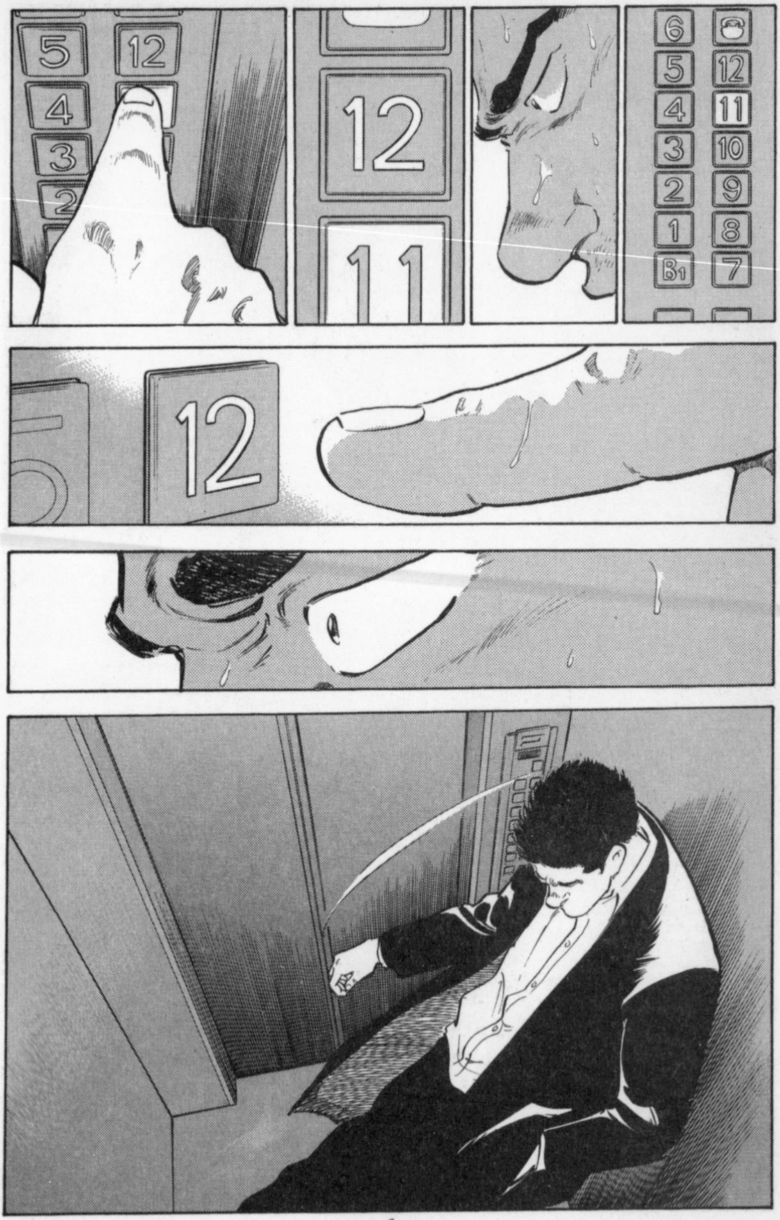
6
5
12
4
11
3
10
2
9
1
8
B1
7
12
11
5
12
4
3
2
12

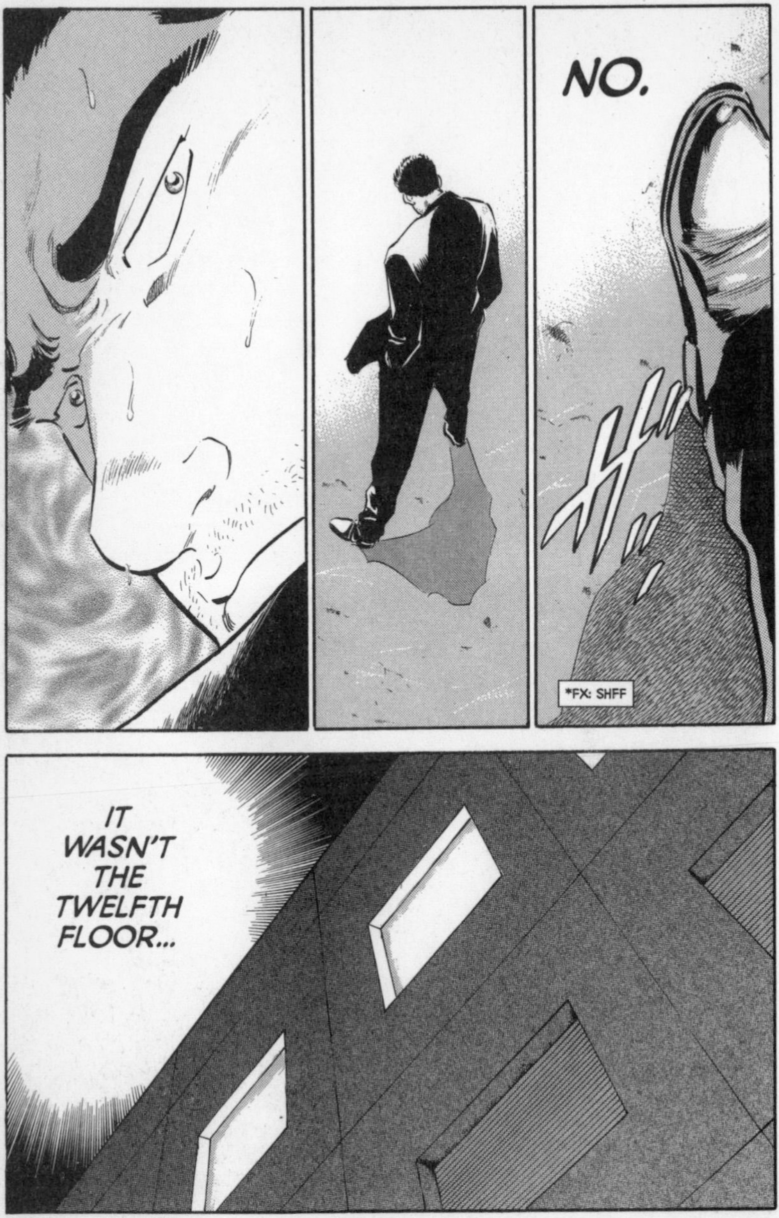
NO.
*FX: SHFF
IT WASN'T THE TWELFTH FLOOR...

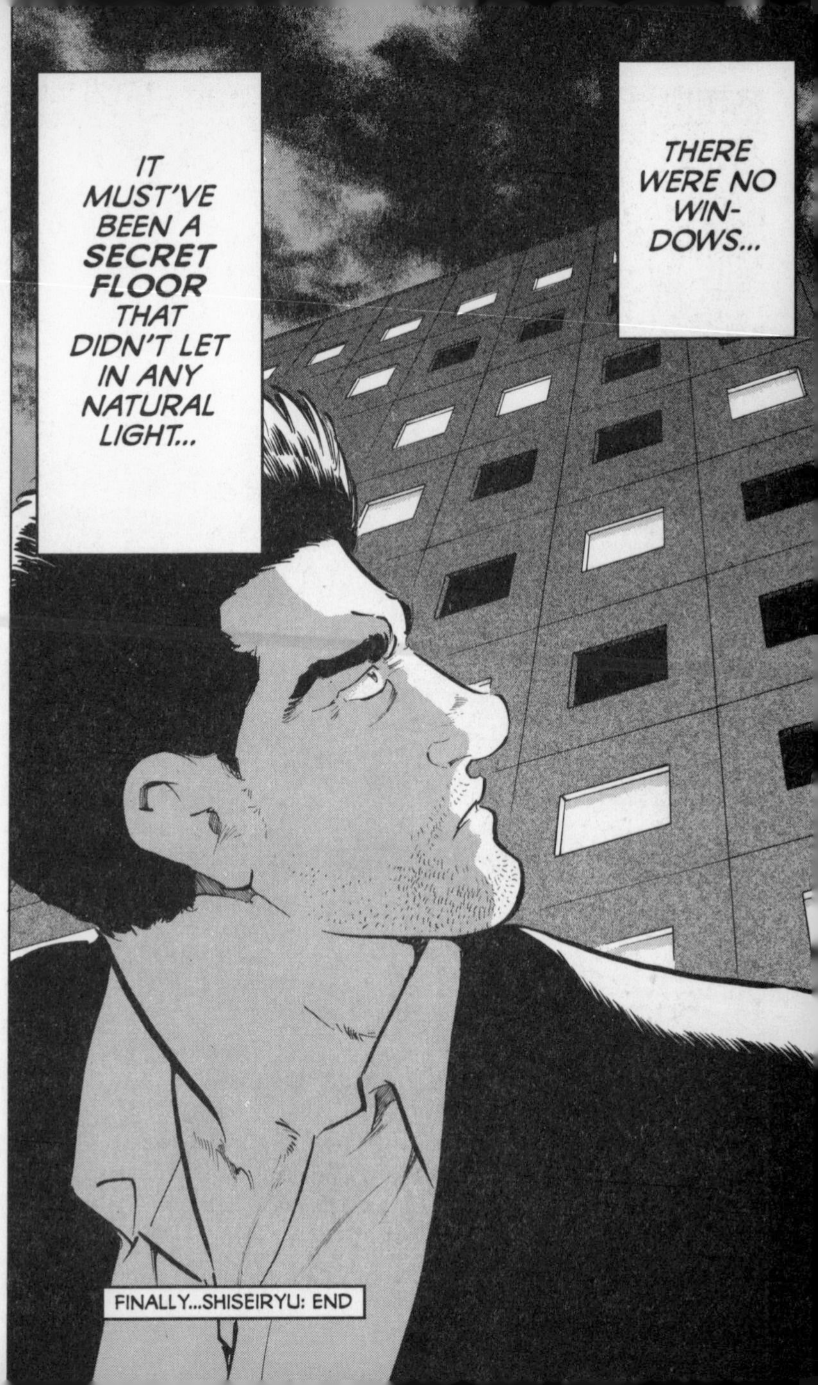
THERE WERE NO WIN-DOWS...
IT MUST'VE BEEN A SECRET FLOOR THAT DIDN'T LET IN ANY NATURAL LIGHT...
FINALLY...SHISEIRYU: END

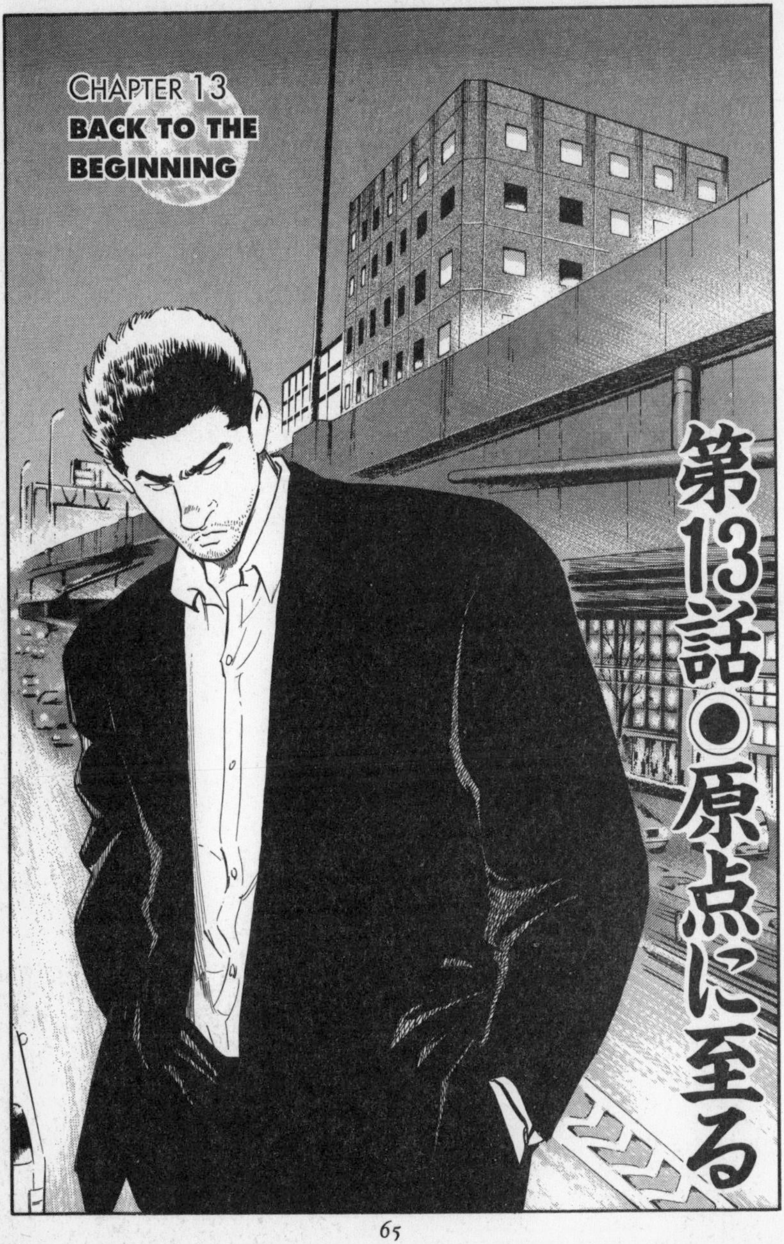
CHAPTER 13
BACK TO THE BEGINNING
第13話●原点に至る

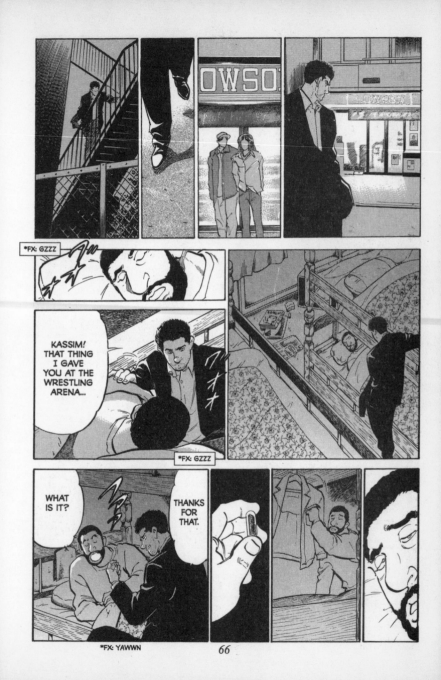

*FX: GZZZ

KASSIM! THAT THING I GAVE YOU AT THE WRESTLING ARENA...

*FX: GZZZ

WHAT IS IT?

THANKS FOR THAT.

*FX: YAWWN

66

MMPH
...

A VERY IMPORTANT "LUCKY CHARM"!

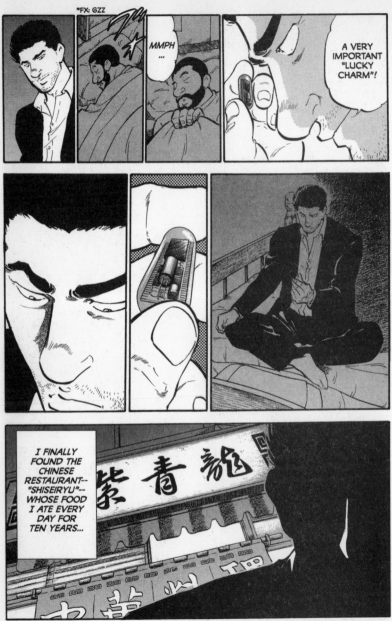

I FINALLY FOUND THE CHINESE RESTAURANT-- "SHISEIRYU"-- WHOSE FOOD I ATE EVERY DAY FOR TEN YEARS...

*SIGN: SHISEIRYU

67

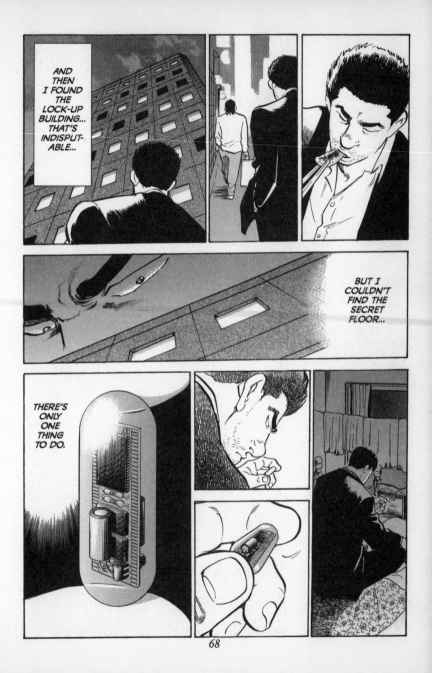

AND THEN I FOUND THE LOCK-UP BUILDING... THAT'S INDISPUTABLE...

BUT I COULDN'T FIND THE SECRET FLOOR...

THERE'S ONLY ONE THING TO DO.

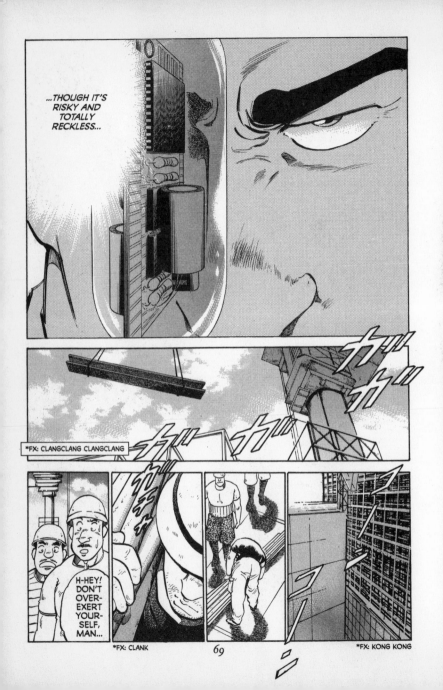

...THOUGH IT'S RISKY AND TOTALLY RECKLESS...

*FX: CLANGCLANG CLANGCLANG

H-HEY! DON'T OVER-EXERT YOUR-SELF, MAN...

*FX: CLANK

69

*FX: KONG KONG

*FX: CLANGCLANGCLANGCLANG GONGONGGONGGONG

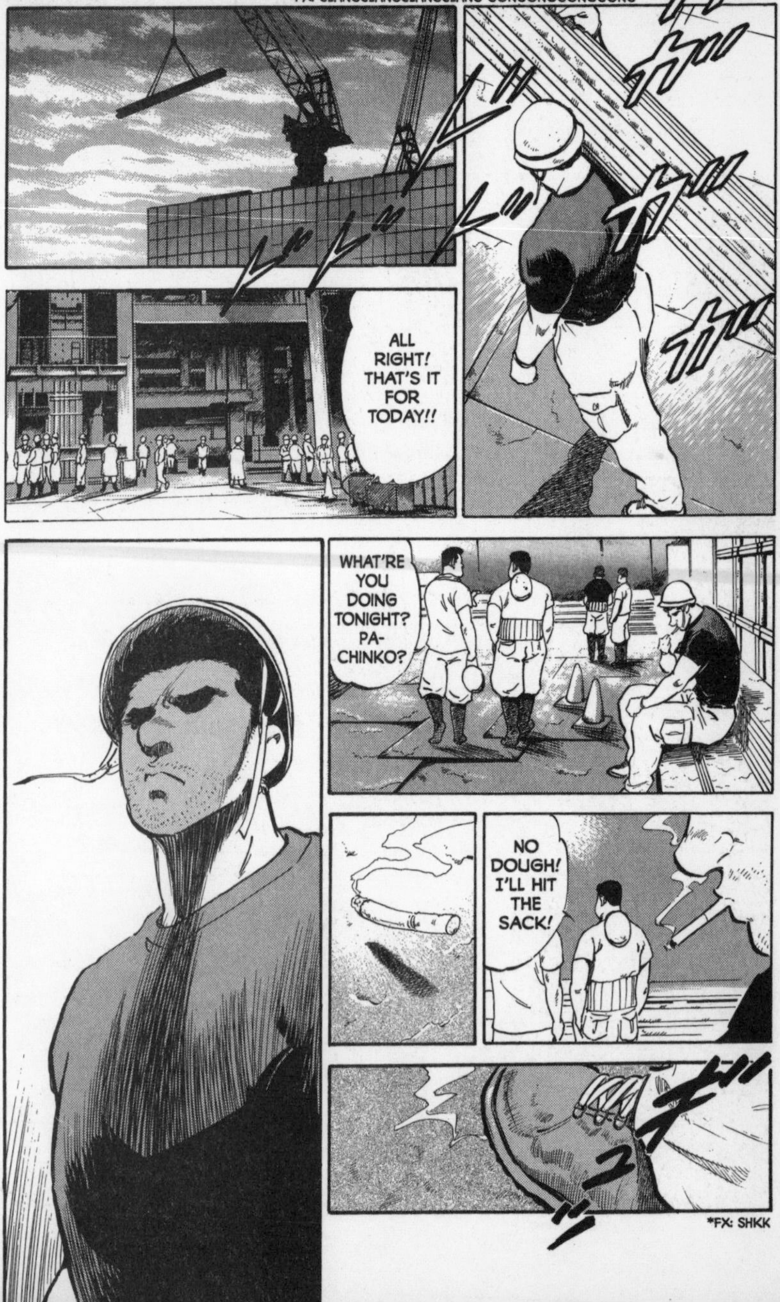
ALL RIGHT! THAT'S IT FOR TODAY!!
WHAT'RE YOU DOING TONIGHT? PA-CHINKO?
NO DOUGH! I'LL HIT THE SACK!

*FX: SHKK

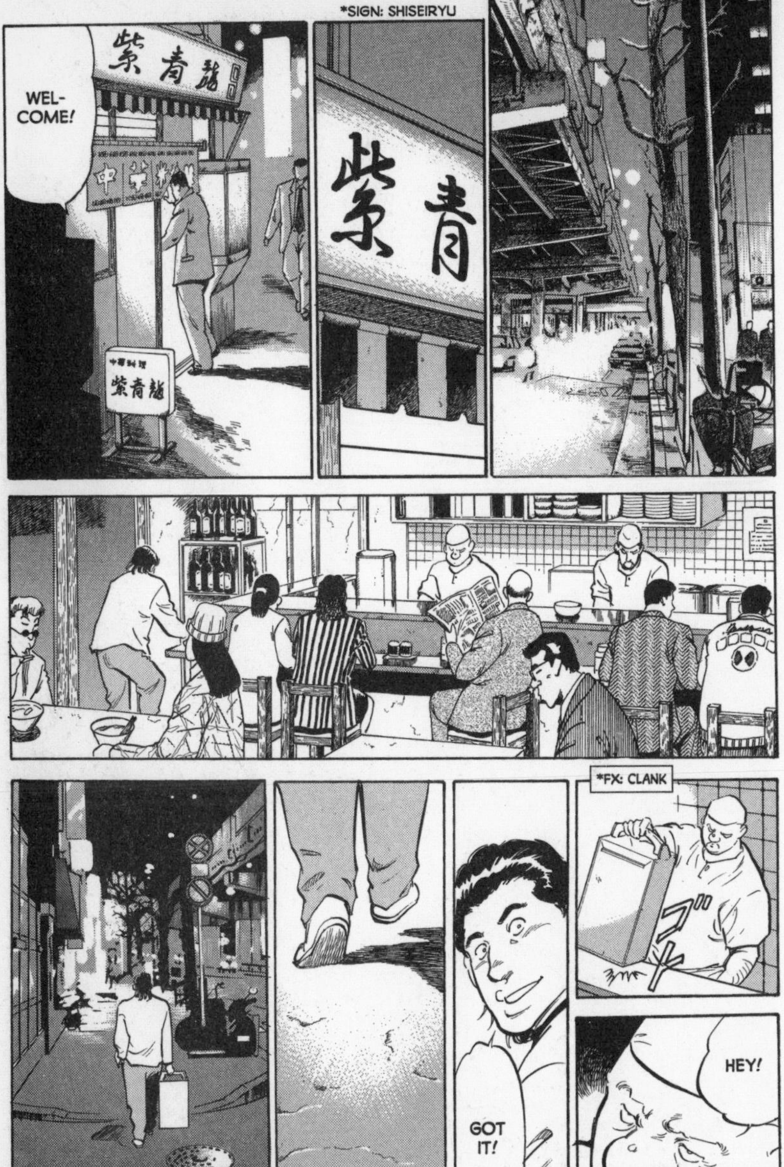
*SIGN: SHISEIRYU
WEL-
COME!
*FX: CLANK
HEY!
GOT
IT!

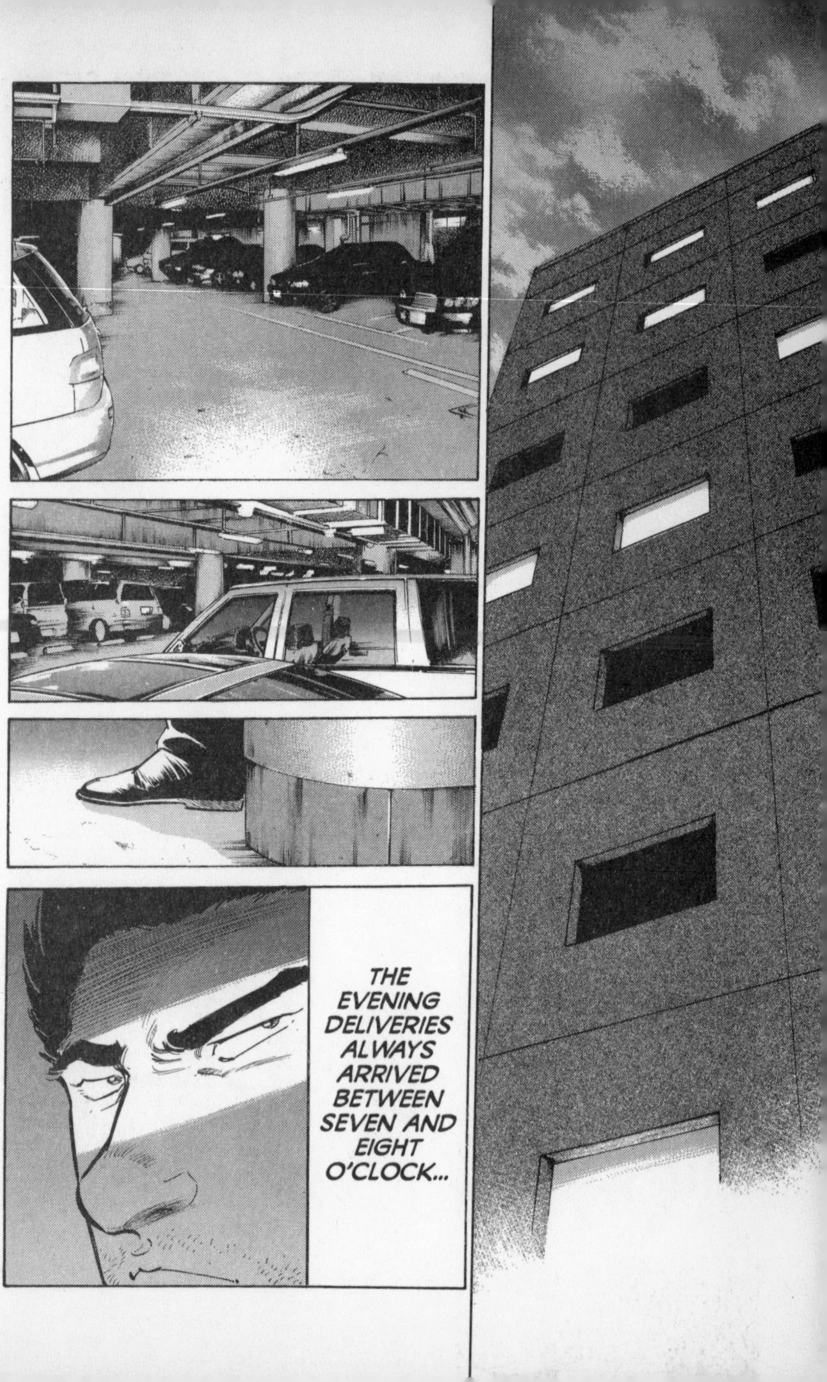
THE EVENING DELIVERIES ALWAYS ARRIVED BETWEEN SEVEN AND EIGHT O'CLOCK...

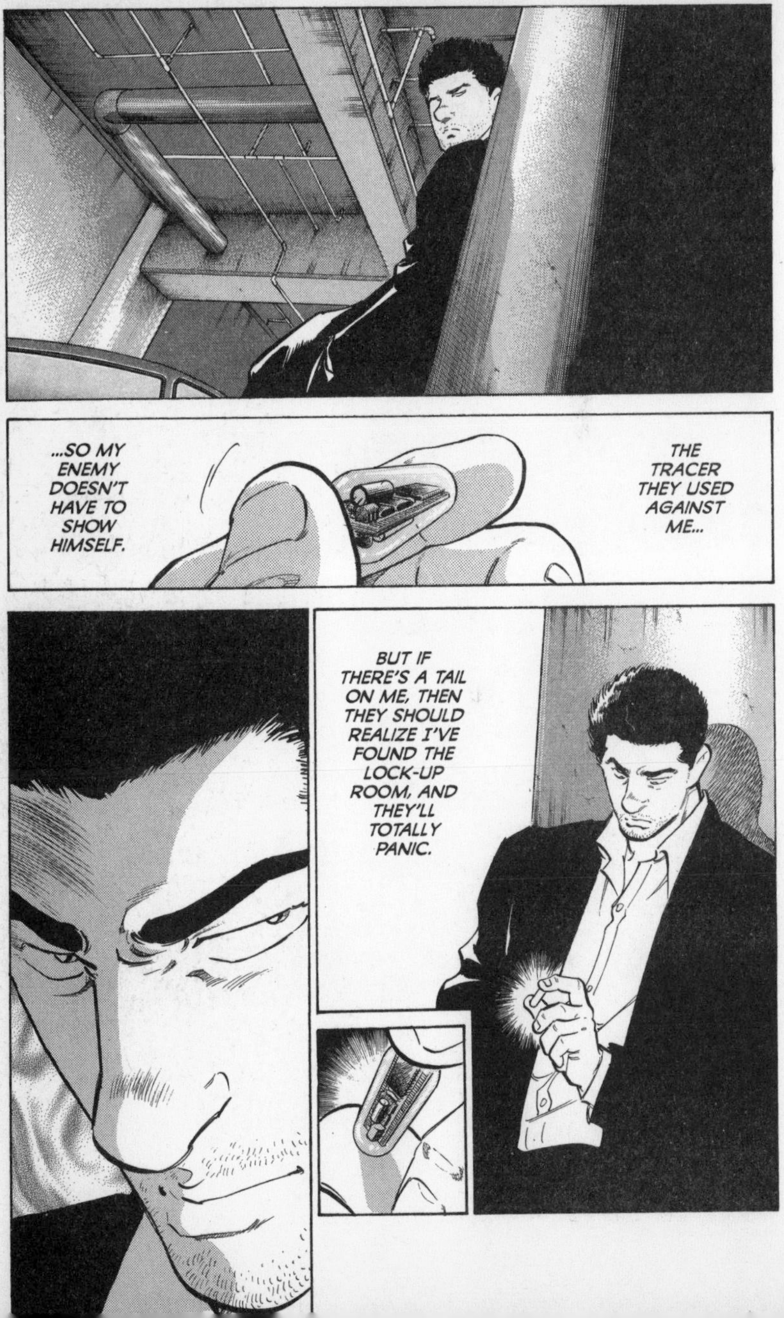
THE TRACER THEY USED AGAINST ME...
...SO MY ENEMY DOESN'T HAVE TO SHOW HIMSELF.
BUT IF THERE'S A TAIL ON ME, THEN THEY SHOULD REALIZE I'VE FOUND THE LOCK-UP ROOM, AND THEY'LL TOTALLY PANIC.

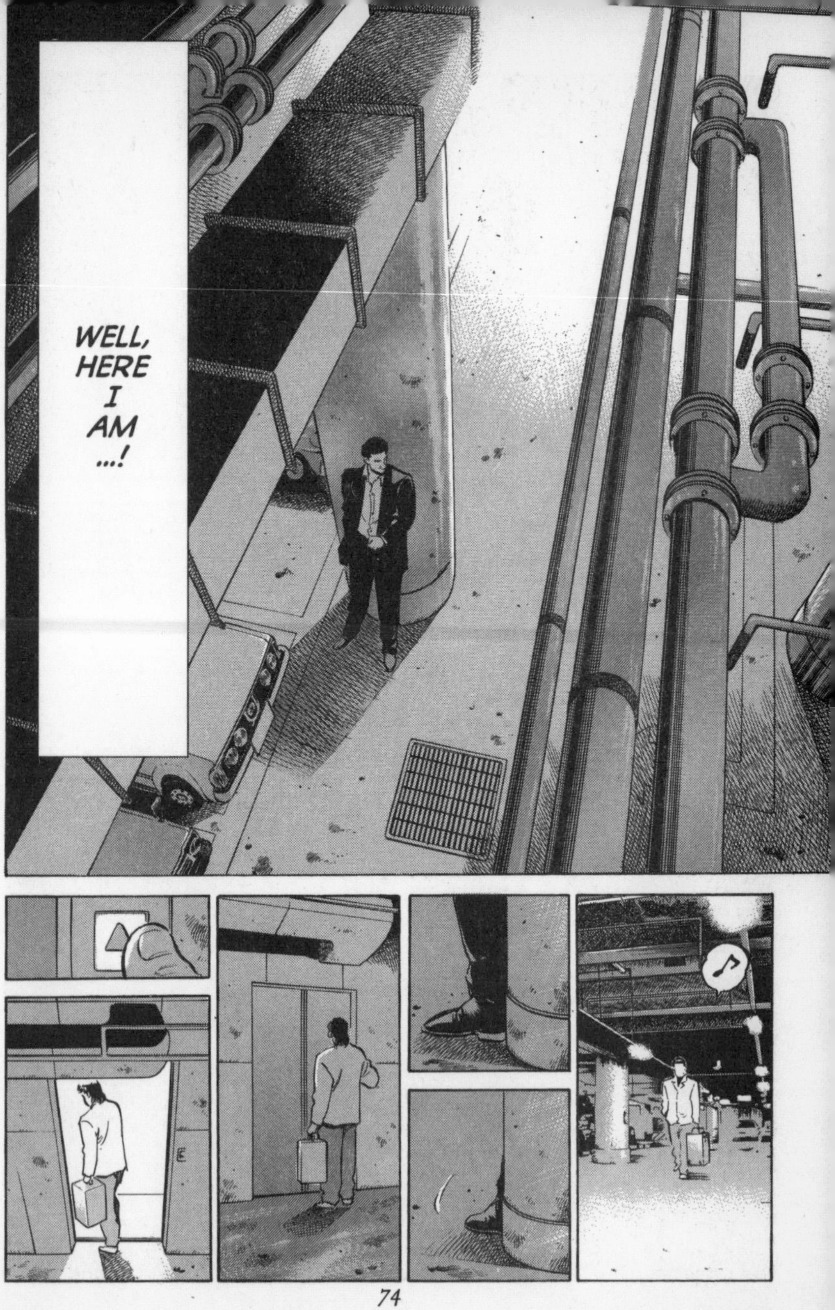
WELL, HERE I AM ...!

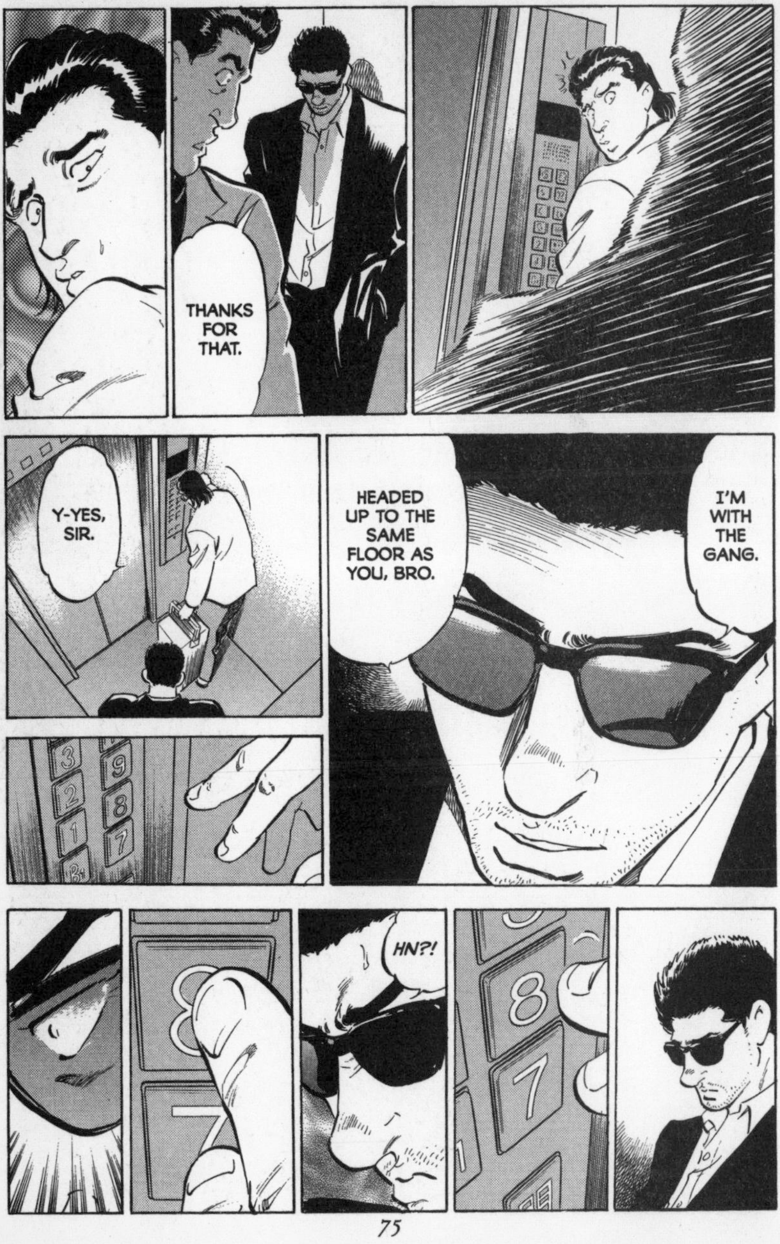
THANKS FOR THAT.
I'M WITH THE GANG.
HEADED UP TO THE SAME FLOOR AS YOU, BRO.
Y-YES, SIR.
HN?!

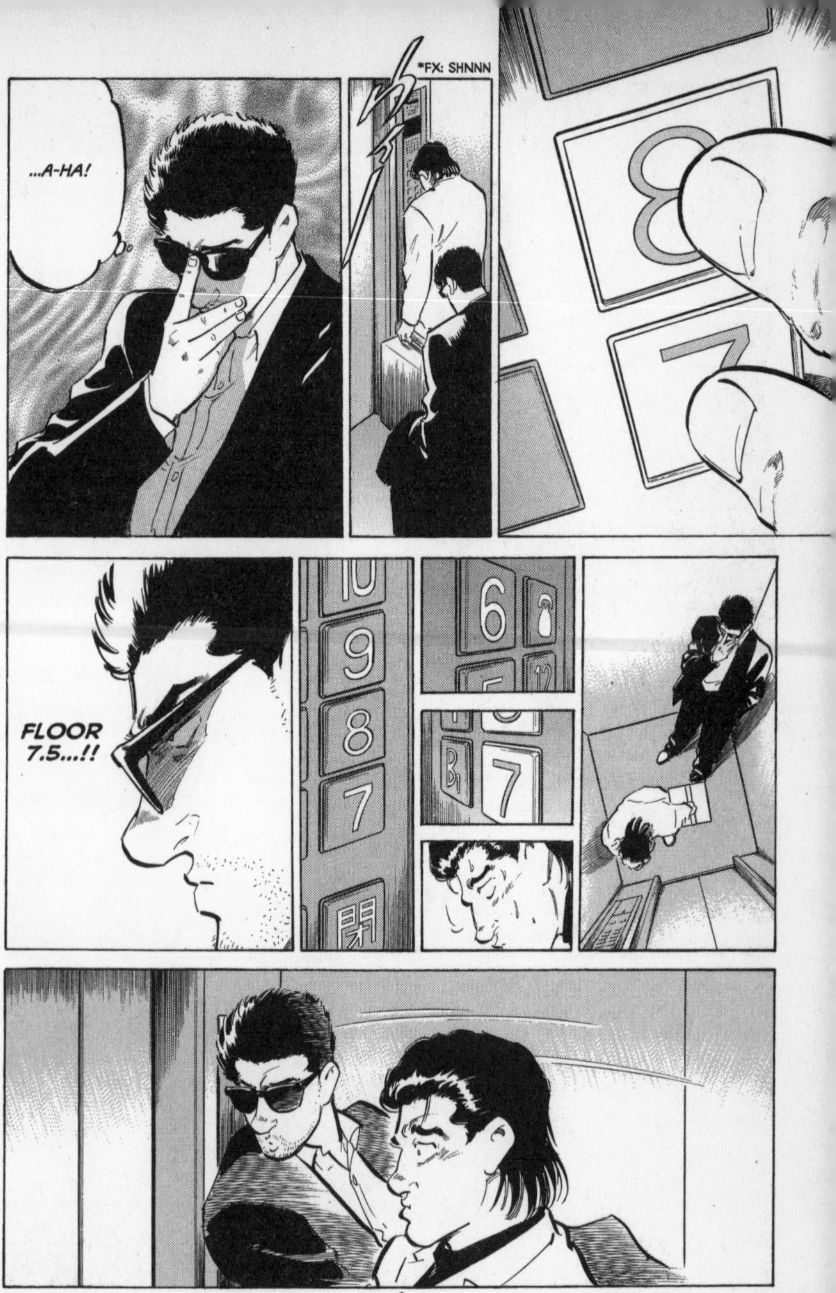
*FX: SHNNN
...A-HA!
FLOOR 7.5...!!

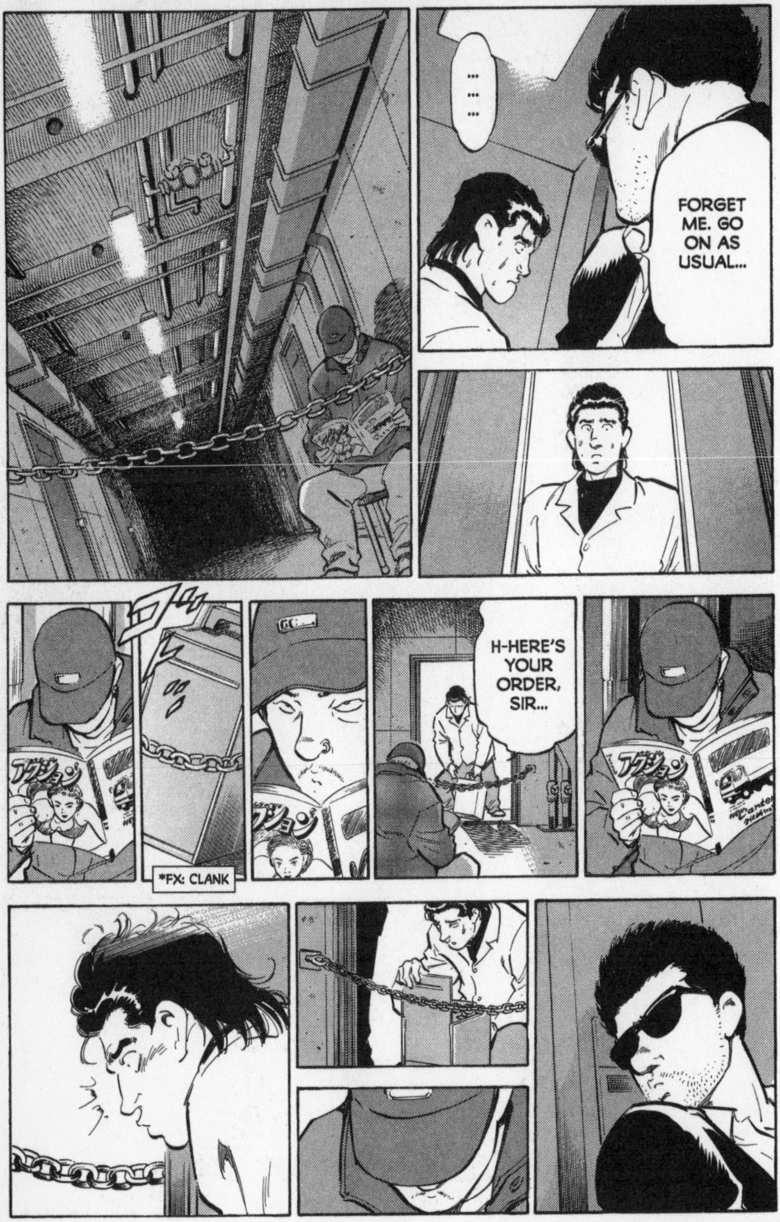
FORGET ME. GO ON AS USUAL...
......
......
......
アクション
H-HERE'S YOUR ORDER, SIR...
アクション
*FX: CLANK

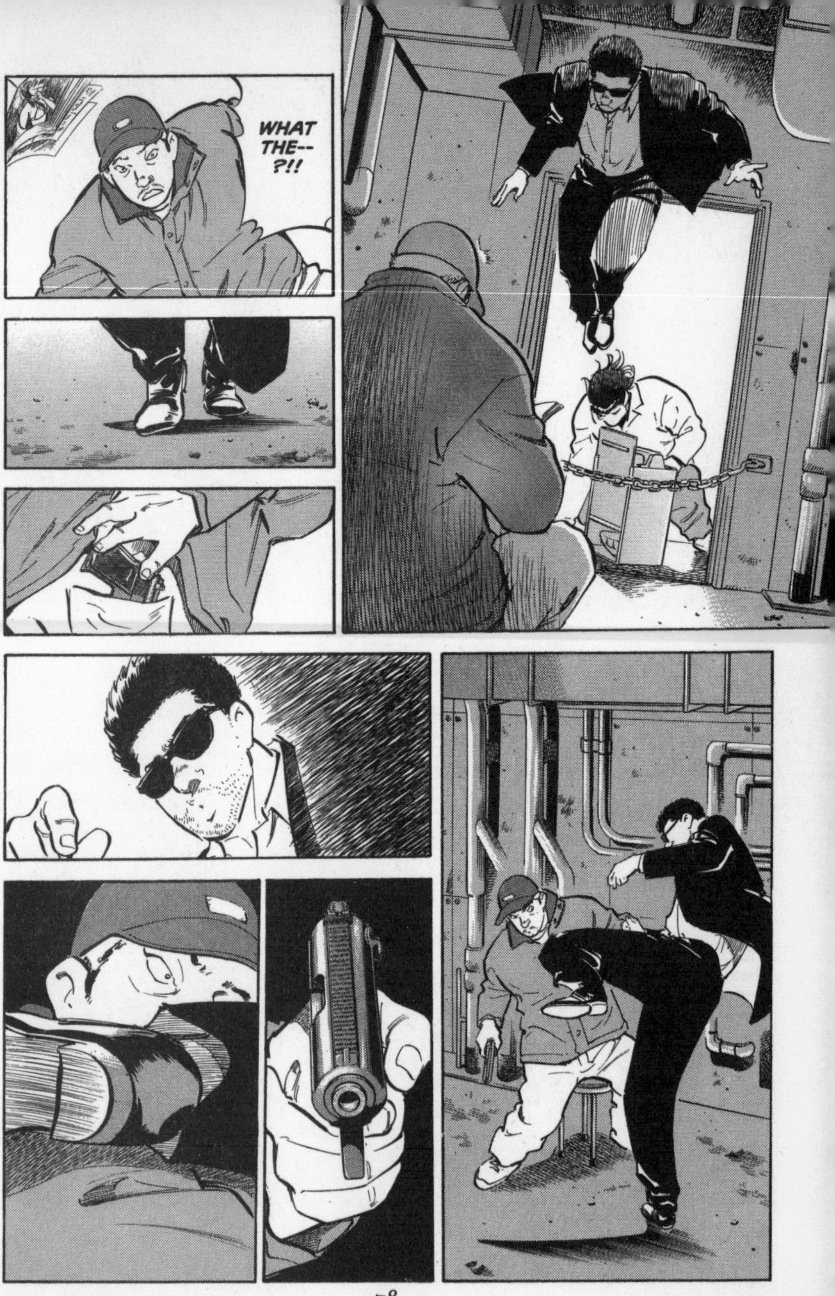
WHAT THE-- ?!!

*FX: BLAM

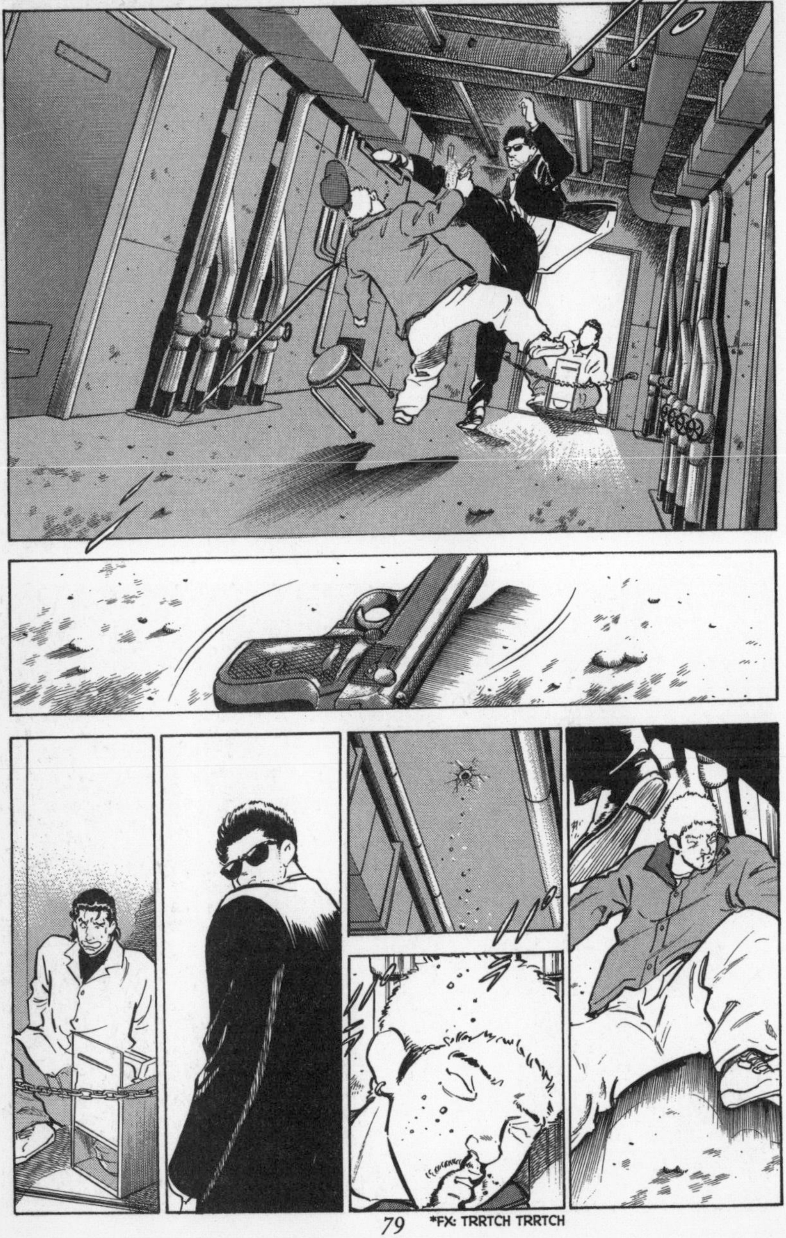

*FX: TRRTCH TRRTCH

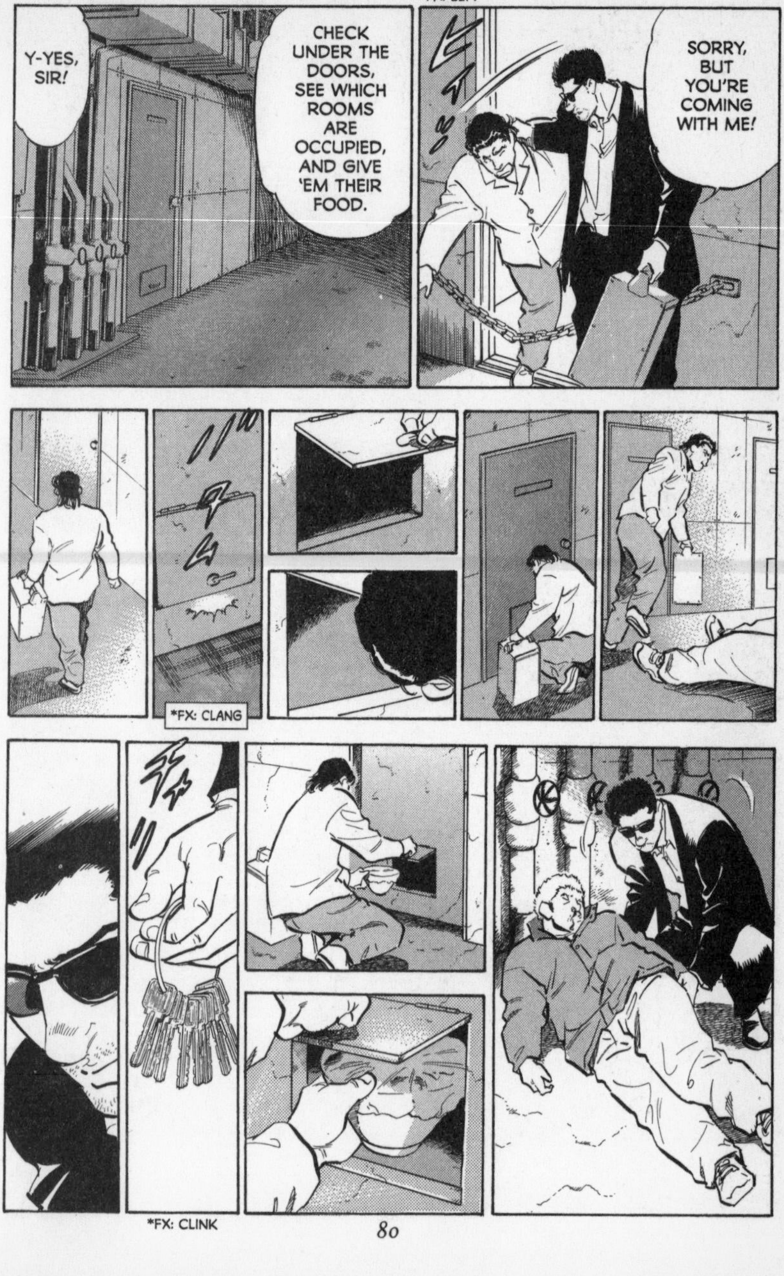
*FX: EEP!
SORRY, BUT YOU'RE COMING WITH ME!
CHECK UNDER THE DOORS, SEE WHICH ROOMS ARE OCCUPIED, AND GIVE 'EM THEIR FOOD.
Y-YES, SIR!
*FX: CLANG
*FX: CLINK

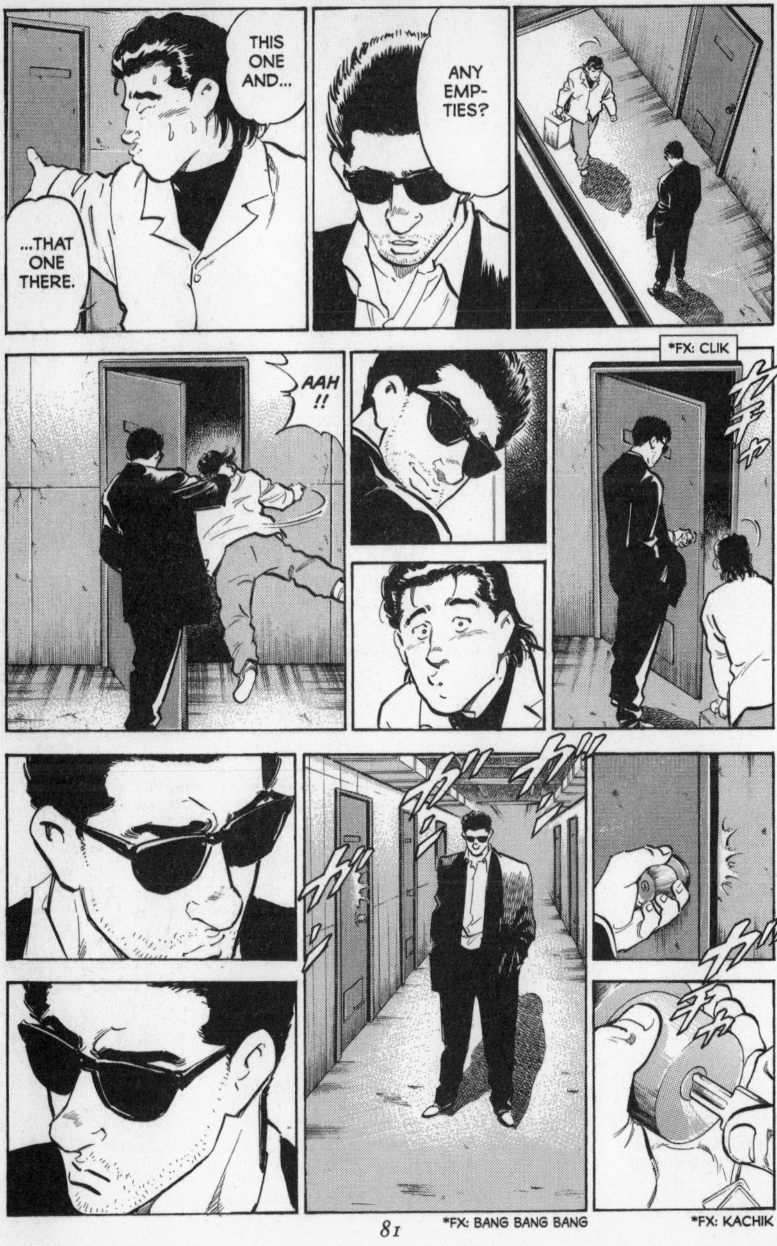
ANY EMP- TIES?
THIS ONE AND...
...THAT ONE THERE.
*FX: CLIK
AAH !!
*FX: KACHIK
*FX: BANG BANG BANG

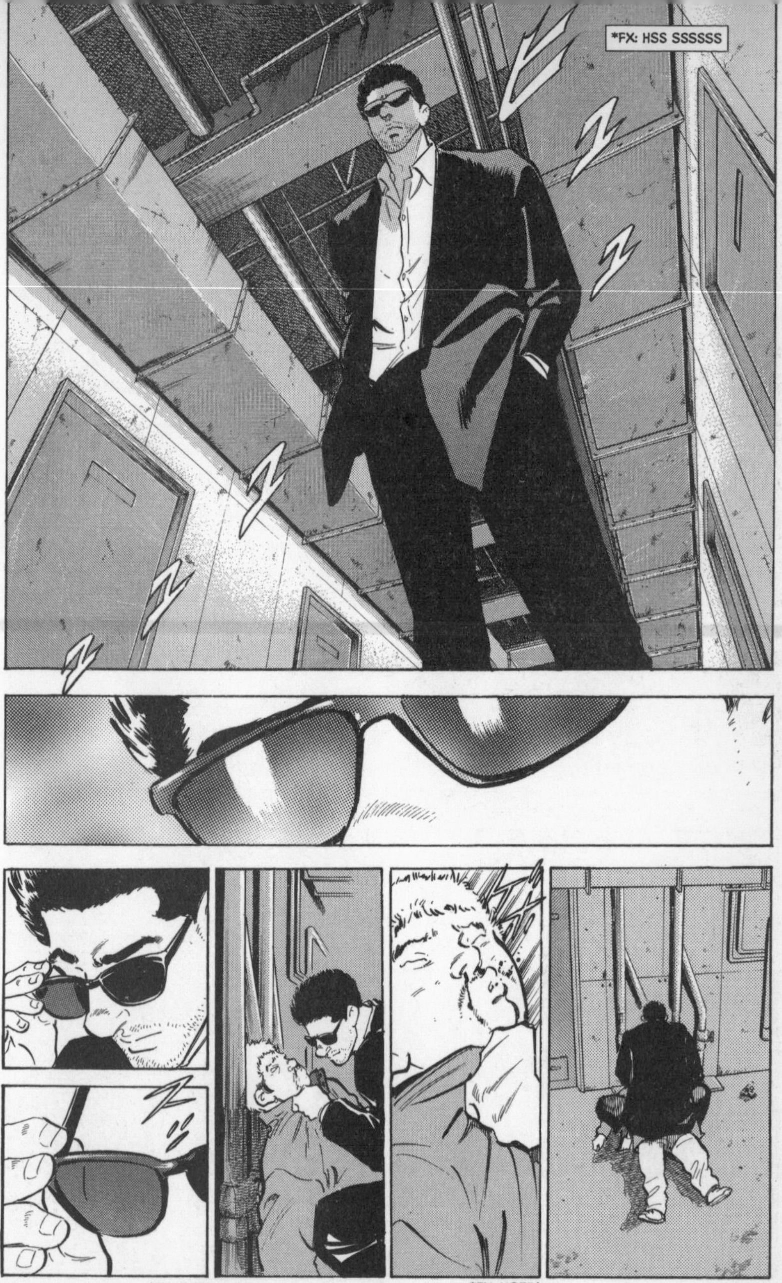
*FX: HSS SSSSSS

*FX: KOFF!

*FX: SHFF

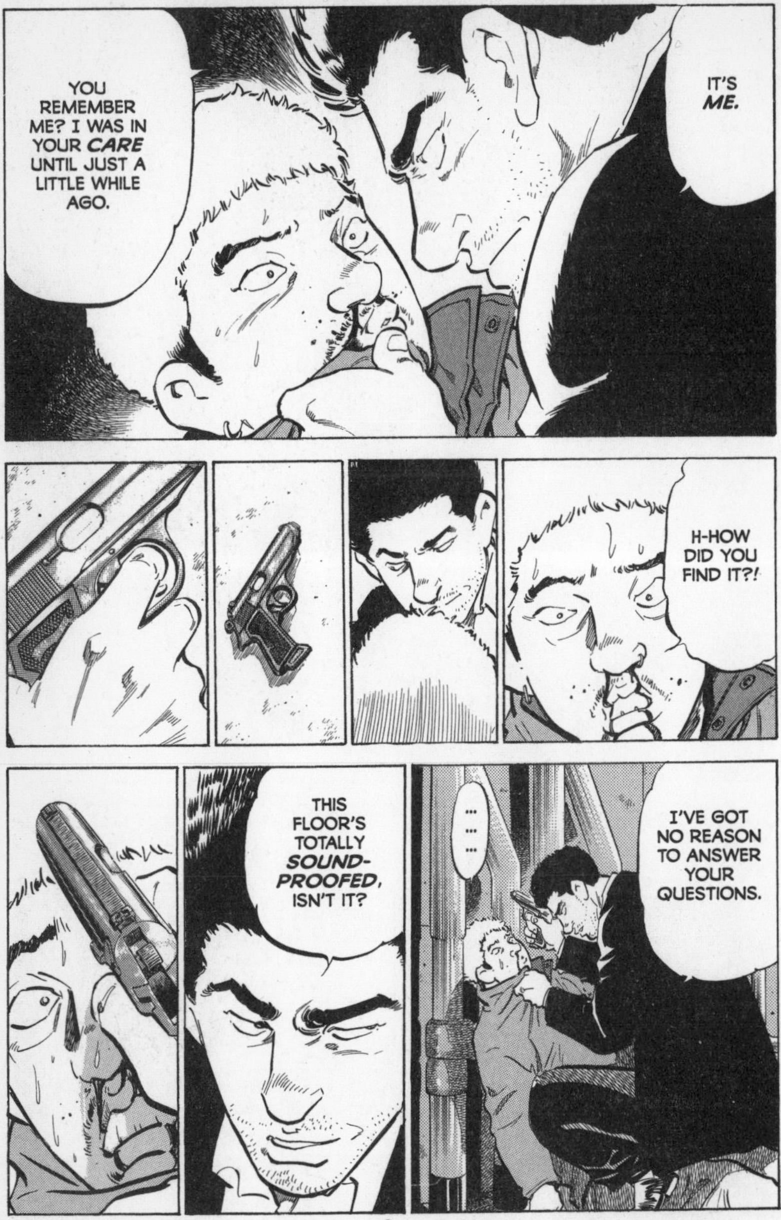
IT'S *ME.*
YOU REMEMBER ME? I WAS IN YOUR *CARE* UNTIL JUST A LITTLE WHILE AGO.
H-HOW DID YOU FIND IT?!
I'VE GOT NO REASON TO ANSWER YOUR QUESTIONS.
... ...
THIS FLOOR'S TOTALLY *SOUND-PROOFED,* ISN'T IT?

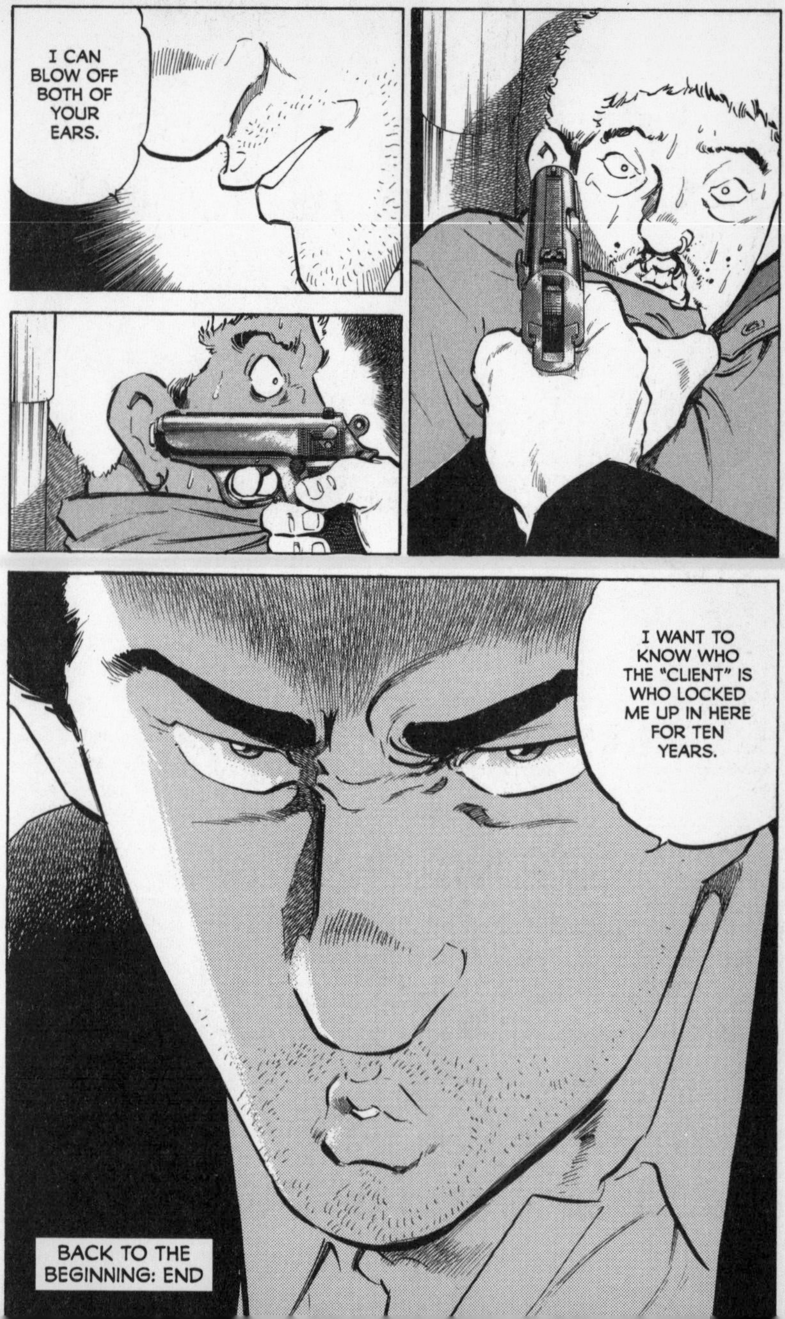
I CAN BLOW OFF BOTH OF YOUR EARS.
I WANT TO KNOW WHO THE "CLIENT" IS WHO LOCKED ME UP IN HERE FOR TEN YEARS.
BACK TO THE BEGINNING: END

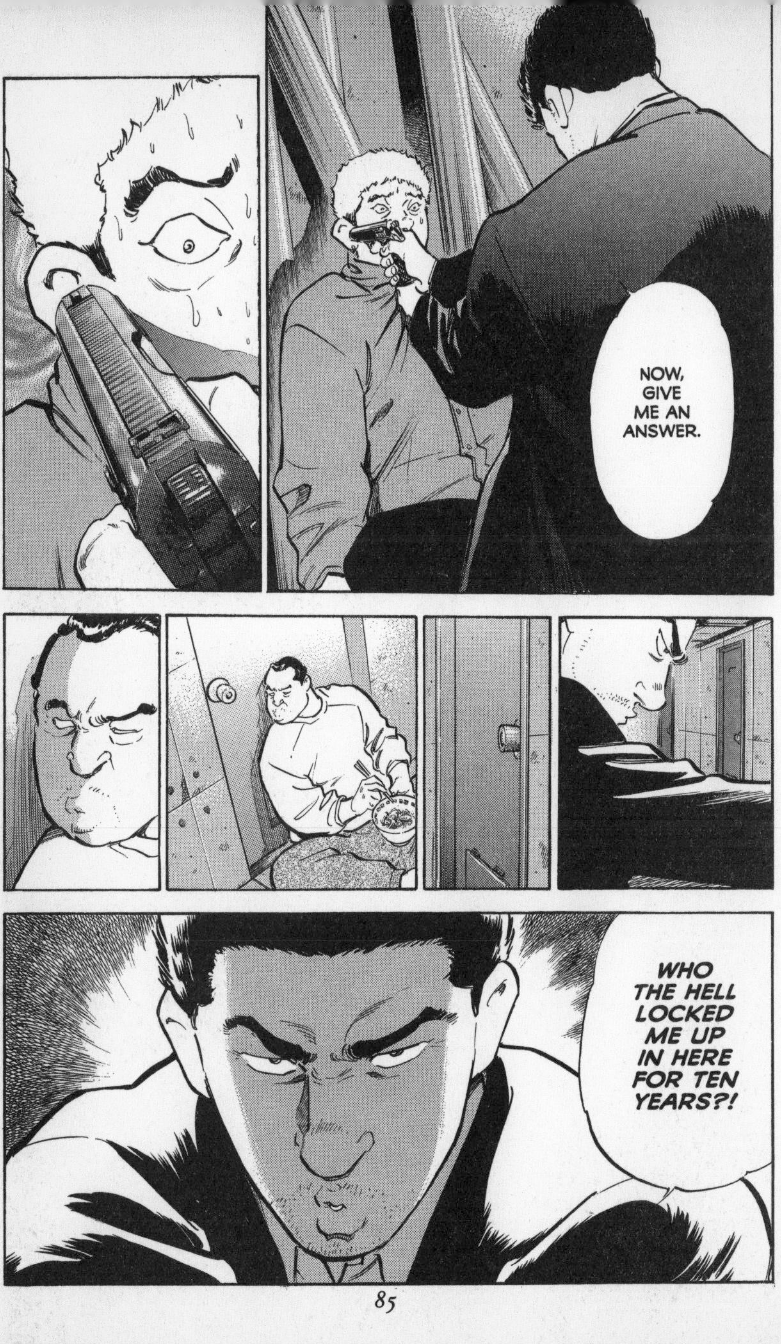
NOW, GIVE ME AN ANSWER.
WHO THE HELL LOCKED ME UP IN HERE FOR TEN YEARS?!

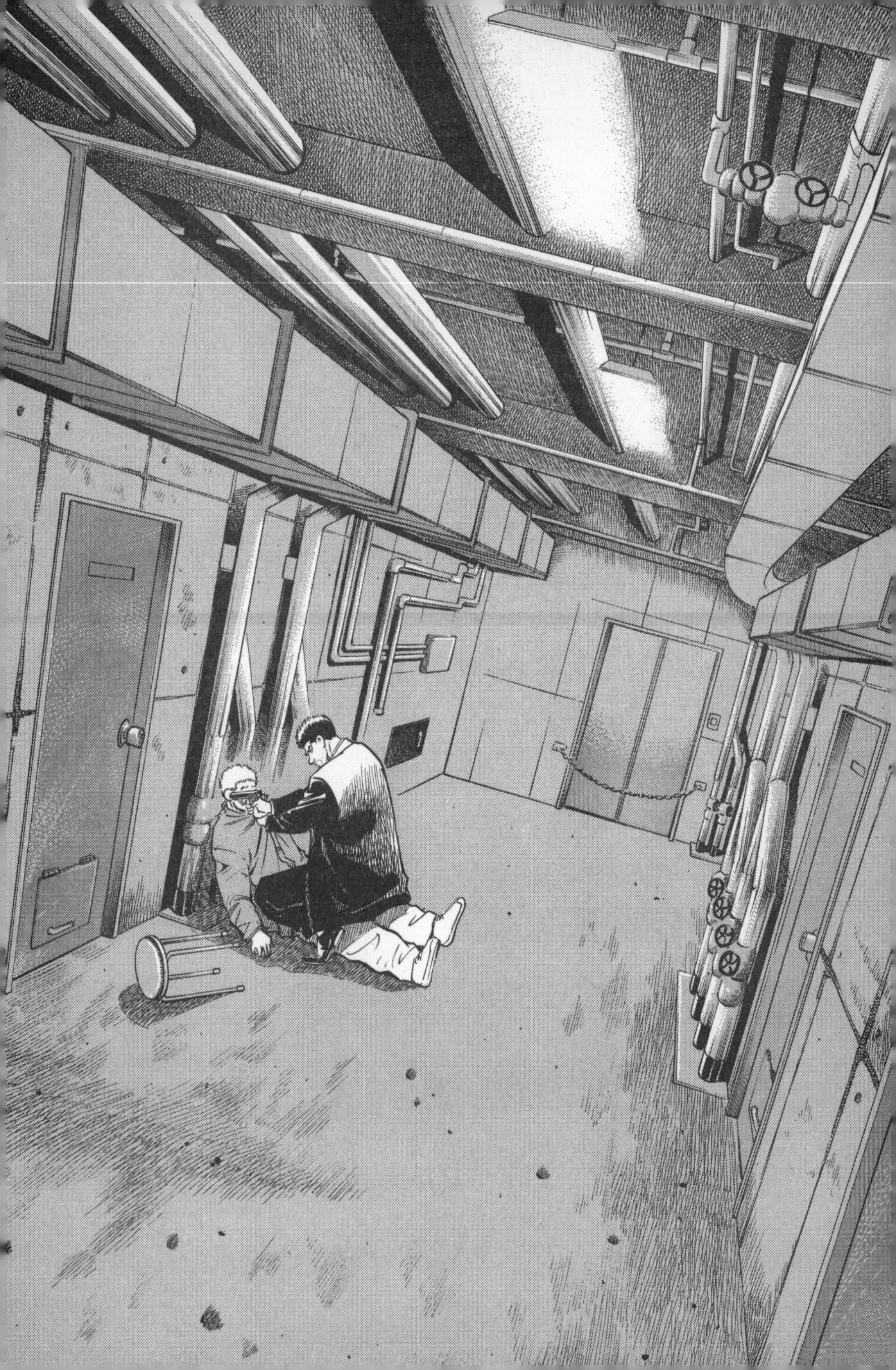

第14話○尾行者あり

CHAPTER 14

TAILED

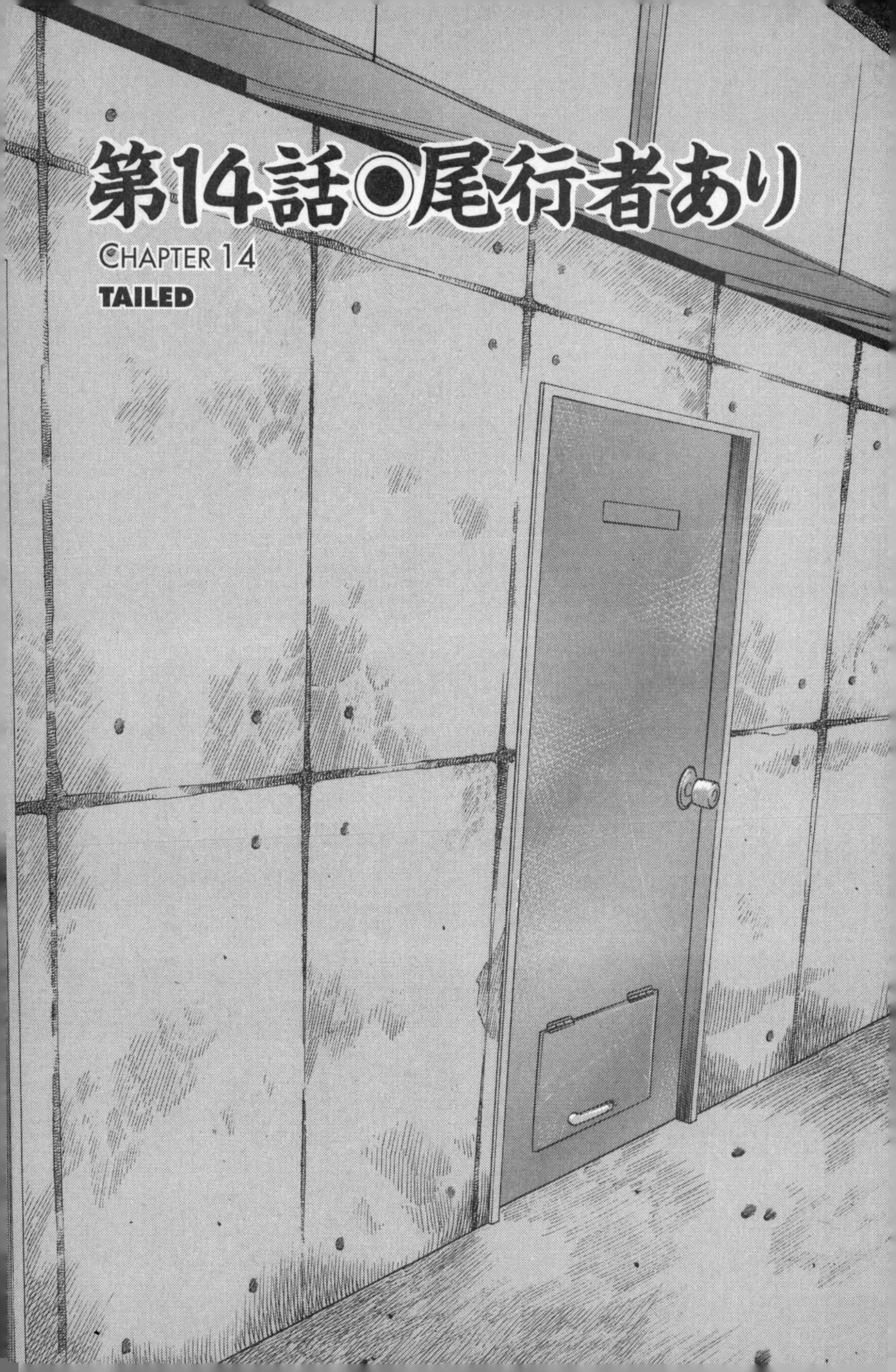

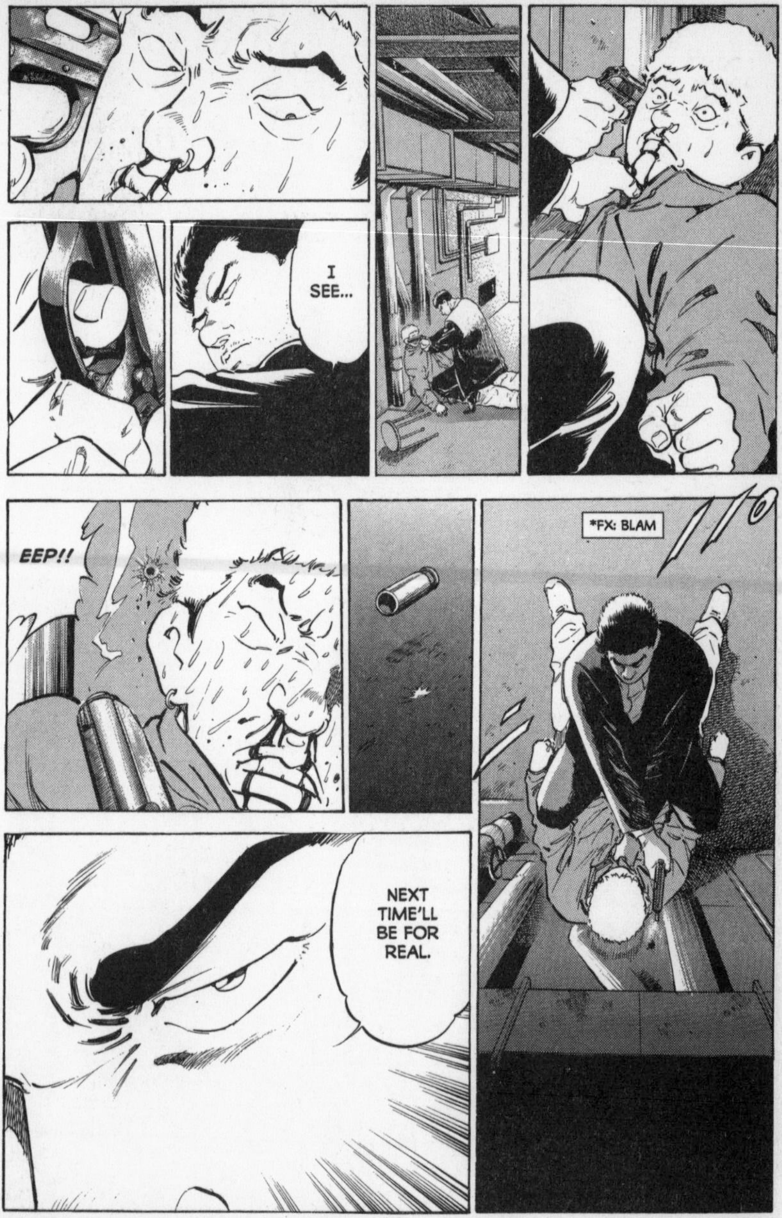
I SEE...
*FX: BLAM
EEP!!
NEXT TIME'LL BE FOR REAL.

*FX: SHRRK

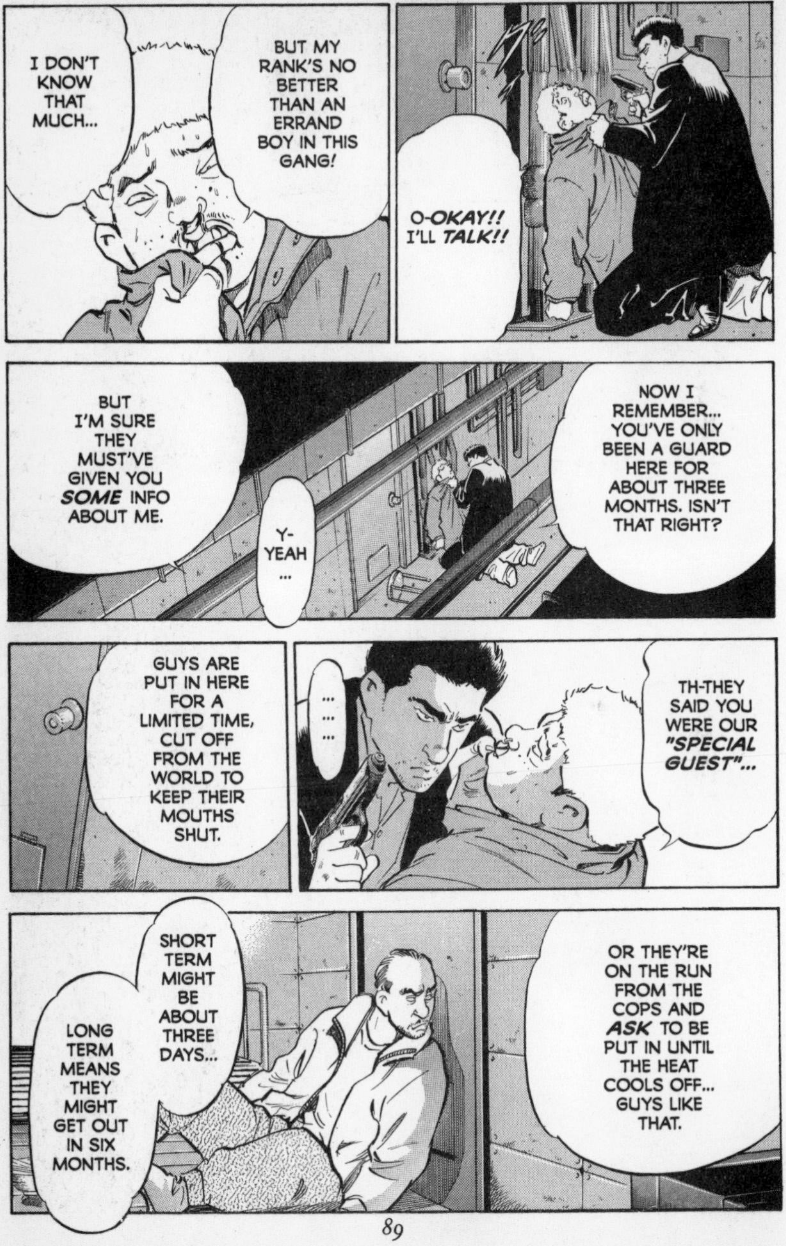
O-OKAY!! I'LL TALK!!
BUT MY RANK'S NO BETTER THAN AN ERRAND BOY IN THIS GANG!
I DON'T KNOW THAT MUCH...
NOW I REMEMBER... YOU'VE ONLY BEEN A GUARD HERE FOR ABOUT THREE MONTHS. ISN'T THAT RIGHT?
Y-YEAH ...
BUT I'M SURE THEY MUST'VE GIVEN YOU SOME INFO ABOUT ME.
TH-THEY SAID YOU WERE OUR "SPECIAL GUEST"...
... ...
GUYS ARE PUT IN HERE FOR A LIMITED TIME, CUT OFF FROM THE WORLD TO KEEP THEIR MOUTHS SHUT.
OR THEY'RE ON THE RUN FROM THE COPS AND ASK TO BE PUT IN UNTIL THE HEAT COOLS OFF... GUYS LIKE THAT.
SHORT TERM MIGHT BE ABOUT THREE DAYS...
LONG TERM MEANS THEY MIGHT GET OUT IN SIX MONTHS.

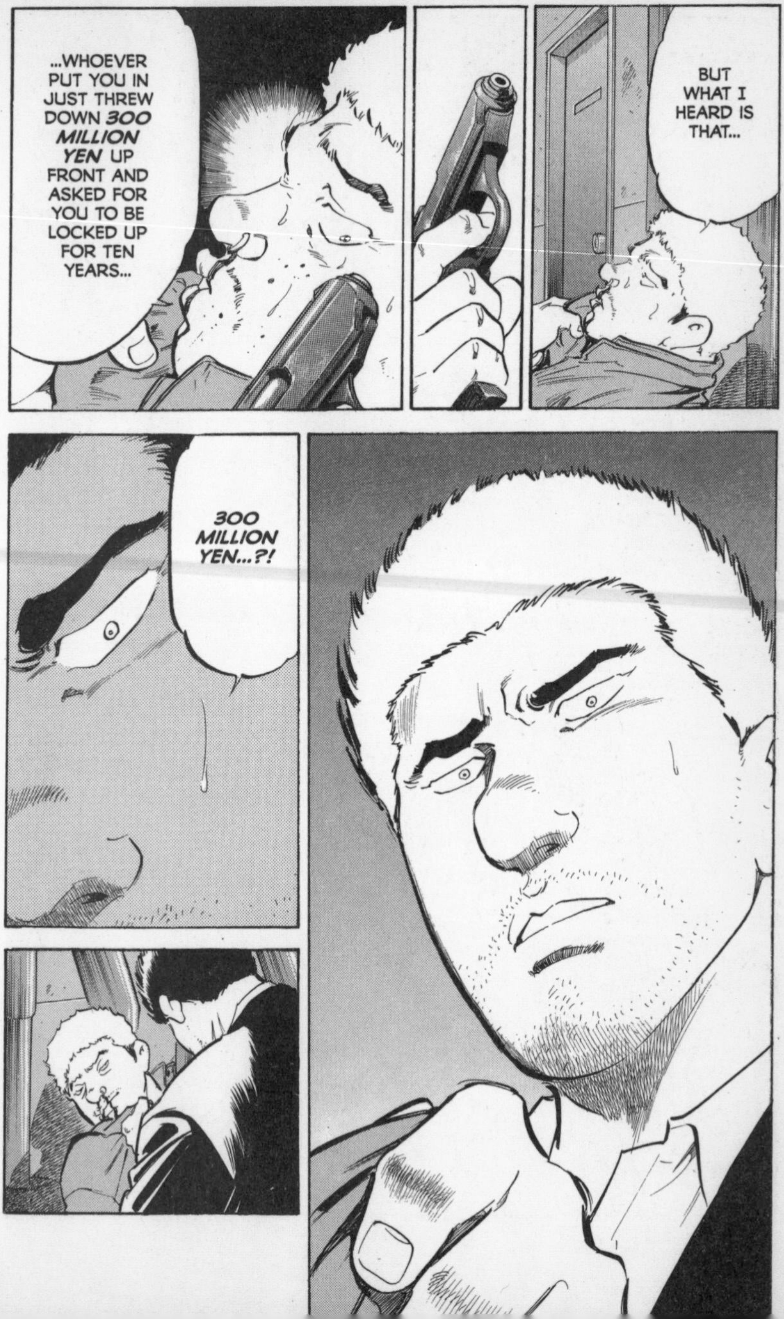
BUT WHAT I HEARD IS THAT...
...WHOEVER PUT YOU IN JUST THREW DOWN *300 MILLION YEN* UP FRONT AND ASKED FOR YOU TO BE LOCKED UP FOR TEN YEARS...
300 MILLION YEN...?!

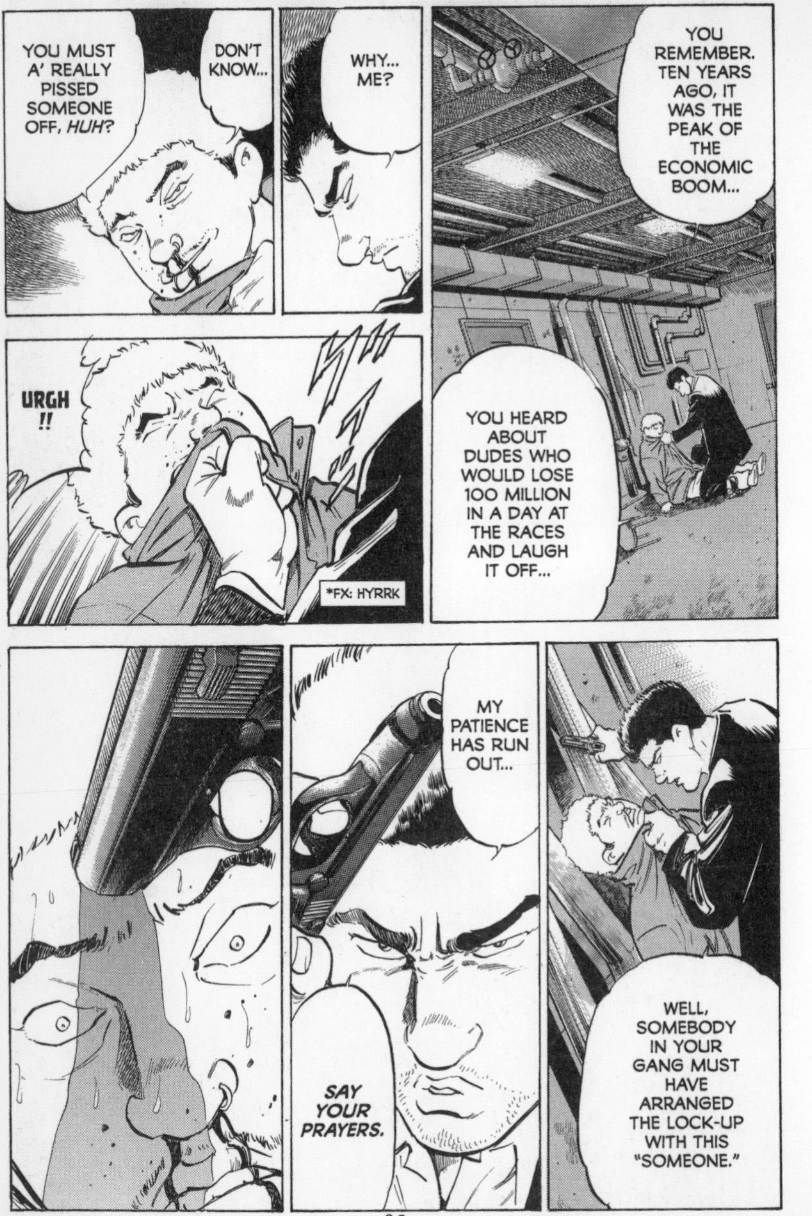

YOU REMEMBER. TEN YEARS AGO, IT WAS THE PEAK OF THE ECONOMIC BOOM...
YOU HEARD ABOUT DUDES WHO WOULD LOSE 100 MILLION IN A DAY AT THE RACES AND LAUGH IT OFF...
WHY... ME?
DON'T KNOW...
YOU MUST A' REALLY PISSED SOMEONE OFF, *HUH*?
*FX: HYRRK
URGH !!
WELL, SOMEBODY IN YOUR GANG MUST HAVE ARRANGED THE LOCK-UP WITH THIS "SOMEONE."
MY PATIENCE HAS RUN OUT...
SAY YOUR PRAYERS.

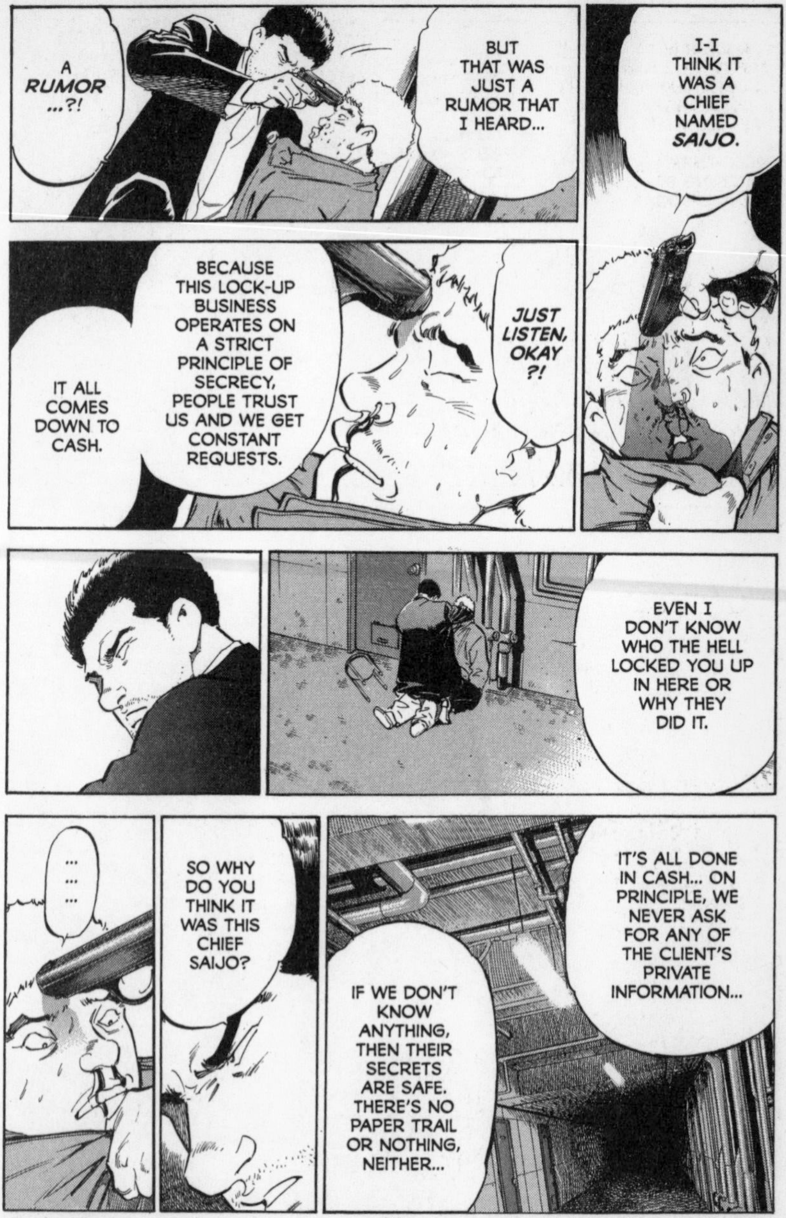

I-I THINK IT WAS A CHIEF NAMED *SAIJO*.
BUT THAT WAS JUST A RUMOR THAT I HEARD...
A *RUMOR* ...?!
JUST LISTEN, OKAY ?!
BECAUSE THIS LOCK-UP BUSINESS OPERATES ON A STRICT PRINCIPLE OF SECRECY, PEOPLE TRUST US AND WE GET CONSTANT REQUESTS.
IT ALL COMES DOWN TO CASH.
EVEN I DON'T KNOW WHO THE HELL LOCKED YOU UP IN HERE OR WHY THEY DID IT.
IT'S ALL DONE IN CASH... ON PRINCIPLE, WE NEVER ASK FOR ANY OF THE CLIENT'S PRIVATE INFORMATION...
IF WE DON'T KNOW ANYTHING, THEN THEIR SECRETS ARE SAFE. THERE'S NO PAPER TRAIL OR NOTHING, NEITHER...
SO WHY DO YOU THINK IT WAS THIS CHIEF SAIJO?
... ...

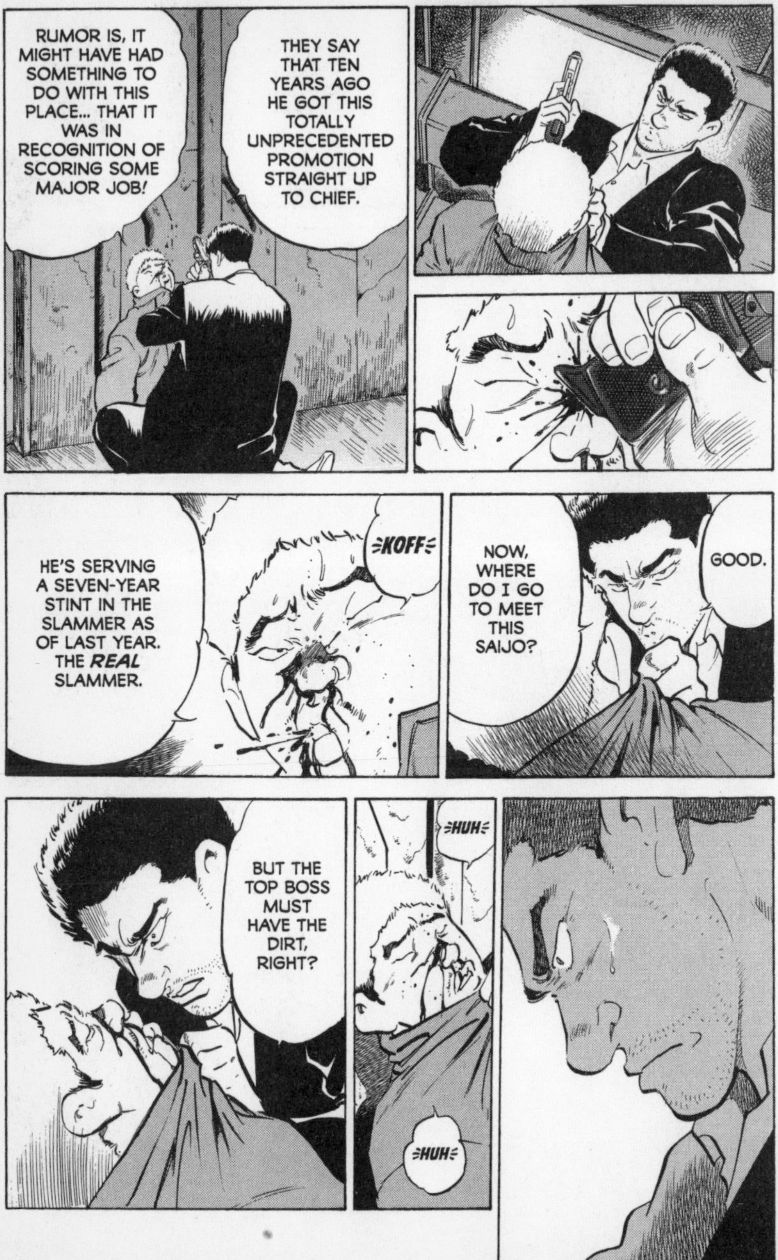
RUMOR IS, IT MIGHT HAVE HAD SOMETHING TO DO WITH THIS PLACE... THAT IT WAS IN RECOGNITION OF SCORING SOME MAJOR JOB!
THEY SAY THAT TEN YEARS AGO HE GOT THIS TOTALLY UNPRECEDENTED PROMOTION STRAIGHT UP TO CHIEF.
HE'S SERVING A SEVEN-YEAR STINT IN THE SLAMMER AS OF LAST YEAR. THE *REAL* SLAMMER.
KOFF
NOW, WHERE DO I GO TO MEET THIS SAIJO?
GOOD.
BUT THE TOP BOSS MUST HAVE THE DIRT, RIGHT?
HUH
HUH

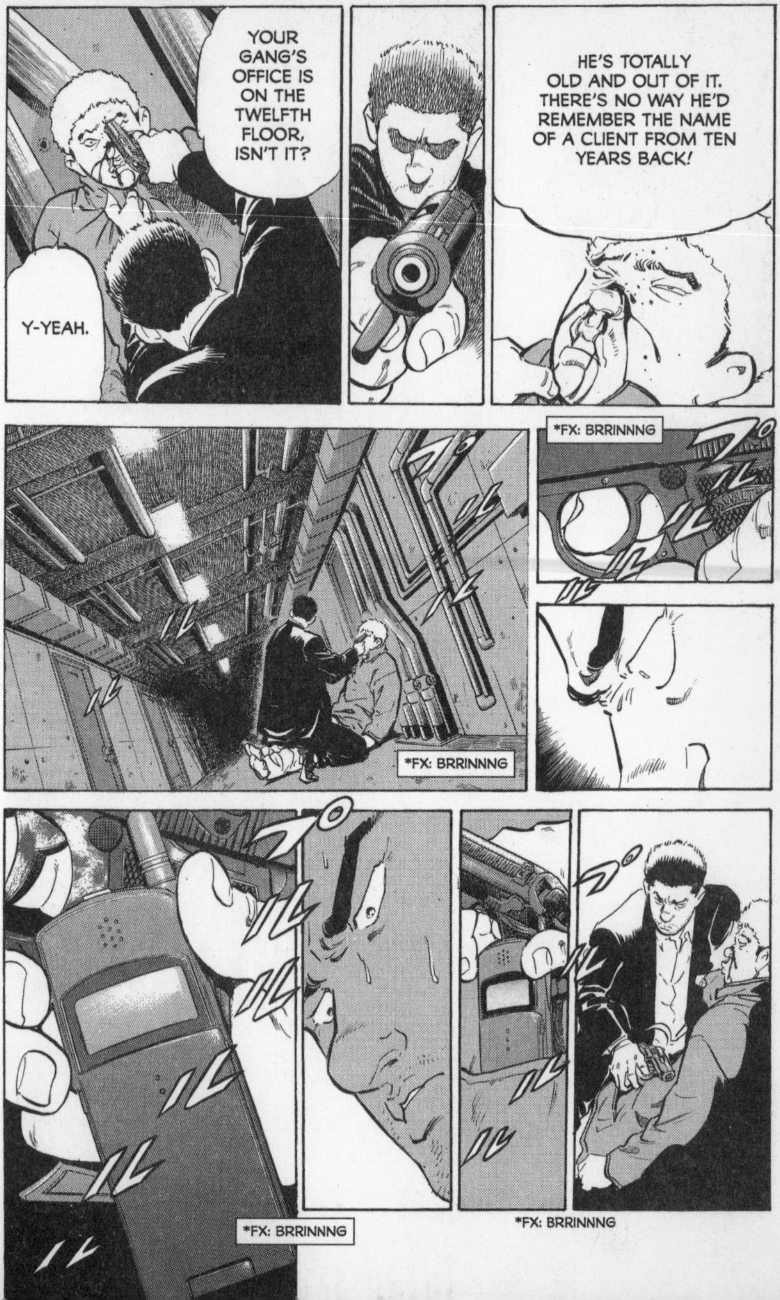
HE'S TOTALLY OLD AND OUT OF IT. THERE'S NO WAY HE'D REMEMBER THE NAME OF A CLIENT FROM TEN YEARS BACK!
YOUR GANG'S OFFICE IS ON THE TWELFTH FLOOR, ISN'T IT?
Y-YEAH.
*FX: BRRINNNG
*FX: BRRINNNG
*FX: BRRINNNG
*FX: BRRINNNG

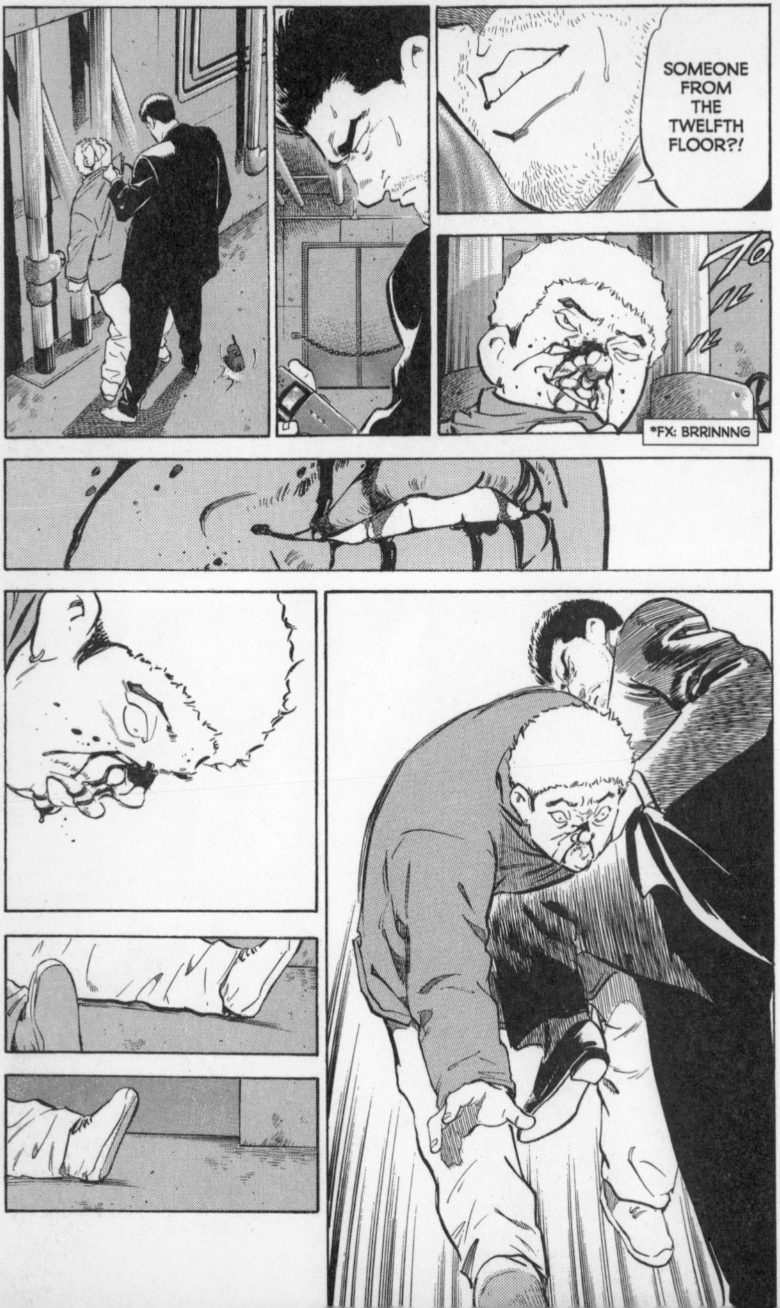
SOMEONE FROM THE TWELFTH FLOOR?!
*FX: BRRINNNG

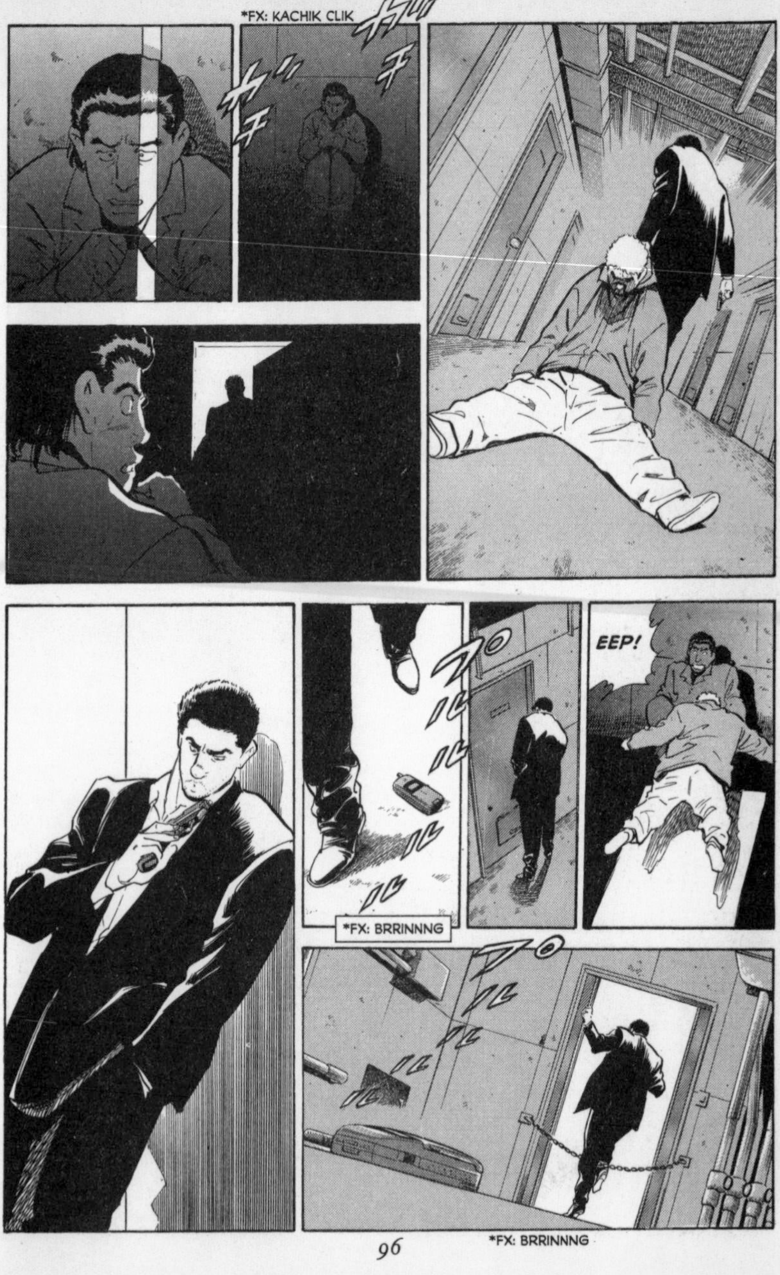
*FX: KACHIK CLIK
EEP!
*FX: BRRINNNG
*FX: BRRINNNG

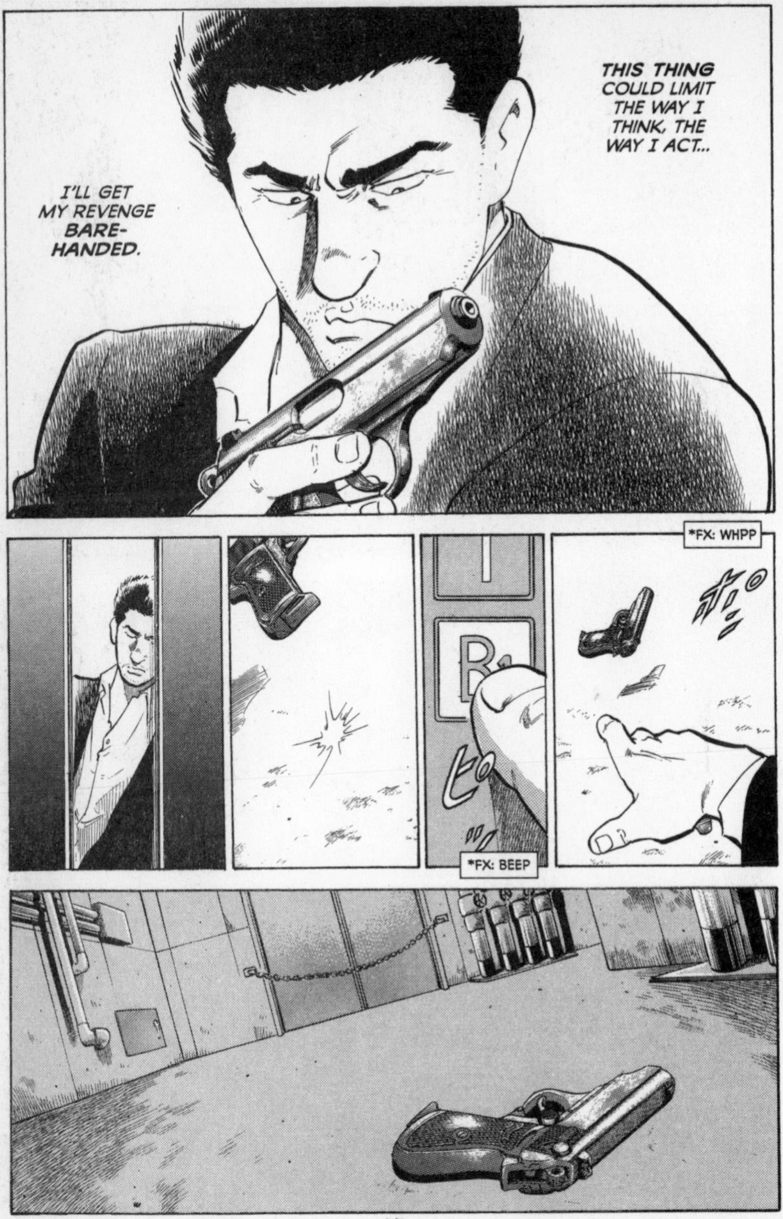
THIS THING COULD LIMIT THE WAY I THINK, THE WAY I ACT...
I'LL GET MY REVENGE BARE-HANDED.
*FX: WHPP
*FX: BEEP

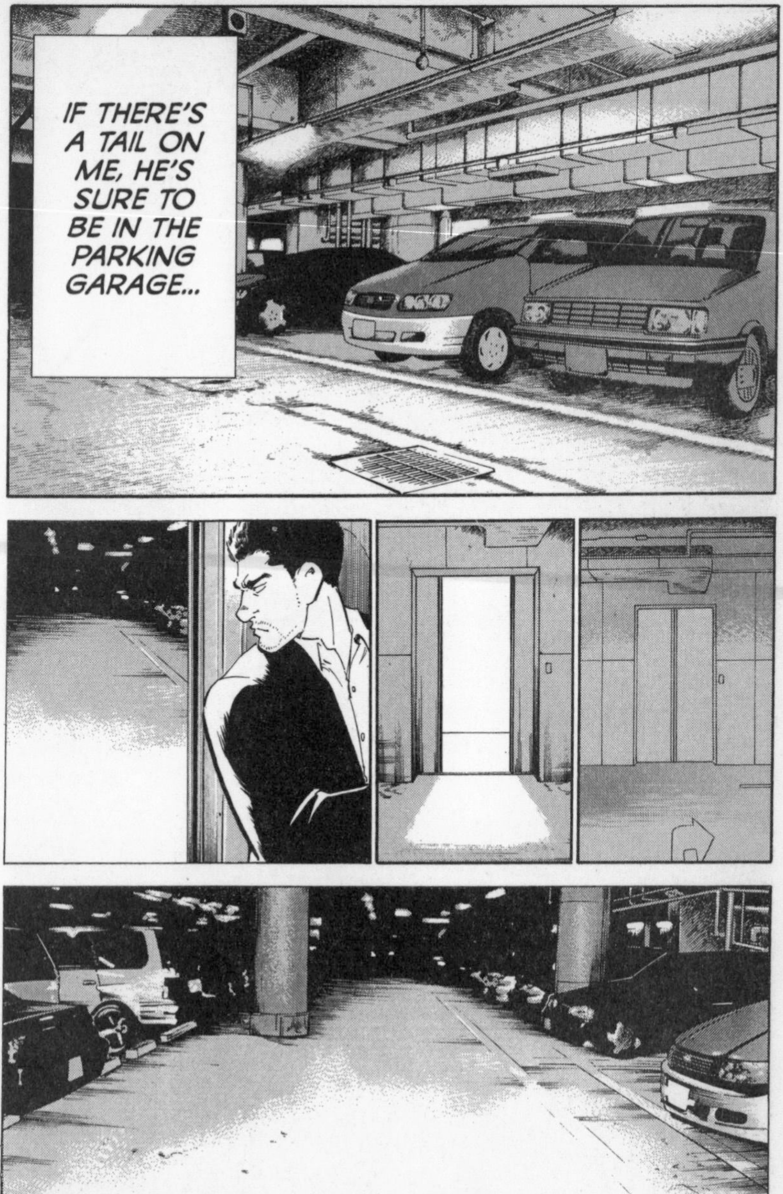
IF THERE'S A TAIL ON ME, HE'S SURE TO BE IN THE PARKING GARAGE...

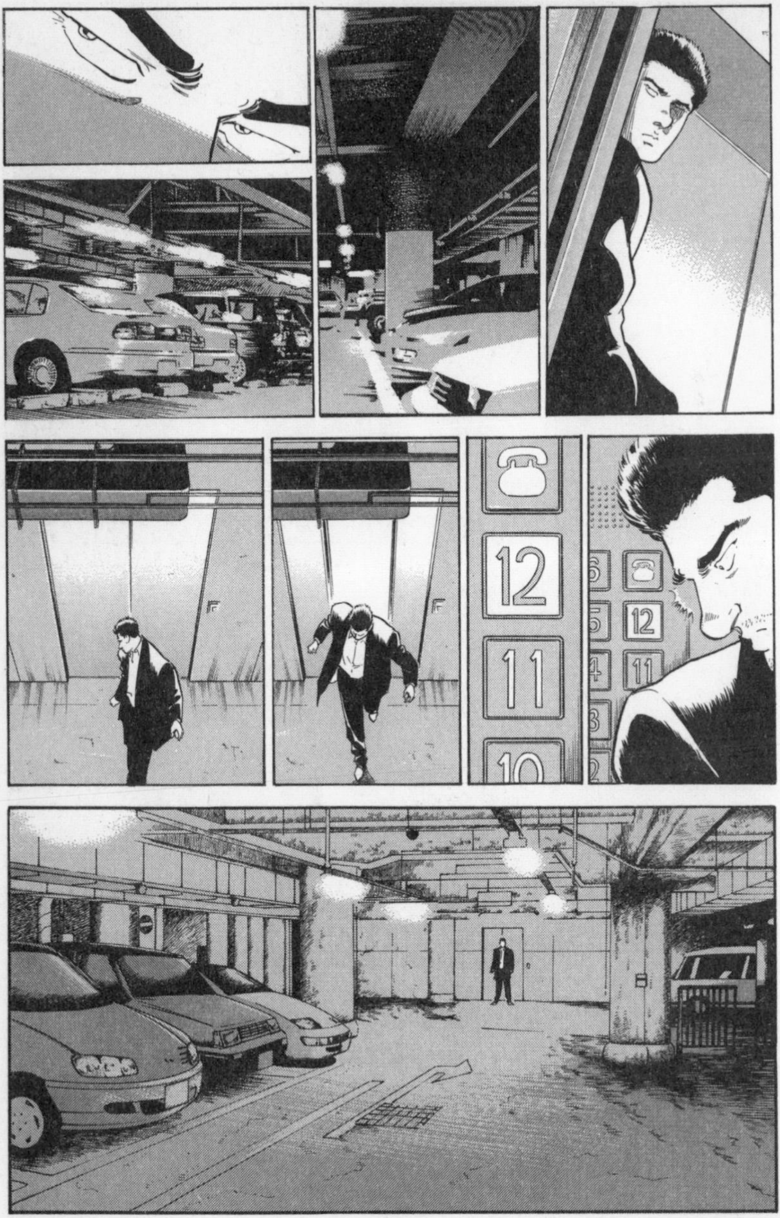
12
11

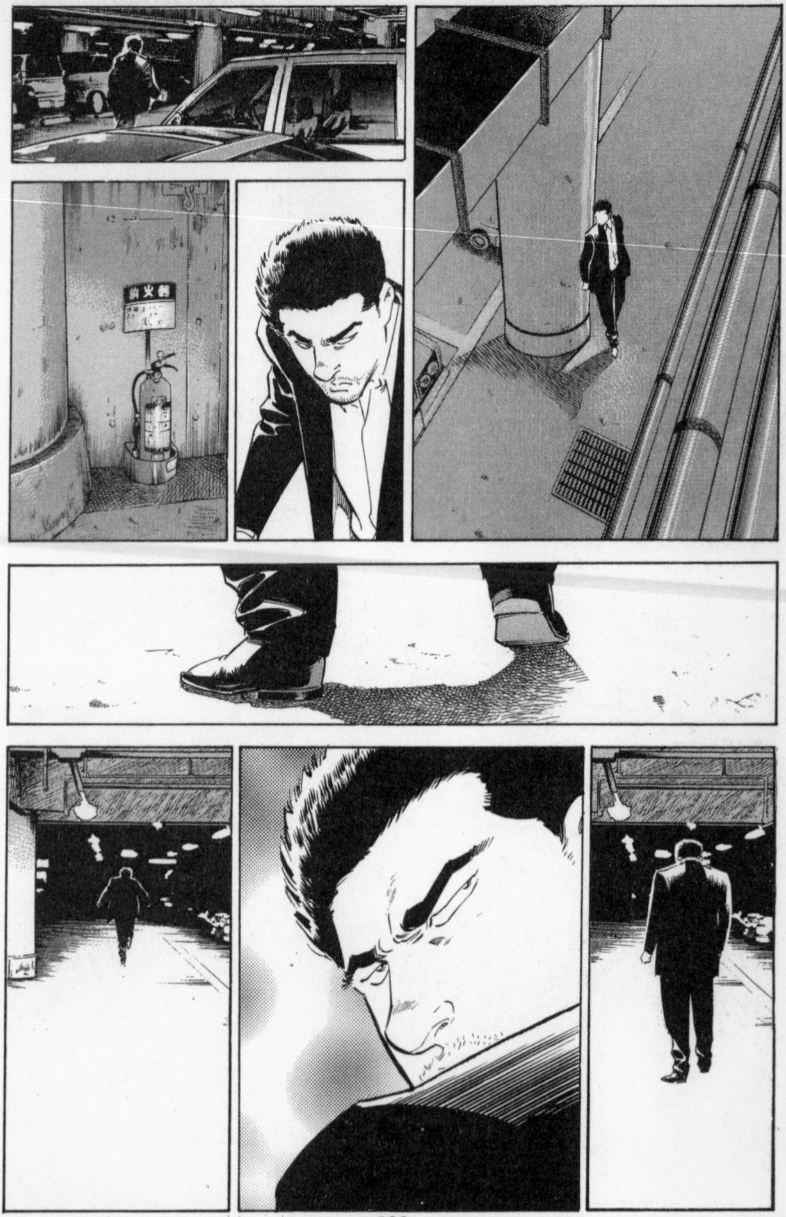

*FX: DING

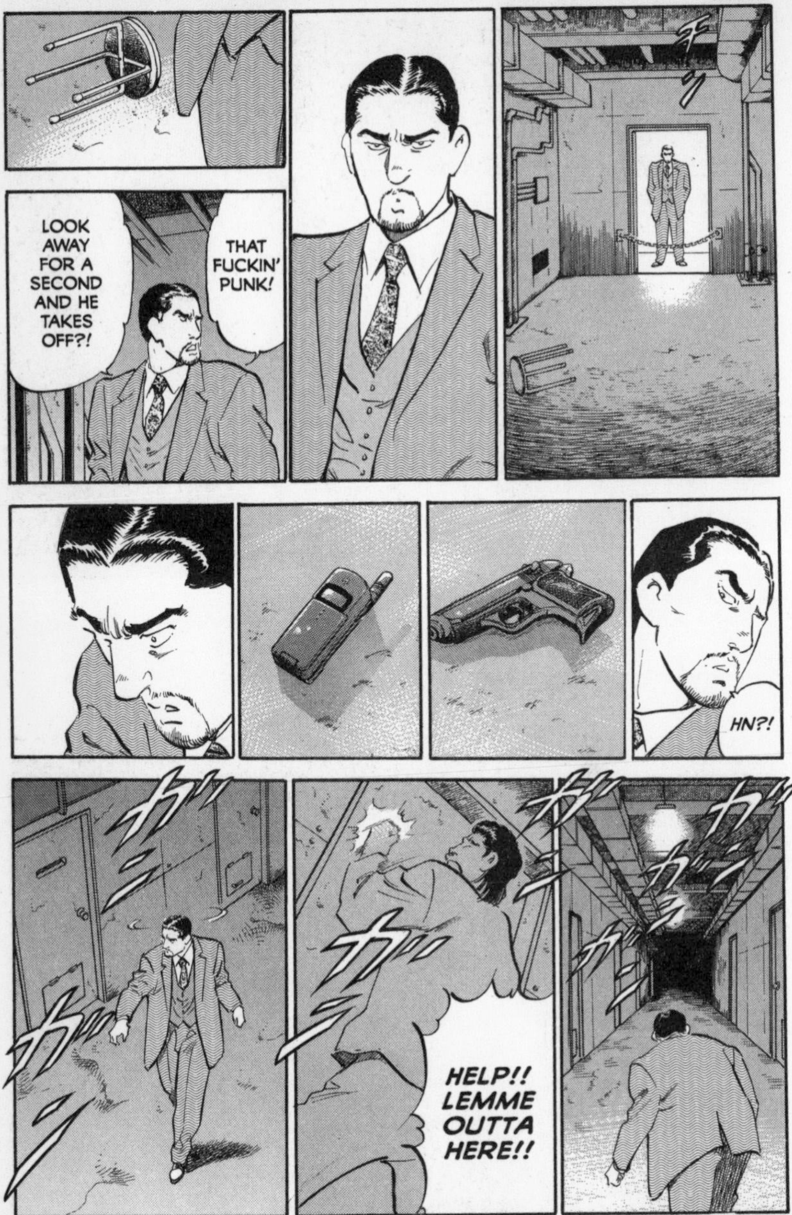
THAT FUCKIN' PUNK!
LOOK AWAY FOR A SECOND AND HE TAKES OFF?!
HN?!
HELP!! LEMME OUTTA HERE!!

*FX: BANG BANG BANG

*FX: BANG BANG

*FX: BANG BANG

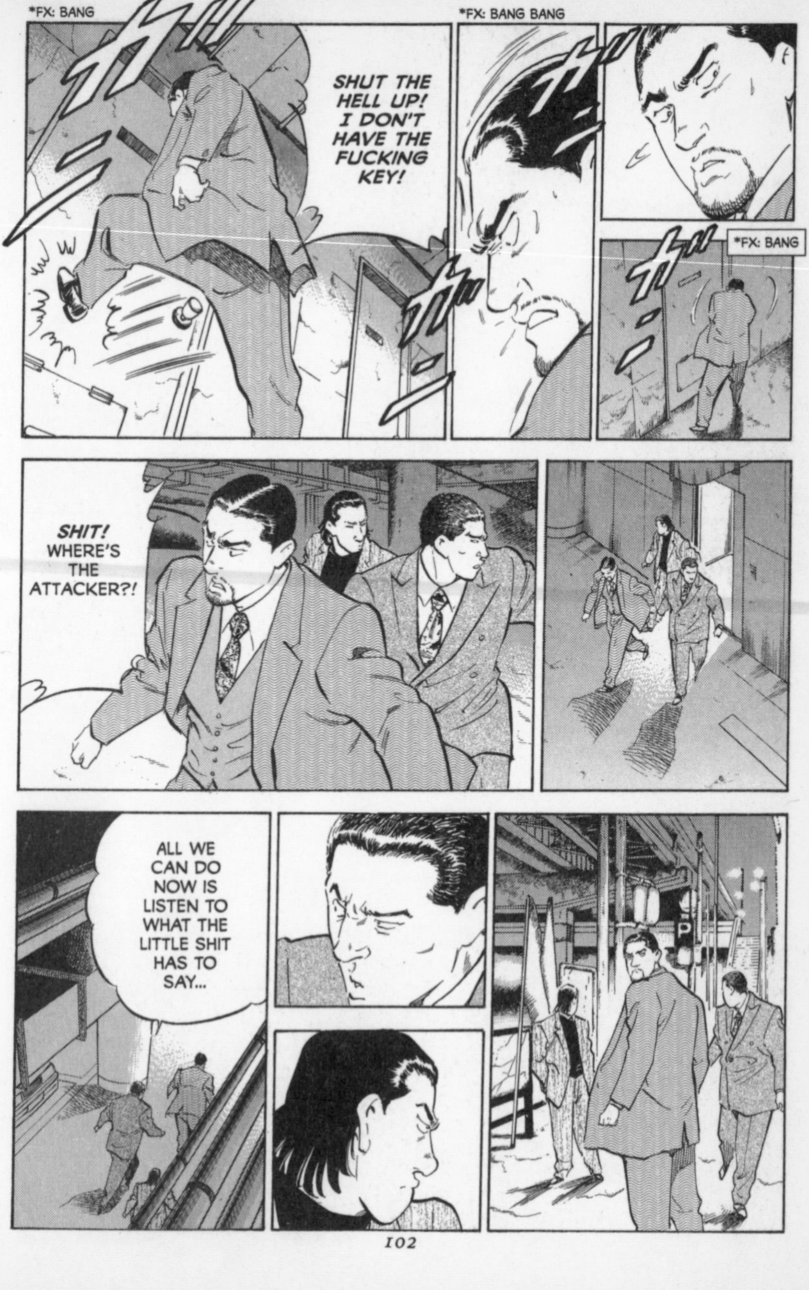
*FX: BANG
*FX: BANG BANG
*FX: BANG
SHUT THE HELL UP! I DON'T HAVE THE FUCKING KEY!
SHIT! WHERE'S THE ATTACKER?!
ALL WE CAN DO NOW IS LISTEN TO WHAT THE LITTLE SHIT HAS TO SAY...

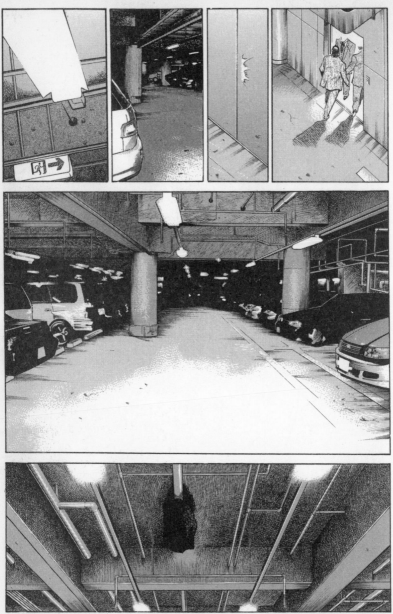

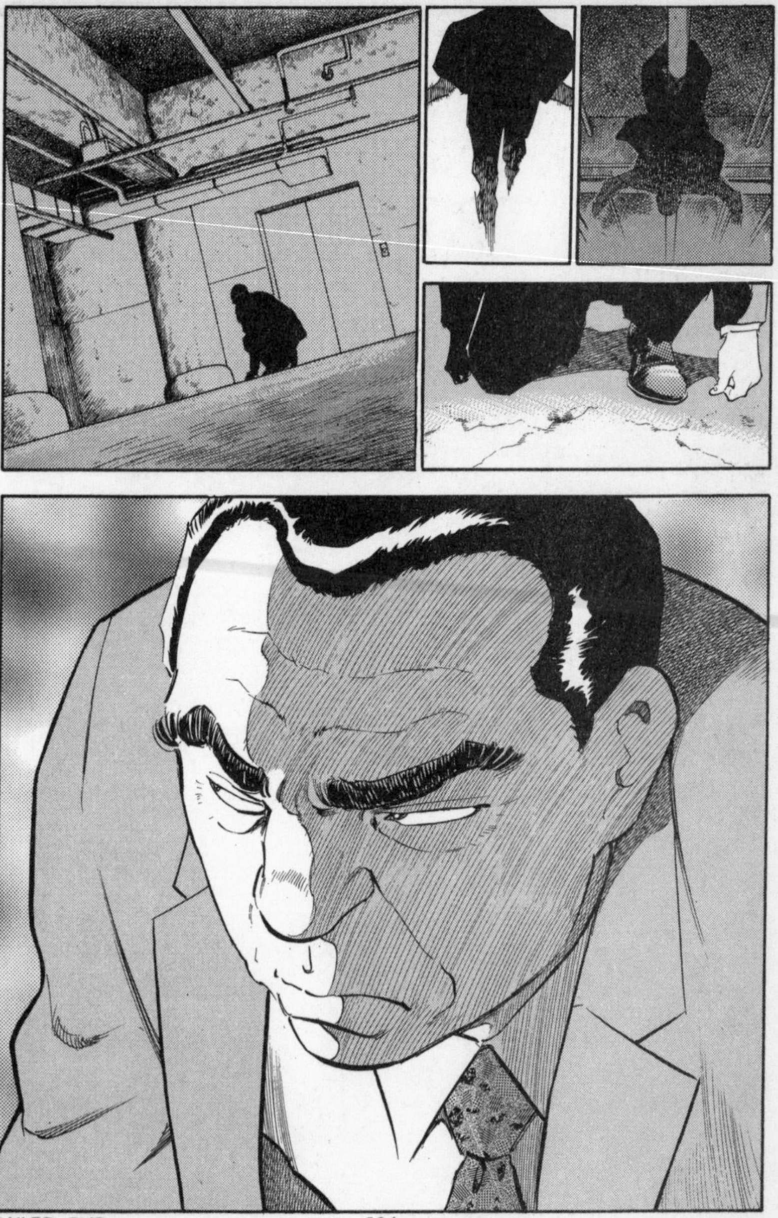

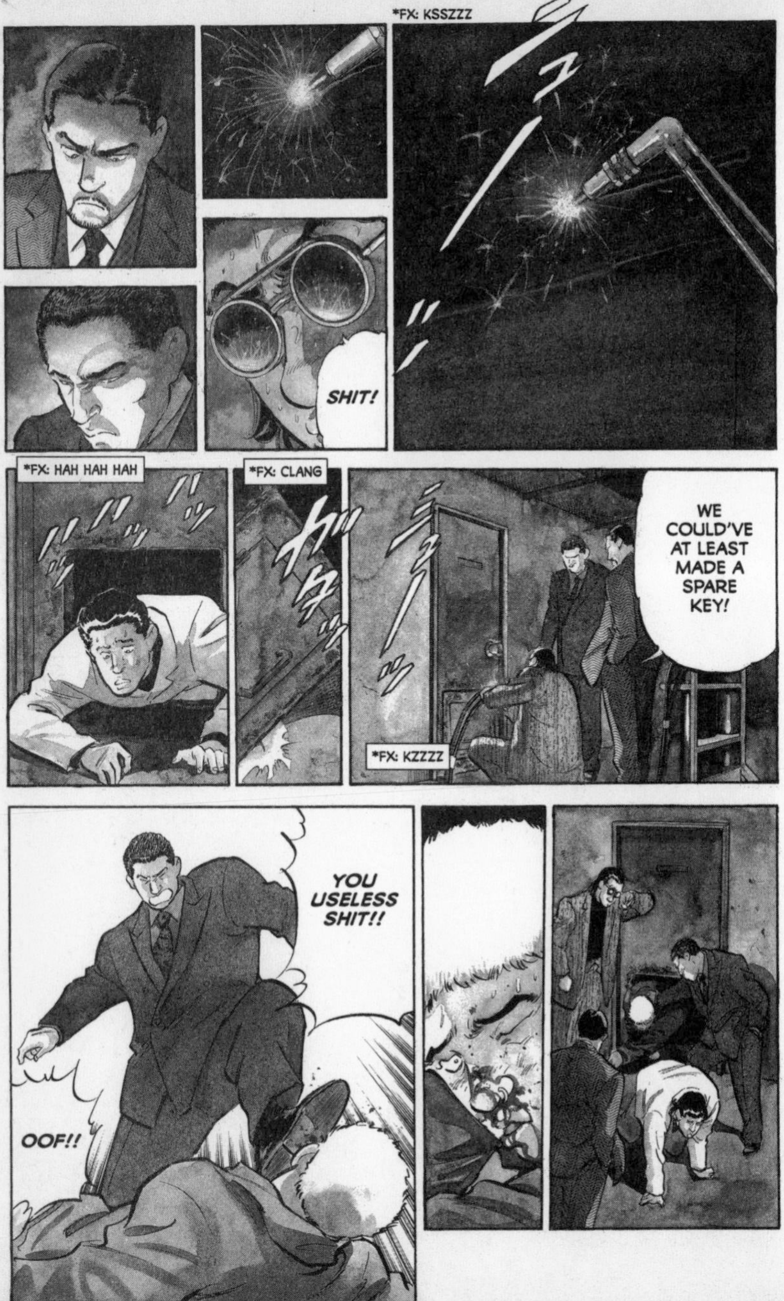
*FX: KSSZZZ
SHIT!
WE COULD'VE AT LEAST MADE A SPARE KEY!
*FX: KZZZZ
*FX: CLANG
*FX: HAH HAH HAH
YOU USELESS SHIT!!
OOF!!

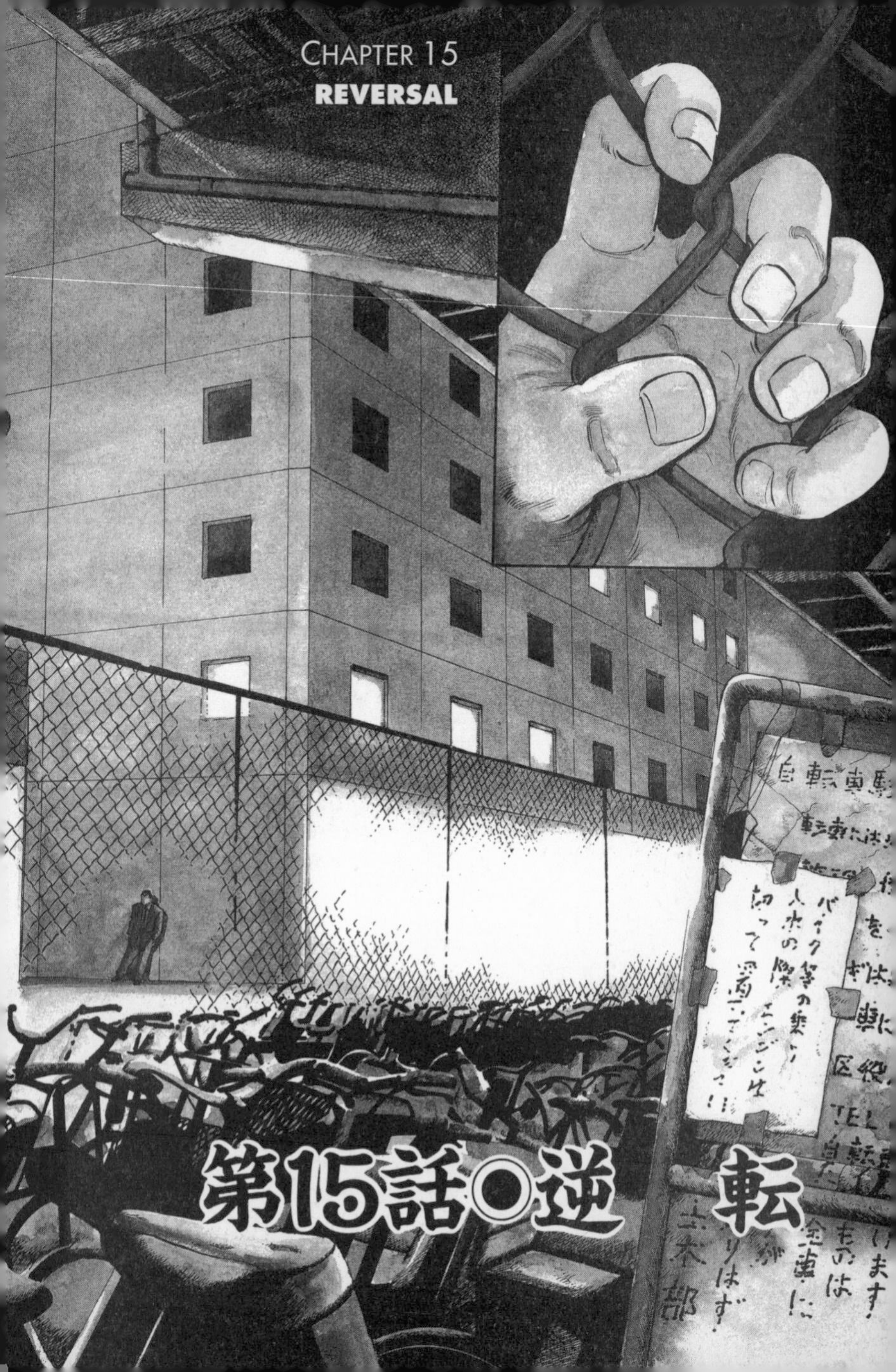
CHAPTER 15
REVERSAL
第15話○逆　転

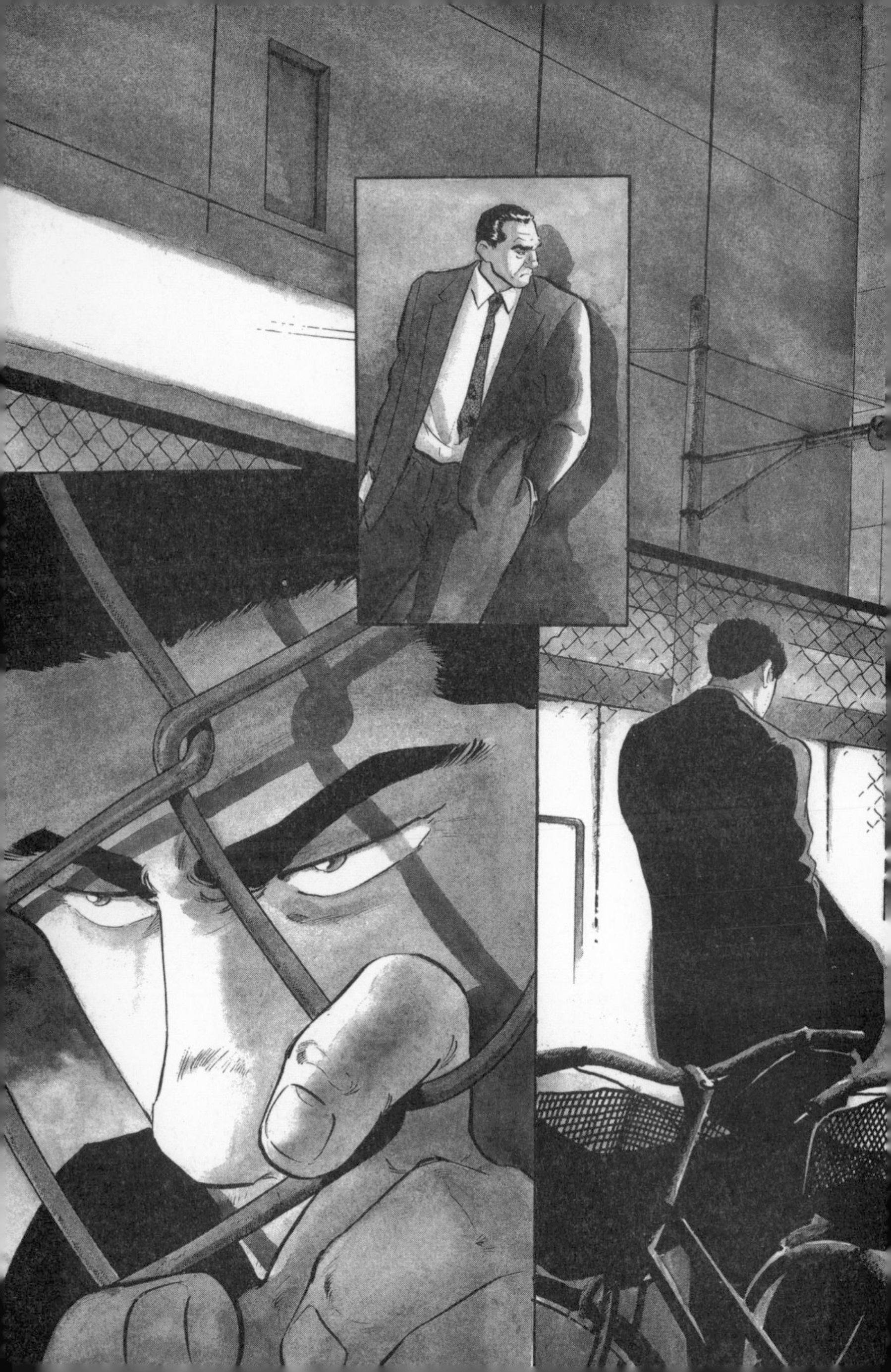

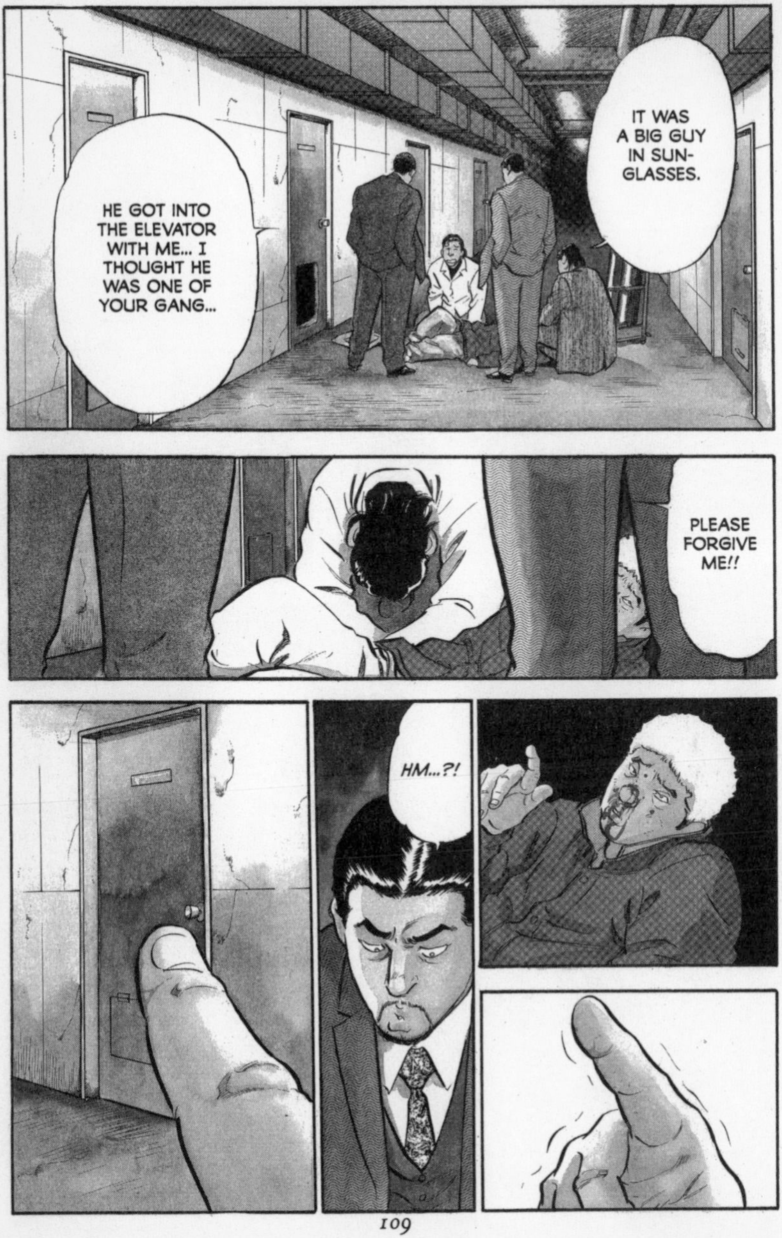
IT WAS A BIG GUY IN SUN-GLASSES.
HE GOT INTO THE ELEVATOR WITH ME... I THOUGHT HE WAS ONE OF YOUR GANG...
PLEASE FORGIVE ME!!
HM...?!

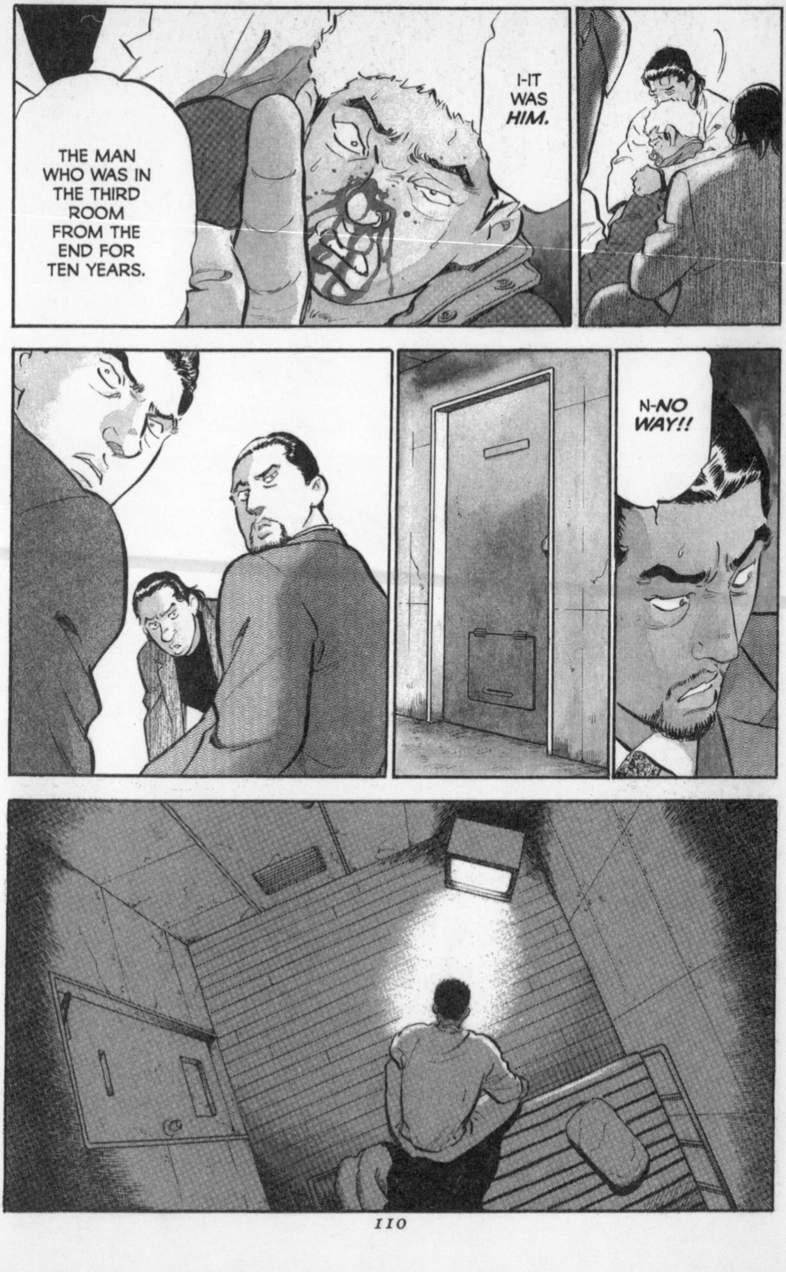
I-IT WAS *HIM.*
THE MAN WHO WAS IN THE THIRD ROOM FROM THE END FOR TEN YEARS.
N-*NO WAY!!*

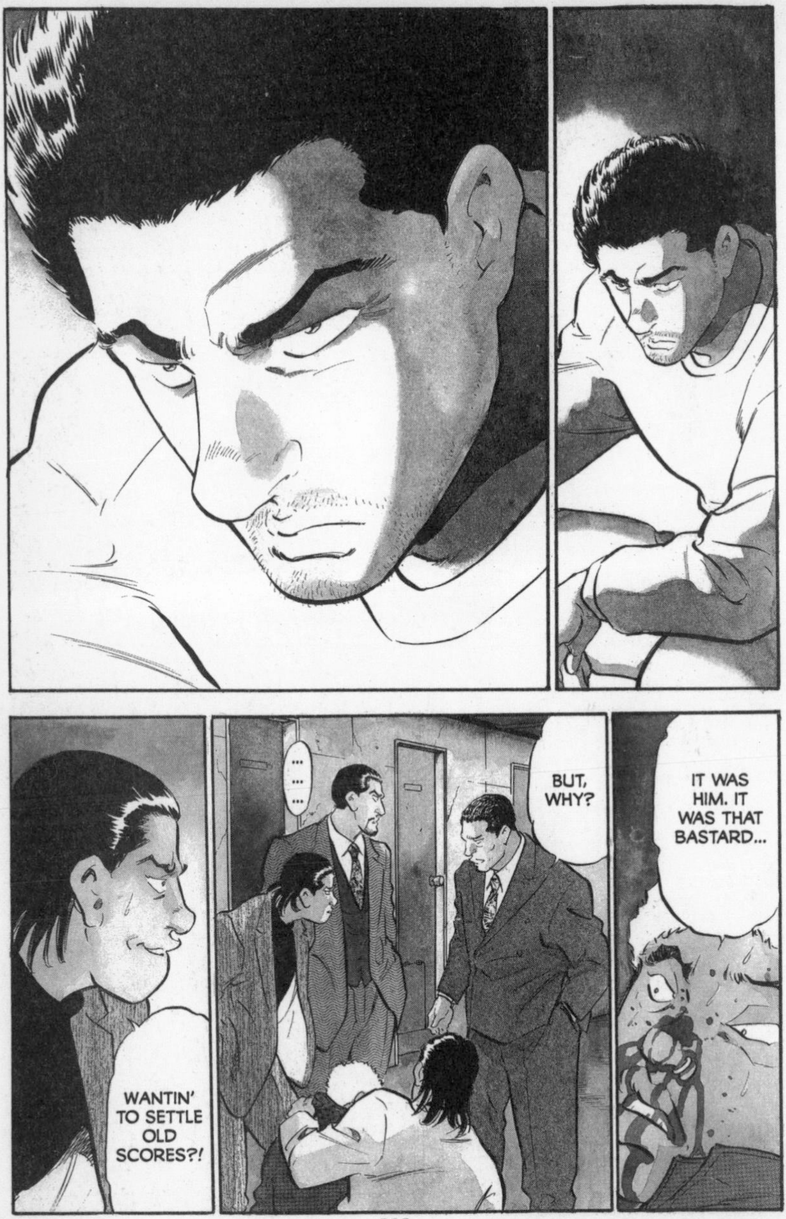
IT WAS HIM. IT WAS THAT BASTARD...
BUT, WHY?
... ...
WANTIN' TO SETTLE OLD SCORES?!

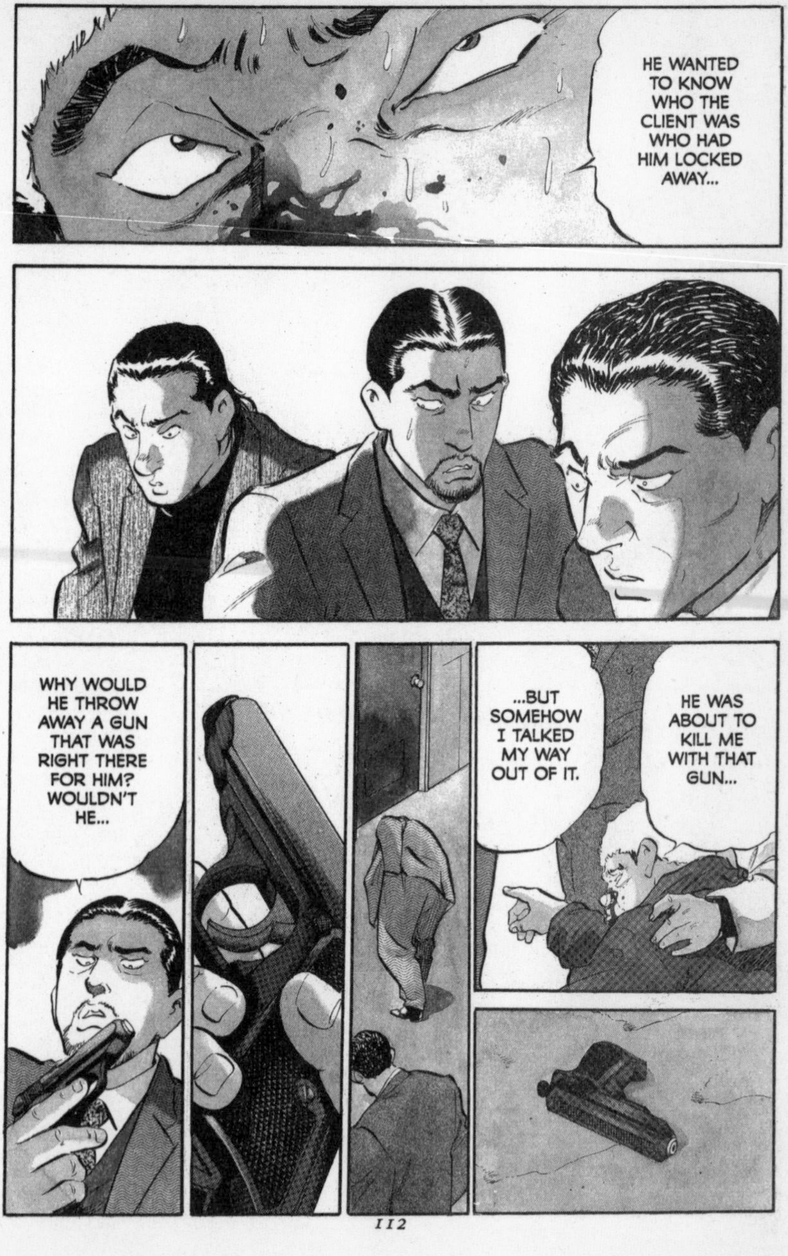
HE WANTED TO KNOW WHO THE CLIENT WAS WHO HAD HIM LOCKED AWAY...
HE WAS ABOUT TO KILL ME WITH THAT GUN...
...BUT SOMEHOW I TALKED MY WAY OUT OF IT.
WHY WOULD HE THROW AWAY A GUN THAT WAS RIGHT THERE FOR HIM? WOULDN'T HE...

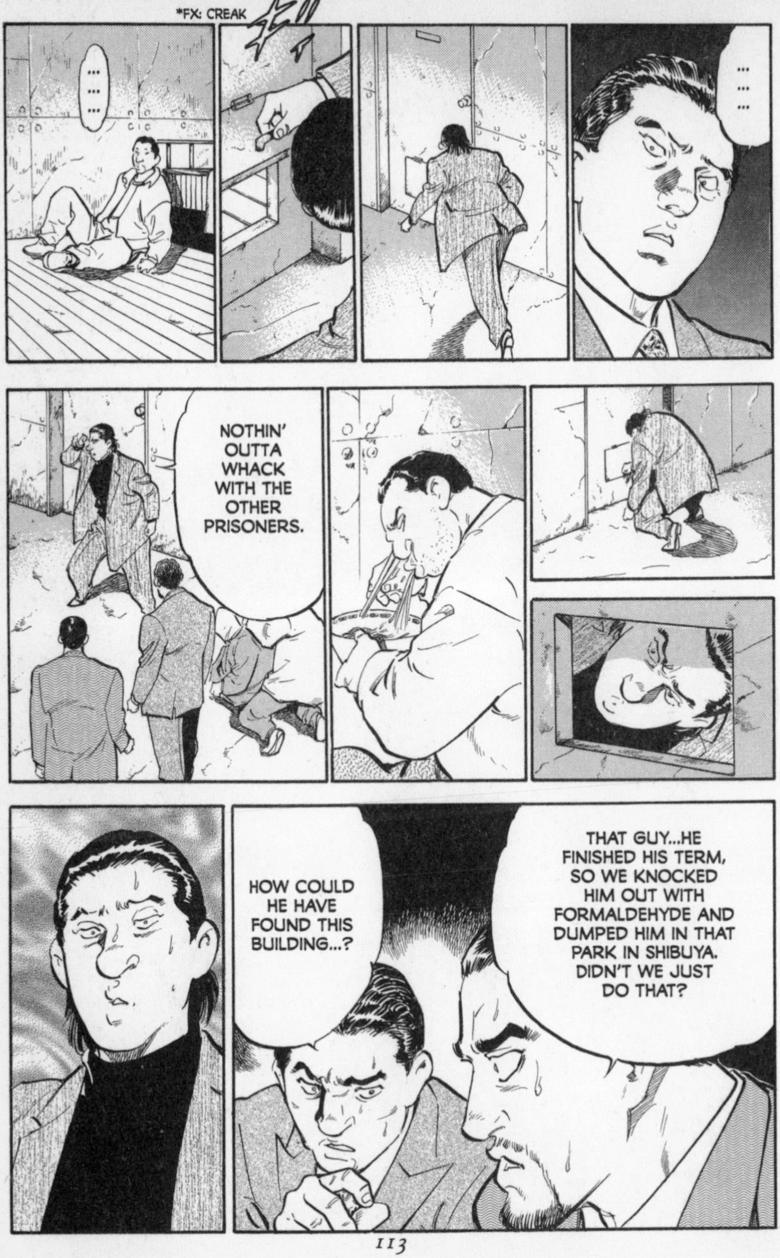
...
...
...
*FX: CREAK
...
...
...
NOTHIN' OUTTA WHACK WITH THE OTHER PRISONERS.
THAT GUY...HE FINISHED HIS TERM, SO WE KNOCKED HIM OUT WITH FORMALDEHYDE AND DUMPED HIM IN THAT PARK IN SHIBUYA. DIDN'T WE JUST DO THAT?
HOW COULD HE HAVE FOUND THIS BUILDING...?

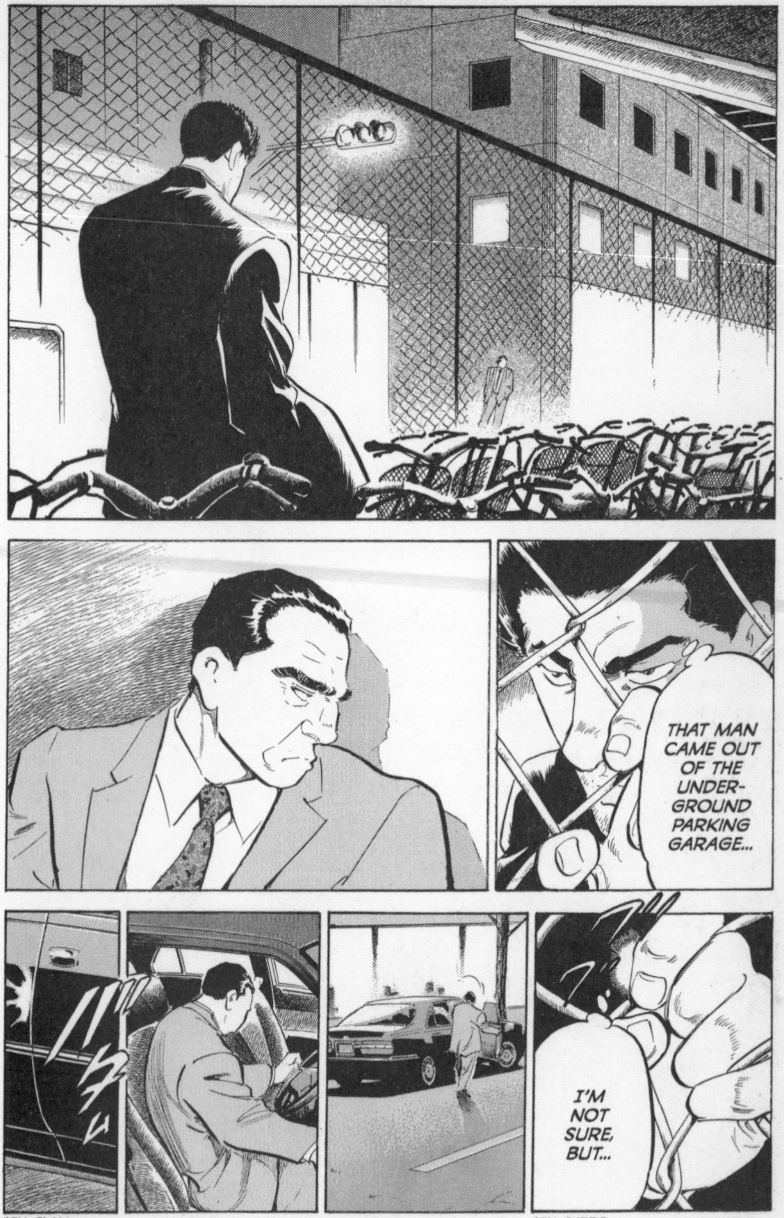
THAT MAN CAME OUT OF THE UNDER-GROUND PARKING GARAGE...
I'M NOT SURE, BUT...

*FX: SHRRG

*FX: SLAM

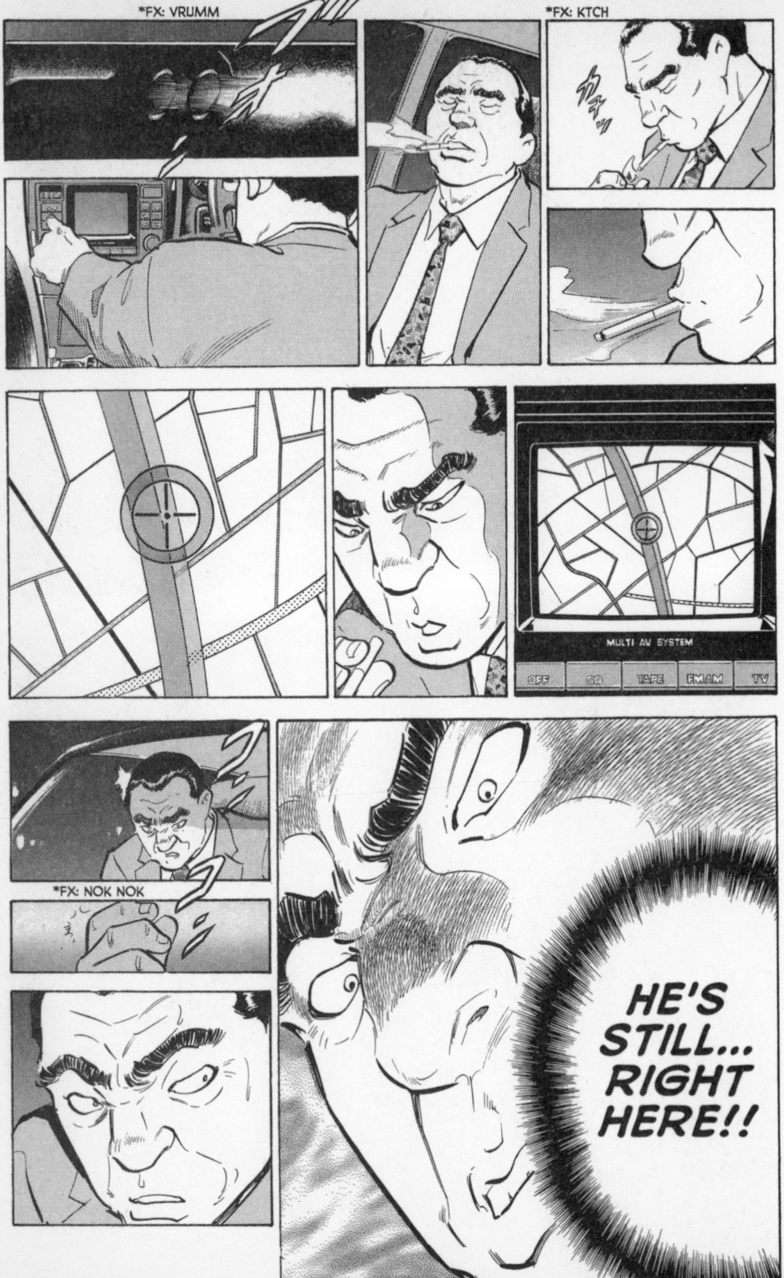
*FX: KTCH
*FX: VRUMM
MULTI AV SYSTEM
OFF
GQ
TAPE
FMAM
TV
HE'S STILL... RIGHT HERE!!
*FX: NOK NOK

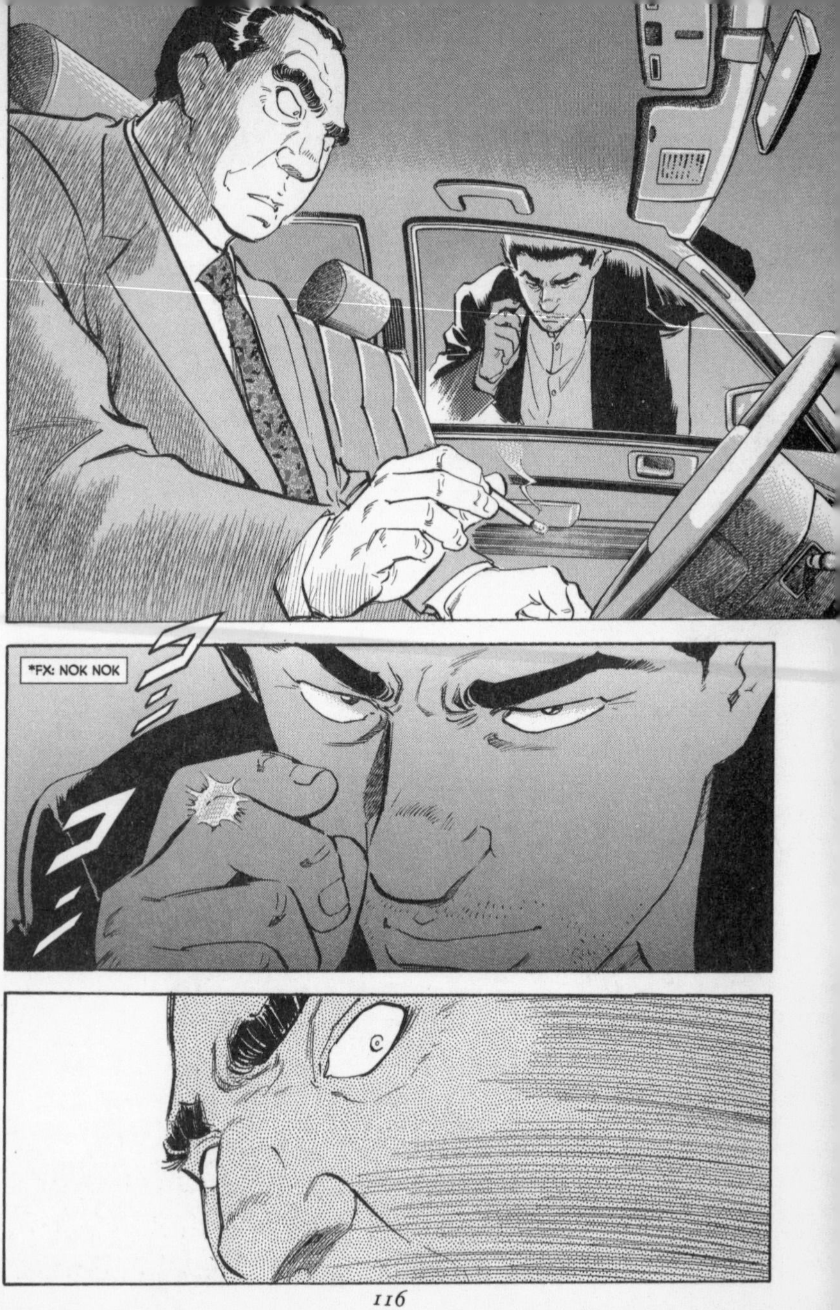
*FX: NOK NOK

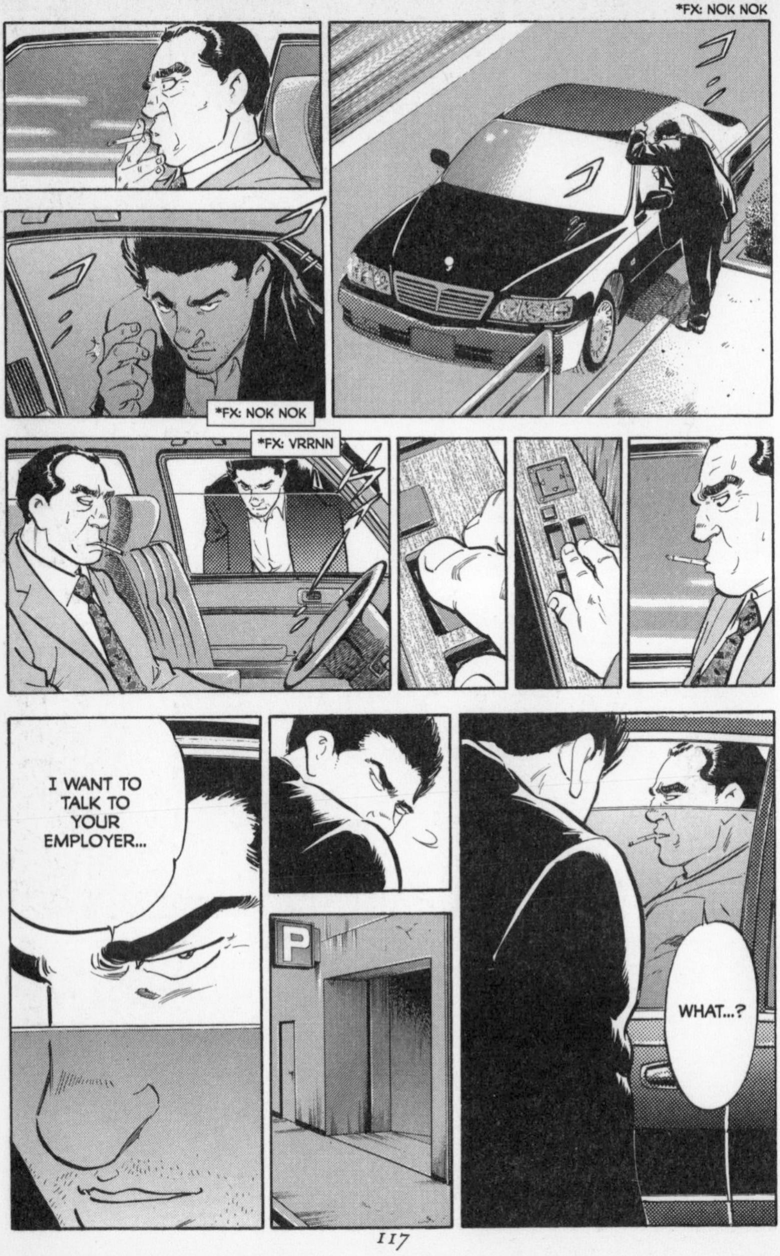

*FX: NOK NOK
*FX: NOK NOK
*FX: VRRNN
WHAT...?
I WANT TO TALK TO YOUR EMPLOYER...

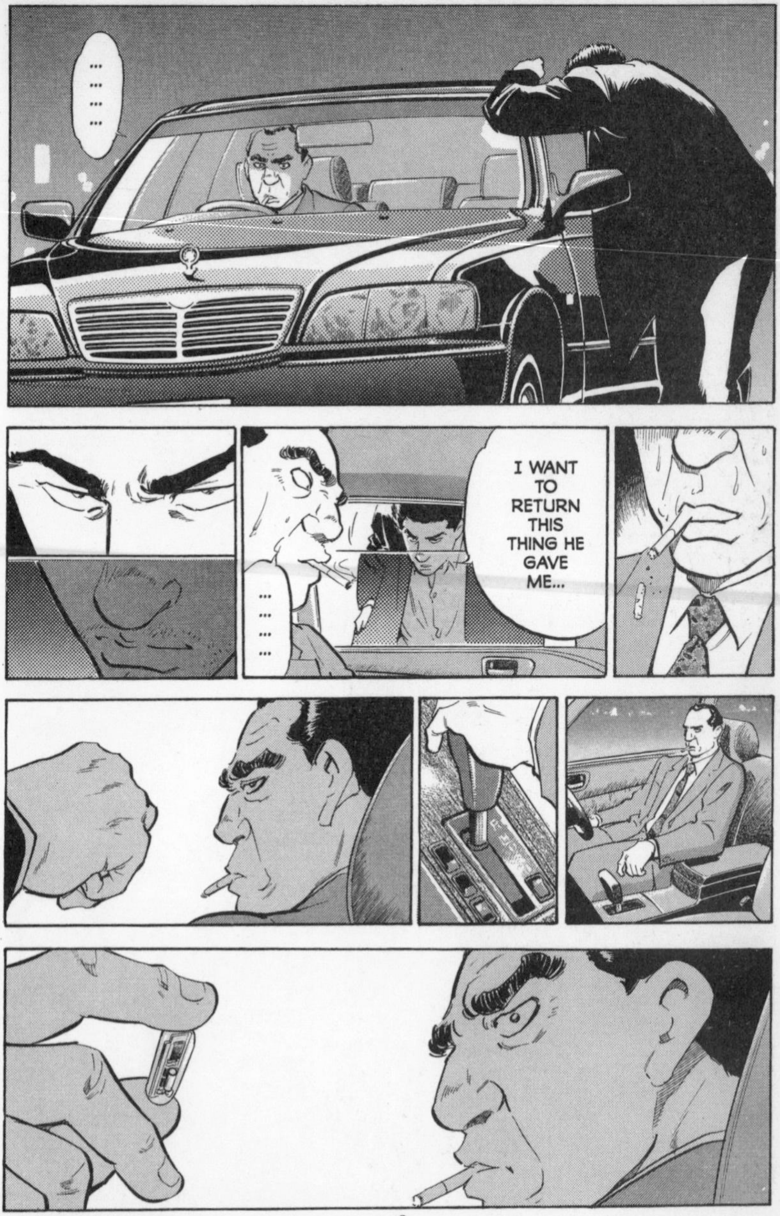
....
I WANT TO RETURN THIS THING HE GAVE ME...
....

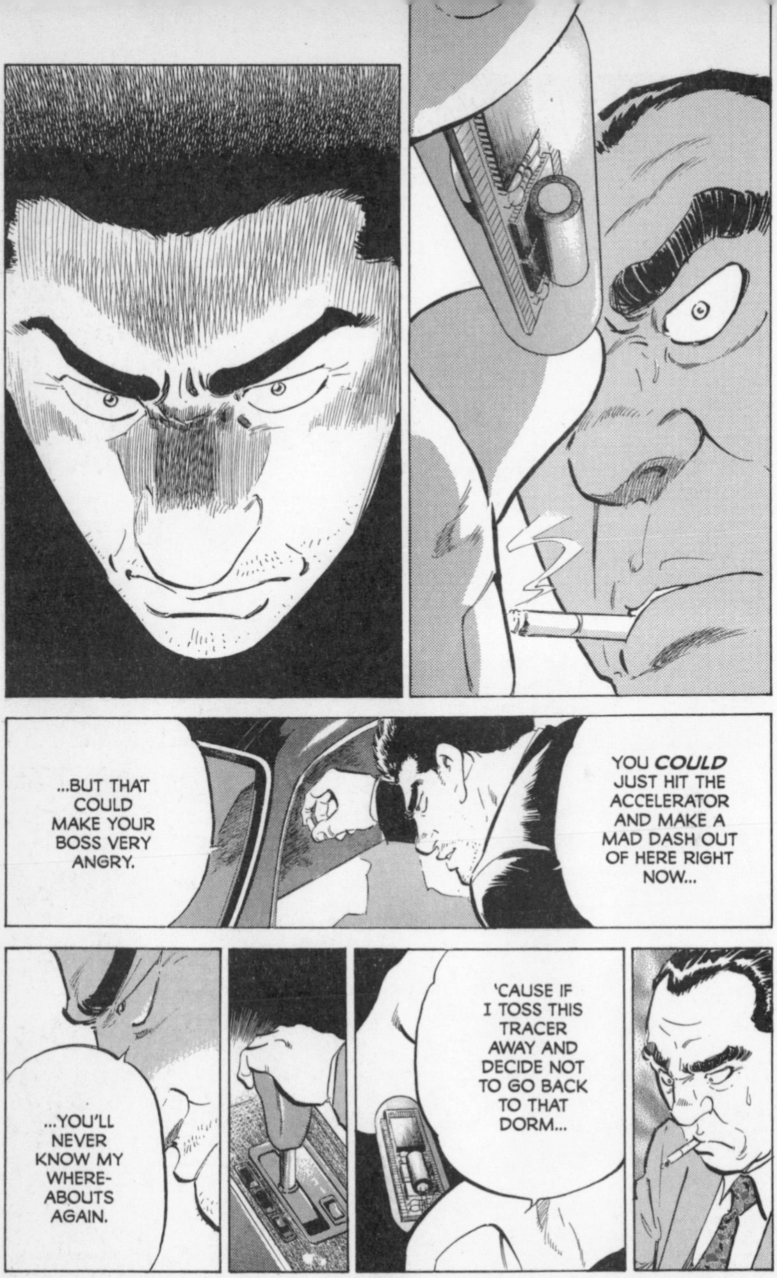
YOU ***COULD*** JUST HIT THE ACCELERATOR AND MAKE A MAD DASH OUT OF HERE RIGHT NOW...
...BUT THAT COULD MAKE YOUR BOSS VERY ANGRY.
'CAUSE IF I TOSS THIS TRACER AWAY AND DECIDE NOT TO GO BACK TO THAT DORM...
...YOU'LL NEVER KNOW MY WHERE-ABOUTS AGAIN.

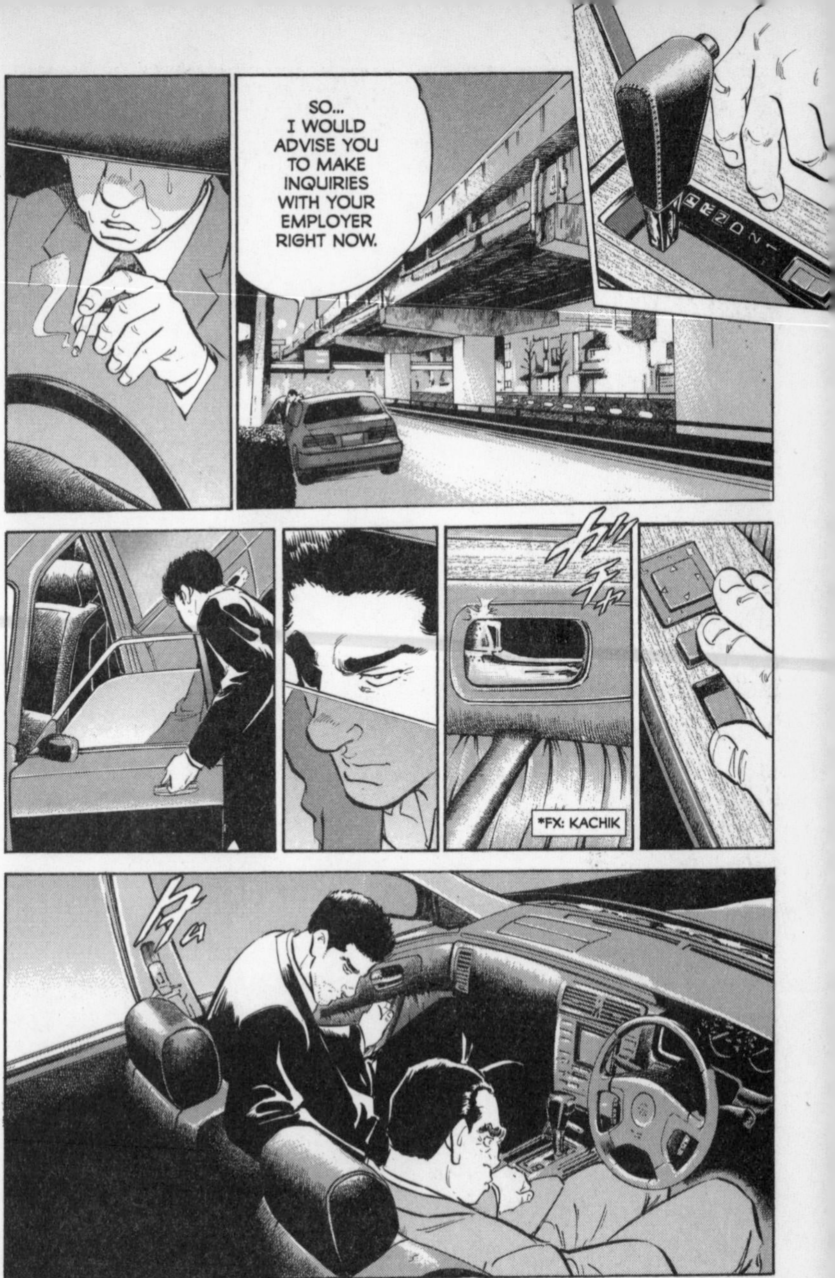
SO... I WOULD ADVISE YOU TO MAKE INQUIRIES WITH YOUR EMPLOYER RIGHT NOW.
*FX: KACHIK

*FX: THUMP

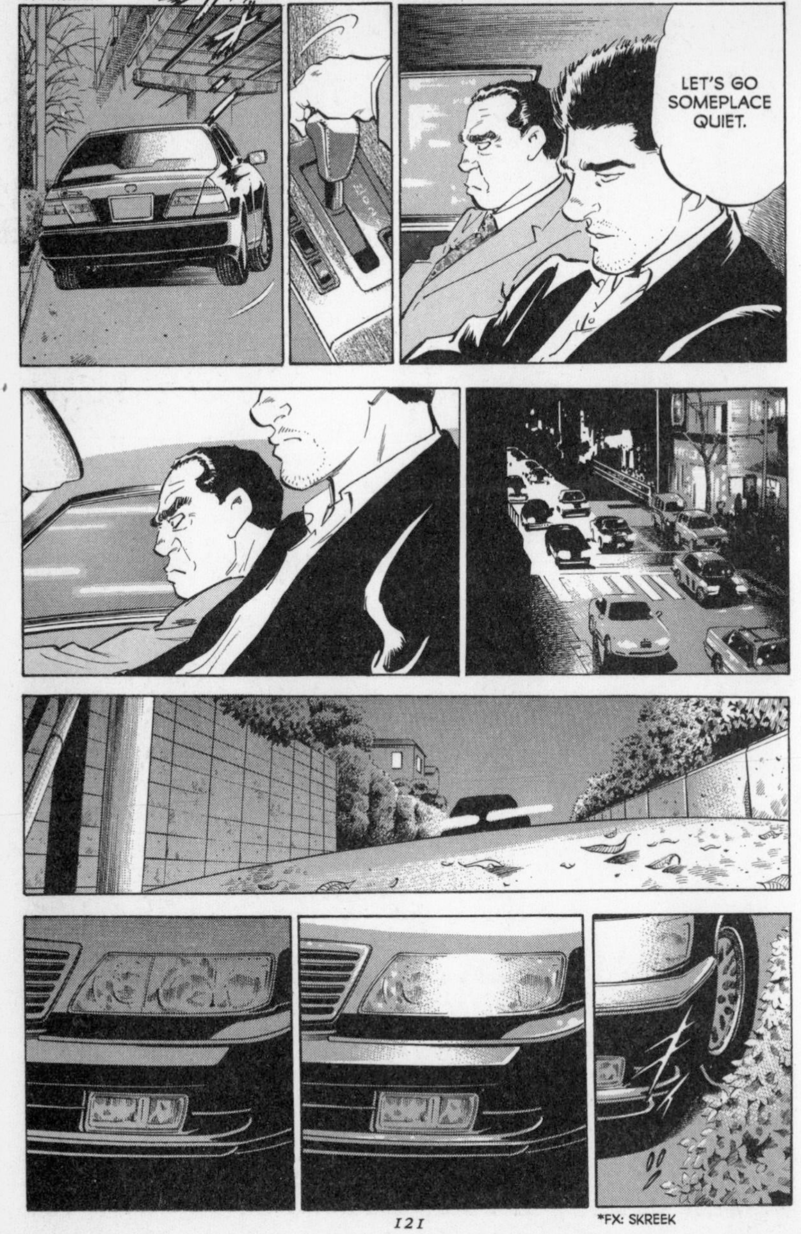
LET'S GO SOMEPLACE QUIET.
*FX: VRUMM
*FX: SKREEK

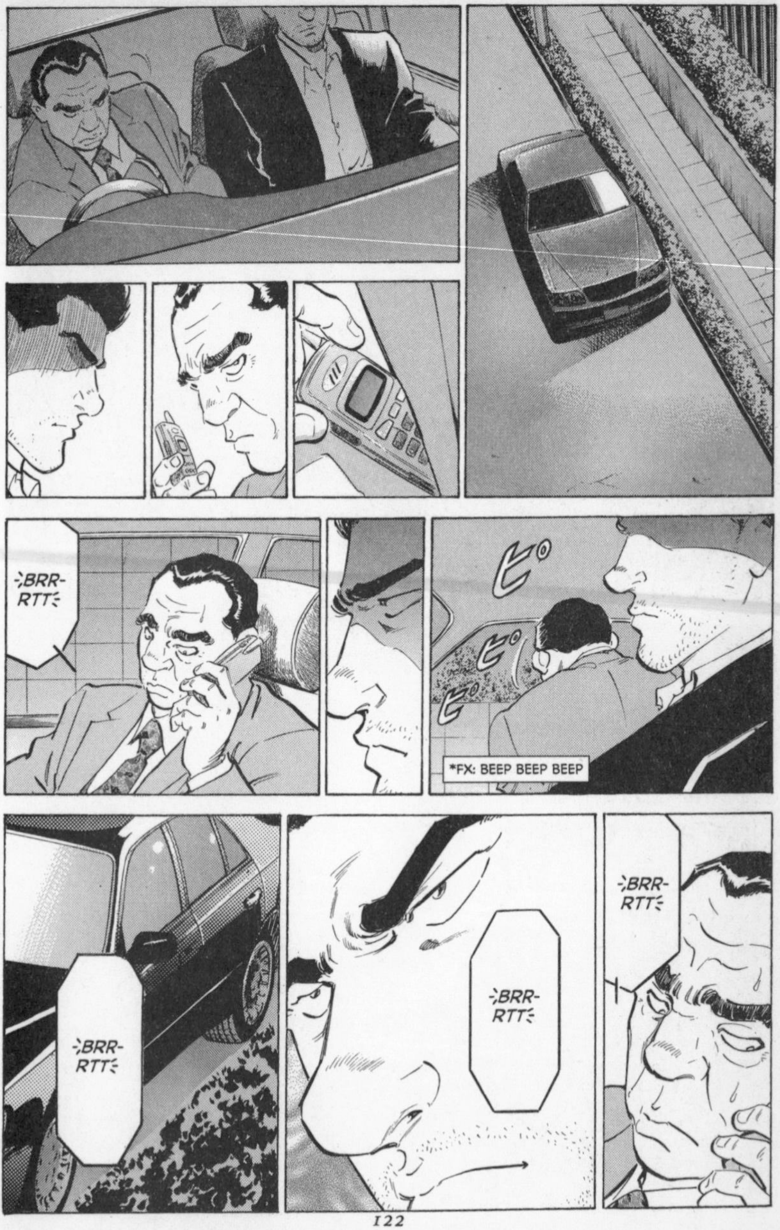
BRR-
RTT
ピ
ピ
ピ
*FX: BEEP BEEP BEEP
BRR-
RTT
BRR-
RTT
BRR-
RTT

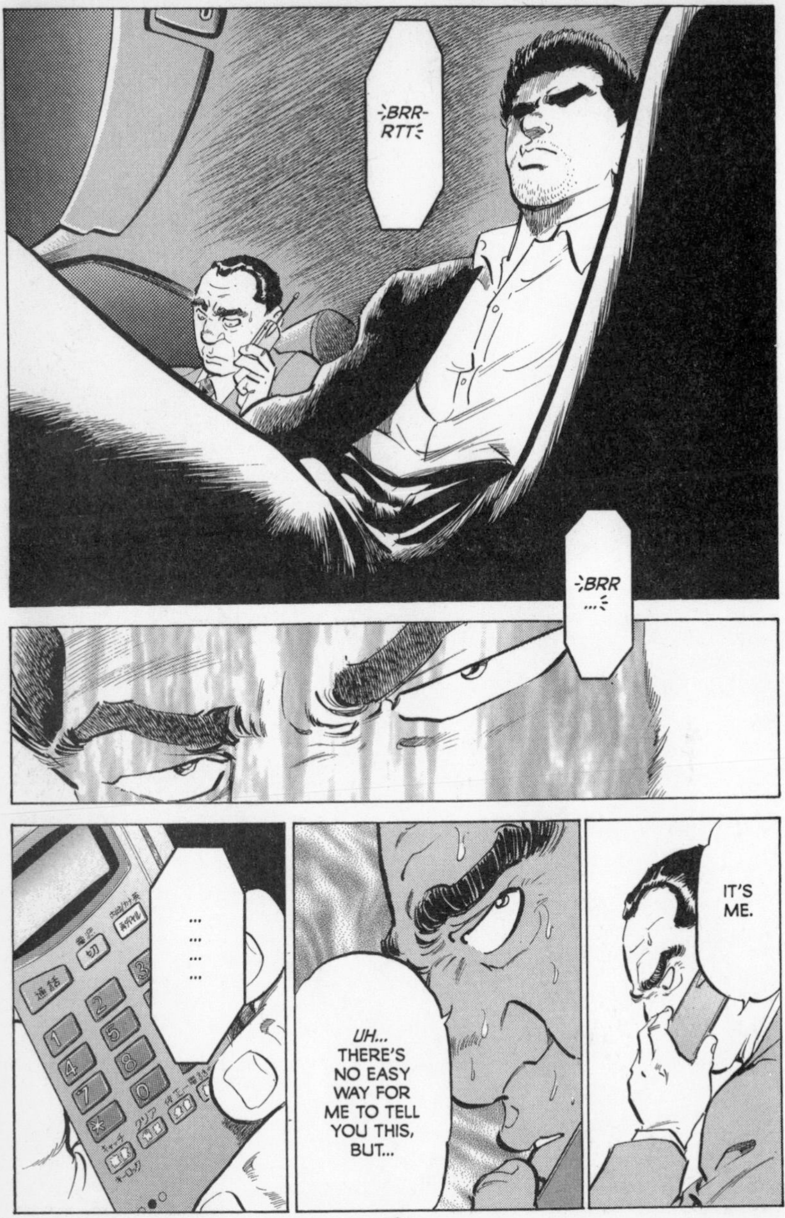
BRR-RTT
BRR...
IT'S ME.
UH... THERE'S NO EASY WAY FOR ME TO TELL YOU THIS, BUT...
... ...

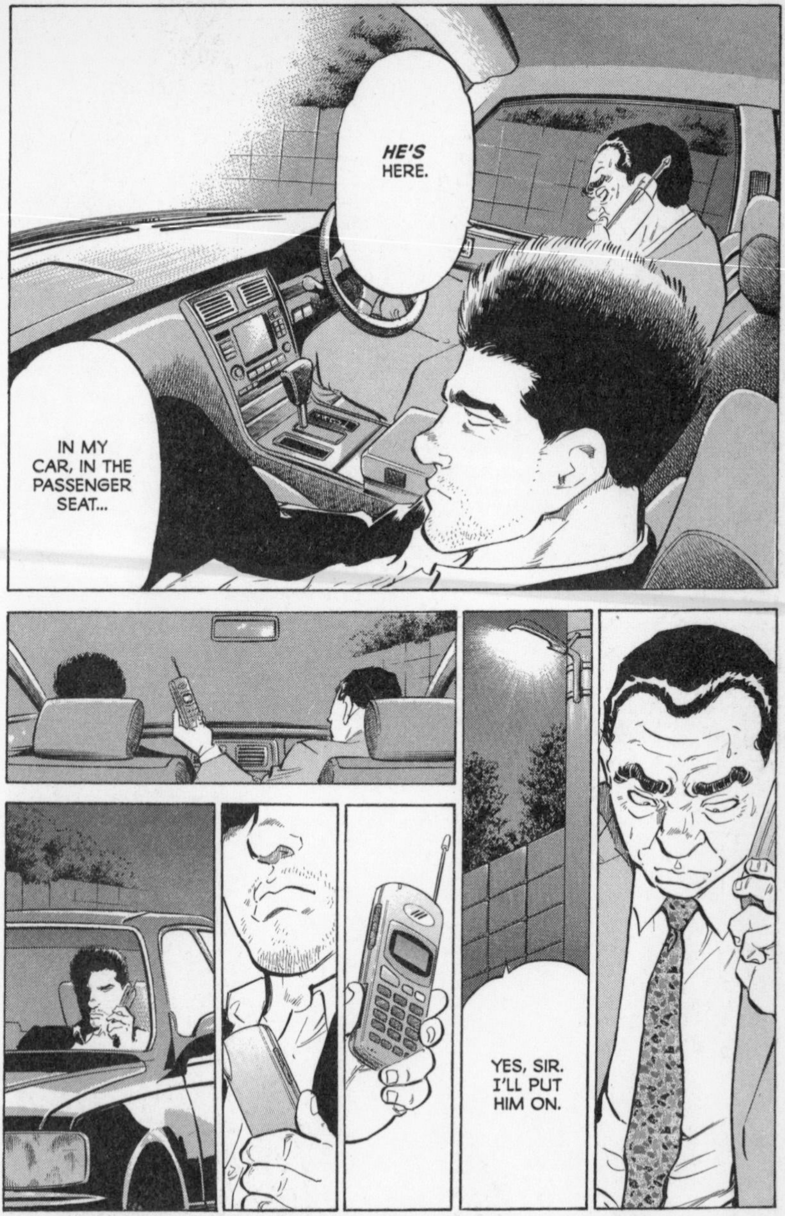
HE'S HERE.
IN MY CAR, IN THE PASSENGER SEAT...
YES, SIR. I'LL PUT HIM ON.

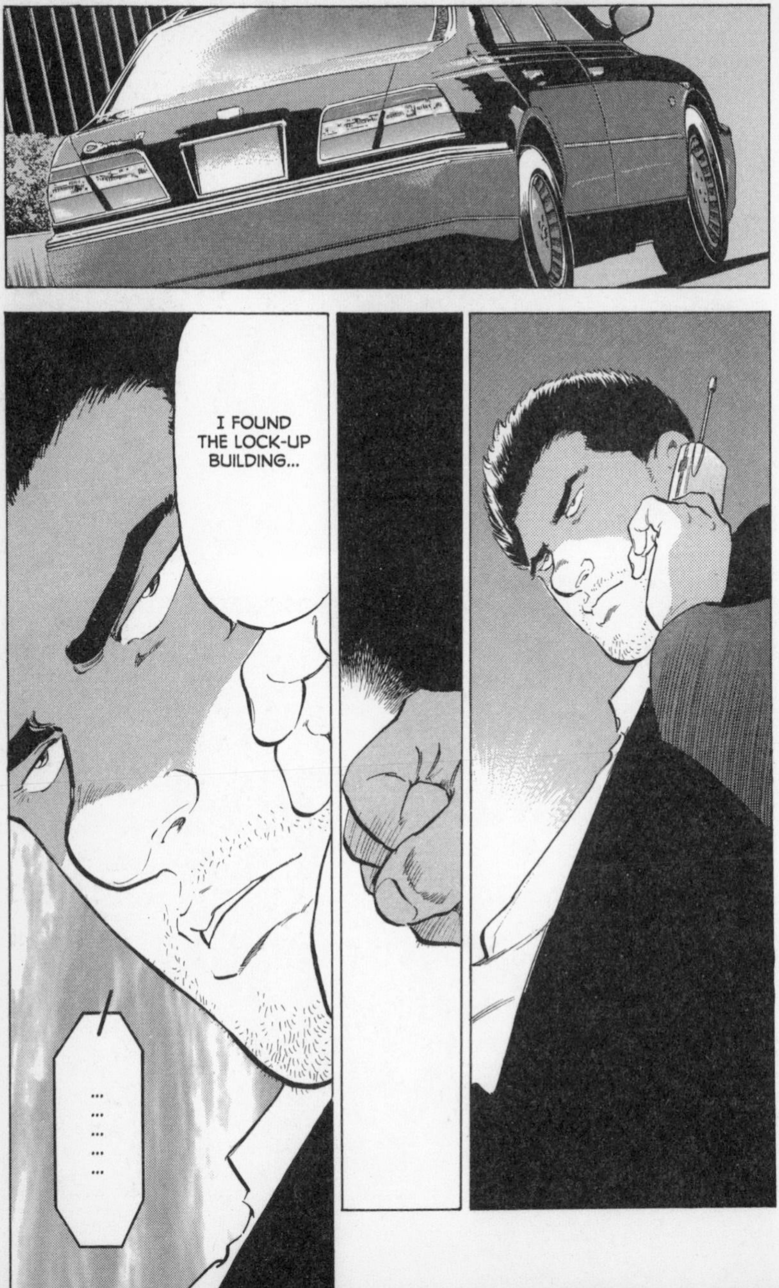
I FOUND THE LOCK-UP BUILDING...
......

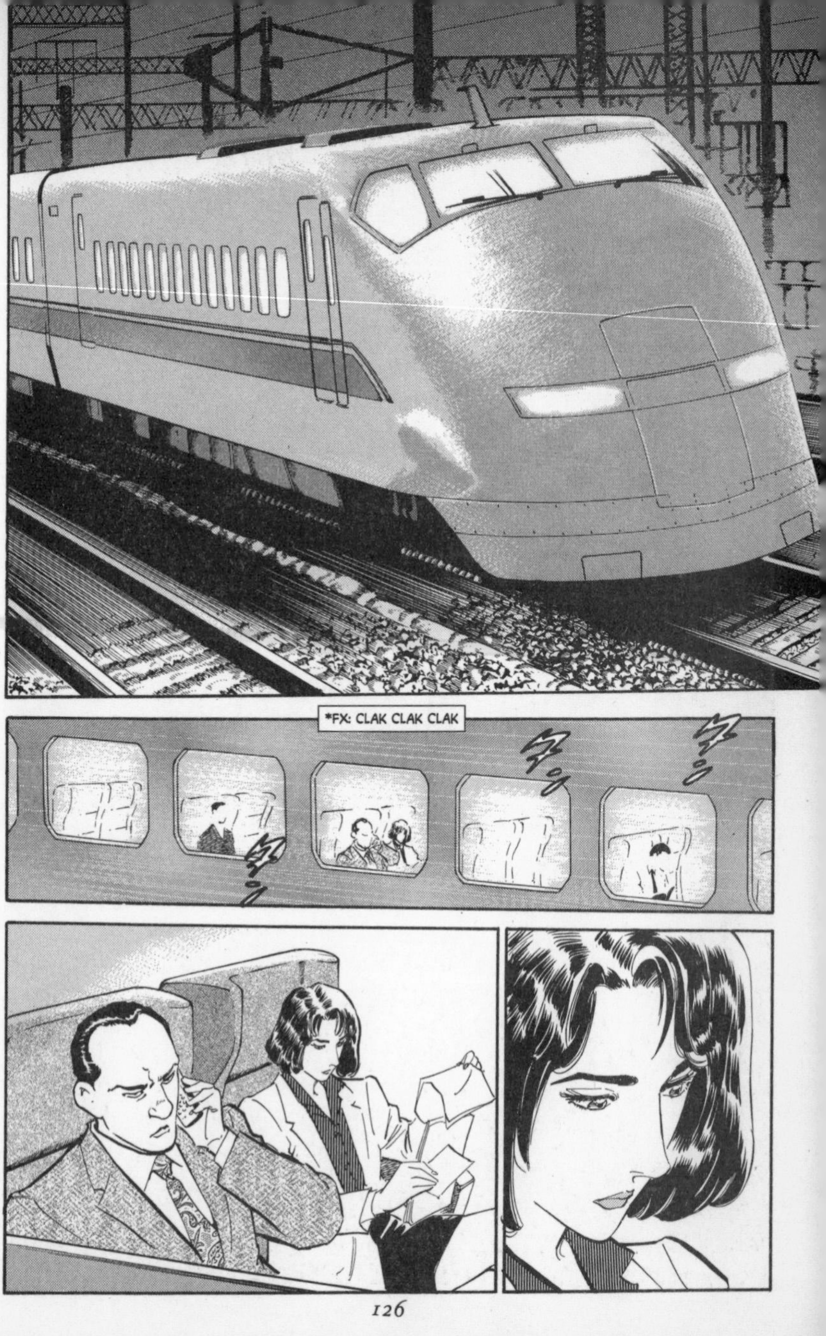
*FX: CLAK CLAK CLAK

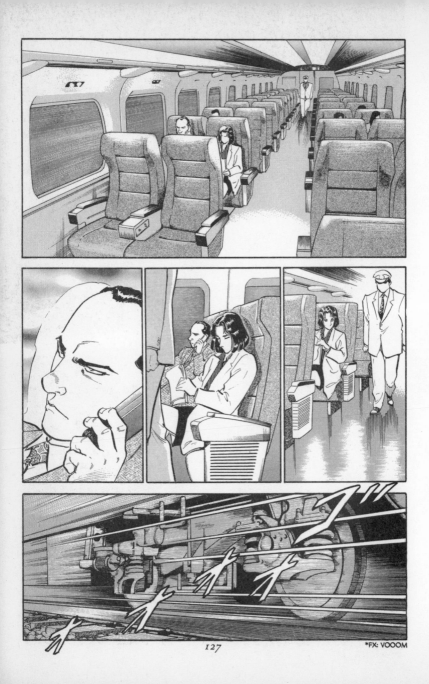

*FX: VOOOM

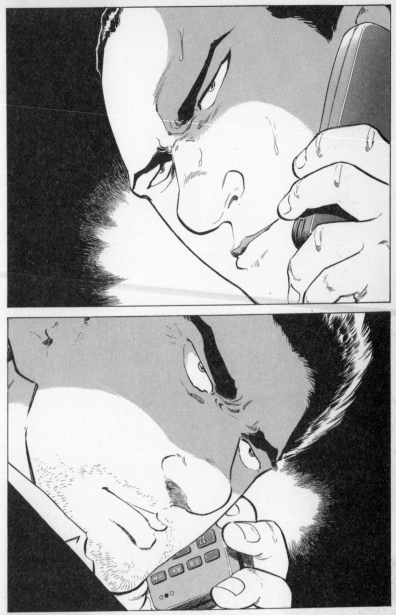

REVERSAL: END

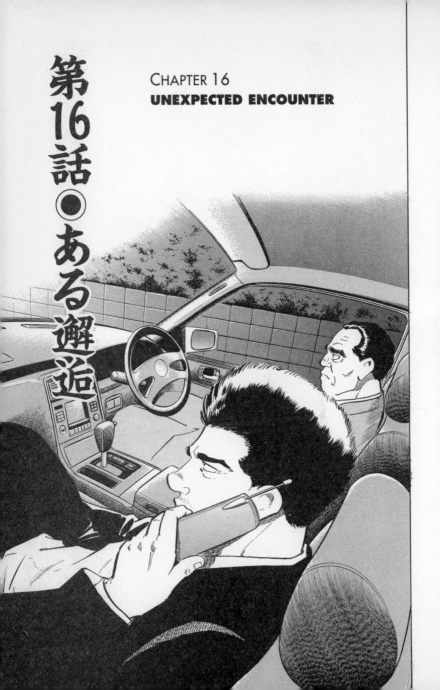

第16話●ある邂逅

CHAPTER 16

UNEXPECTED ENCOUNTER

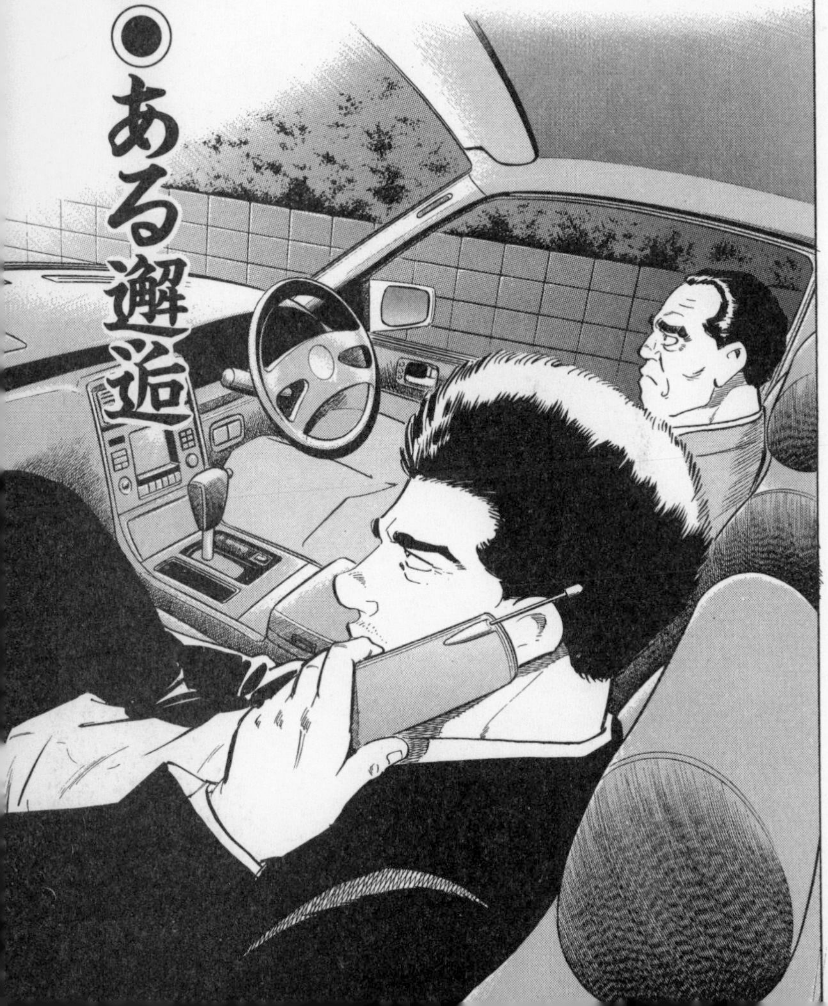

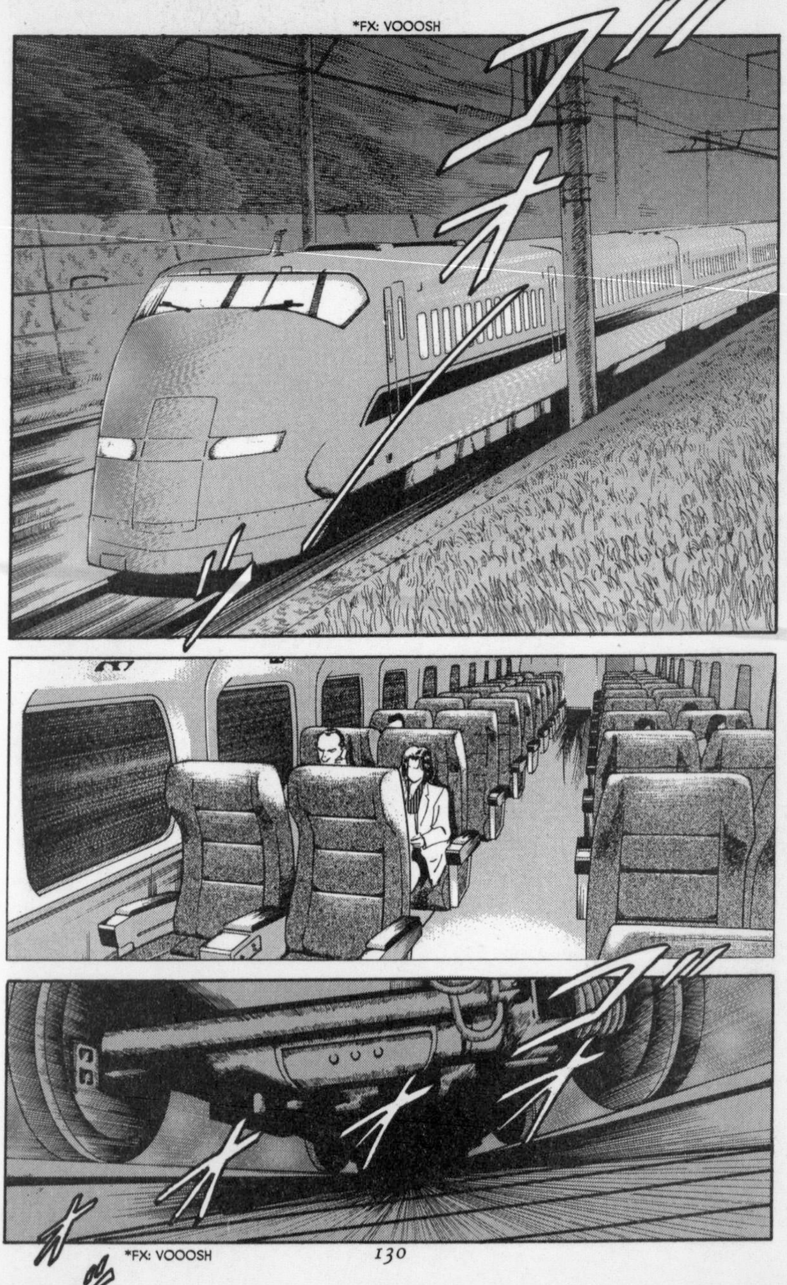
*FX: VOOOSH
*FX: VOOOSH

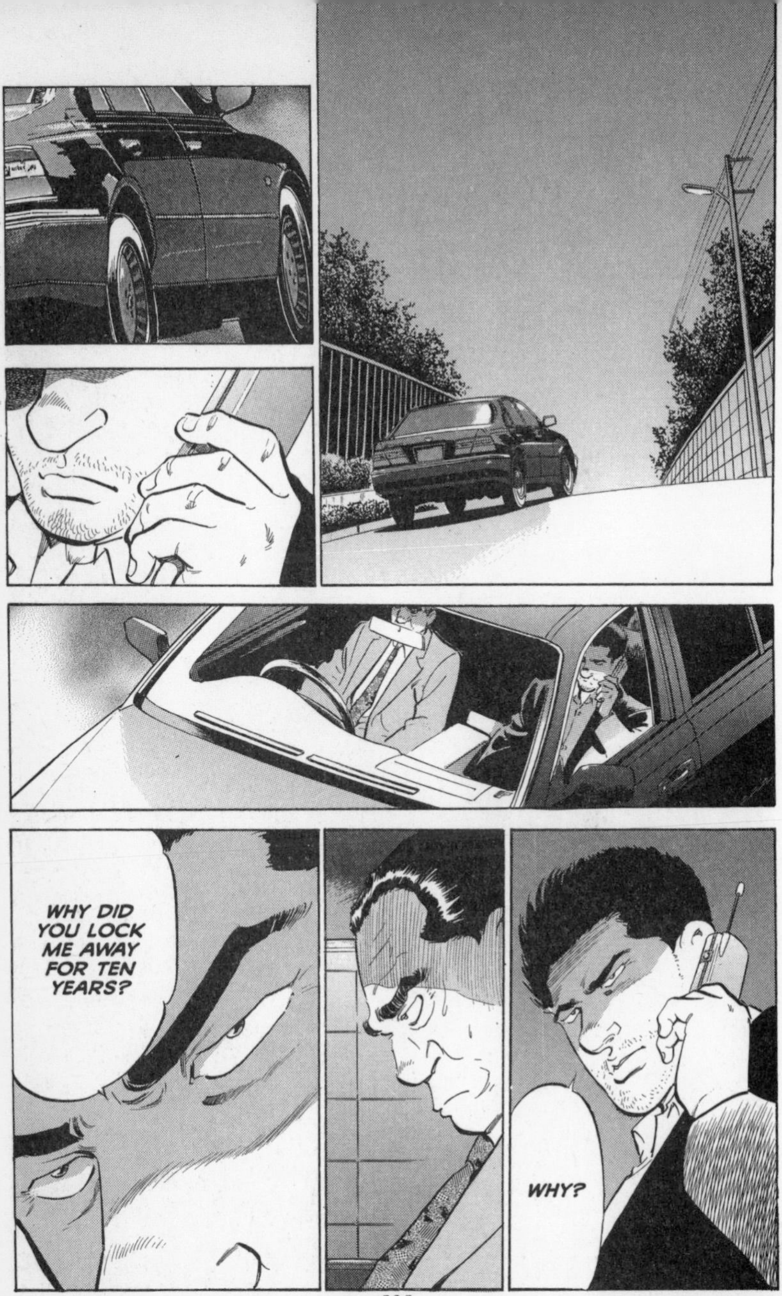
WHY?
WHY DID YOU LOCK ME AWAY FOR TEN YEARS?

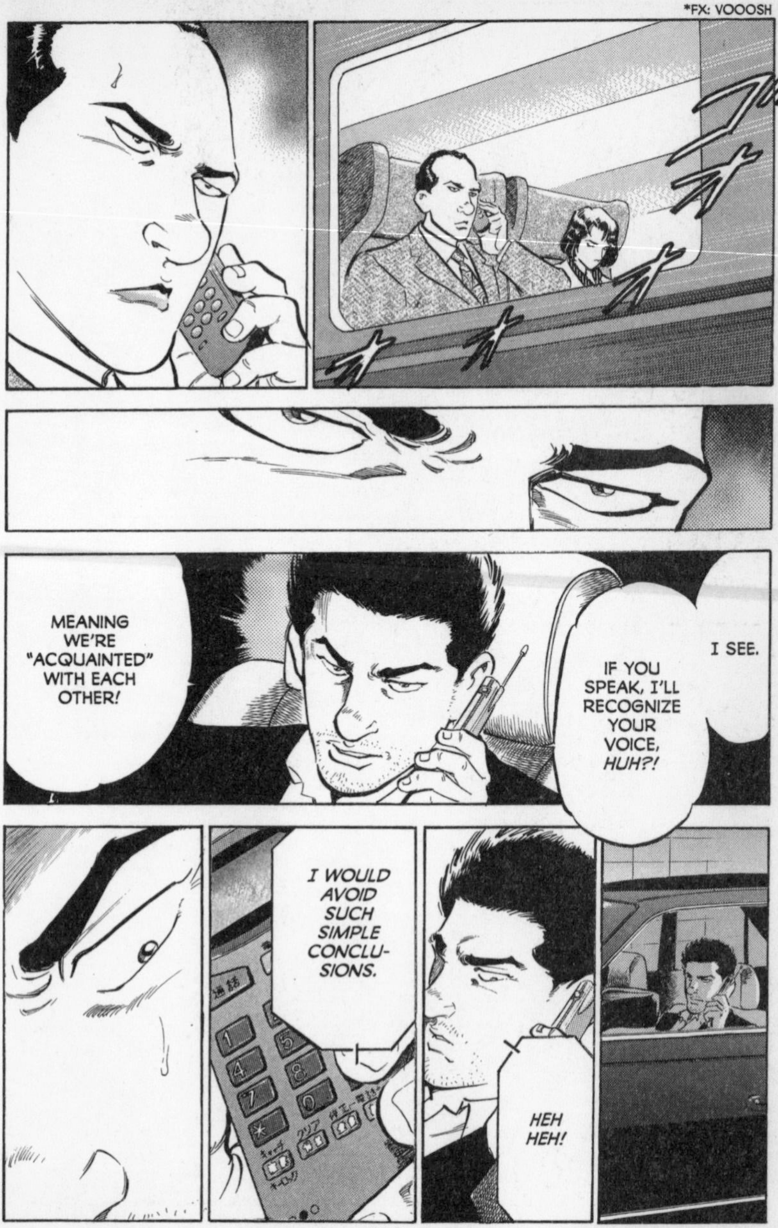
*FX: VOOOSH
I SEE.
IF YOU SPEAK, I'LL RECOGNIZE YOUR VOICE, *HUH?!*
MEANING WE'RE "ACQUAINTED" WITH EACH OTHER!
HEH HEH!
I WOULD AVOID SUCH SIMPLE CONCLU-SIONS.

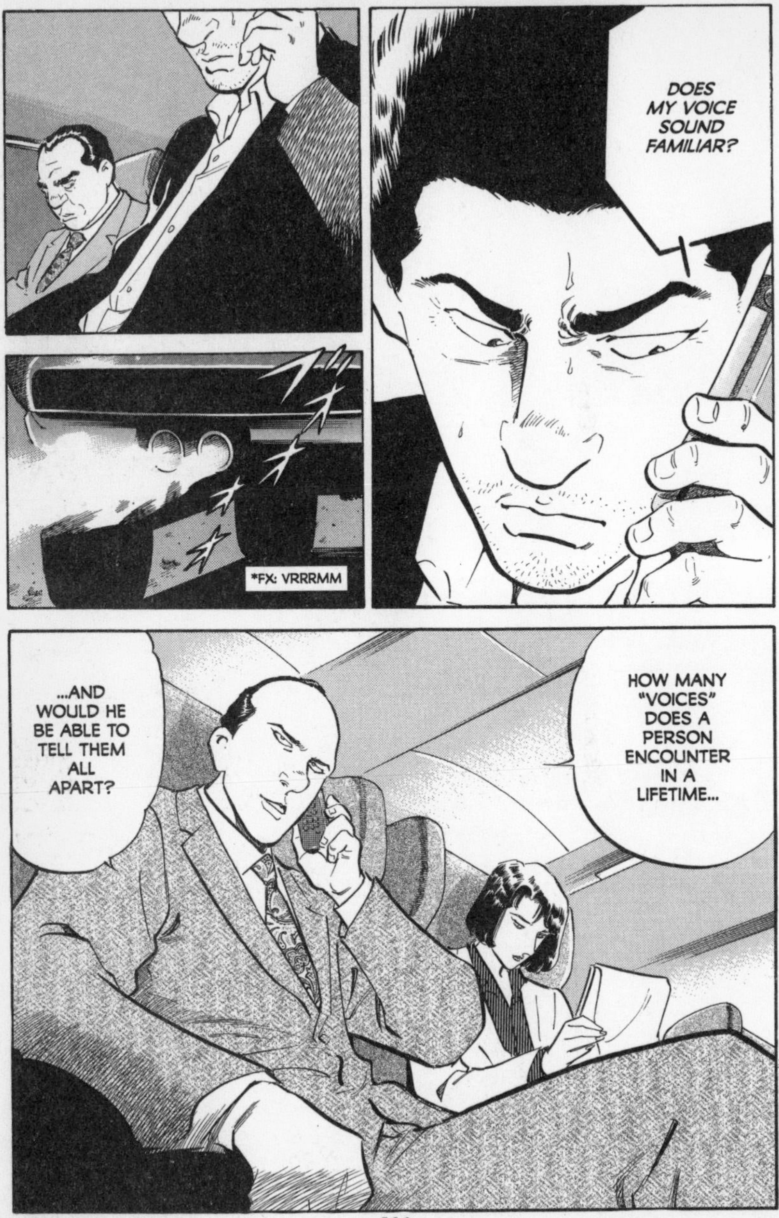
DOES MY VOICE SOUND FAMILIAR?
*FX: VRRRMM
HOW MANY "VOICES" DOES A PERSON ENCOUNTER IN A LIFETIME...
...AND WOULD HE BE ABLE TO TELL THEM ALL APART?

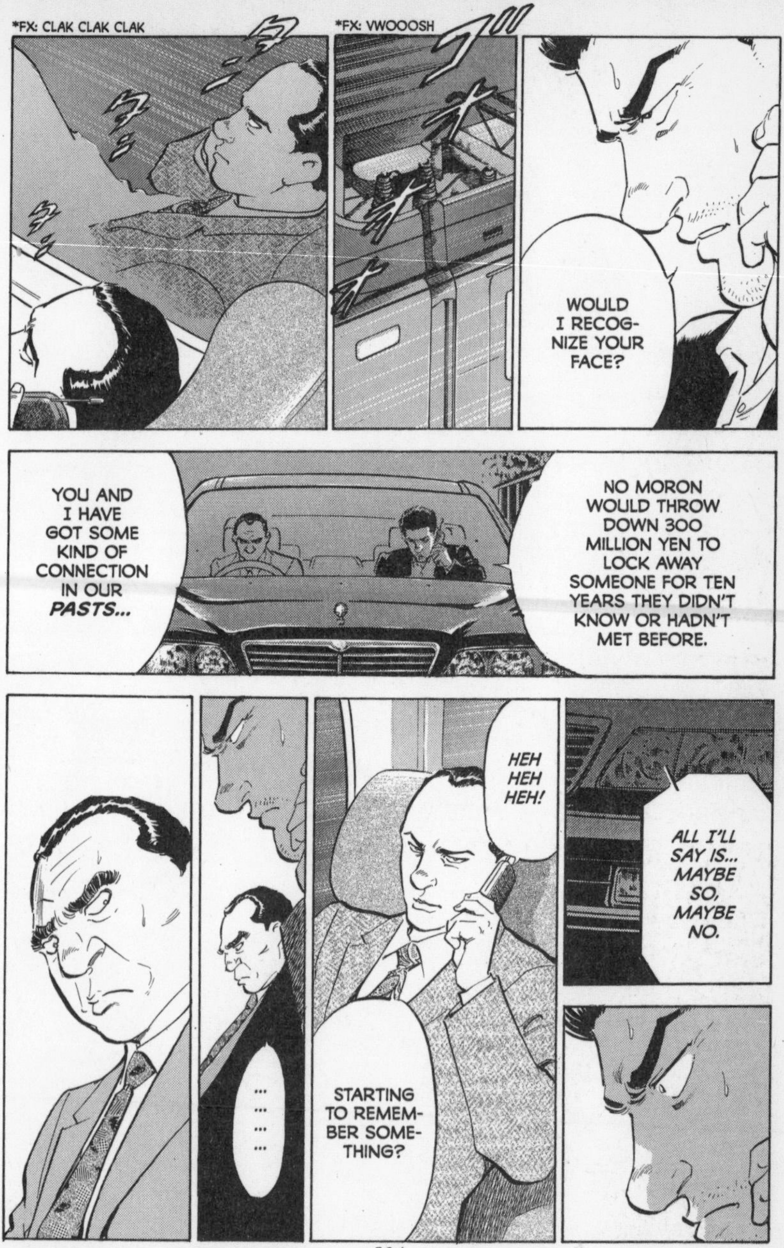
WOULD I RECOGNIZE YOUR FACE?
*FX: VWOOOSH
*FX: CLAK CLAK CLAK
NO MORON WOULD THROW DOWN 300 MILLION YEN TO LOCK AWAY SOMEONE FOR TEN YEARS THEY DIDN'T KNOW OR HADN'T MET BEFORE.
YOU AND I HAVE GOT SOME KIND OF CONNECTION IN OUR *PASTS...*
ALL I'LL SAY IS... MAYBE SO, MAYBE NO.
HEH HEH HEH!
STARTING TO REMEMBER SOMETHING?
....

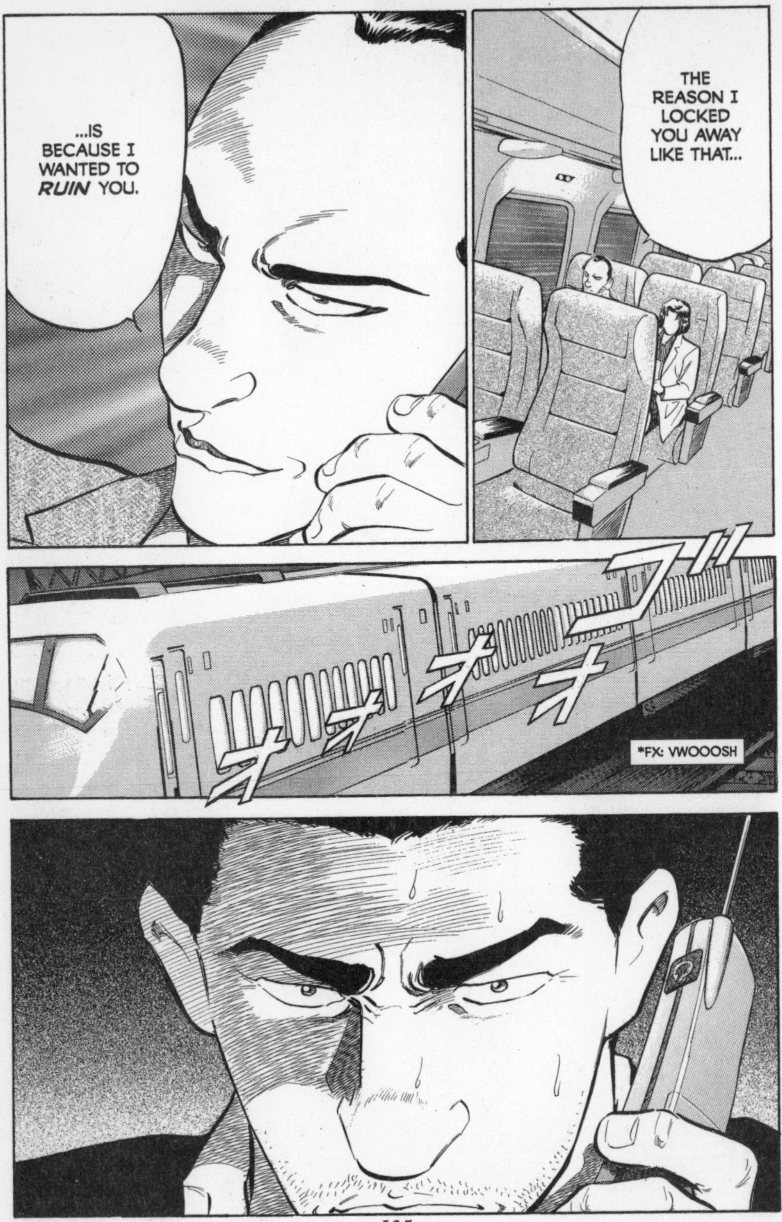
THE REASON I LOCKED YOU AWAY LIKE THAT...
...IS BECAUSE I WANTED TO *RUIN* YOU.
ゴオオオオ
*FX: VWOOOSH

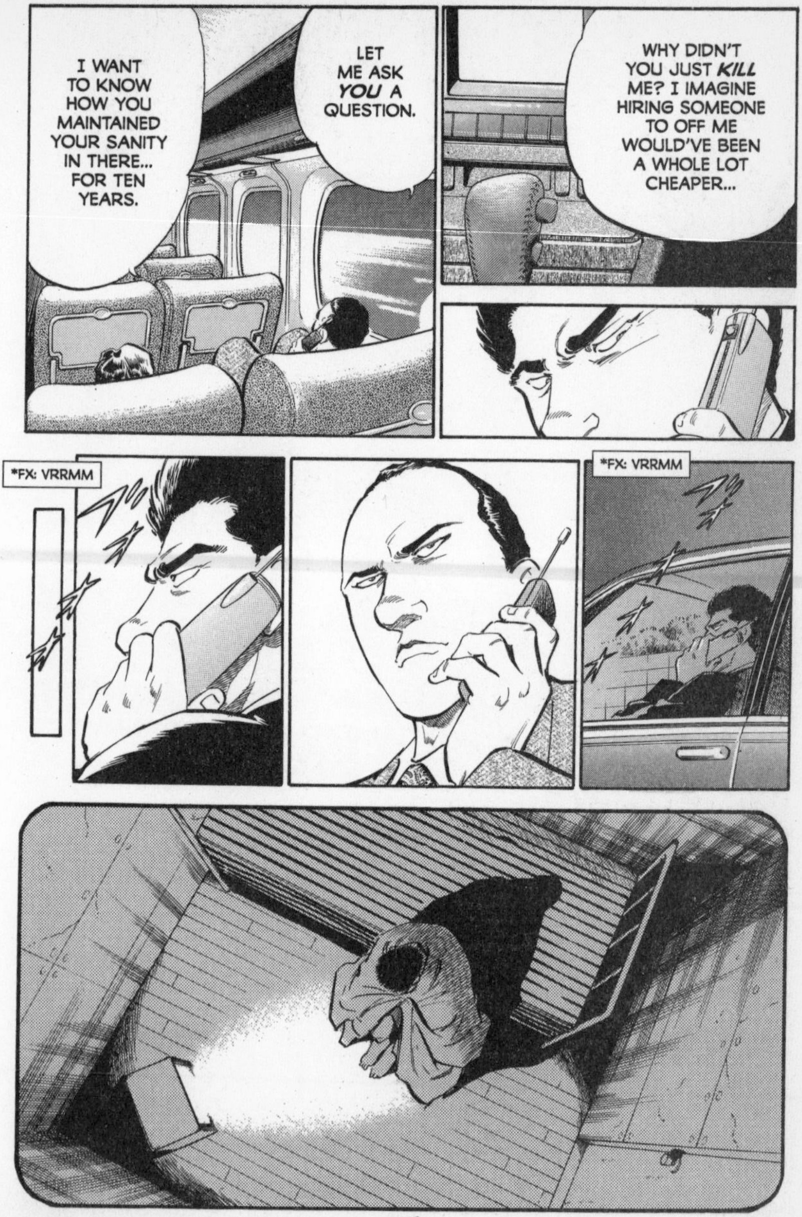
I WANT TO KNOW HOW YOU MAINTAINED YOUR SANITY IN THERE... FOR TEN YEARS.
LET ME ASK YOU A QUESTION.
WHY DIDN'T YOU JUST KILL ME? I IMAGINE HIRING SOMEONE TO OFF ME WOULD'VE BEEN A WHOLE LOT CHEAPER...
*FX: VRRMM
*FX: VRRMM

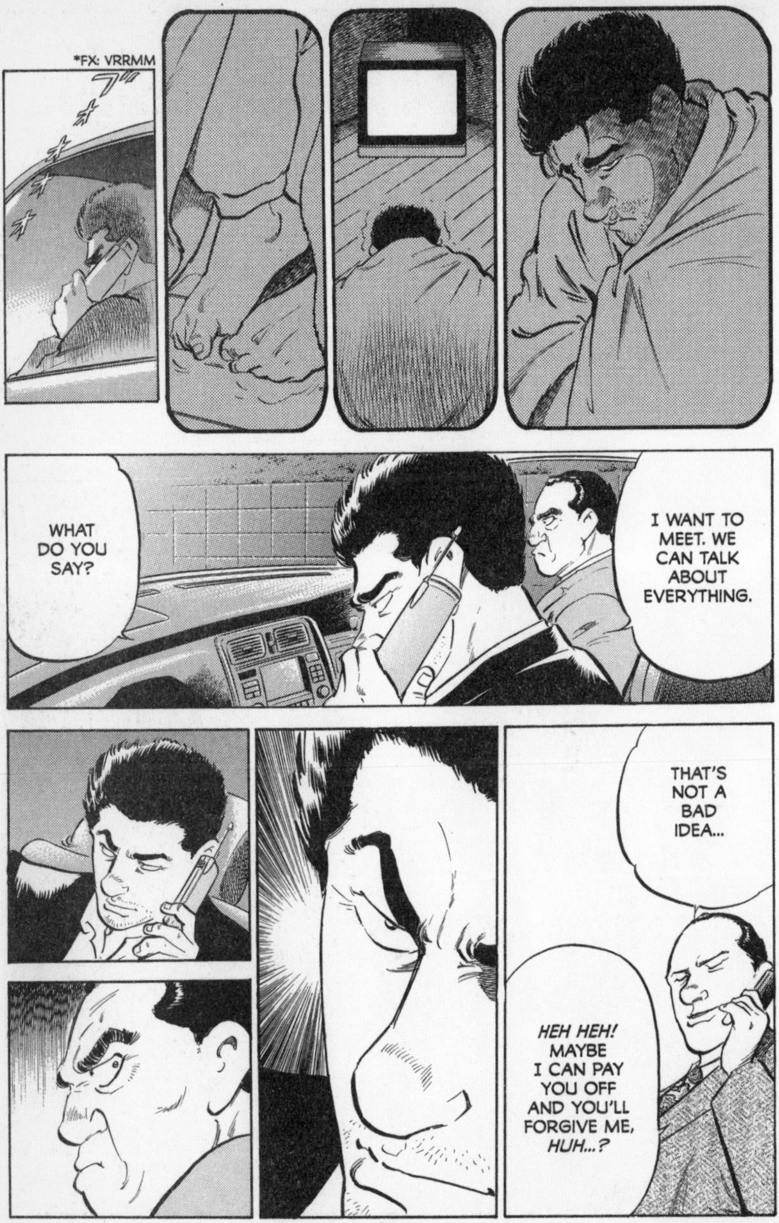
*FX: VRRMM
I WANT TO MEET. WE CAN TALK ABOUT EVERYTHING.
WHAT DO YOU SAY?
THAT'S NOT A BAD IDEA...
HEH HEH! MAYBE I CAN PAY YOU OFF AND YOU'LL FORGIVE ME, *HUH...?*

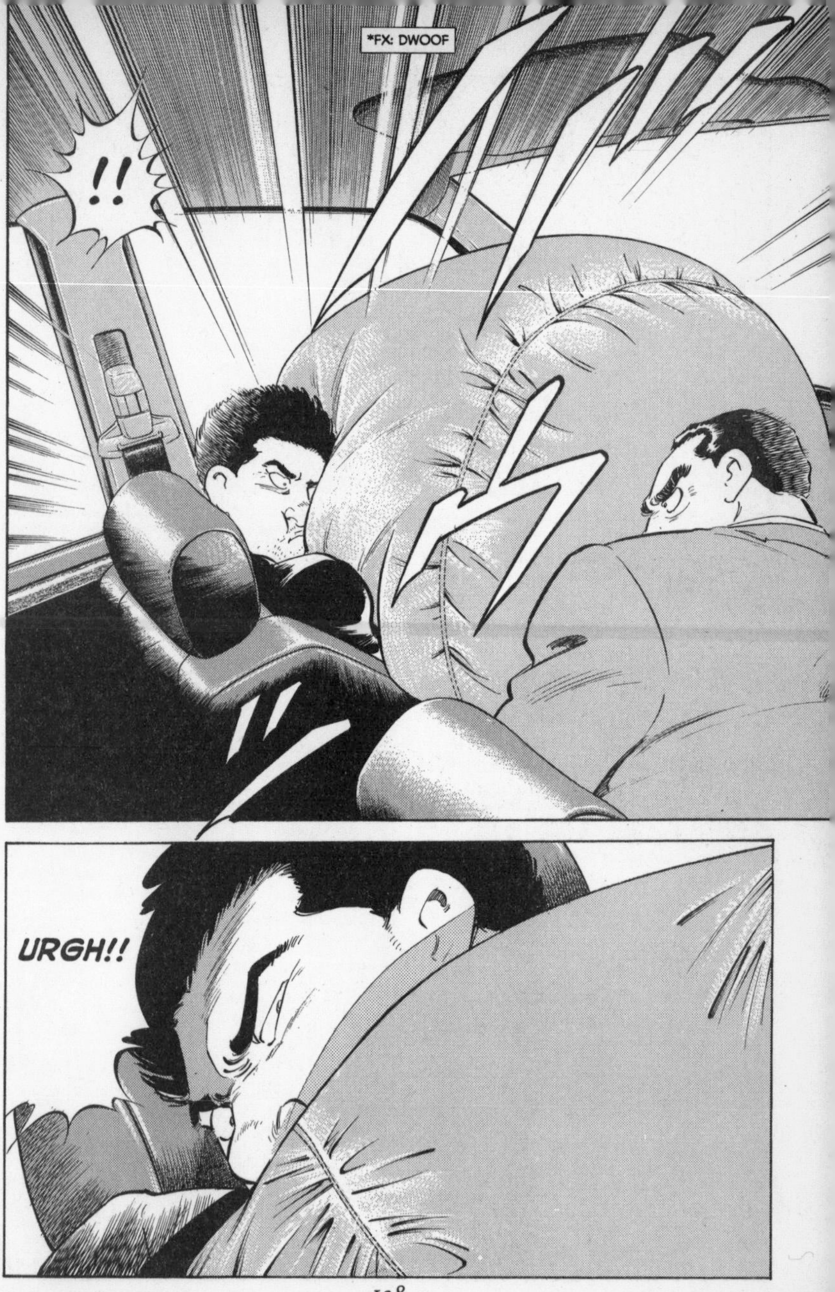
*FX: DWOOF
!!
URGH!!

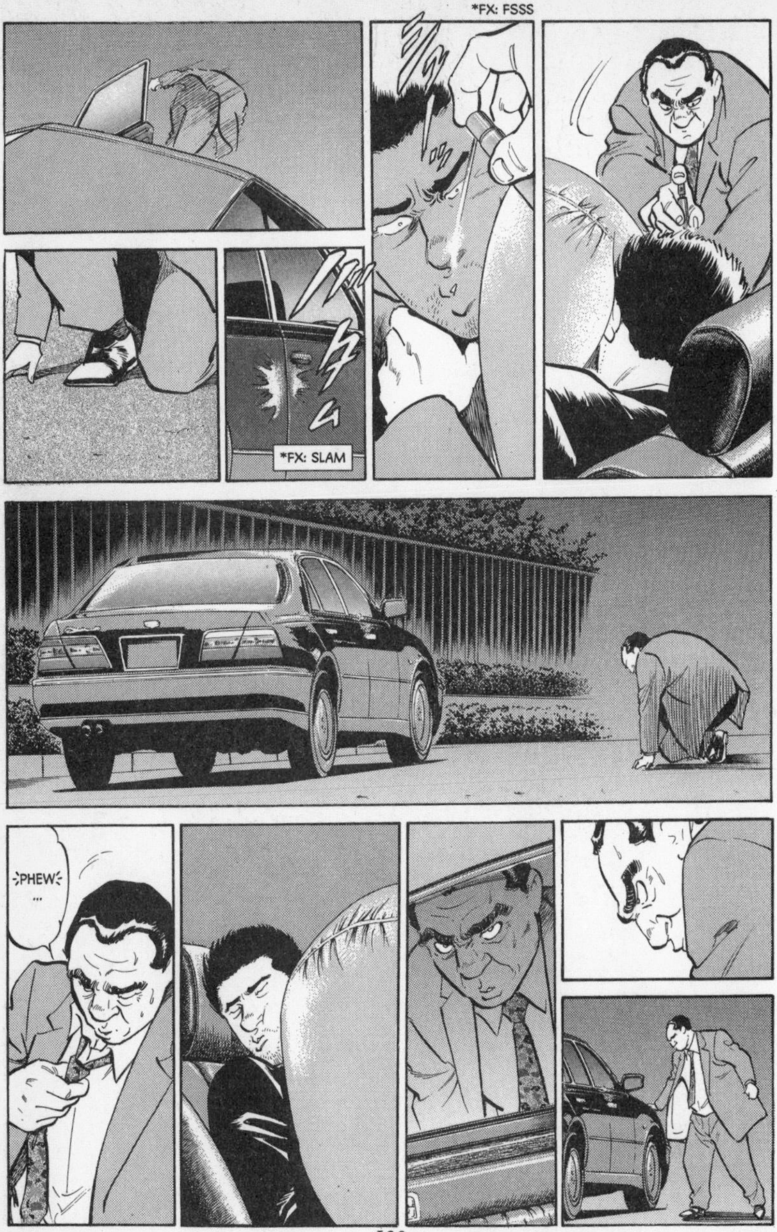
*FX: FSSS
*FX: SLAM
PHEW ...

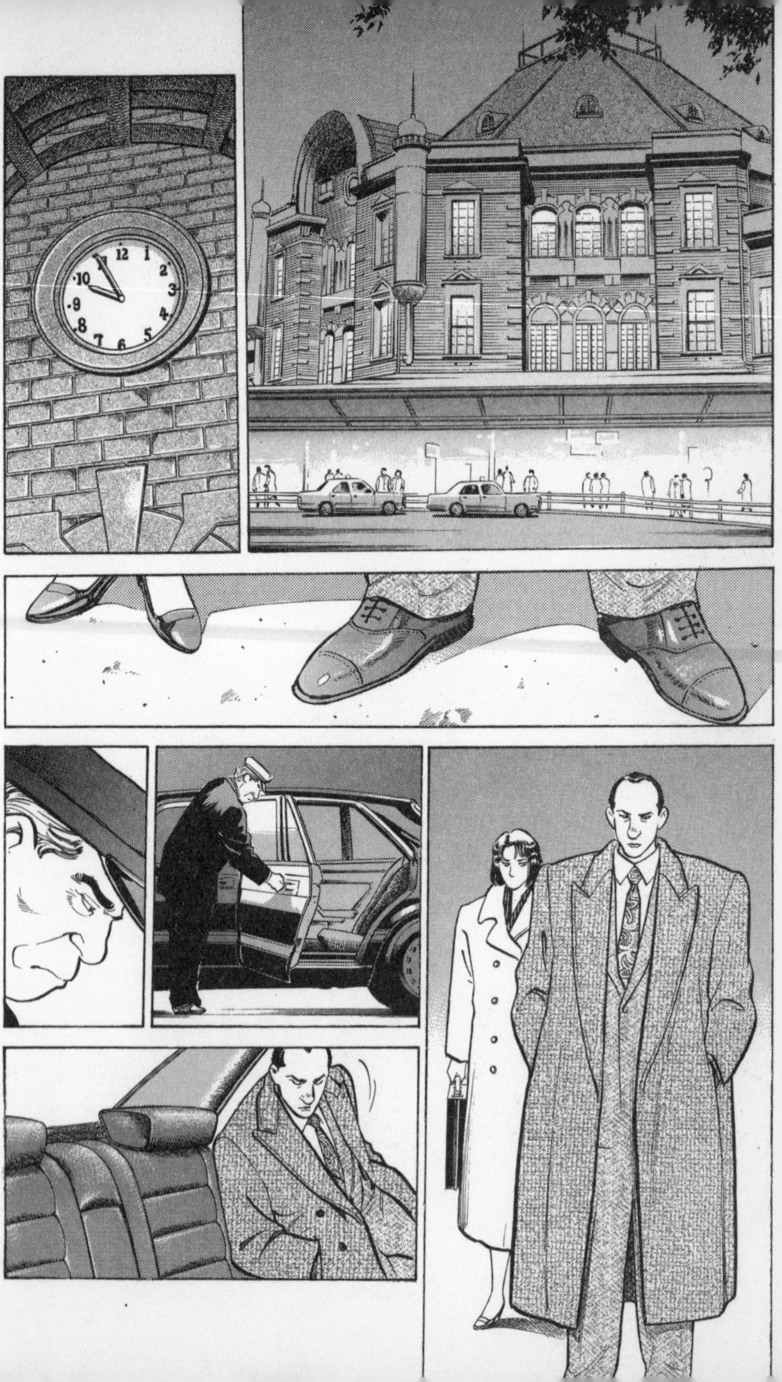

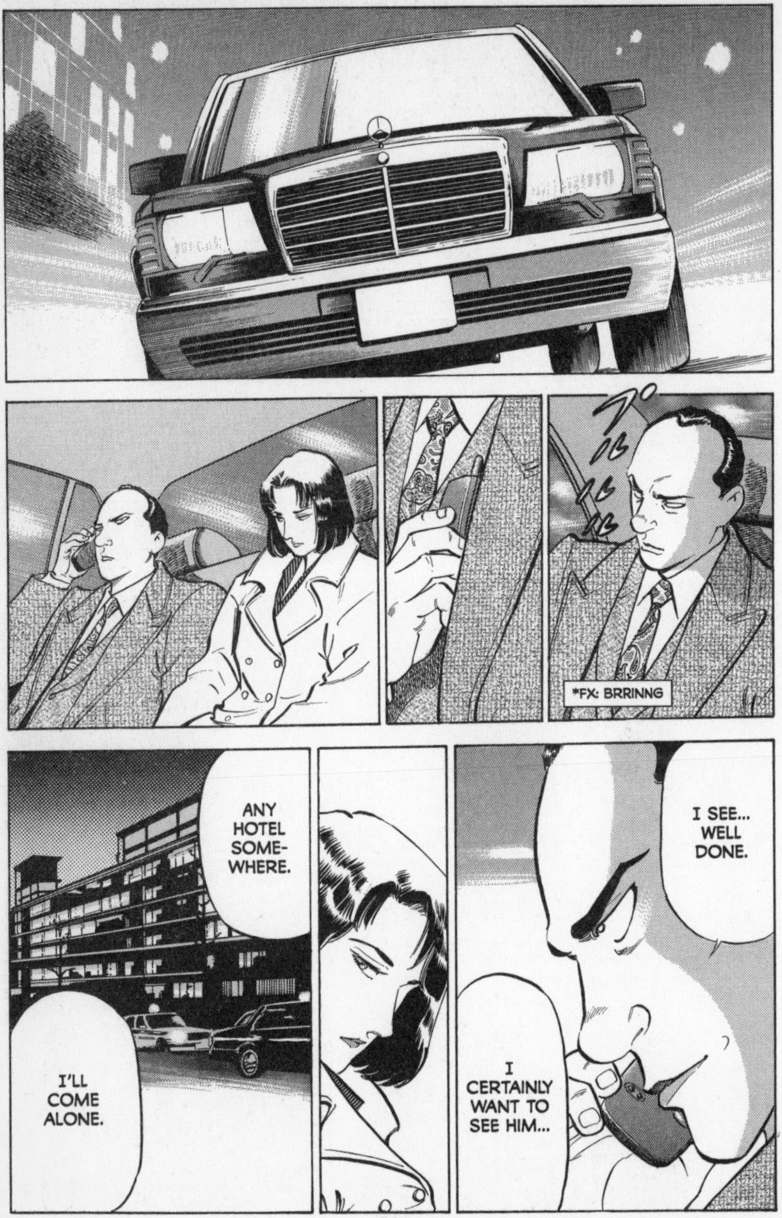
ブルルル
*FX: BRRINNG
I SEE... WELL DONE.
I CERTAINLY WANT TO SEE HIM...
ANY HOTEL SOME-WHERE.
I'LL COME ALONE.

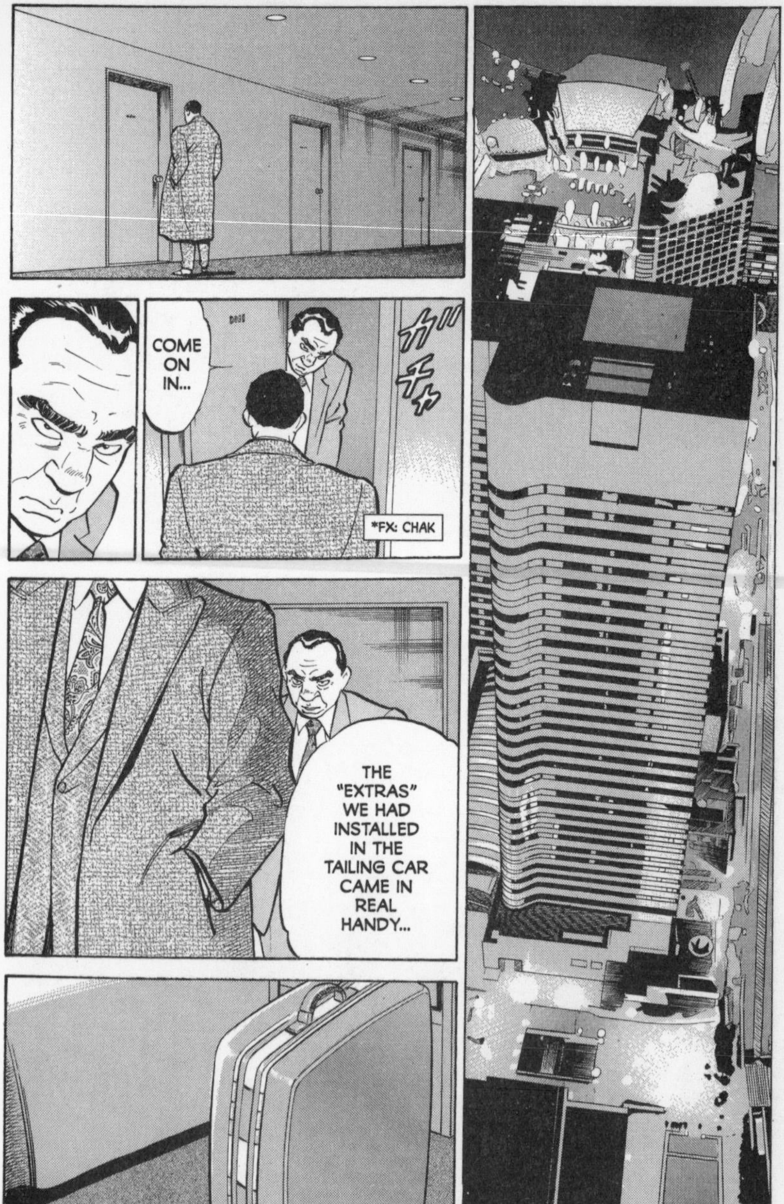
COME ON IN...
カチャ
*FX: CHAK
THE "EXTRAS" WE HAD INSTALLED IN THE TAILING CAR CAME IN REAL HANDY...

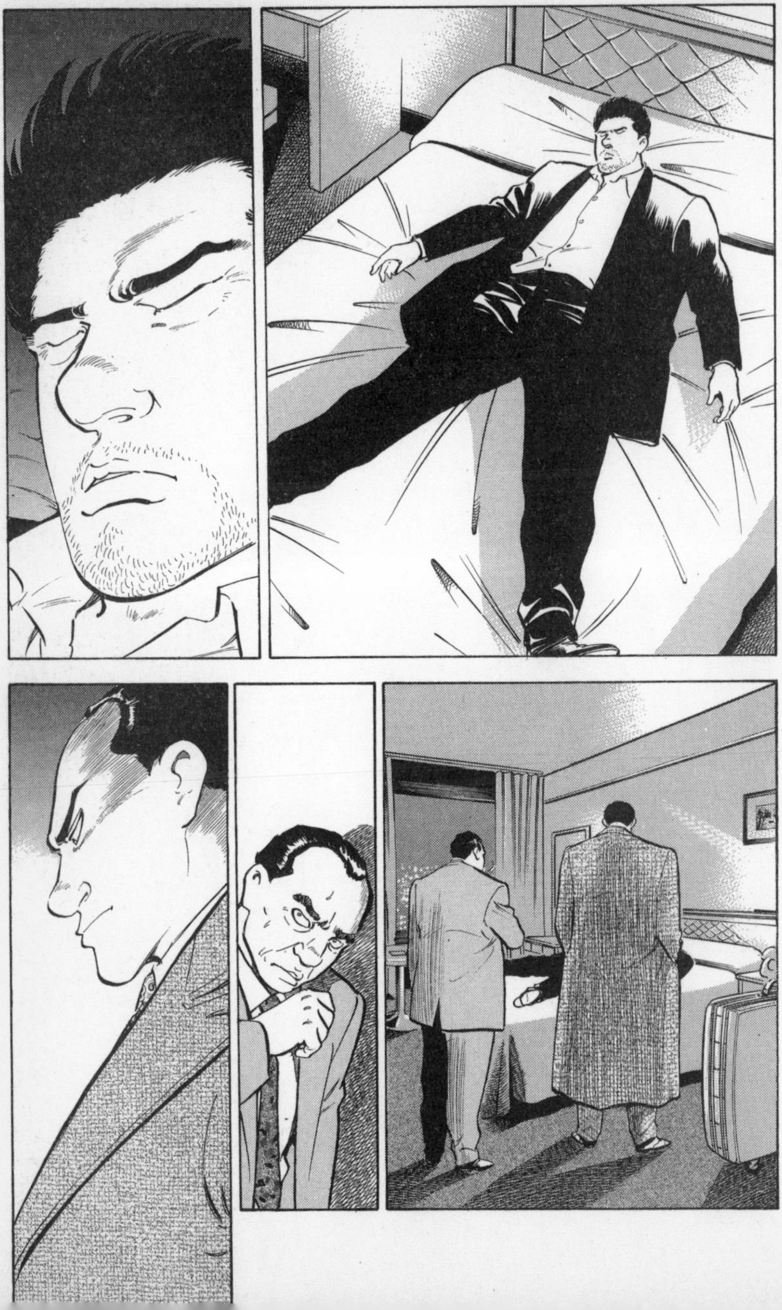

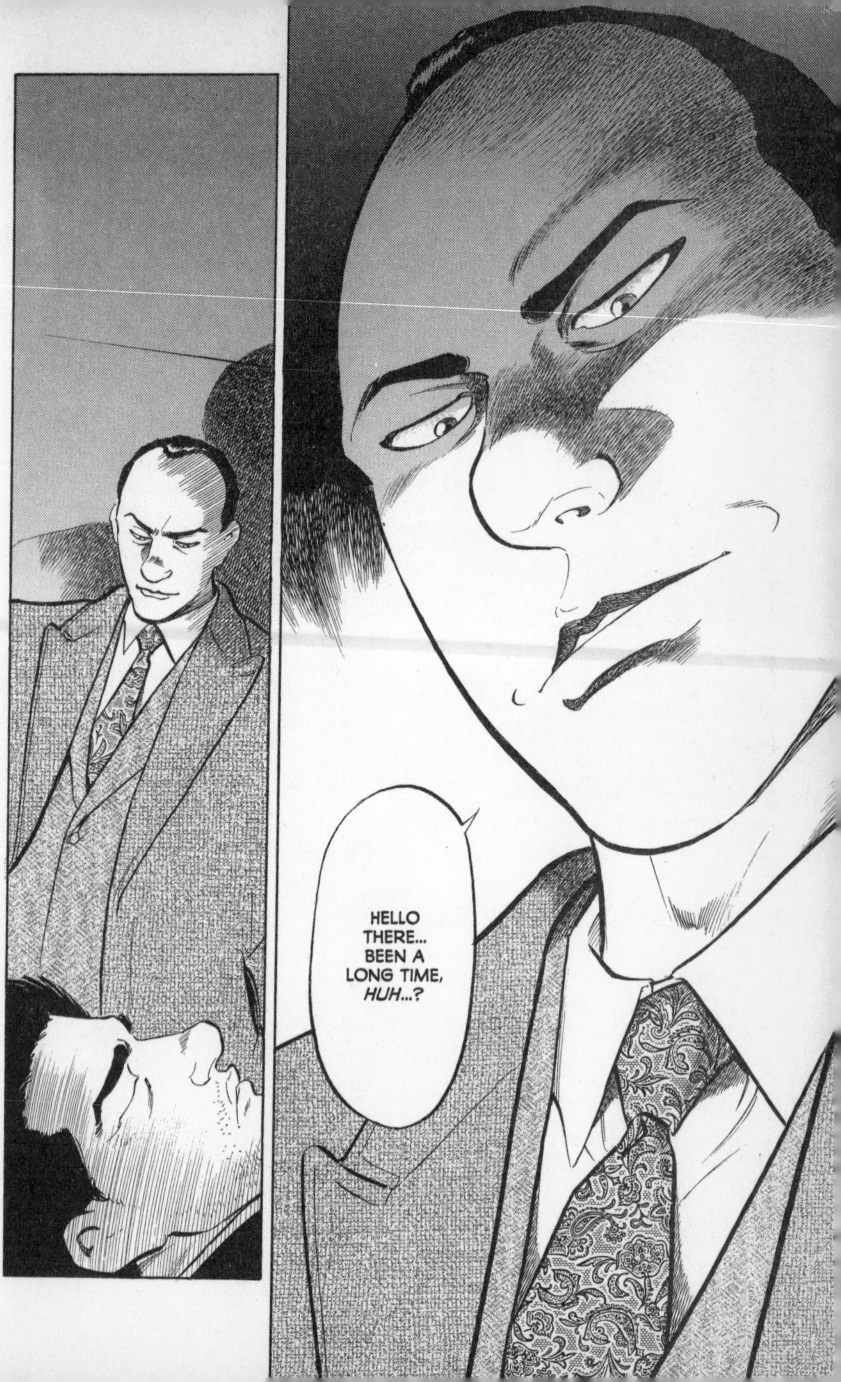
HELLO THERE... BEEN A LONG TIME, *HUH*...?

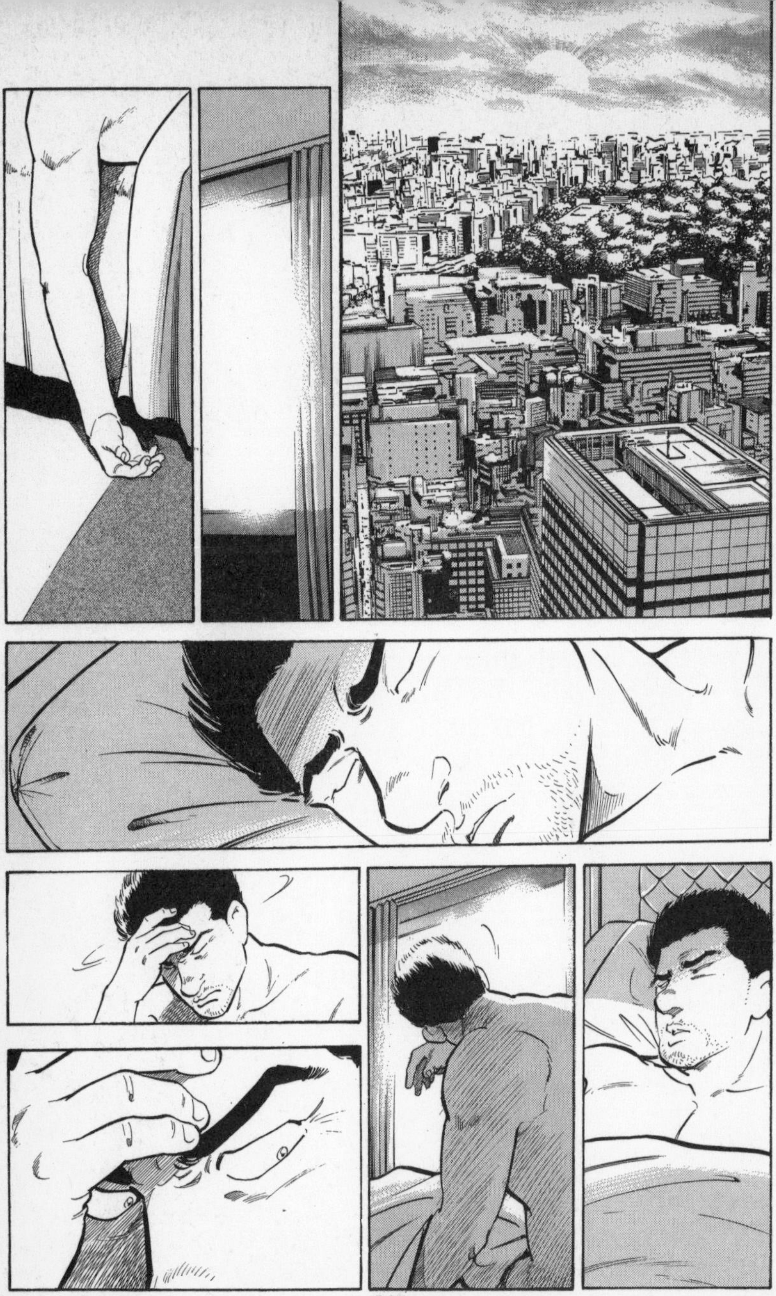

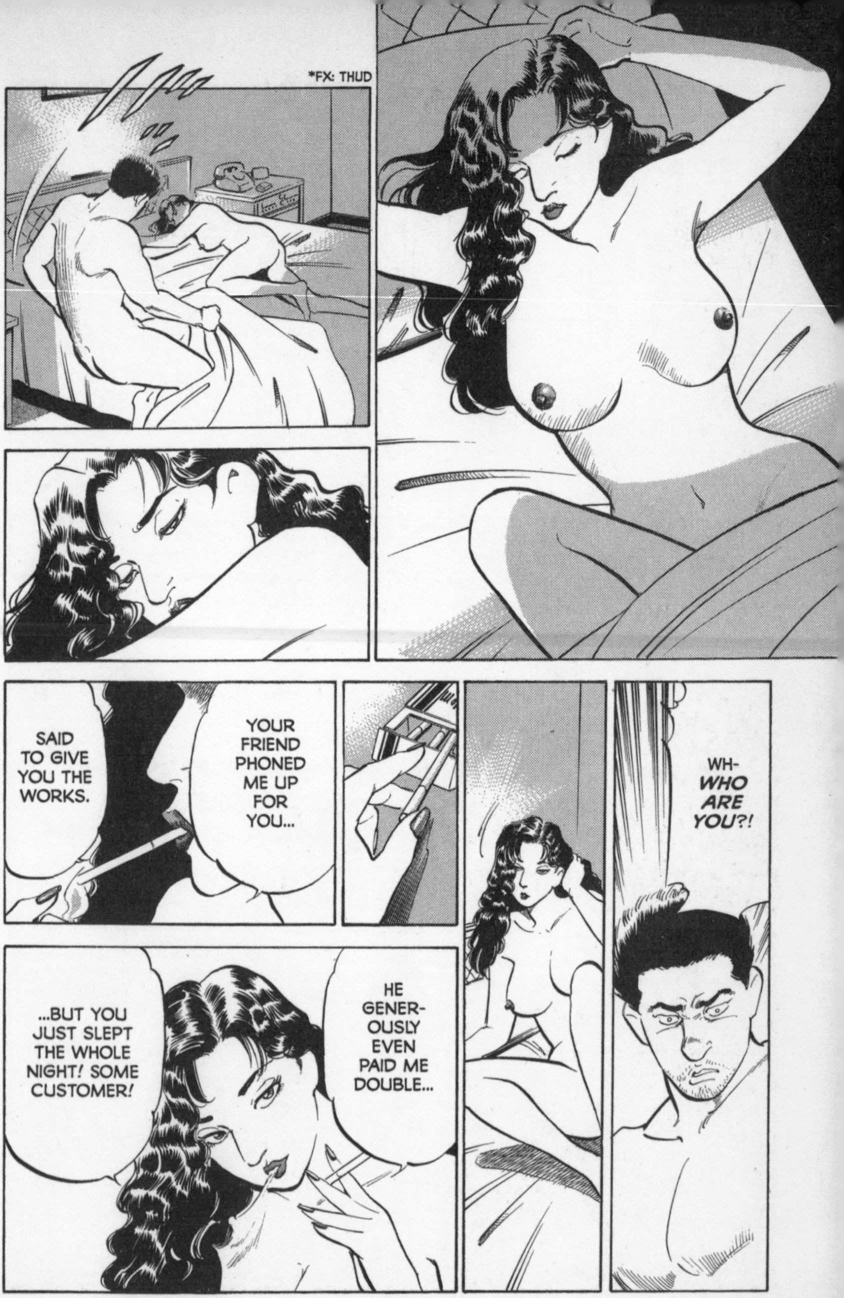
*FX: THUD
WH- WHO ARE YOU?!
YOUR FRIEND PHONED ME UP FOR YOU...
SAID TO GIVE YOU THE WORKS.
HE GENEROUSLY EVEN PAID ME DOUBLE...
...BUT YOU JUST SLEPT THE WHOLE NIGHT! SOME CUSTOMER!

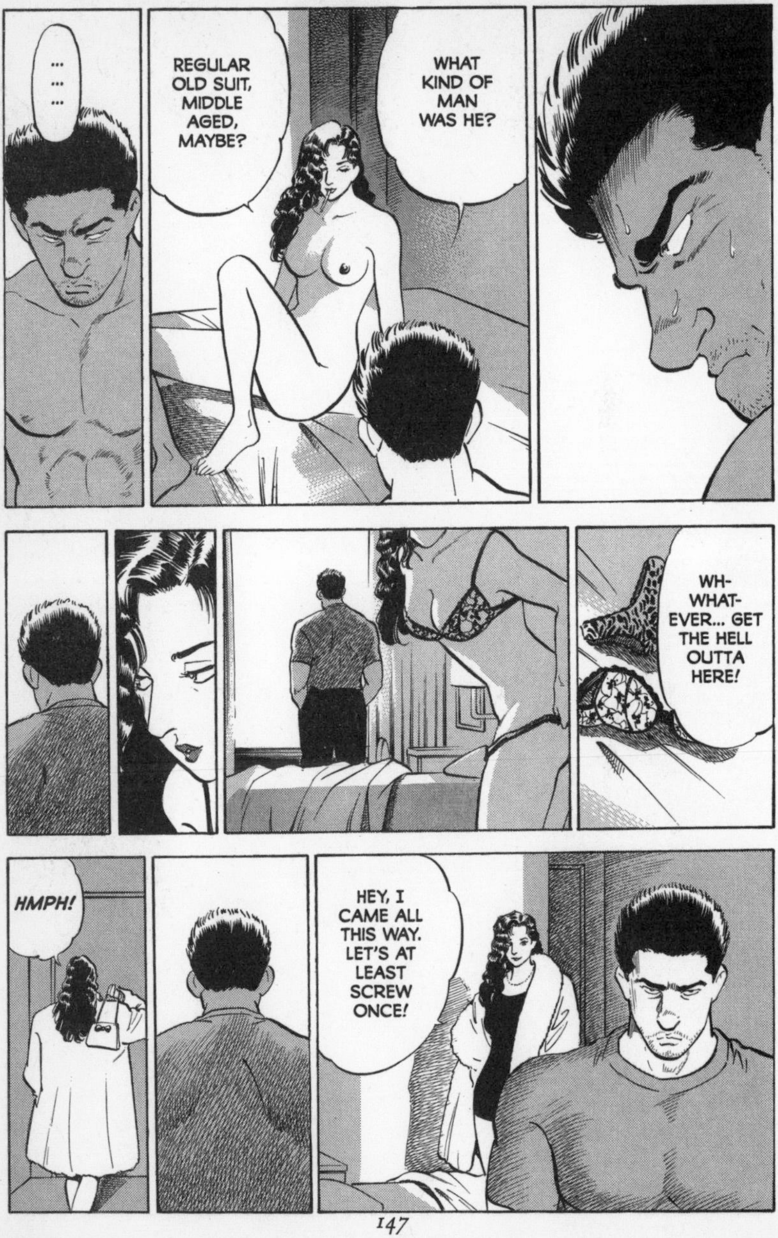
WHAT KIND OF MAN WAS HE?
REGULAR OLD SUIT, MIDDLE AGED, MAYBE?
... ...
WH- WHAT- EVER... GET THE HELL OUTTA HERE!
HEY, I CAME ALL THIS WAY. LET'S AT LEAST SCREW ONCE!
HMPH!

*FX: SLAM

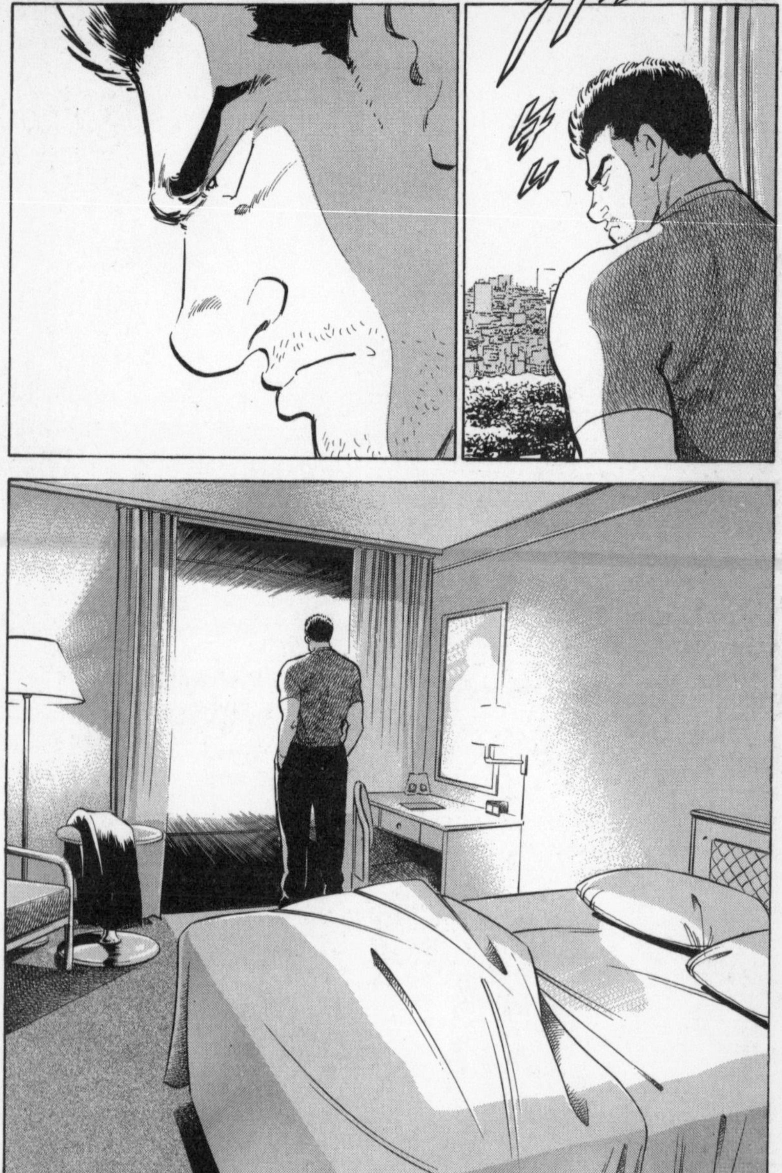

UNEXPECTED ENCOUNTER: END

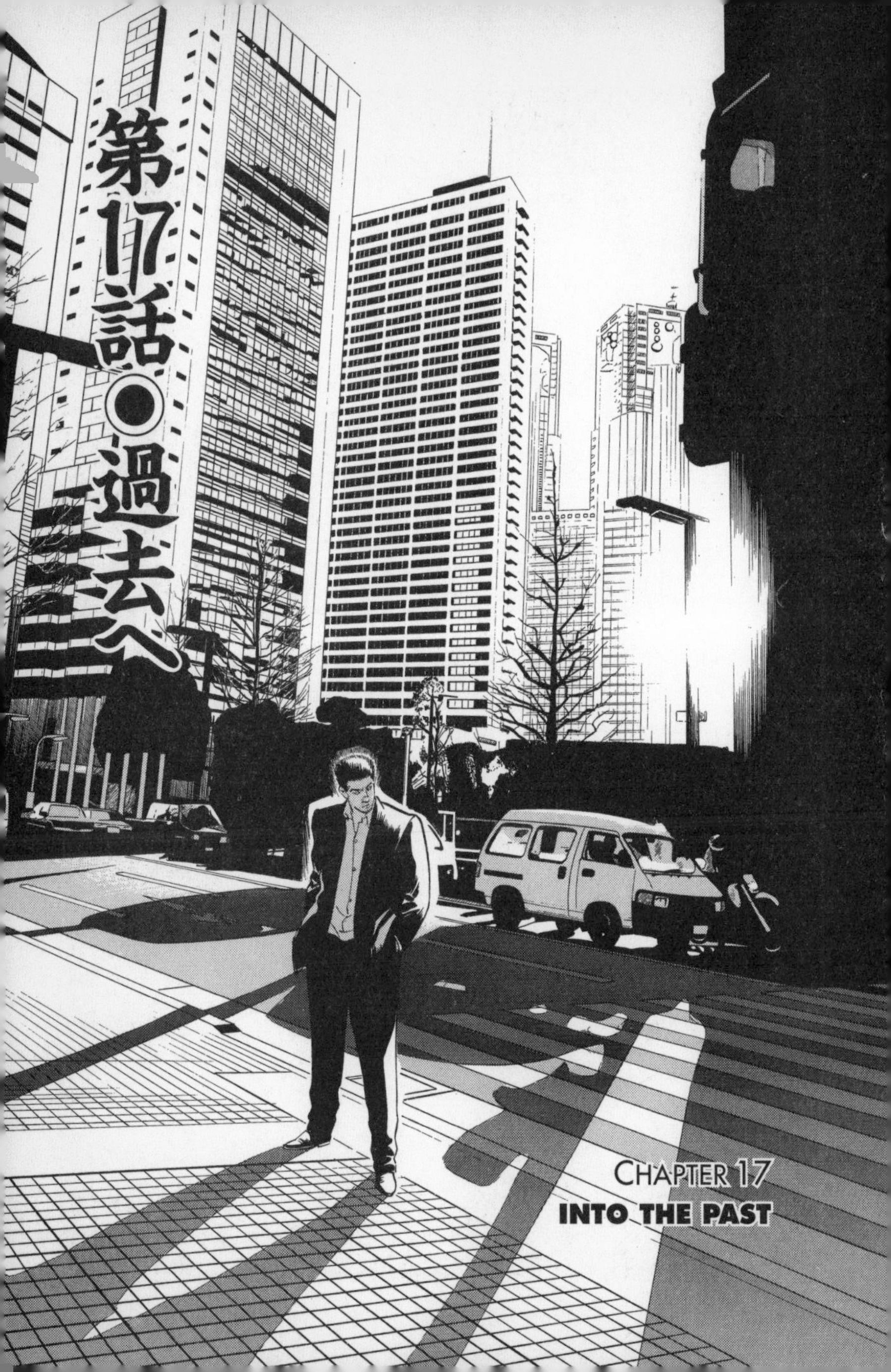
第17話●過去へ
CHAPTER 17
INTO THE PAST

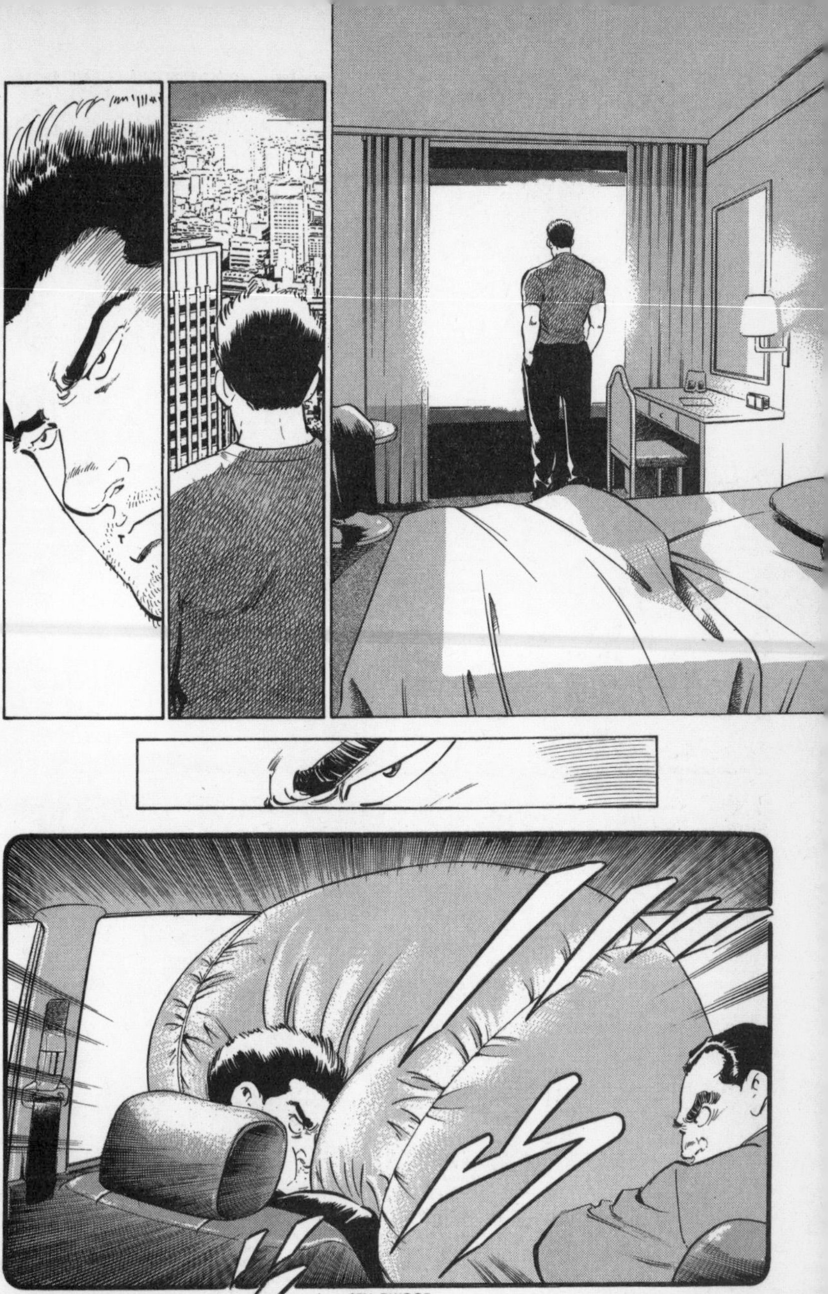

*FX: DWOOF

*FX: FSSS

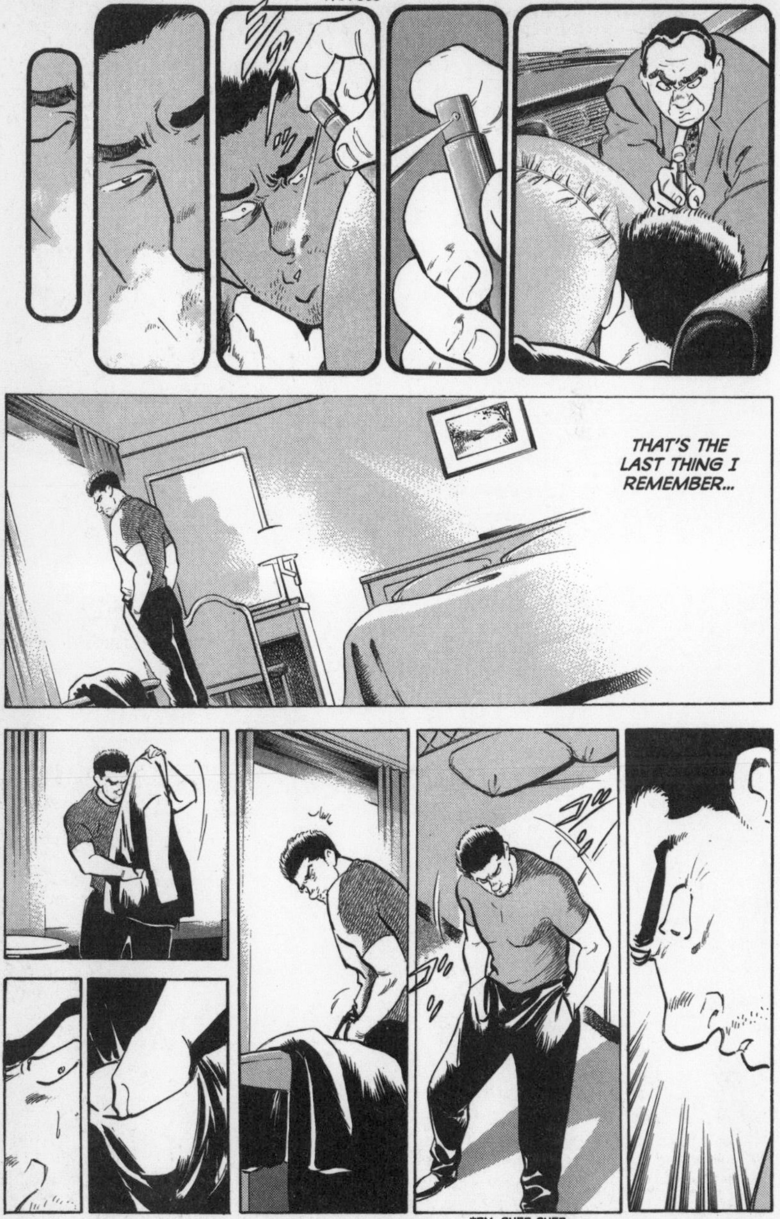
THAT'S THE LAST THING I REMEMBER...

*FX: SHFF SHFF

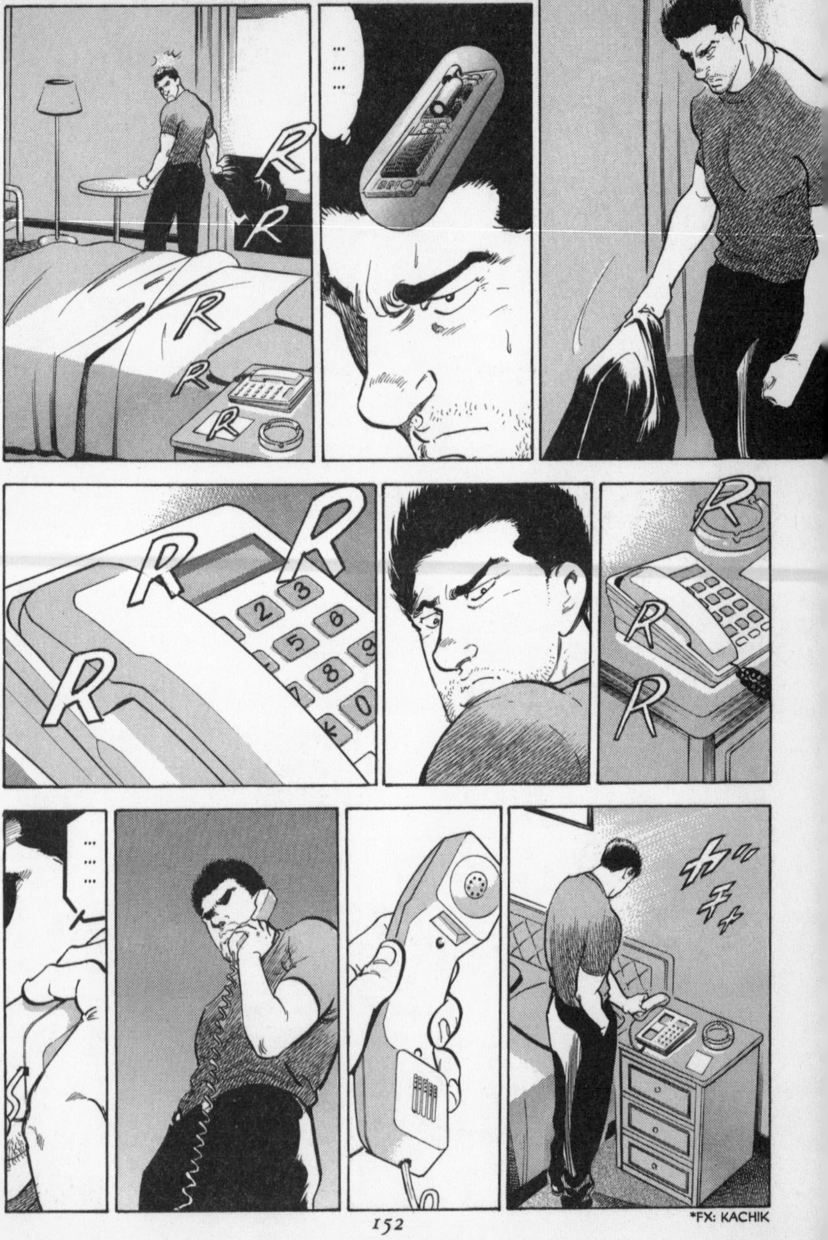
......
R
R
R
R
R
R
R
R
R
R
R
R
カチッ
......

*FX: KACHIK

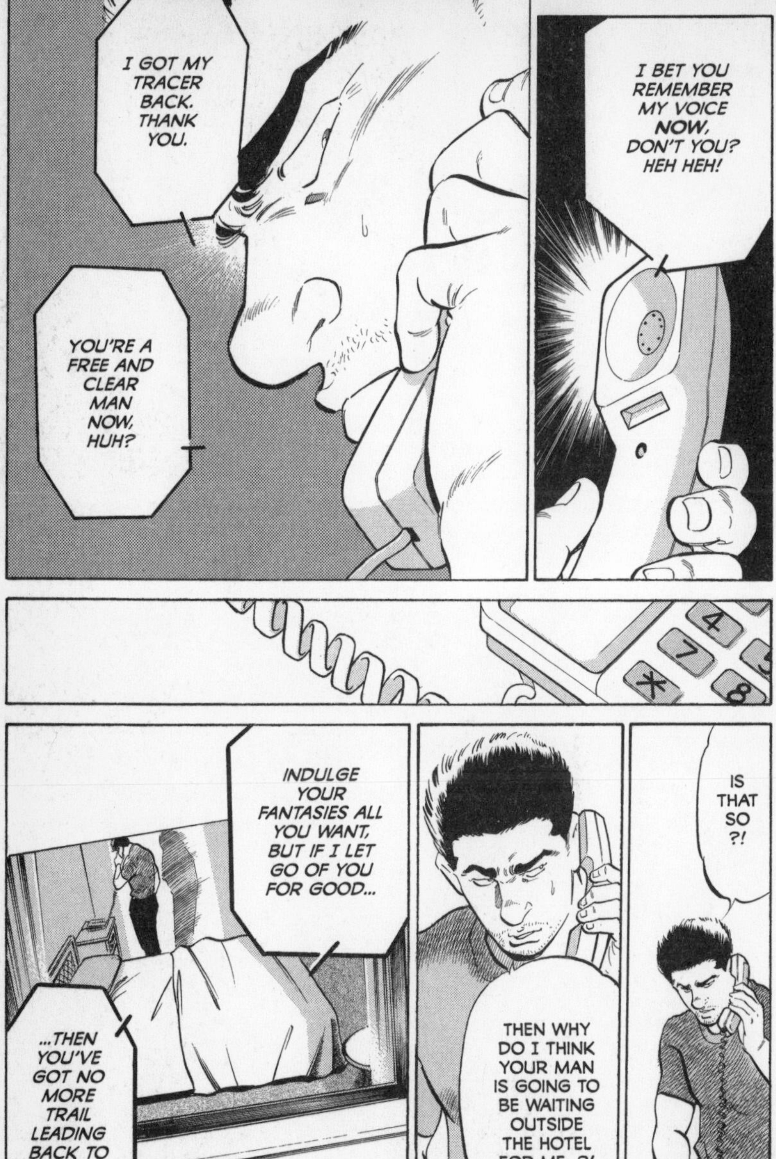
I BET YOU REMEMBER MY VOICE NOW, DON'T YOU? HEH HEH!
I GOT MY TRACER BACK. THANK YOU.
YOU'RE A FREE AND CLEAR MAN NOW, HUH?
IS THAT SO?!
THEN WHY DO I THINK YOUR MAN IS GOING TO BE WAITING OUTSIDE THE HOTEL FOR ME...?!
INDULGE YOUR FANTASIES ALL YOU WANT, BUT IF I LET GO OF YOU FOR GOOD...
...THEN YOU'VE GOT NO MORE TRAIL LEADING BACK TO ME.

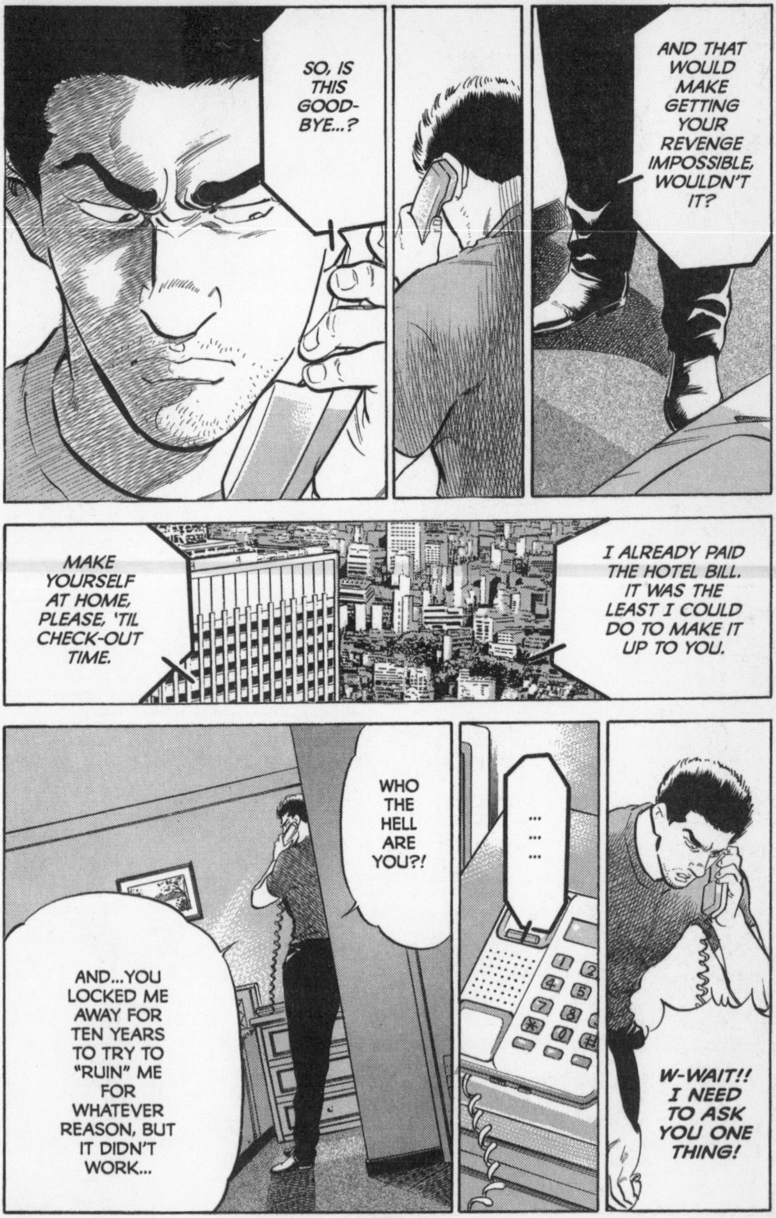
AND THAT WOULD MAKE GETTING YOUR REVENGE IMPOSSIBLE, WOULDN'T IT?
SO, IS THIS GOOD-BYE...?
I ALREADY PAID THE HOTEL BILL. IT WAS THE LEAST I COULD DO TO MAKE IT UP TO YOU.
MAKE YOURSELF AT HOME, PLEASE, 'TIL CHECK-OUT TIME.
W-WAIT!! I NEED TO ASK YOU ONE THING!
... ...
WHO THE HELL ARE YOU?!
AND...YOU LOCKED ME AWAY FOR TEN YEARS TO TRY TO "RUIN" ME FOR WHATEVER REASON, BUT IT DIDN'T WORK...

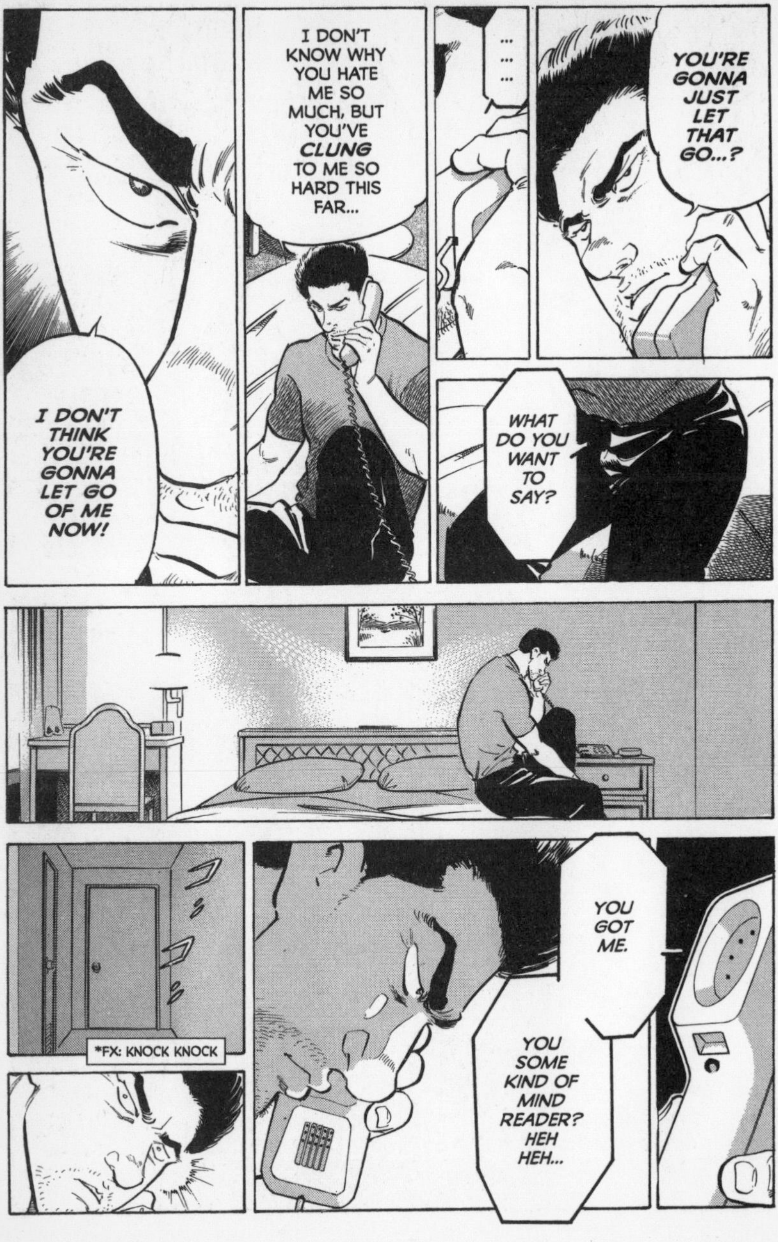

YOU'RE GONNA JUST LET THAT GO...?
... ...
WHAT DO YOU WANT TO SAY?
I DON'T KNOW WHY YOU HATE ME SO MUCH, BUT YOU'VE CLUNG TO ME SO HARD THIS FAR...
I DON'T THINK YOU'RE GONNA LET GO OF ME NOW!
YOU GOT ME.
YOU SOME KIND OF MIND READER? HEH HEH...
*FX: KNOCK KNOCK

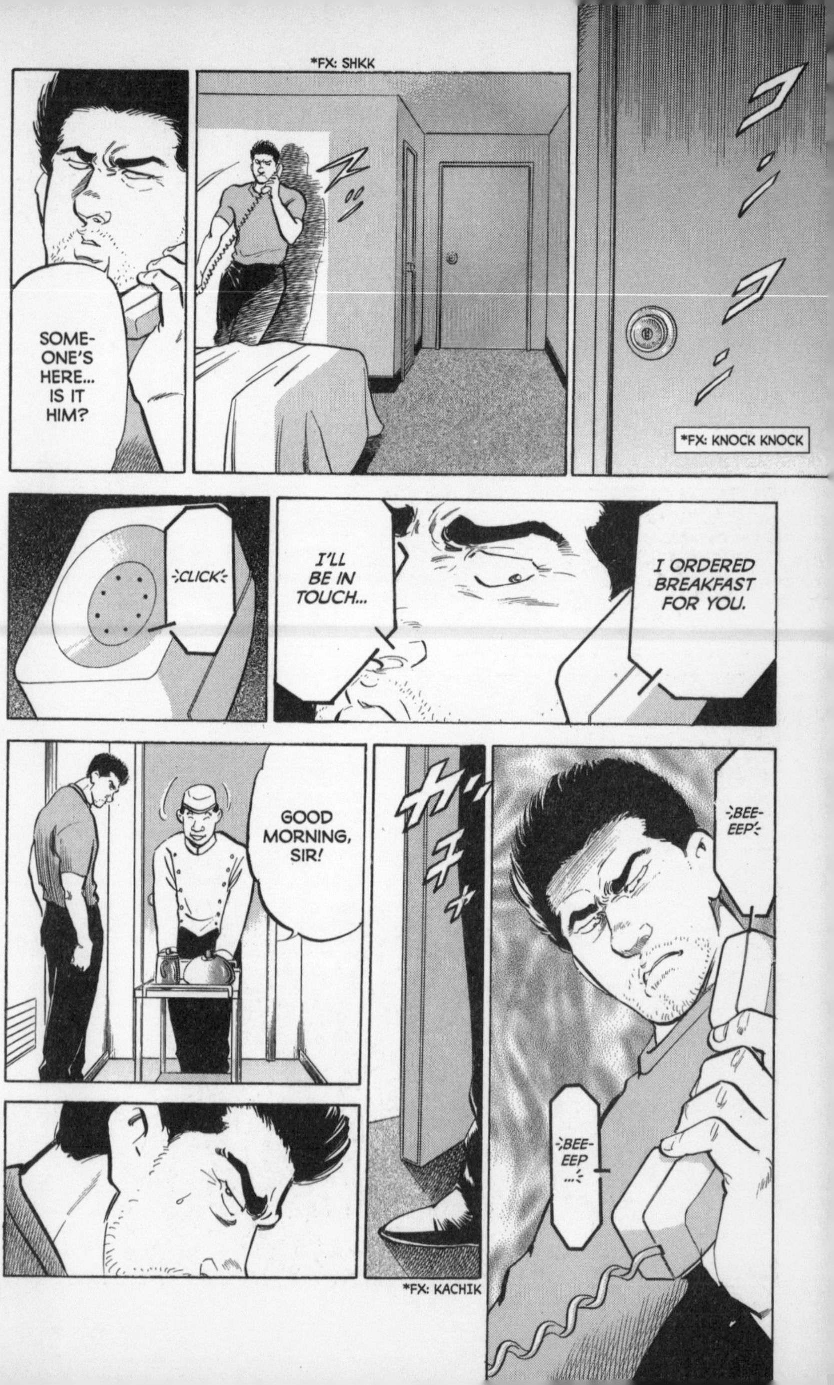
*FX: KNOCK KNOCK
*FX: SHKK
SOME-ONE'S HERE... IS IT HIM?
I ORDERED BREAKFAST FOR YOU.
I'LL BE IN TOUCH...
CLICK
BEE-EEP
BEE-EEP...
*FX: KACHIK
GOOD MORNING, SIR!

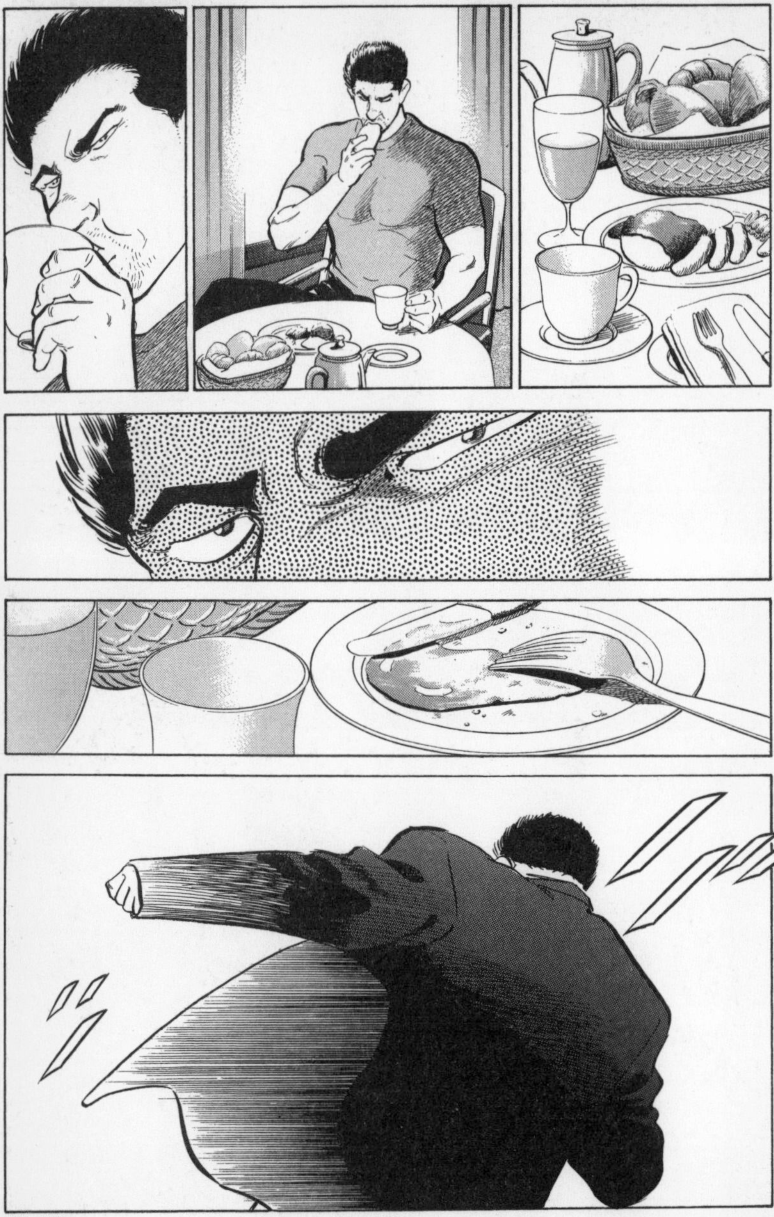
*FX: SHFF

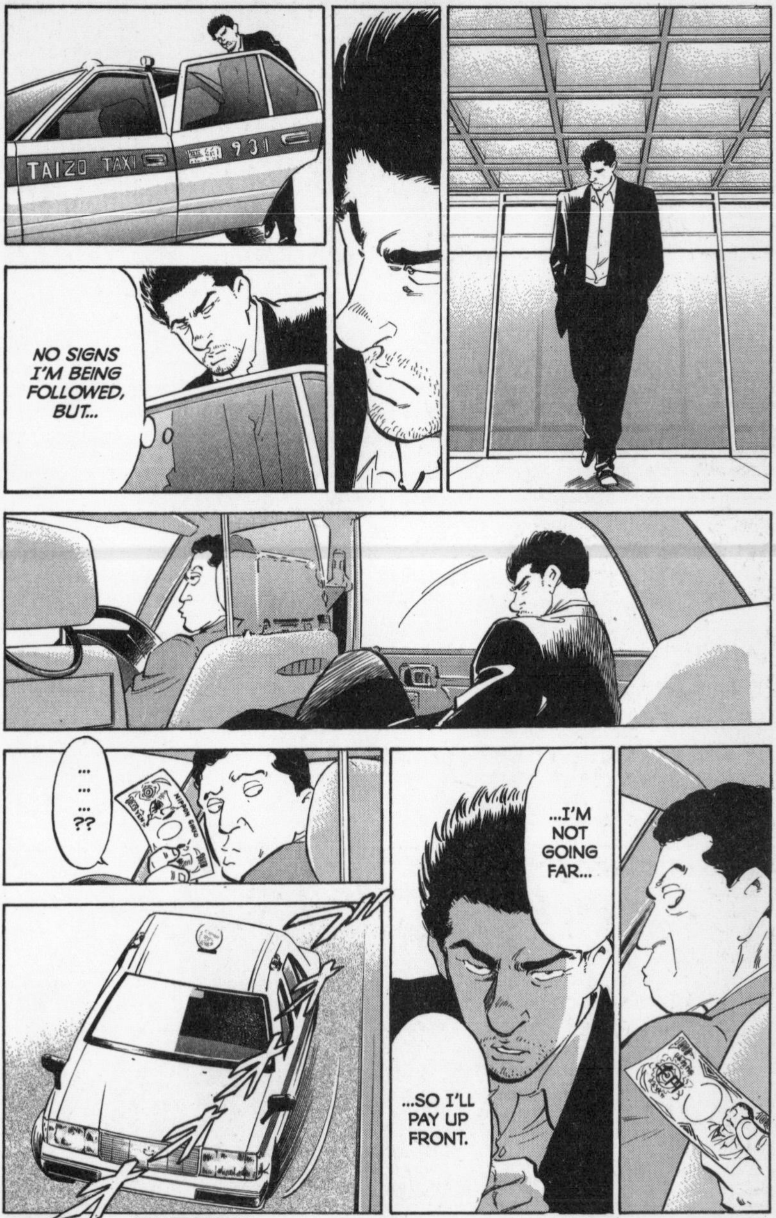
TAIZO TAXI
931
NO SIGNS I'M BEING FOLLOWED, BUT...
...I'M NOT GOING FAR...
...SO I'LL PAY UP FRONT.
...
...
...
??

*FX: VROOOOMM

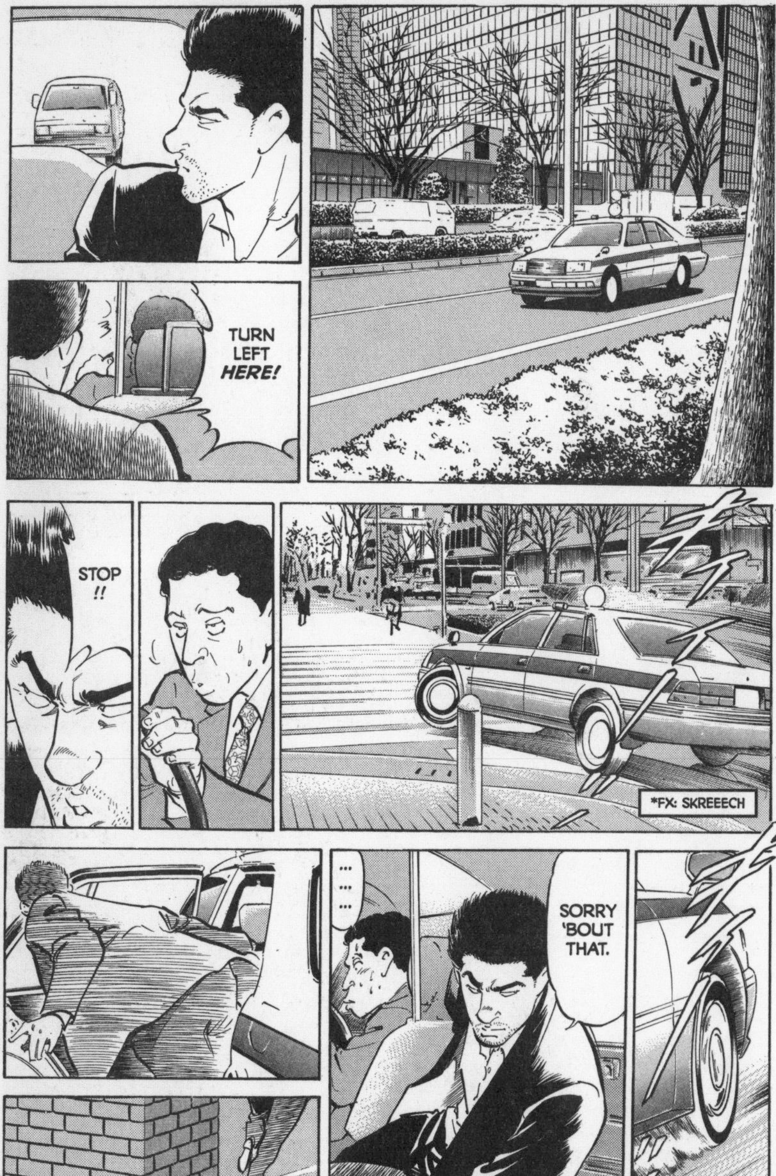
TURN LEFT HERE!
*FX: SKREEECH
STOP !!
SORRY 'BOUT THAT.
...
...
...
*FX: SKREECH

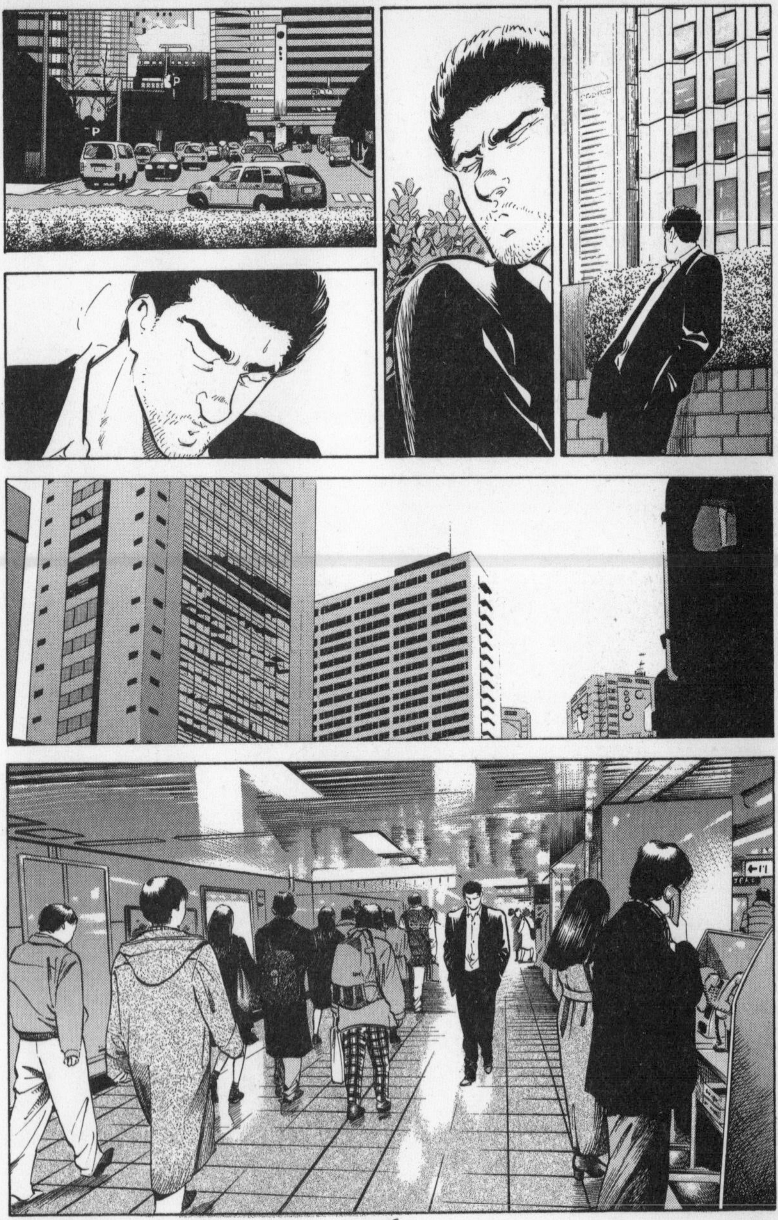

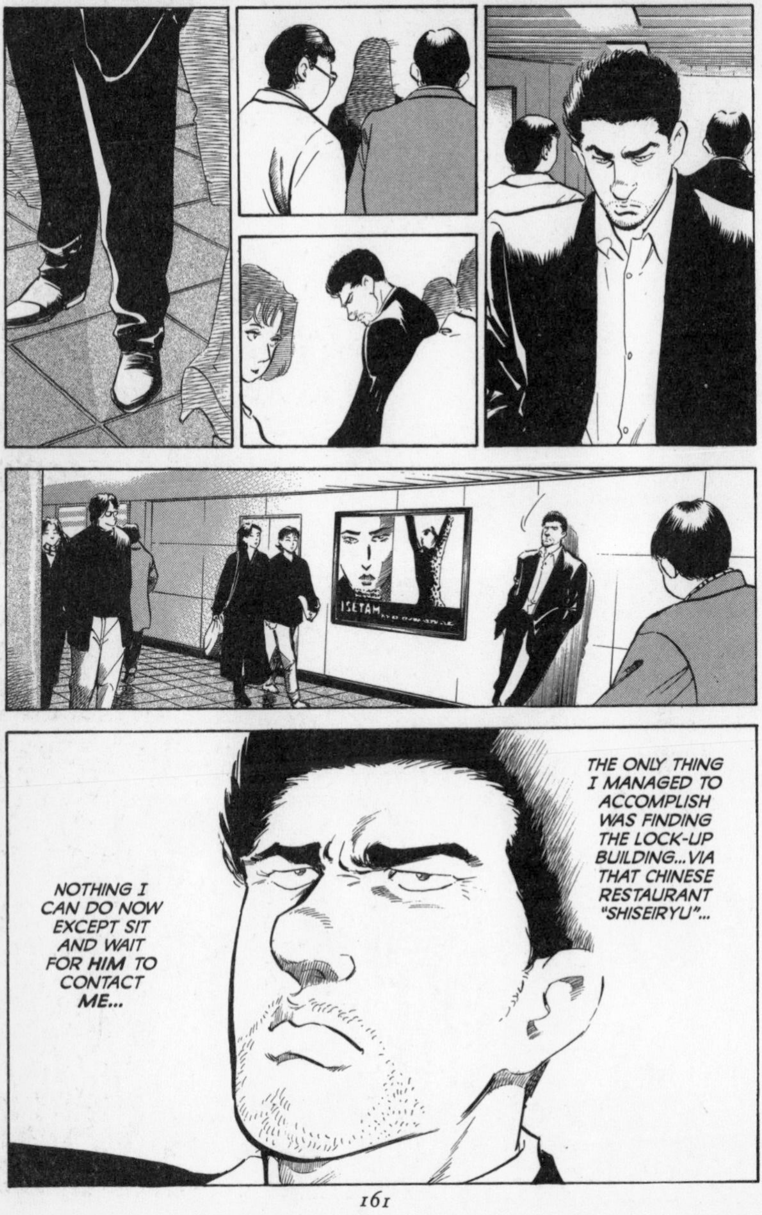
THE ONLY THING I MANAGED TO ACCOMPLISH WAS FINDING THE LOCK-UP BUILDING...VIA THAT CHINESE RESTAURANT "SHISEIRYU"...
NOTHING I CAN DO NOW EXCEPT SIT AND WAIT FOR HIM TO CONTACT ME...
ISETAN

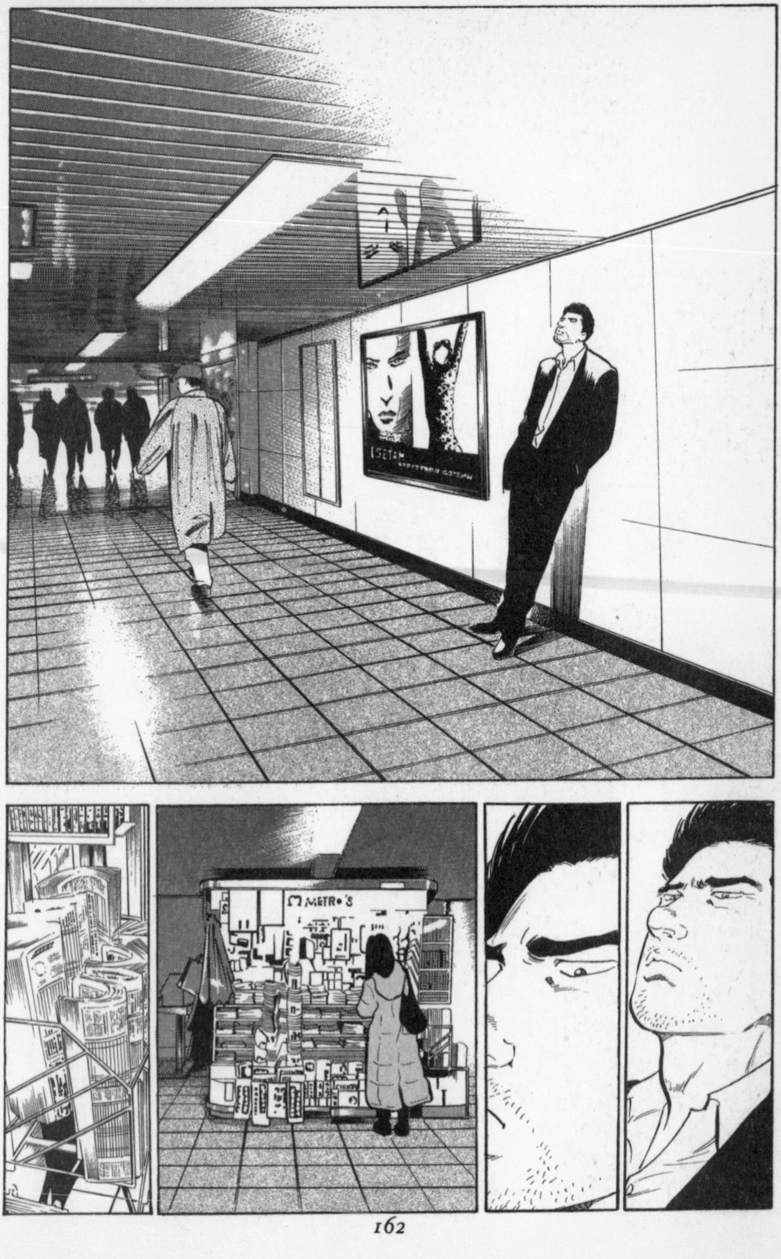
METRO'S

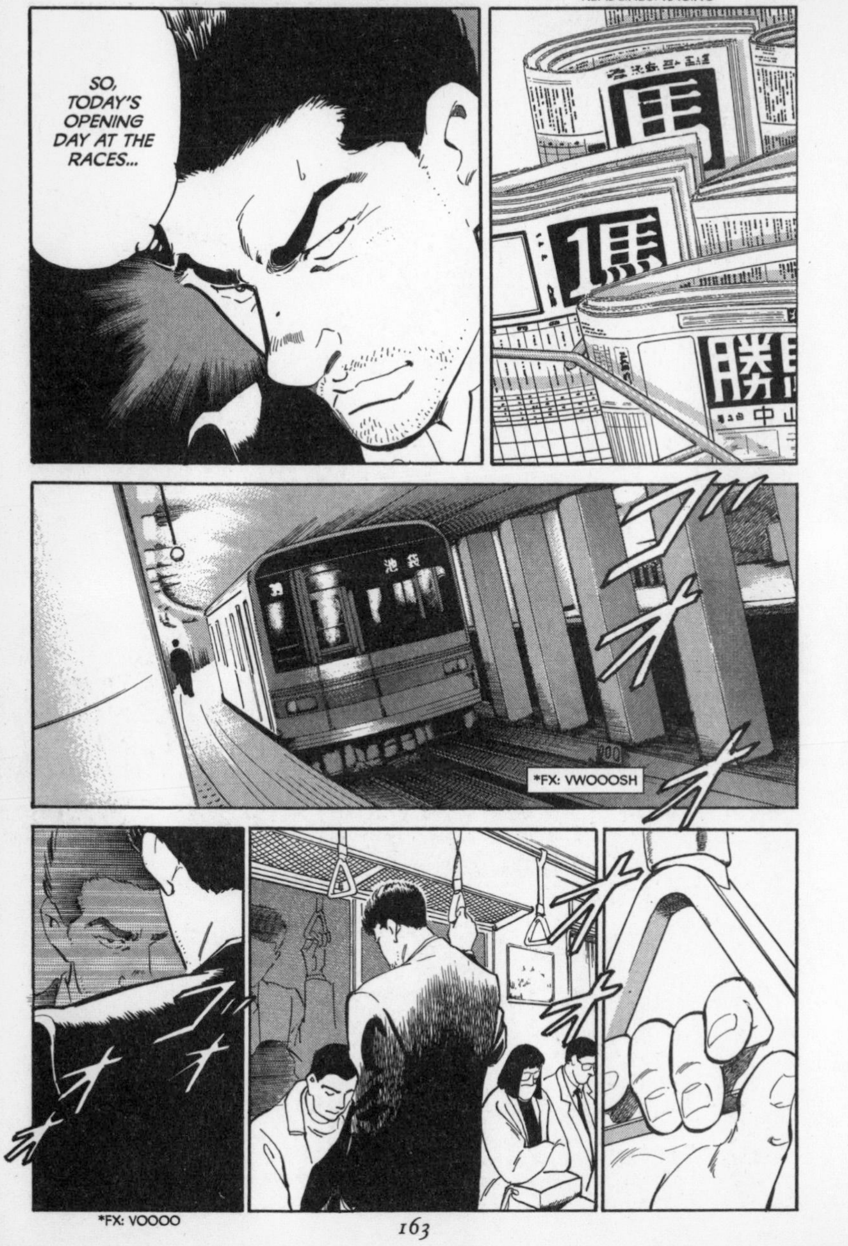
*HEADLINES: RACING
SO, TODAY'S OPENING DAY AT THE RACES...
*FX: VWOOOSH
*FX: VOOOO

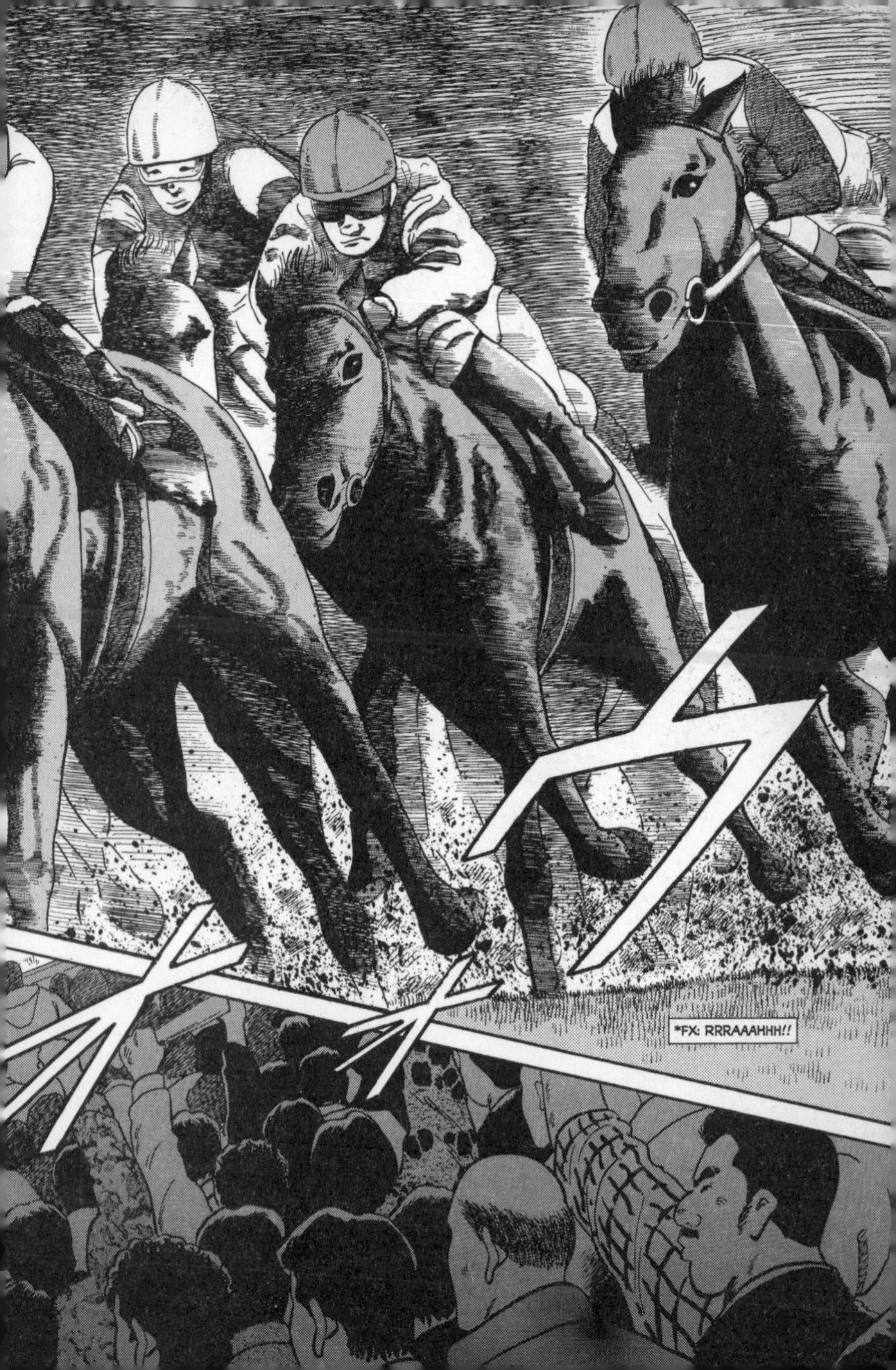
*FX: RRRAAAHHH!!

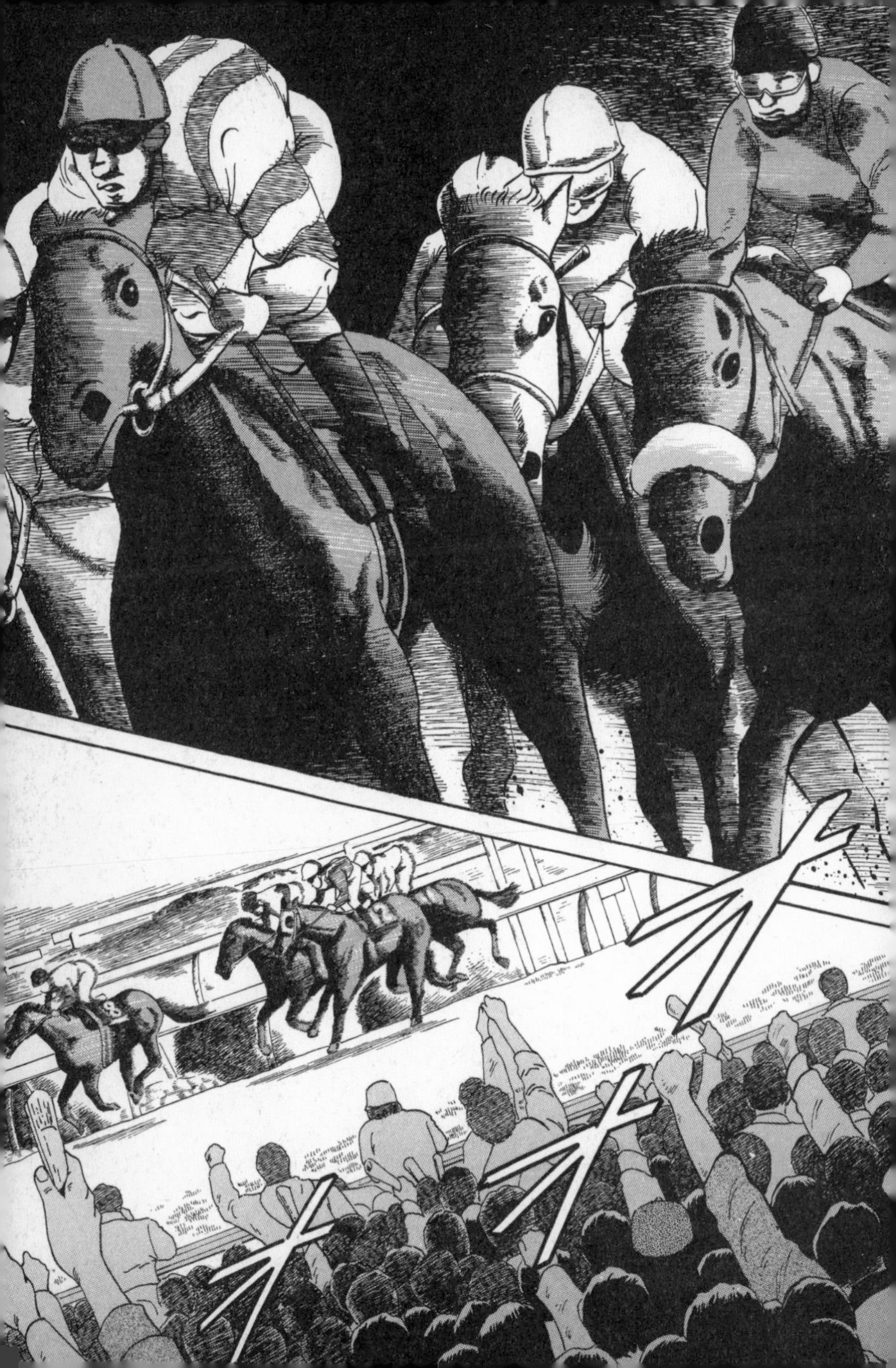

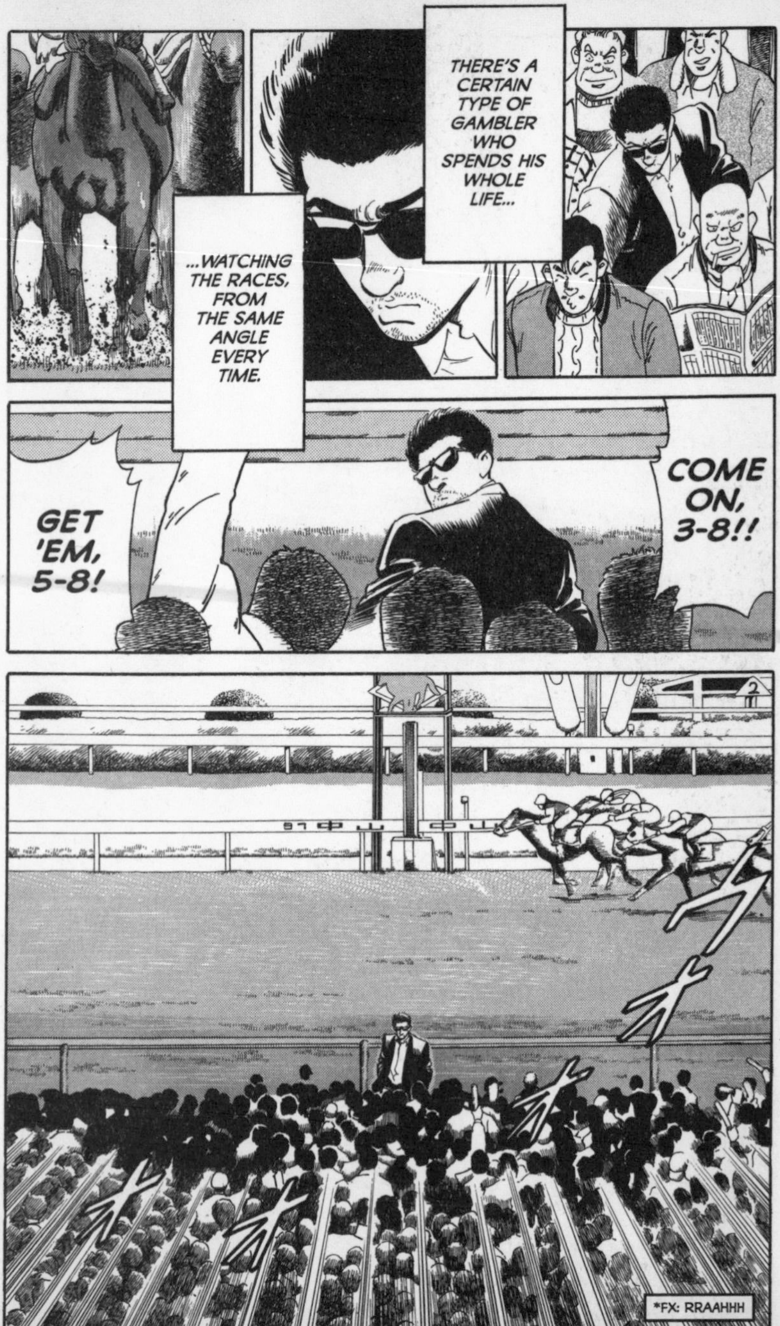

THERE'S A CERTAIN TYPE OF GAMBLER WHO SPENDS HIS WHOLE LIFE...
...WATCHING THE RACES, FROM THE SAME ANGLE EVERY TIME.
COME ON, 3-8!!
GET 'EM, 5-8!
*FX: RRAAHHH

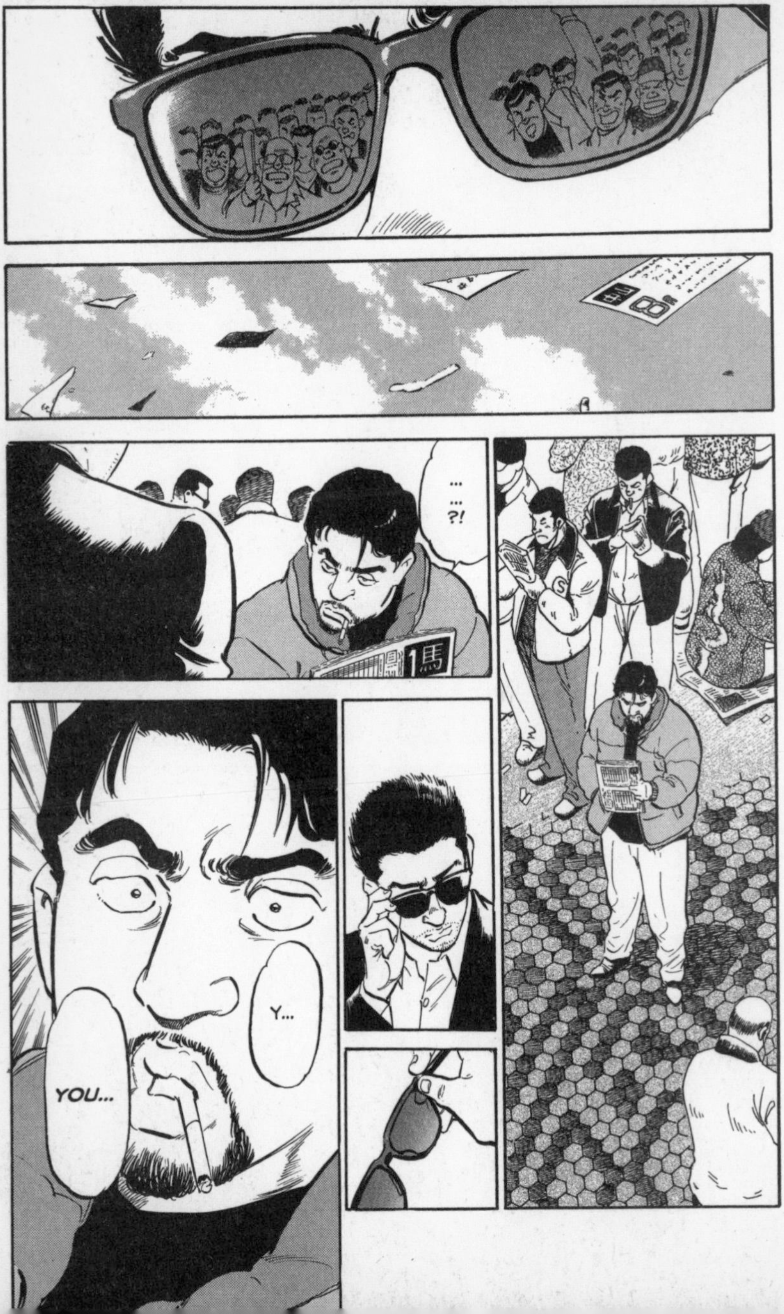

...
...
?!
Y...
YOU...

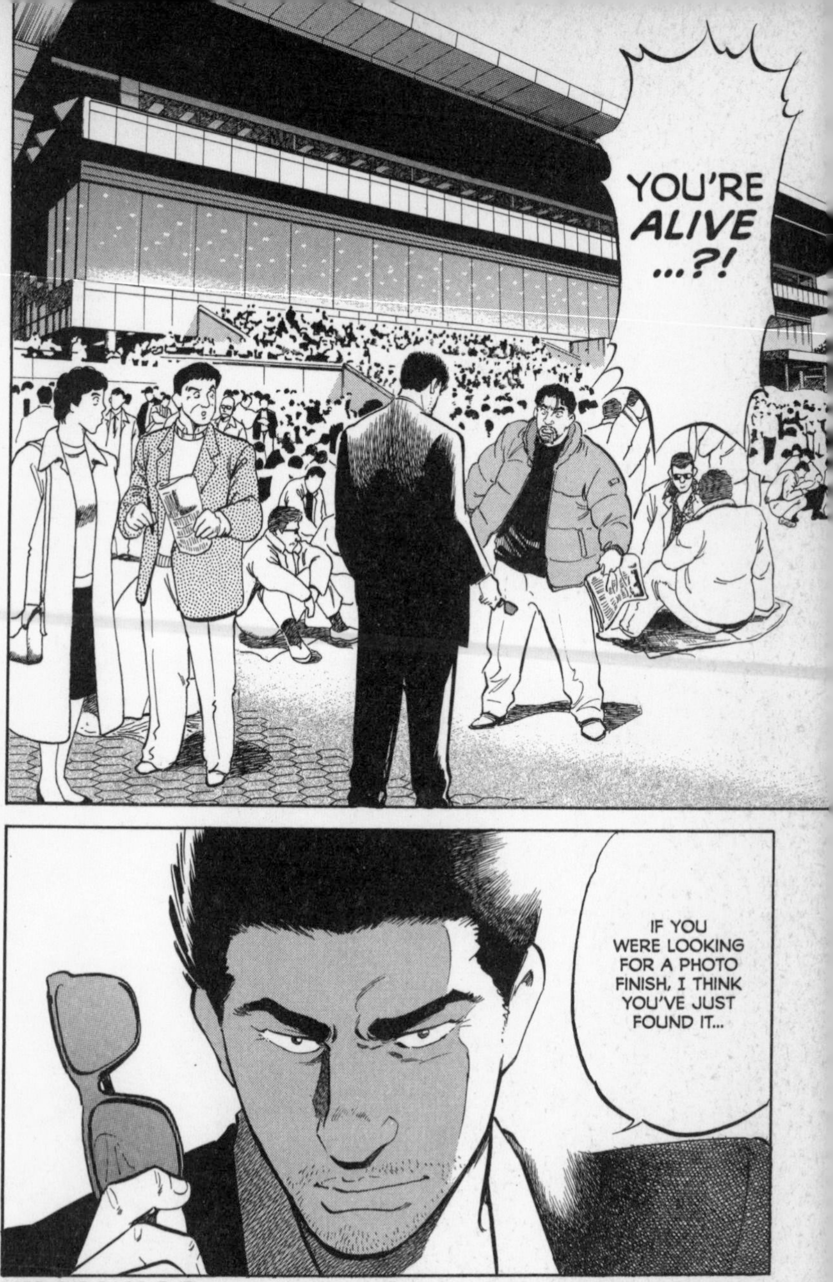
YOU'RE ALIVE ...?!
IF YOU WERE LOOKING FOR A PHOTO FINISH, I THINK YOU'VE JUST FOUND IT...

INTO THE PAST: END

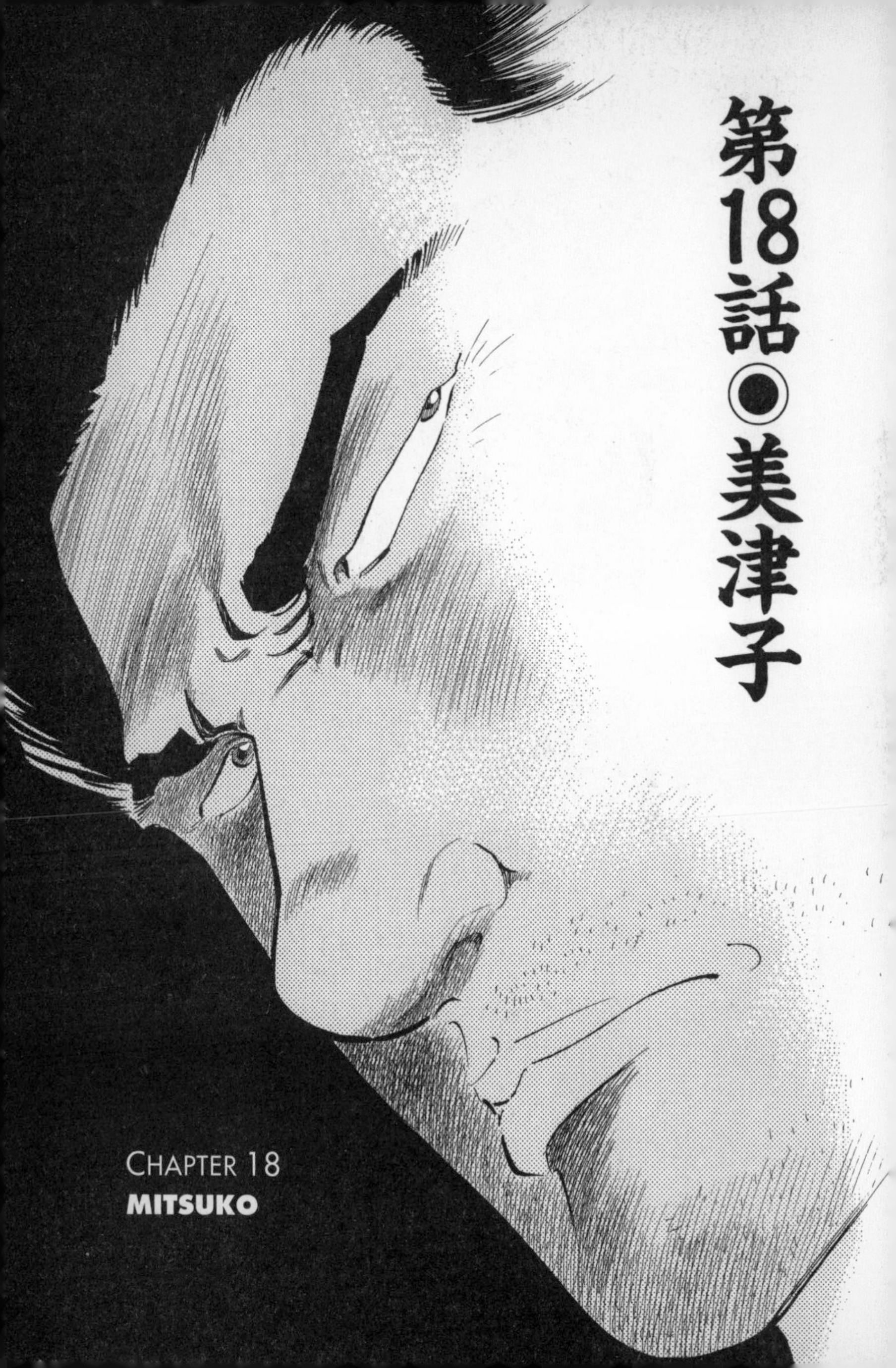

第18話◉美津子

CHAPTER 18
MITSUKO

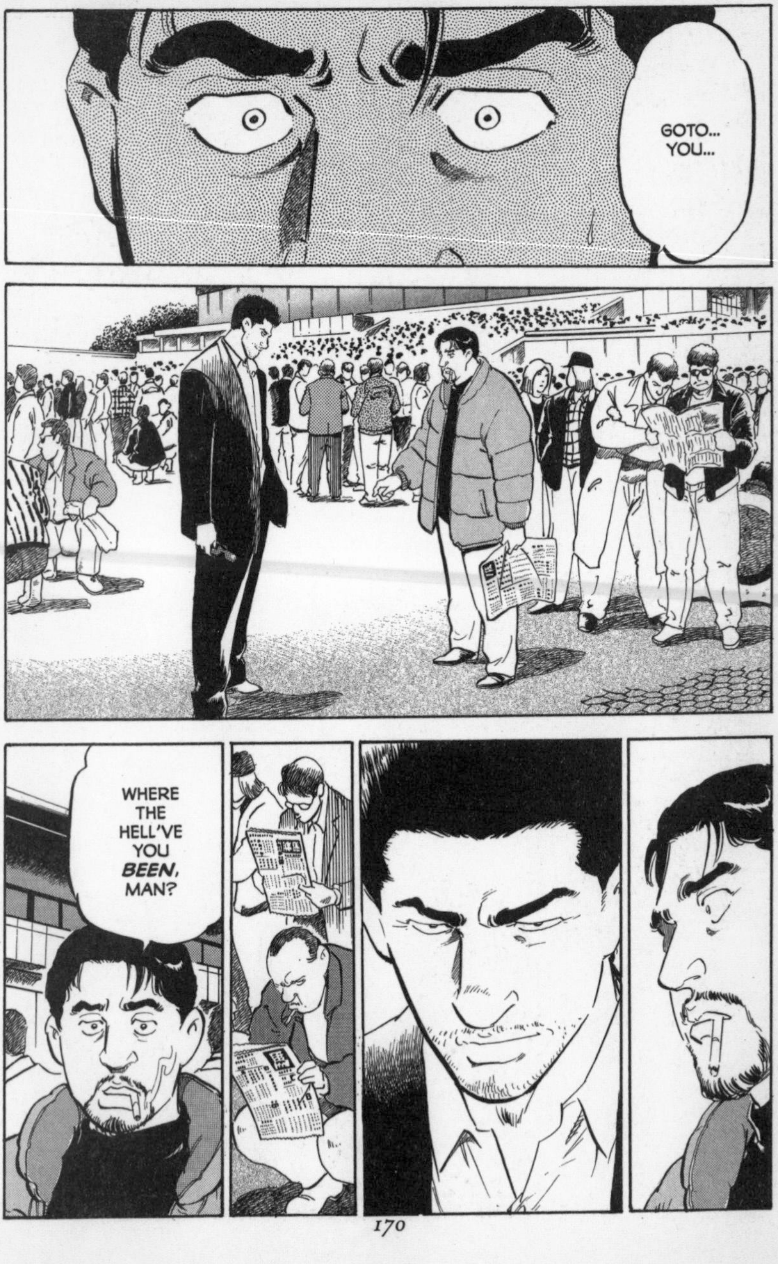
GOTO... YOU...
WHERE THE HELL'VE YOU *BEEN*, MAN?

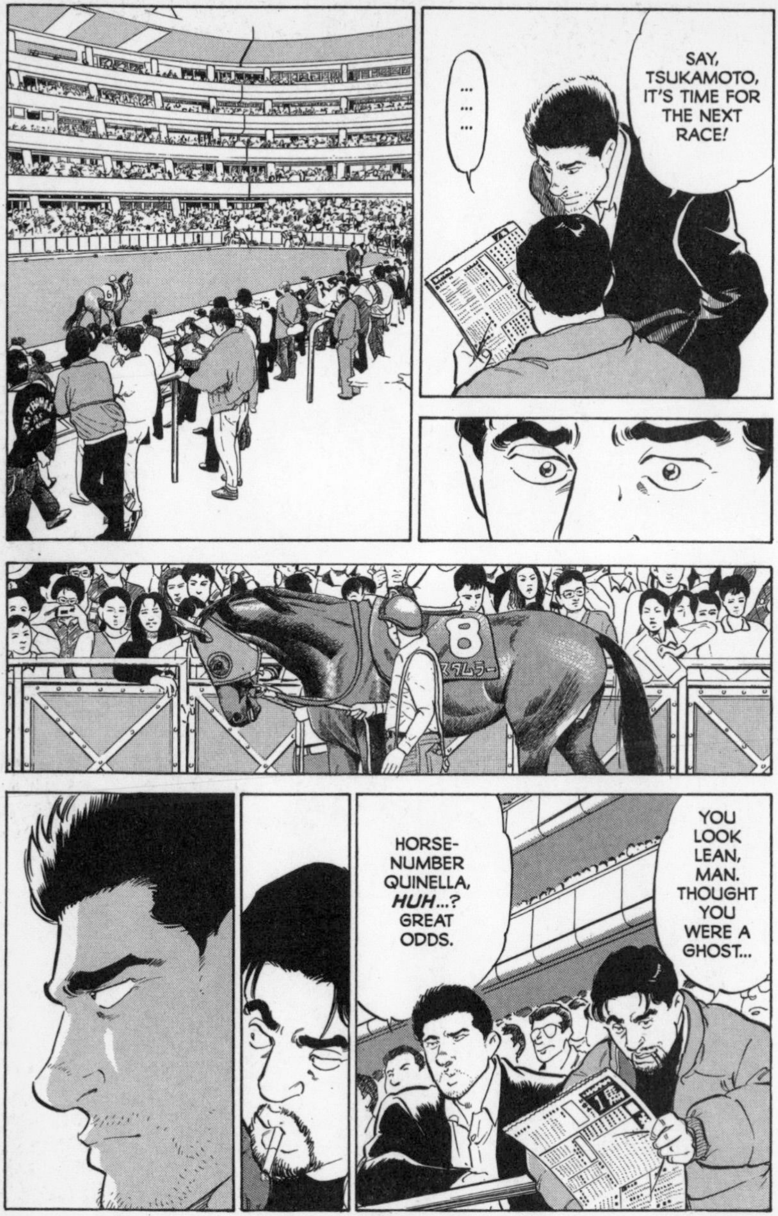
SAY, TSUKAMOTO, IT'S TIME FOR THE NEXT RACE!
... ...
8
YOU LOOK LEAN, MAN. THOUGHT YOU WERE A GHOST...
HORSE-NUMBER QUINELLA, ***HUH***...? GREAT ODDS.

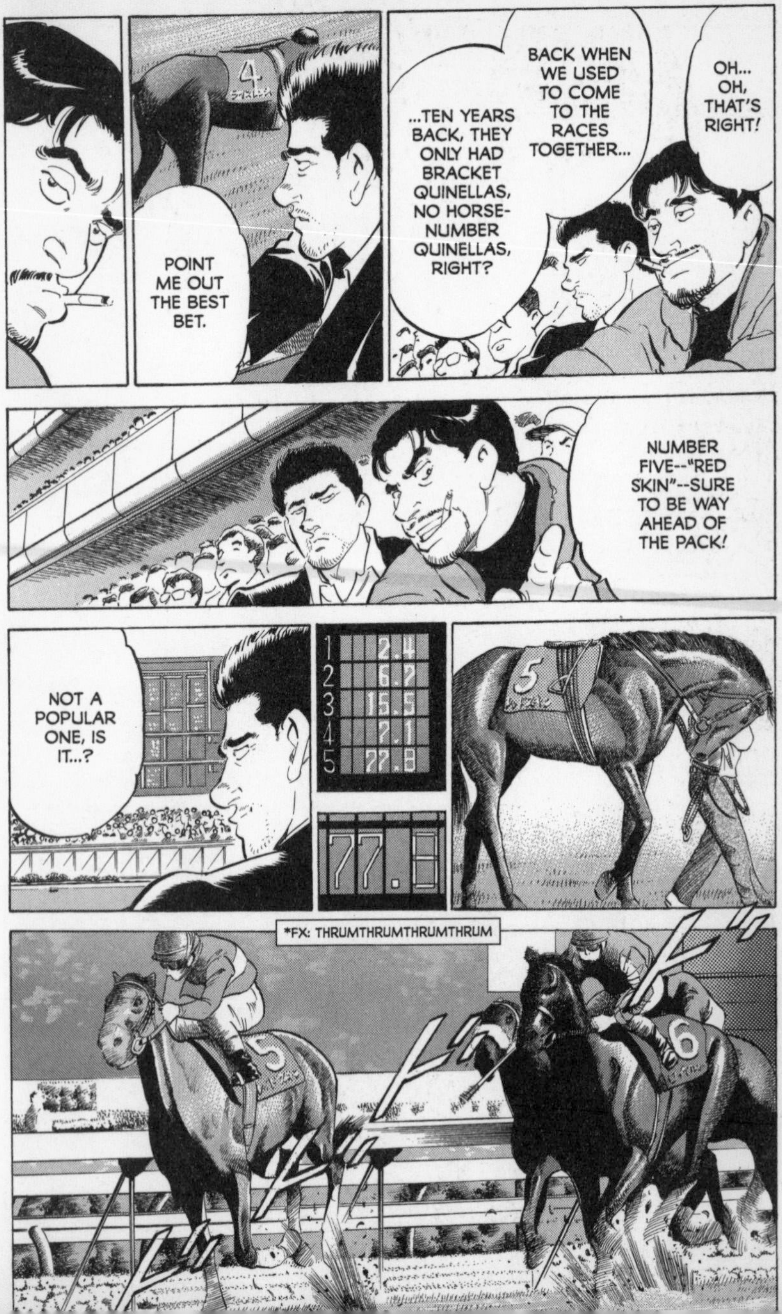
OH... OH, THAT'S RIGHT!
BACK WHEN WE USED TO COME TO THE RACES TOGETHER...
...TEN YEARS BACK, THEY ONLY HAD BRACKET QUINELLAS, NO HORSE-NUMBER QUINELLAS, RIGHT?
POINT ME OUT THE BEST BET.
NUMBER FIVE--"RED SKIN"--SURE TO BE WAY AHEAD OF THE PACK!
1 2.4
2 6.7
3 15.5
4 7.1
5 77.8
77.8
NOT A POPULAR ONE, IS IT...?
*FX: THRUMTHRUMTHRUMTHRUM

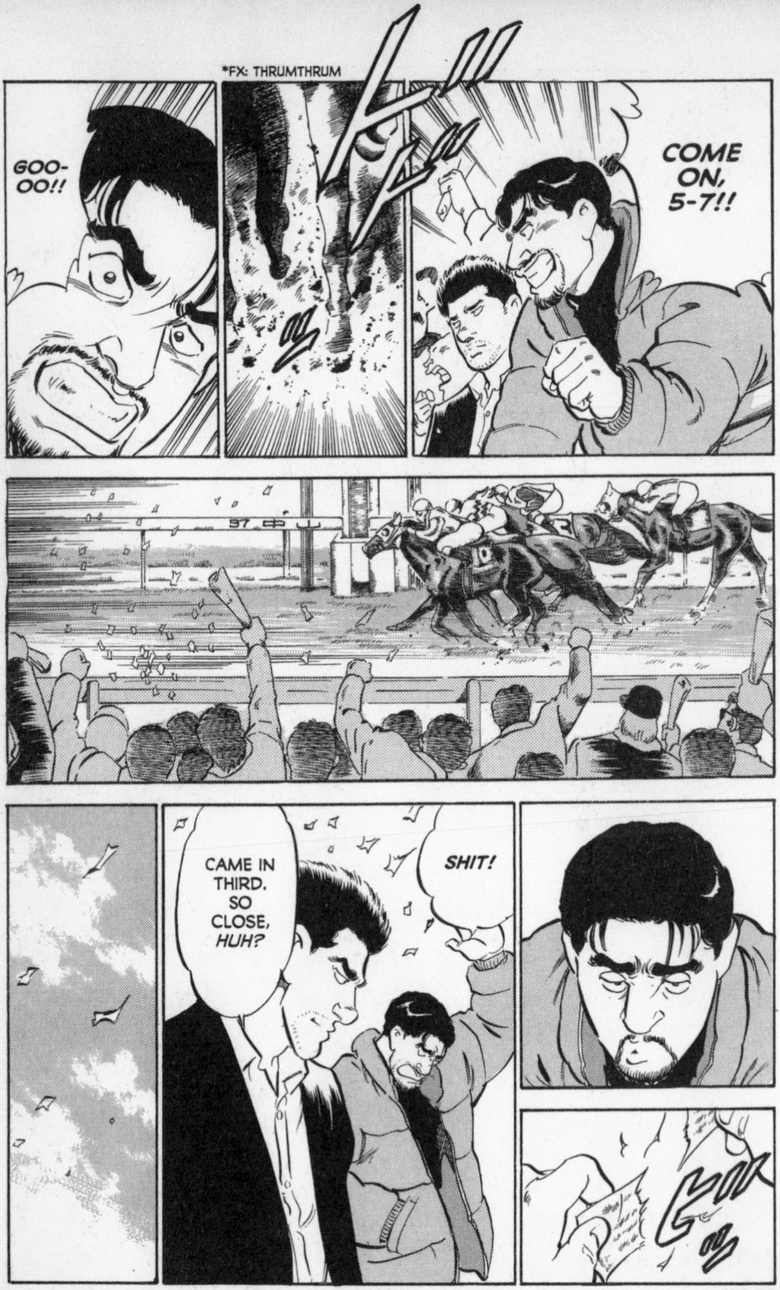
COME ON, 5-7!!
GOO-OO!!
SHIT!
CAME IN THIRD. SO CLOSE, HUH?

*FX: THRUMTHRUM

*FX: RIP

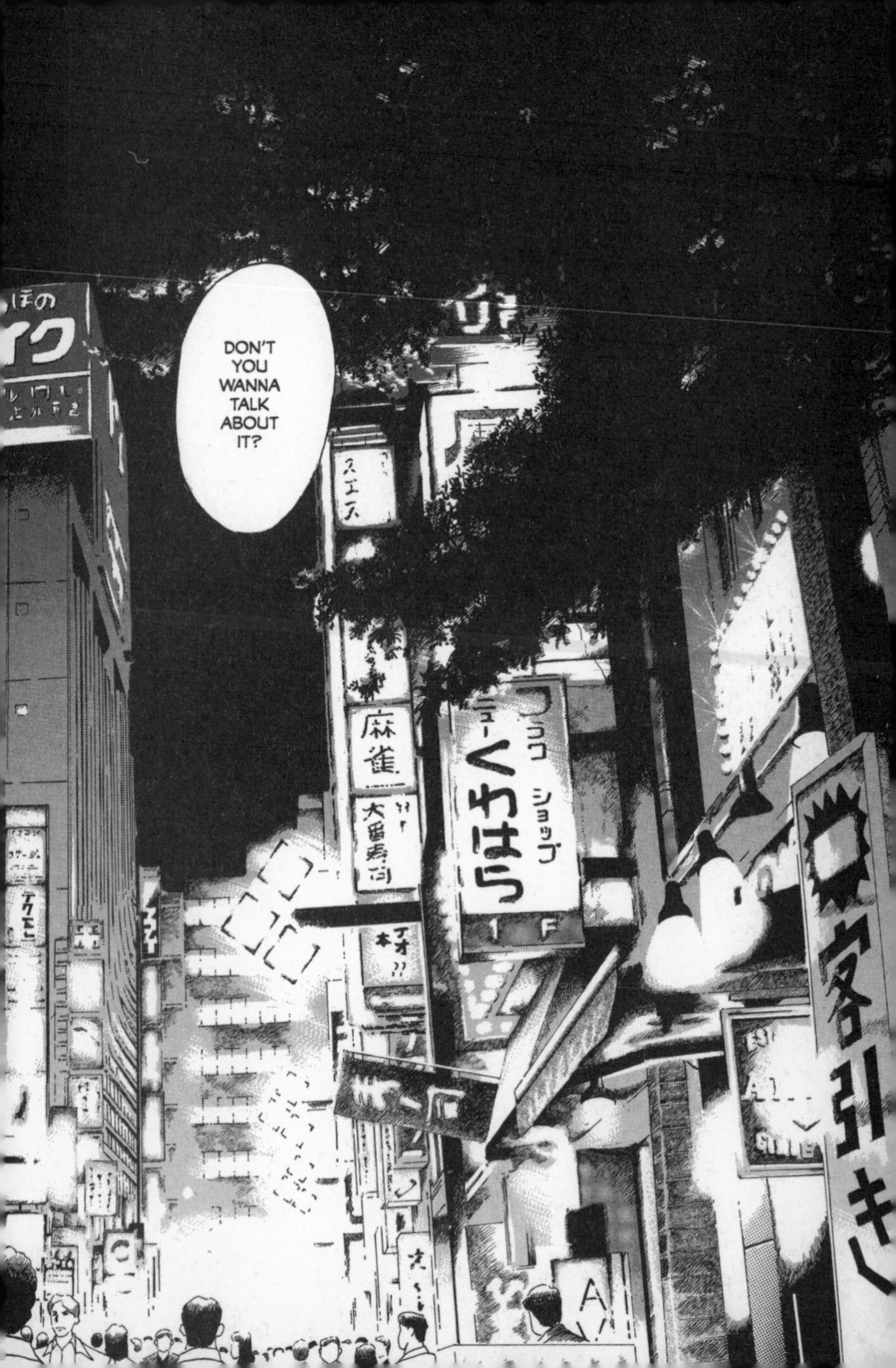
DON'T YOU WANNA TALK ABOUT IT?
ニューくわはら
ショップ
1F
麻雀

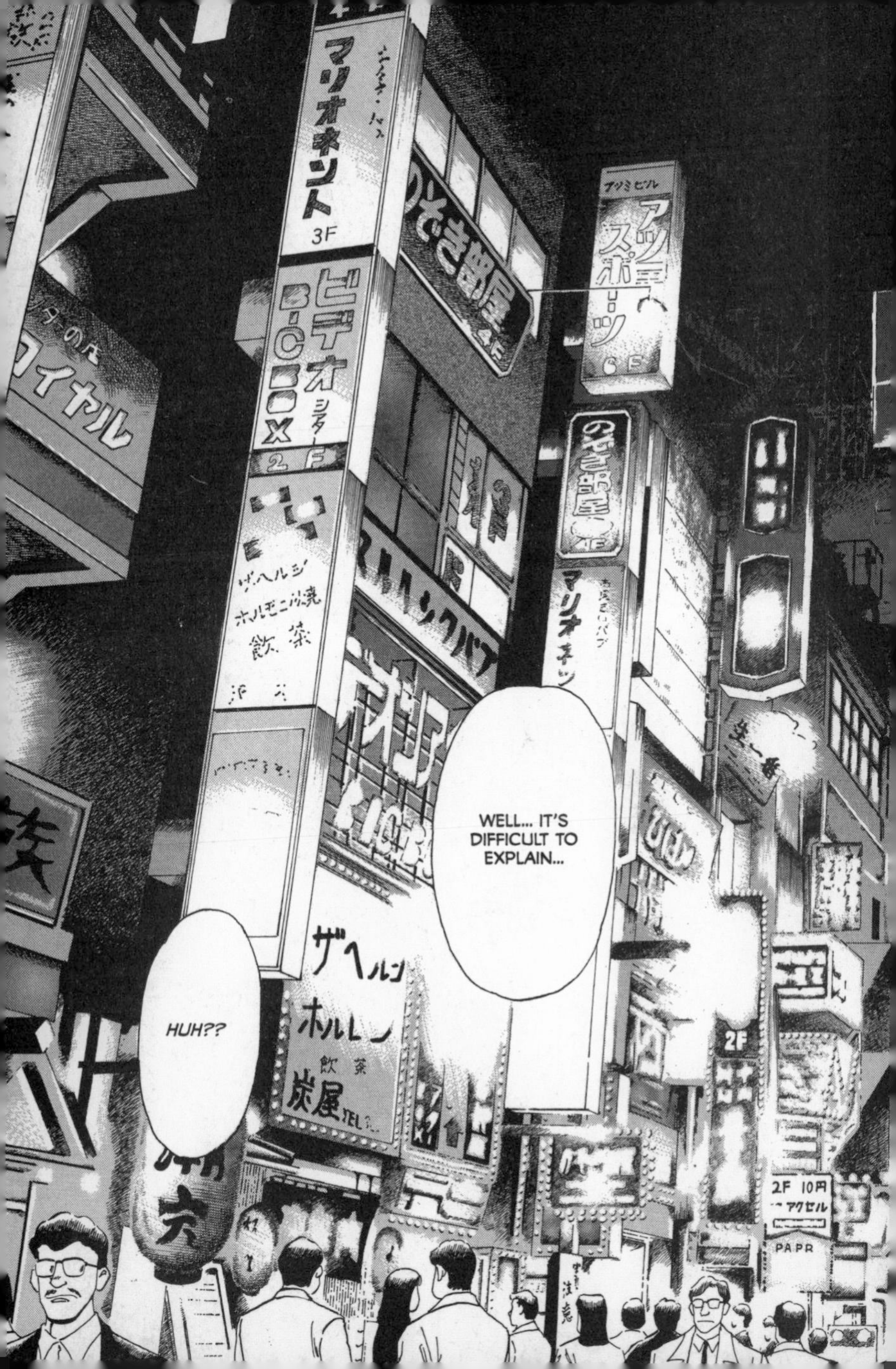
WELL... IT'S DIFFICULT TO EXPLAIN...
HUH??

*SIGN: GOLDEN GAI

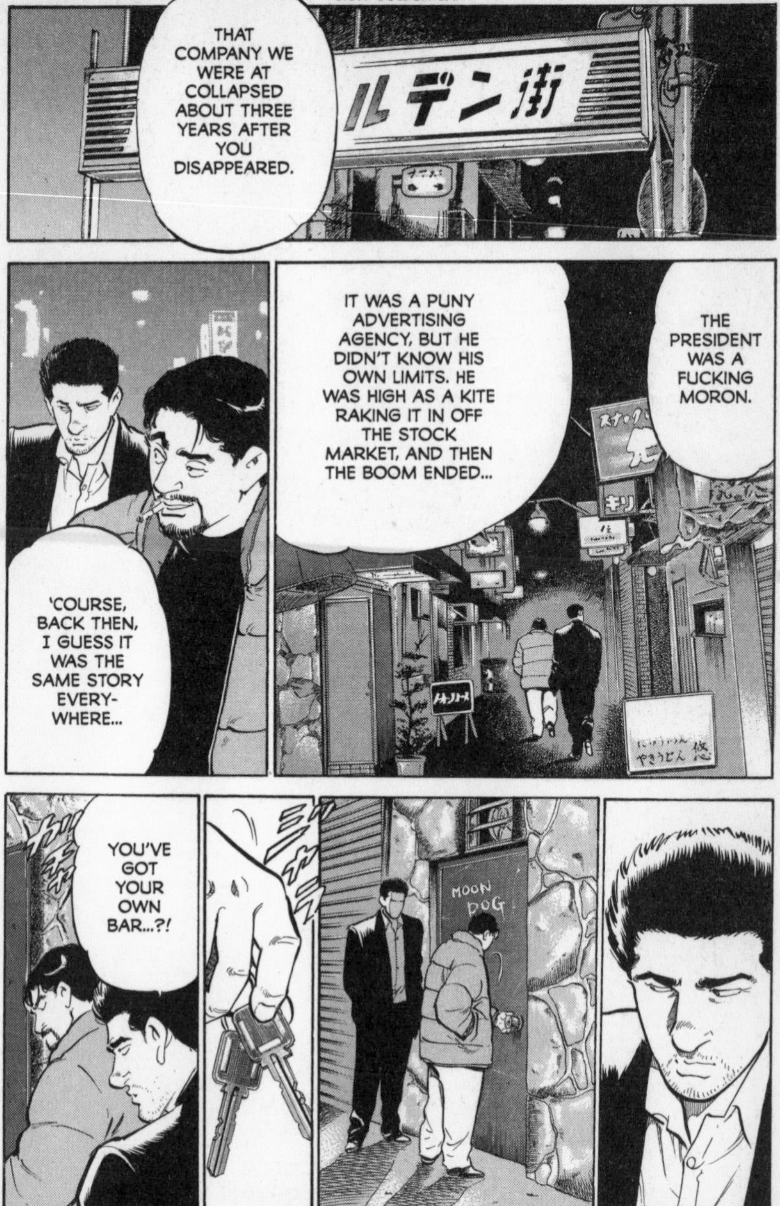
THAT COMPANY WE WERE AT COLLAPSED ABOUT THREE YEARS AFTER YOU DISAPPEARED.
THE PRESIDENT WAS A FUCKING MORON.
IT WAS A PUNY ADVERTISING AGENCY, BUT HE DIDN'T KNOW HIS OWN LIMITS. HE WAS HIGH AS A KITE RAKING IT IN OFF THE STOCK MARKET, AND THEN THE BOOM ENDED...
'COURSE, BACK THEN, I GUESS IT WAS THE SAME STORY EVERY-WHERE...
MOON DOG
YOU'VE GOT YOUR OWN BAR...?!

*FX: CHIK *FX: CLINK

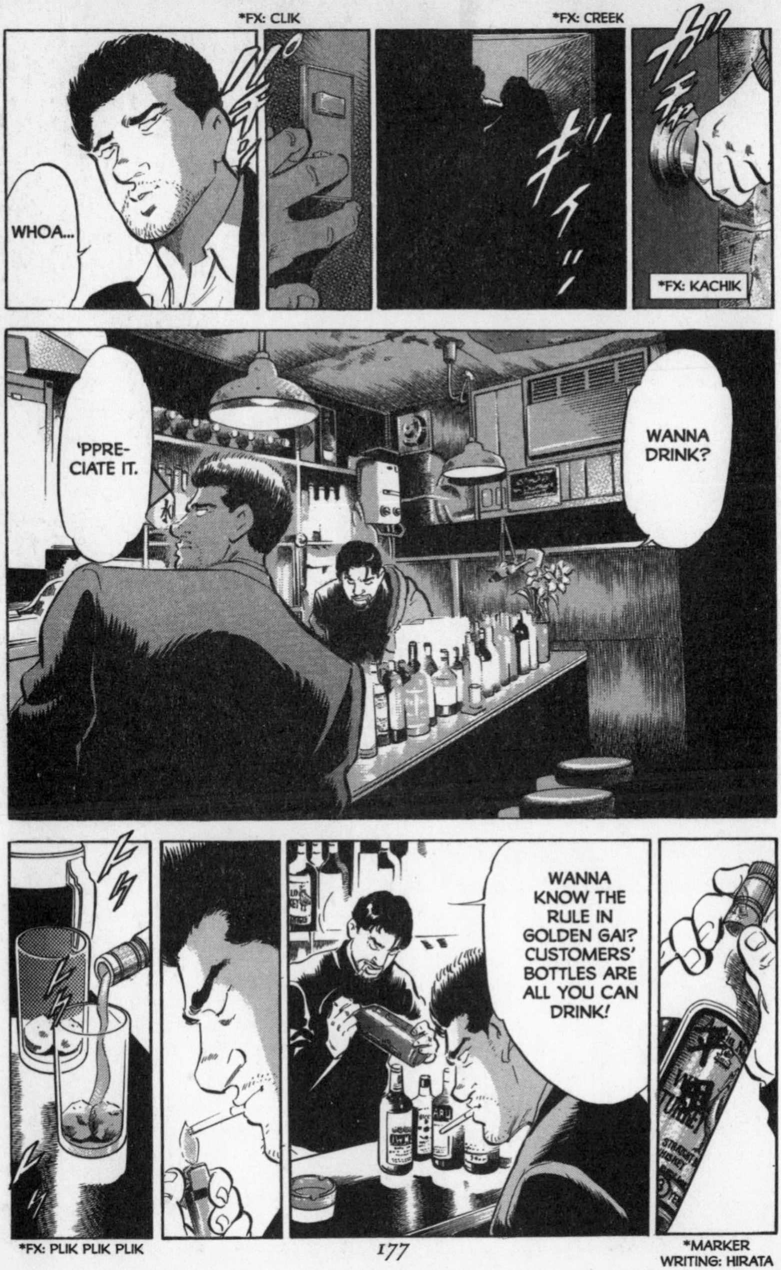
*FX: KACHIK
*FX: CREEK
*FX: CLIK
WHOA...
WANNA DRINK?
'PPRE-CIATE IT.
*MARKER WRITING: HIRATA
WANNA KNOW THE RULE IN GOLDEN GAI? CUSTOMERS' BOTTLES ARE ALL YOU CAN DRINK!
*FX: PLIK PLIK PLIK

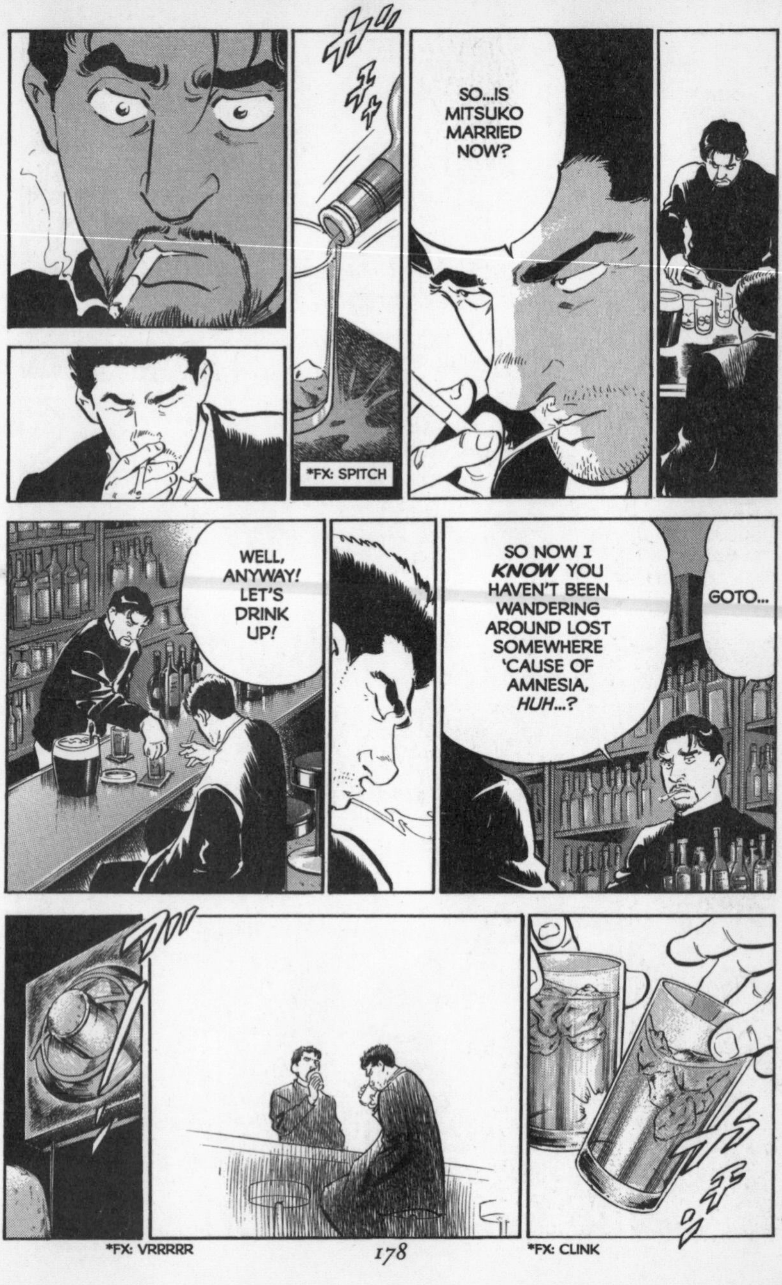
SO...IS MITSUKO MARRIED NOW?
*FX: SPITCH
GOTO...
SO NOW I *KNOW* YOU HAVEN'T BEEN WANDERING AROUND LOST SOMEWHERE 'CAUSE OF AMNESIA, *HUH*...?
WELL, ANYWAY! LET'S DRINK UP!

*FX: CLINK

*FX: VRRRR

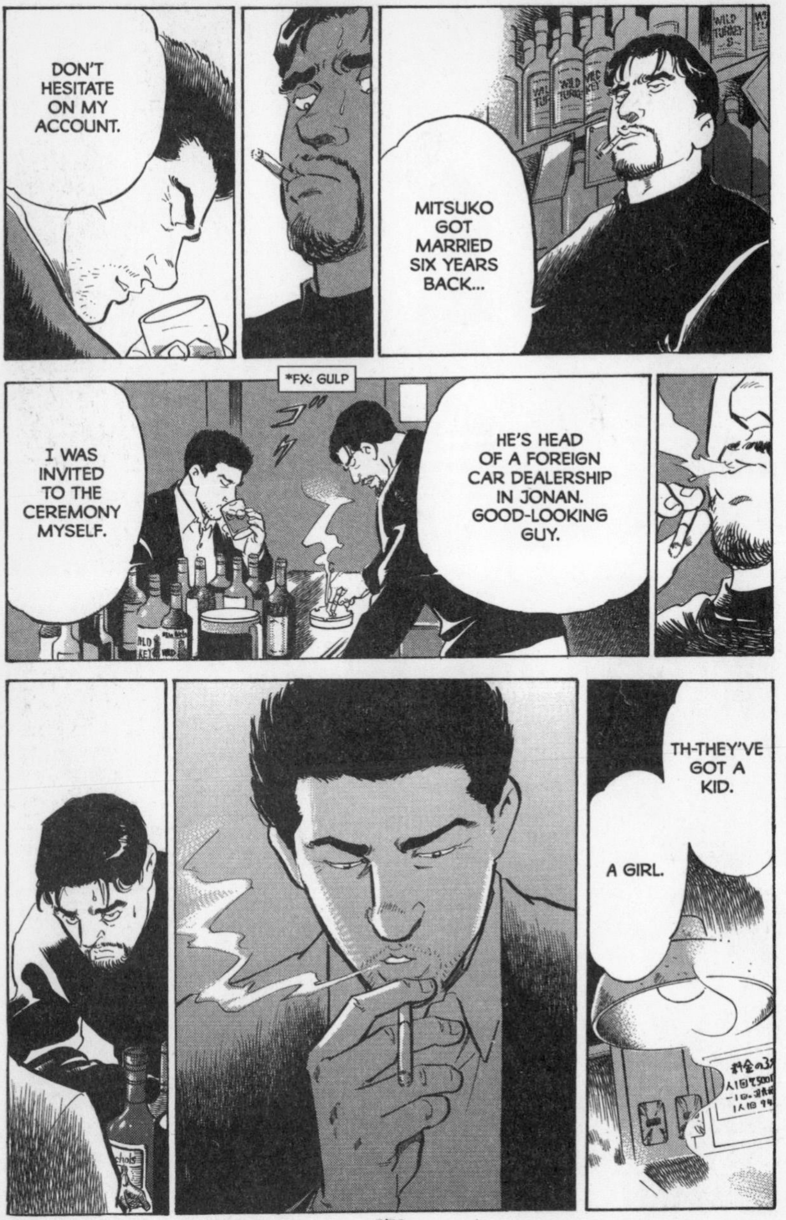
MITSUKO GOT MARRIED SIX YEARS BACK...
DON'T HESITATE ON MY ACCOUNT.
HE'S HEAD OF A FOREIGN CAR DEALERSHIP IN JONAN. GOOD-LOOKING GUY.
*FX: GULP
I WAS INVITED TO THE CEREMONY MYSELF.
TH-THEY'VE GOT A KID.
A GIRL.

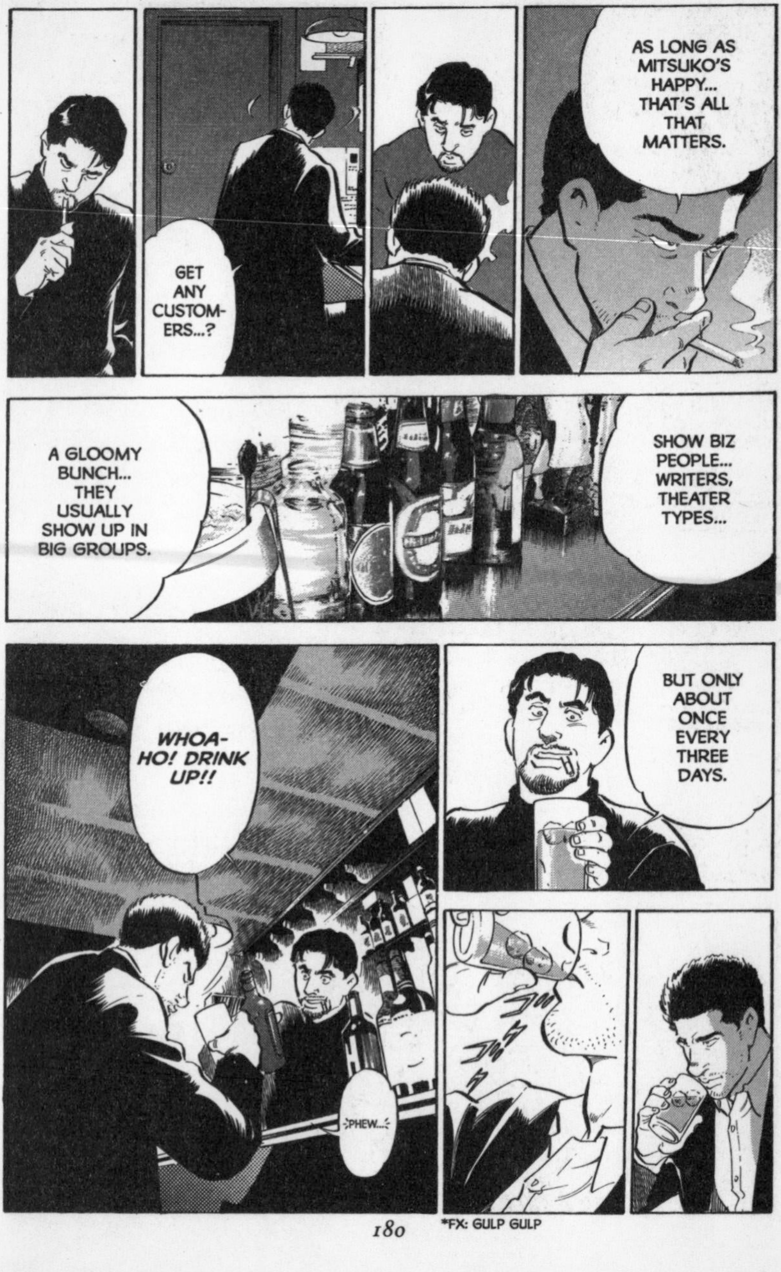
AS LONG AS MITSUKO'S HAPPY... THAT'S ALL THAT MATTERS.
GET ANY CUSTOM-ERS...?
SHOW BIZ PEOPLE... WRITERS, THEATER TYPES...
A GLOOMY BUNCH... THEY USUALLY SHOW UP IN BIG GROUPS.
BUT ONLY ABOUT ONCE EVERY THREE DAYS.
WHOA-HO! DRINK UP!!
PHEW...

*FX: GULP GULP

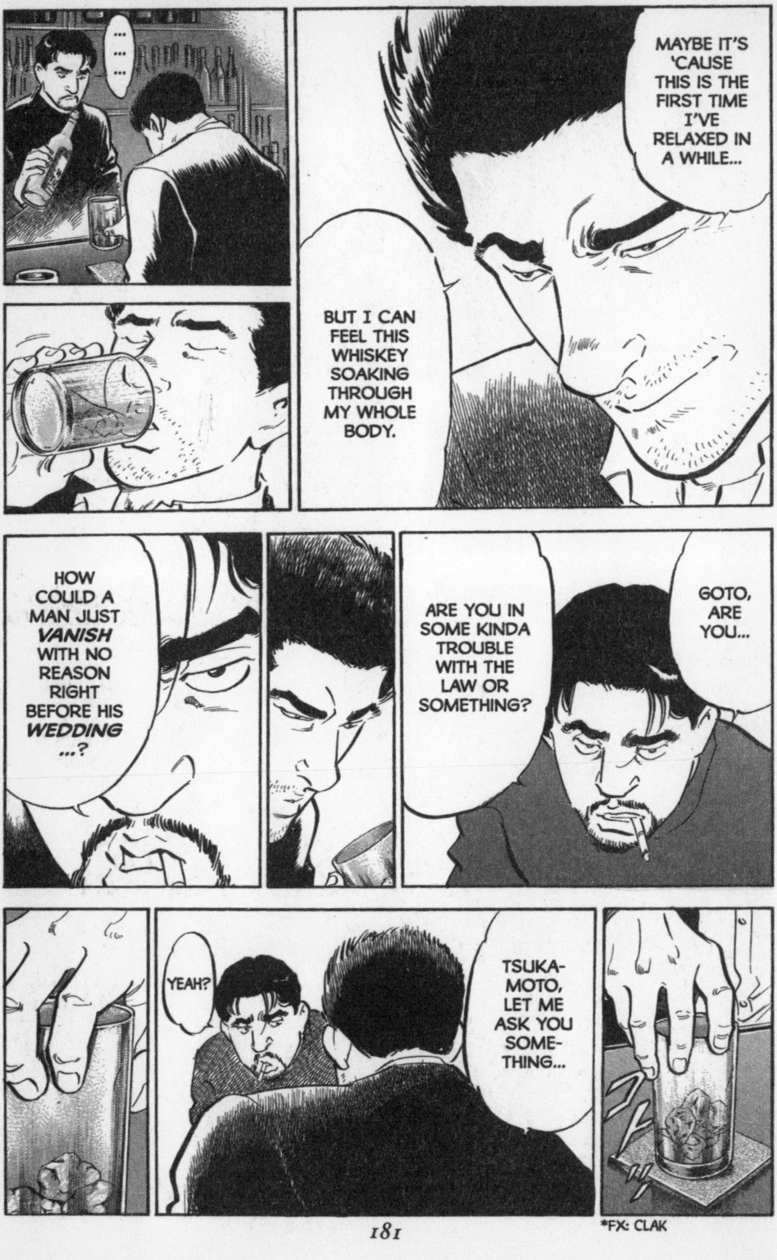

MAYBE IT'S 'CAUSE THIS IS THE FIRST TIME I'VE RELAXED IN A WHILE...
BUT I CAN FEEL THIS WHISKEY SOAKING THROUGH MY WHOLE BODY.
... ...
GOTO, ARE YOU...
ARE YOU IN SOME KINDA TROUBLE WITH THE LAW OR SOMETHING?
HOW COULD A MAN JUST *VANISH* WITH NO REASON RIGHT BEFORE HIS *WEDDING* ...?
TSUKA-MOTO, LET ME ASK YOU SOME-THING...
YEAH?

*FX: CLAK

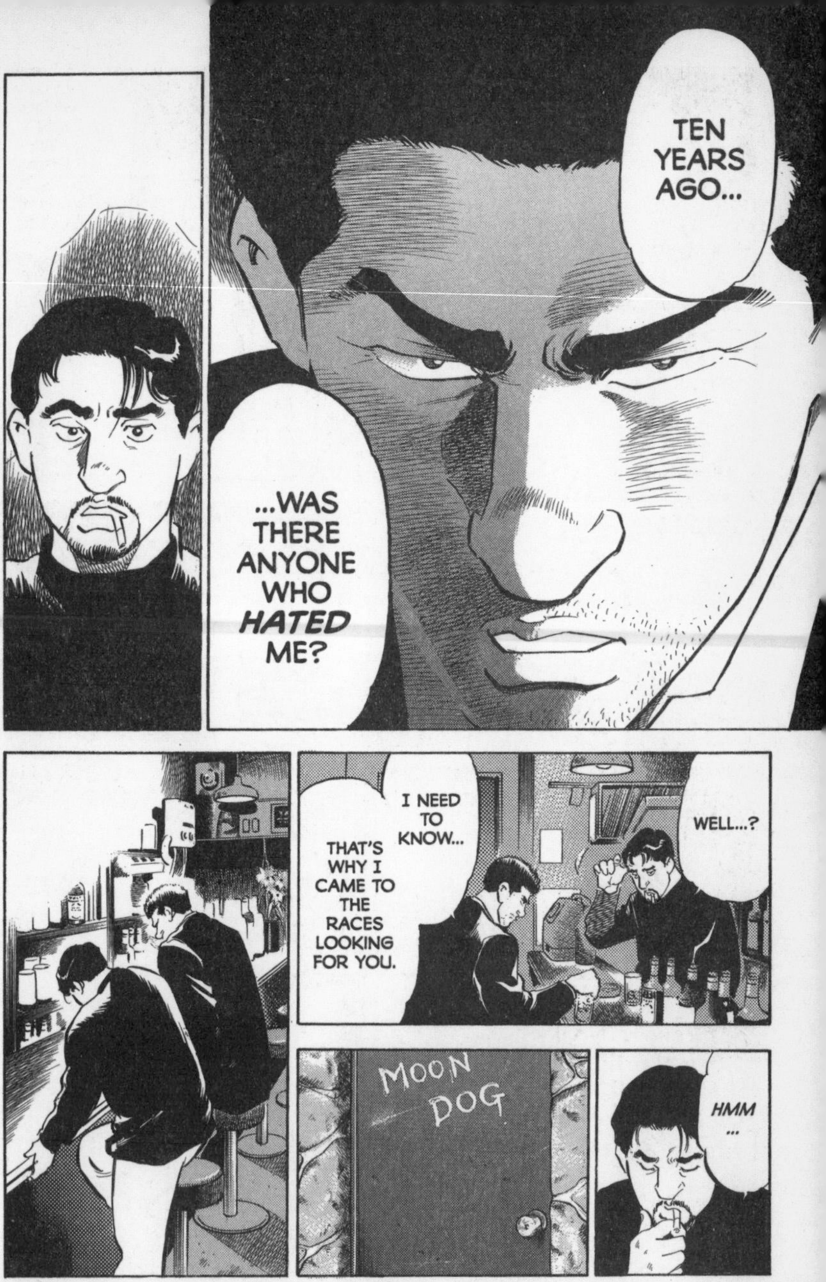
TEN YEARS AGO...
...WAS THERE ANYONE WHO *HATED* ME?
WELL...?
I NEED TO KNOW...
THAT'S WHY I CAME TO THE RACES LOOKING FOR YOU.
HMM ...
MOON DOG

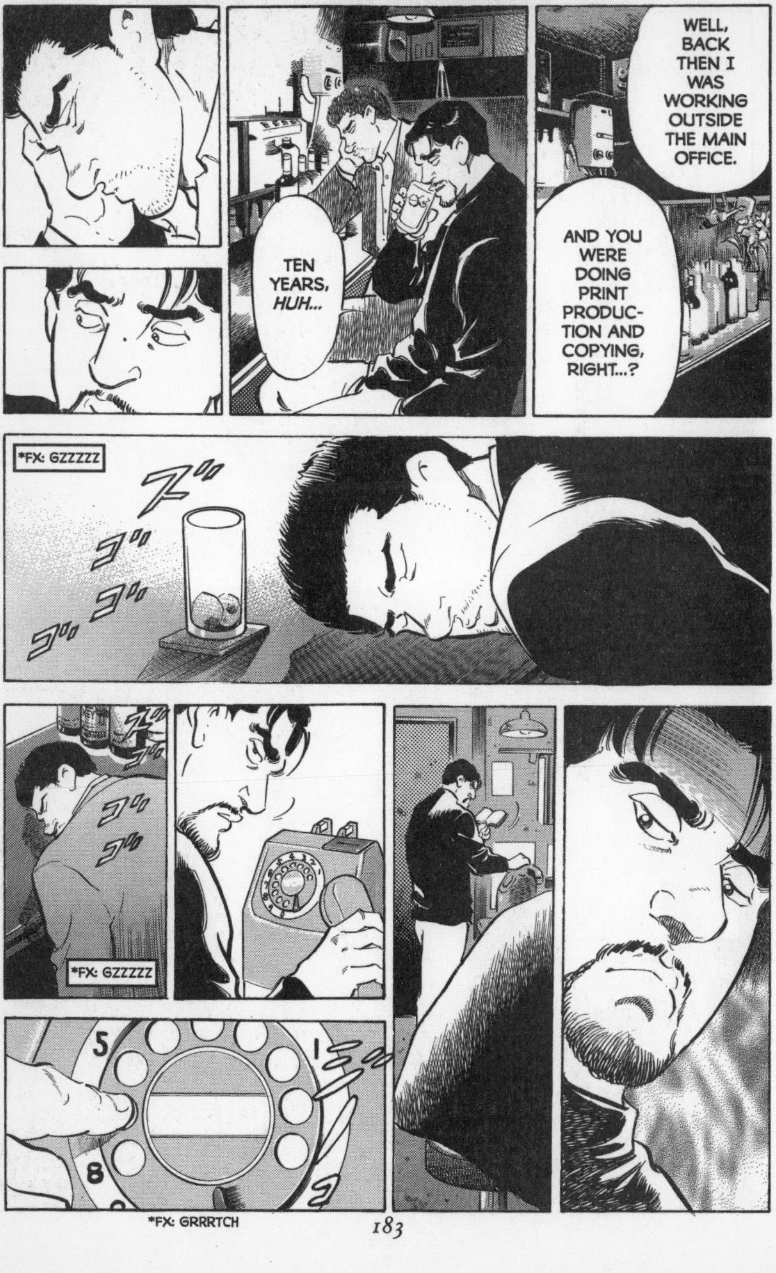
WELL, BACK THEN I WAS WORKING OUTSIDE THE MAIN OFFICE.
AND YOU WERE DOING PRINT PRODUCTION AND COPYING, RIGHT...?
TEN YEARS, *HUH*...
*FX: GZZZZZ
*FX: GZZZZZ

*FX: GRRRTCH

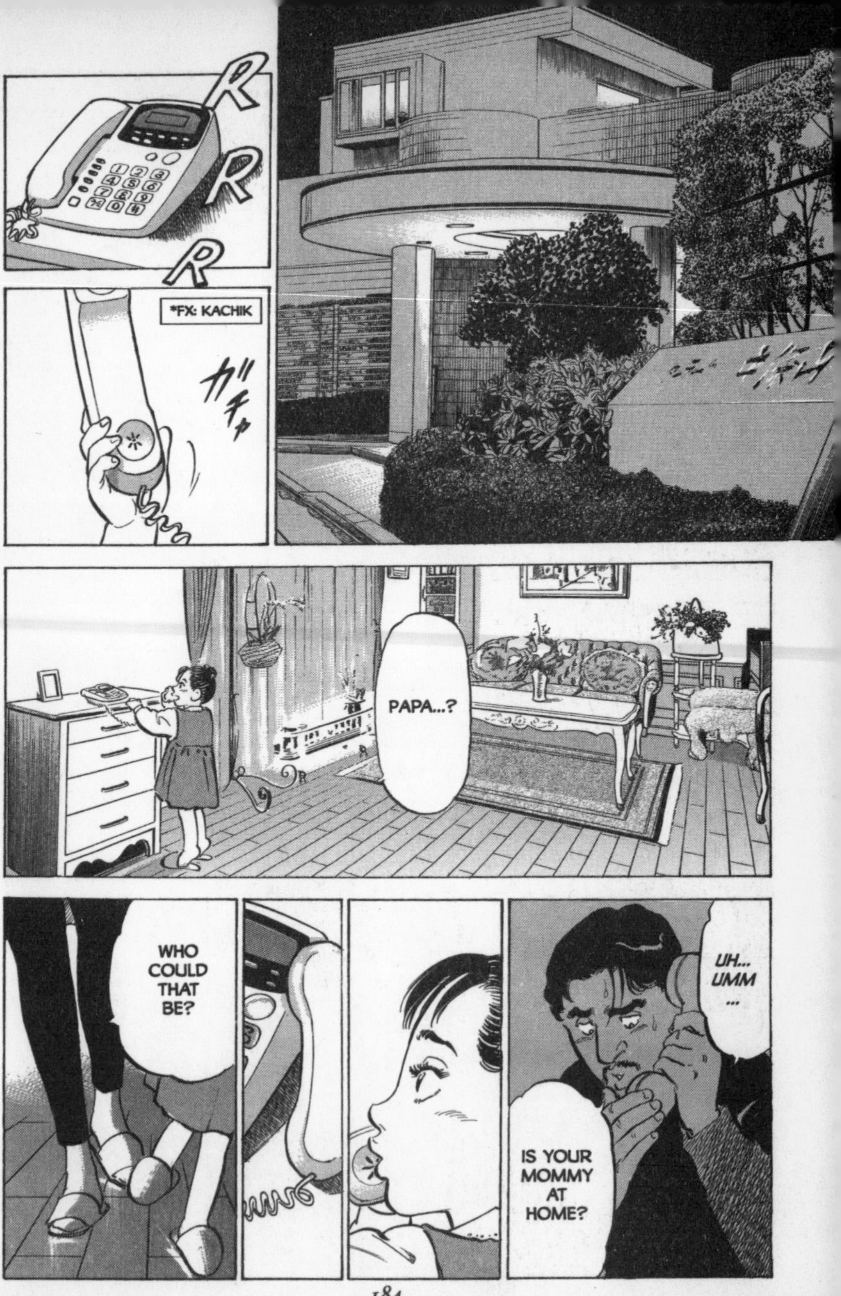
R
R
R
*FX: KACHIK
ガチャ
PAPA...?
UH... UMM ...
IS YOUR MOMMY AT HOME?
WHO COULD THAT BE?

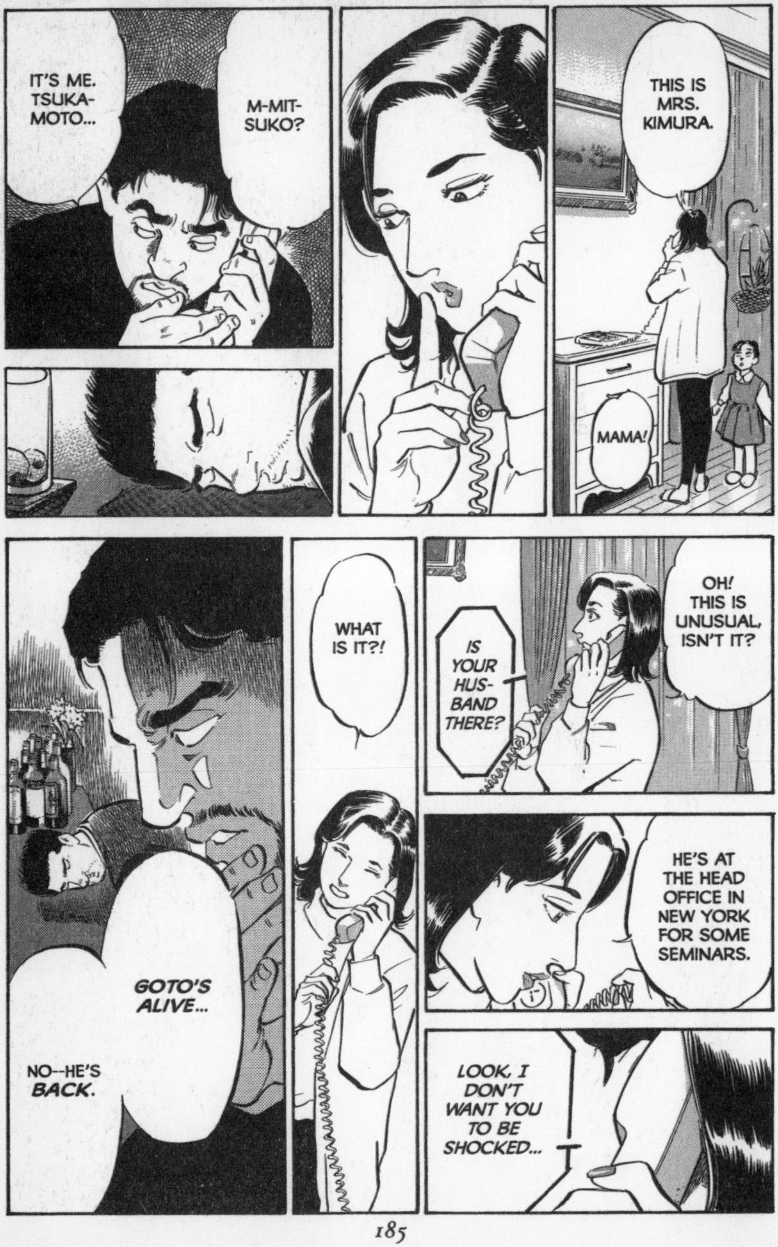
THIS IS MRS. KIMURA.
MAMA!
M-MIT-SUKO?
IT'S ME. TSUKA-MOTO...
OH! THIS IS UNUSUAL, ISN'T IT?
IS YOUR HUS-BAND THERE?
HE'S AT THE HEAD OFFICE IN NEW YORK FOR SOME SEMINARS.
LOOK, I DON'T WANT YOU TO BE SHOCKED...
WHAT IS IT?!
GOTO'S ALIVE...
NO--HE'S BACK.

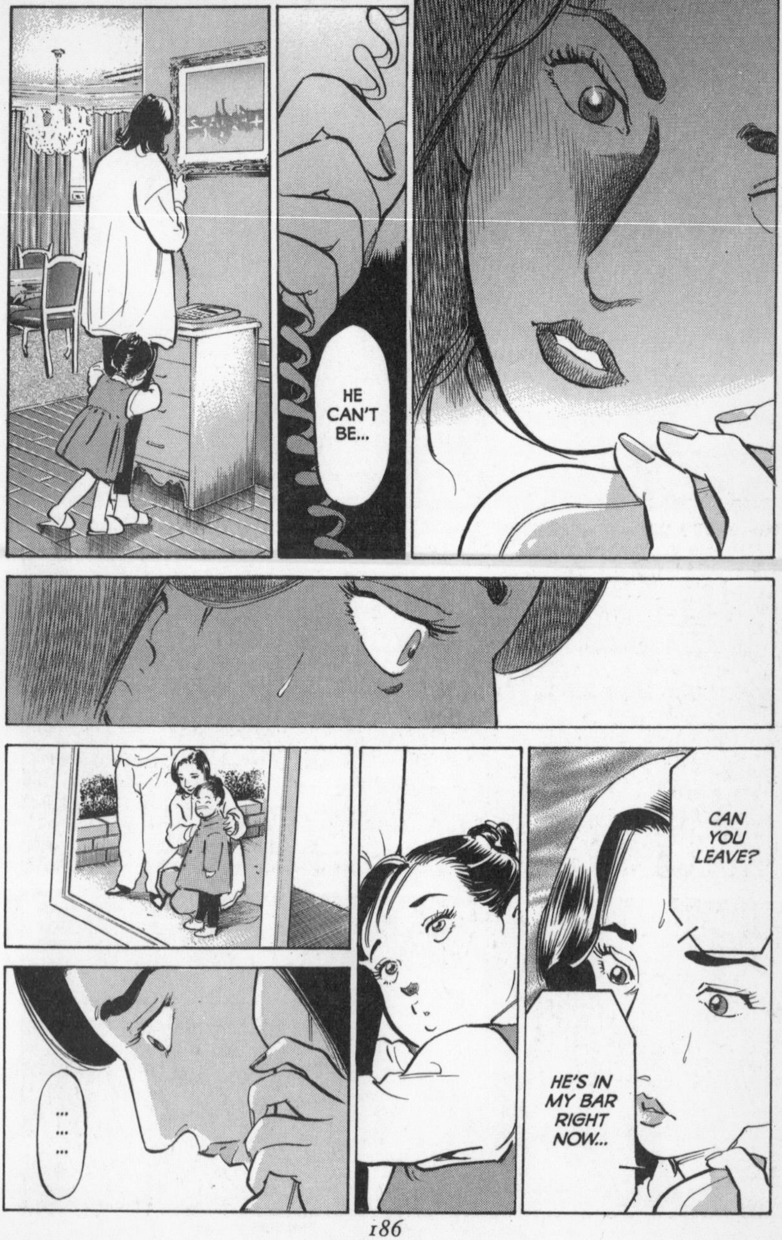
HE CAN'T BE...
CAN YOU LEAVE?
HE'S IN MY BAR RIGHT NOW...
... ...

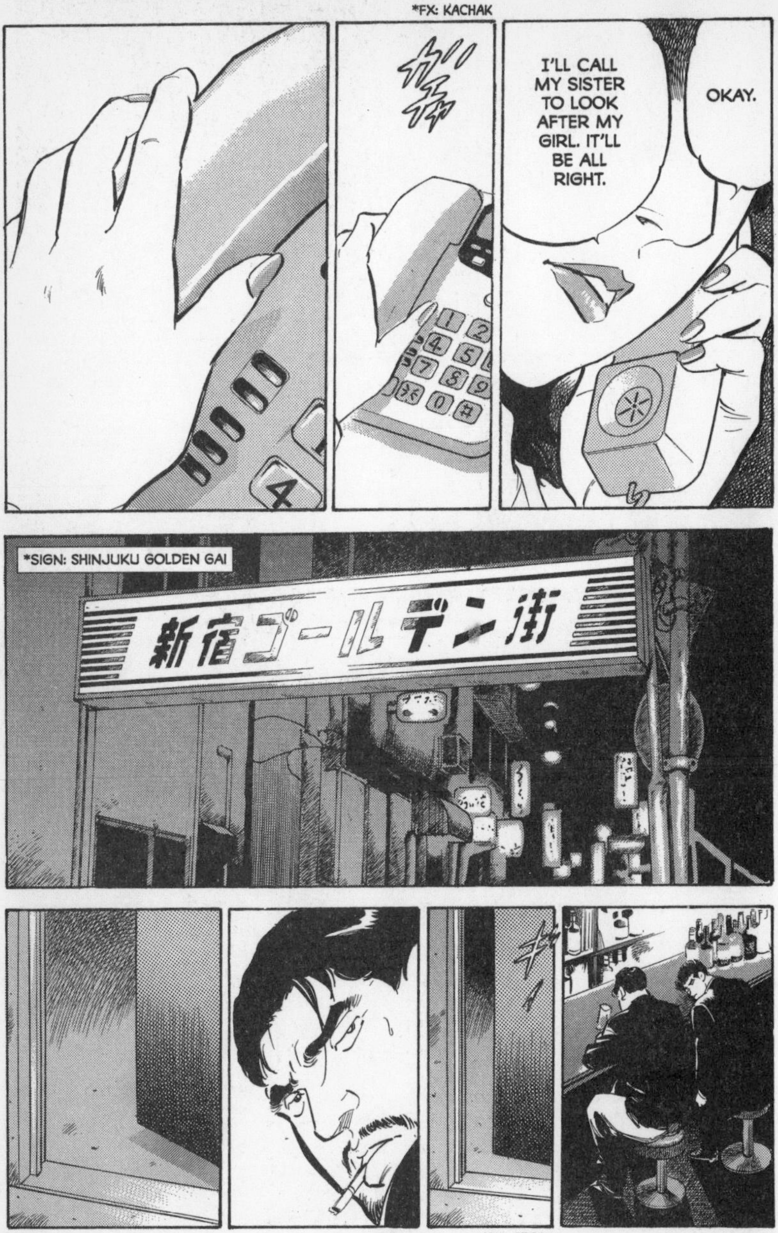
OKAY.
I'LL CALL MY SISTER TO LOOK AFTER MY GIRL. IT'LL BE ALL RIGHT.
*FX: KACHAK
*SIGN: SHINJUKU GOLDEN GAI
新宿ゴールデン街
*FX: CREEK

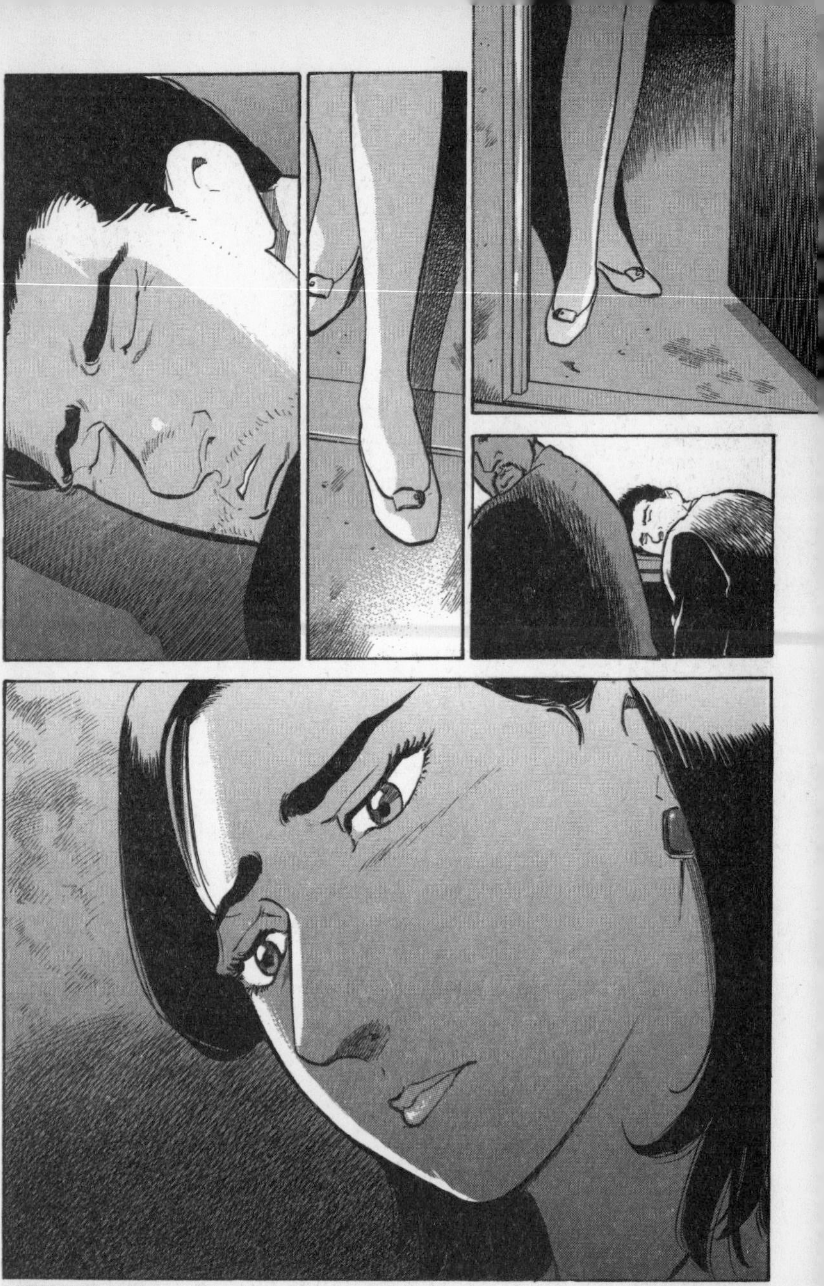

MITSUKO: END

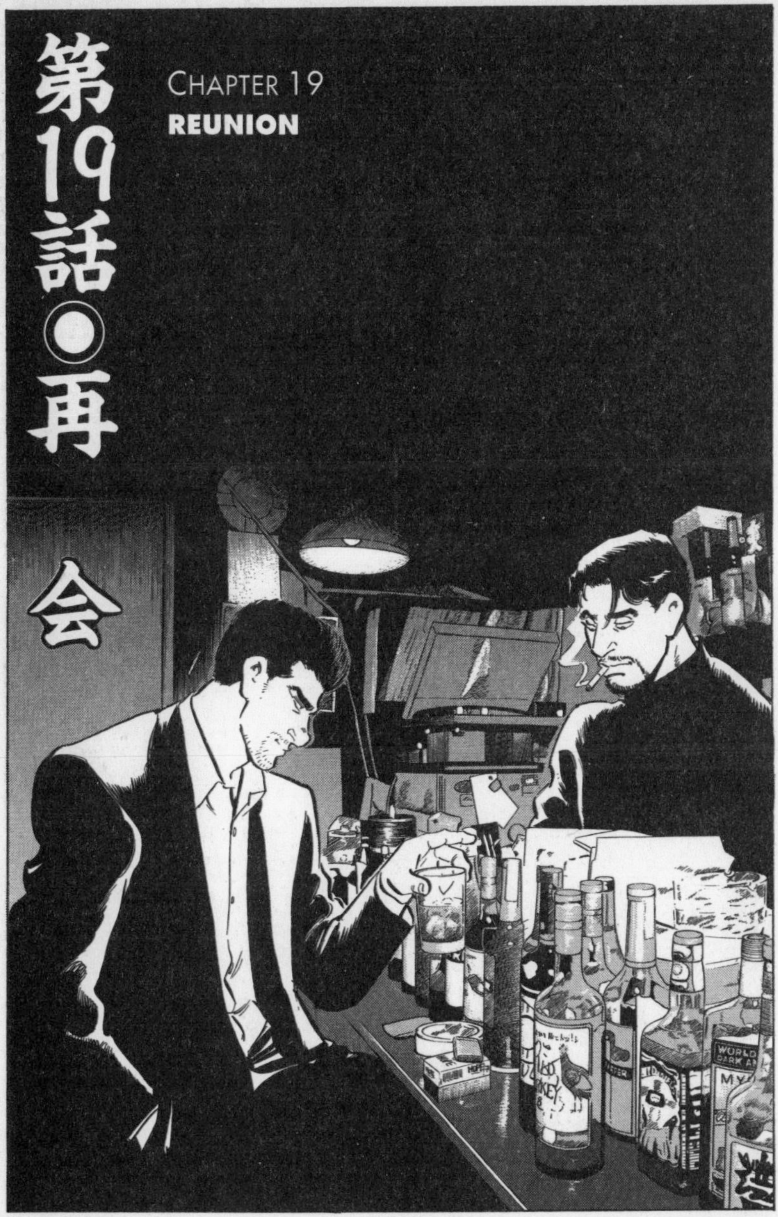
第19話◎再会
CHAPTER 19
REUNION

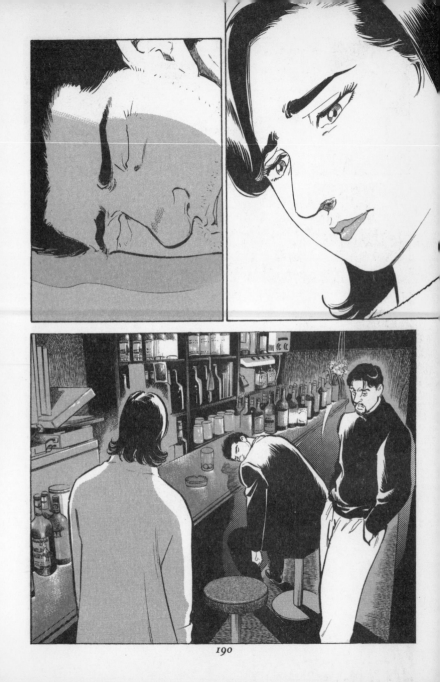

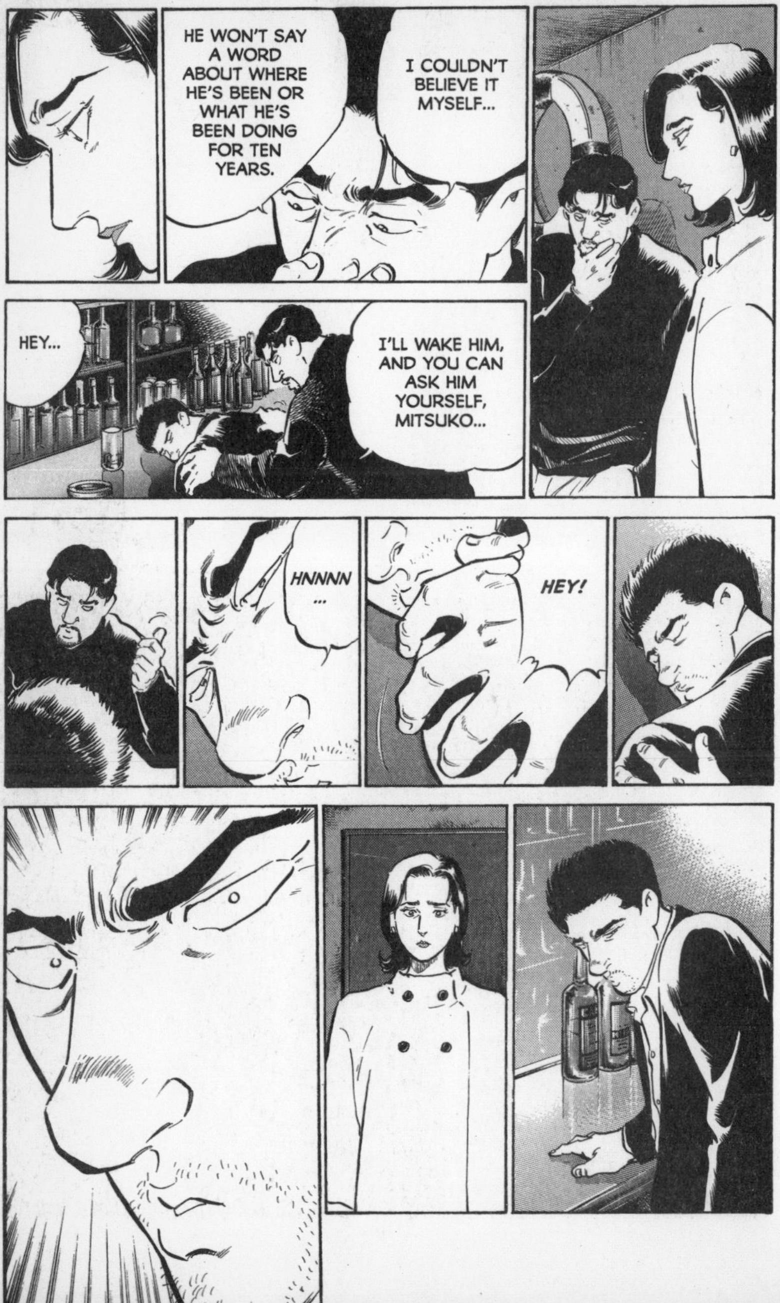
I COULDN'T BELIEVE IT MYSELF...
HE WON'T SAY A WORD ABOUT WHERE HE'S BEEN OR WHAT HE'S BEEN DOING FOR TEN YEARS.
I'LL WAKE HIM, AND YOU CAN ASK HIM YOURSELF, MITSUKO...
HEY...
HEY!
HNNNN ...

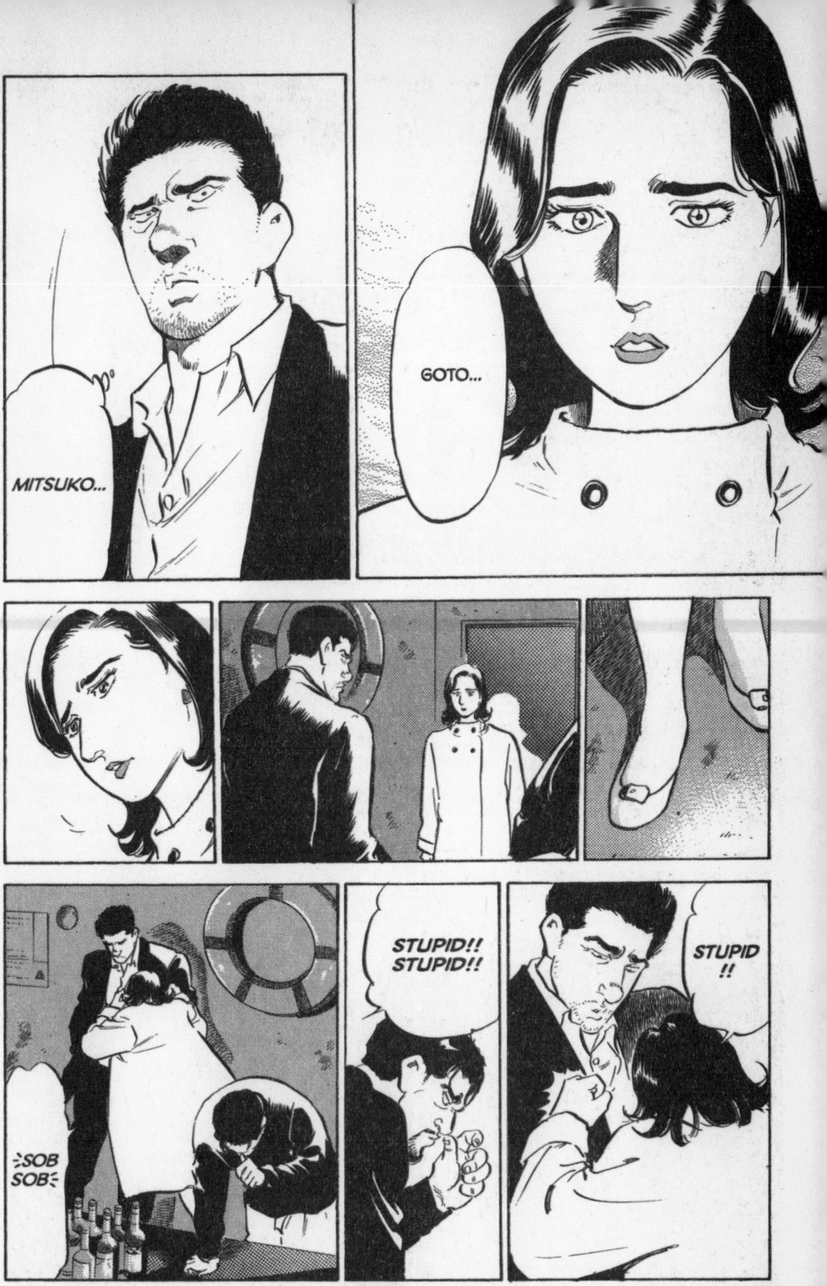
GOTO...
MITSUKO...
STUPID
!!
STUPID!!
STUPID!!
SOB
SOB

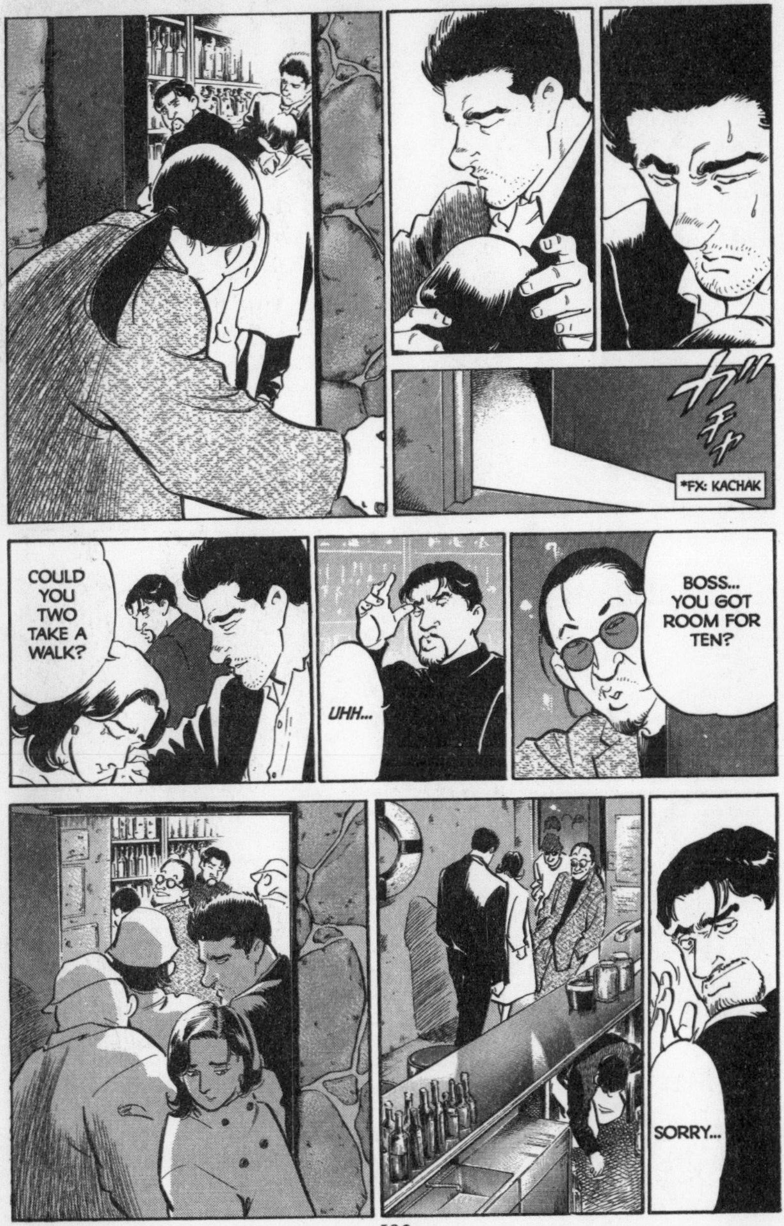
*FX: KACHAK
BOSS... YOU GOT ROOM FOR TEN?
UHH...
COULD YOU TWO TAKE A WALK?
SORRY...

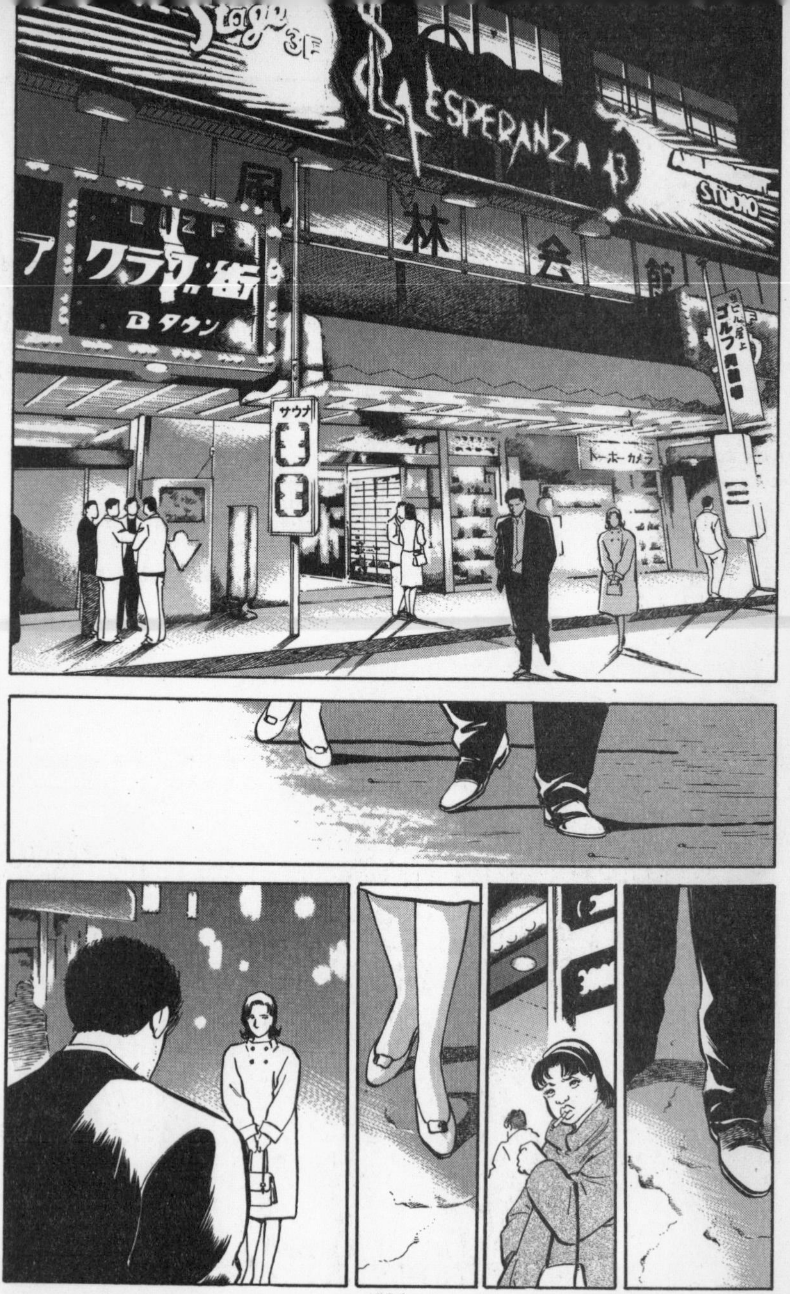
ESPERANZA
STUDIO
風林会館
クラブ街
Bタウン
サウナ
トーホーカメラ
ゴルフ

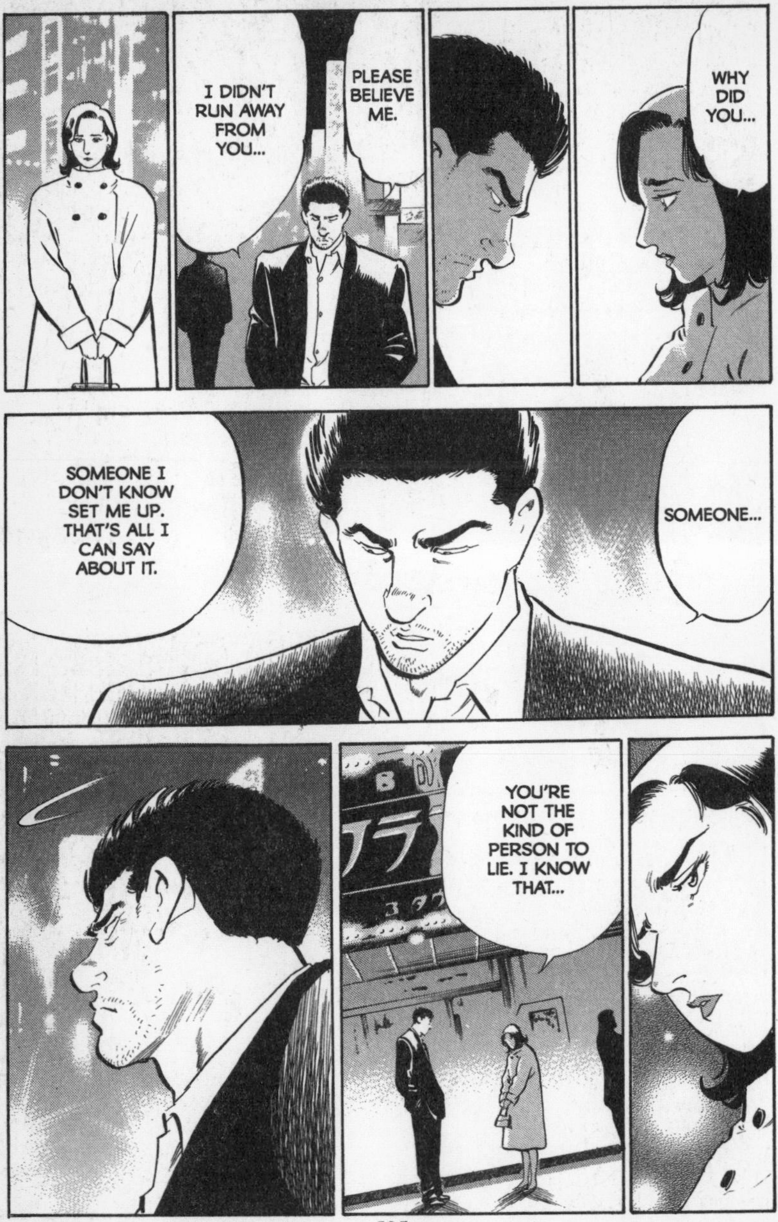
WHY DID YOU...
PLEASE BELIEVE ME.
I DIDN'T RUN AWAY FROM YOU...
SOMEONE...
SOMEONE I DON'T KNOW SET ME UP. THAT'S ALL I CAN SAY ABOUT IT.
YOU'RE NOT THE KIND OF PERSON TO LIE. I KNOW THAT...

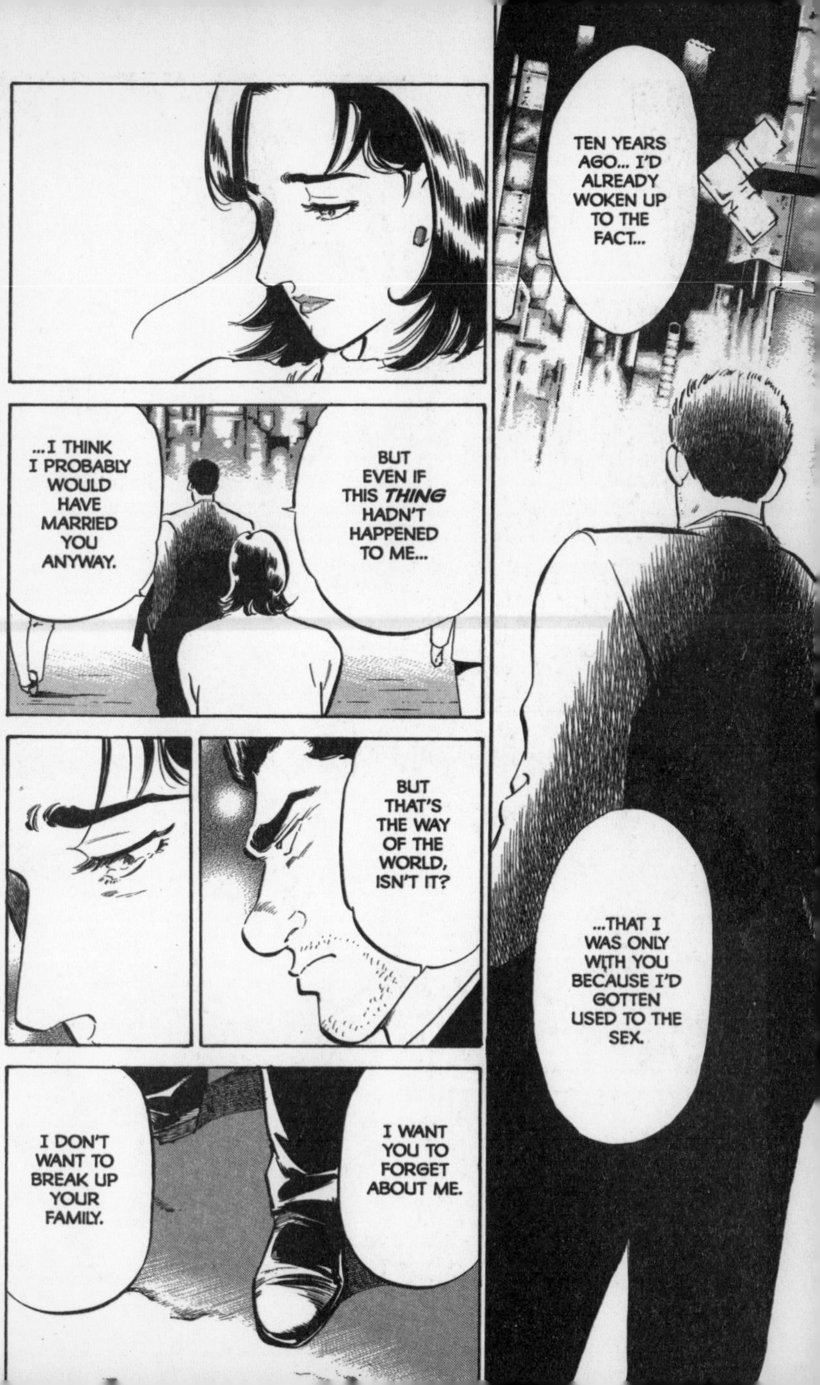
TEN YEARS AGO... I'D ALREADY WOKEN UP TO THE FACT...
...THAT I WAS ONLY WITH YOU BECAUSE I'D GOTTEN USED TO THE SEX.
BUT EVEN IF THIS *THING* HADN'T HAPPENED TO ME...
...I THINK I PROBABLY WOULD HAVE MARRIED YOU ANYWAY.
BUT THAT'S THE WAY OF THE WORLD, ISN'T IT?
I WANT YOU TO FORGET ABOUT ME.
I DON'T WANT TO BREAK UP YOUR FAMILY.

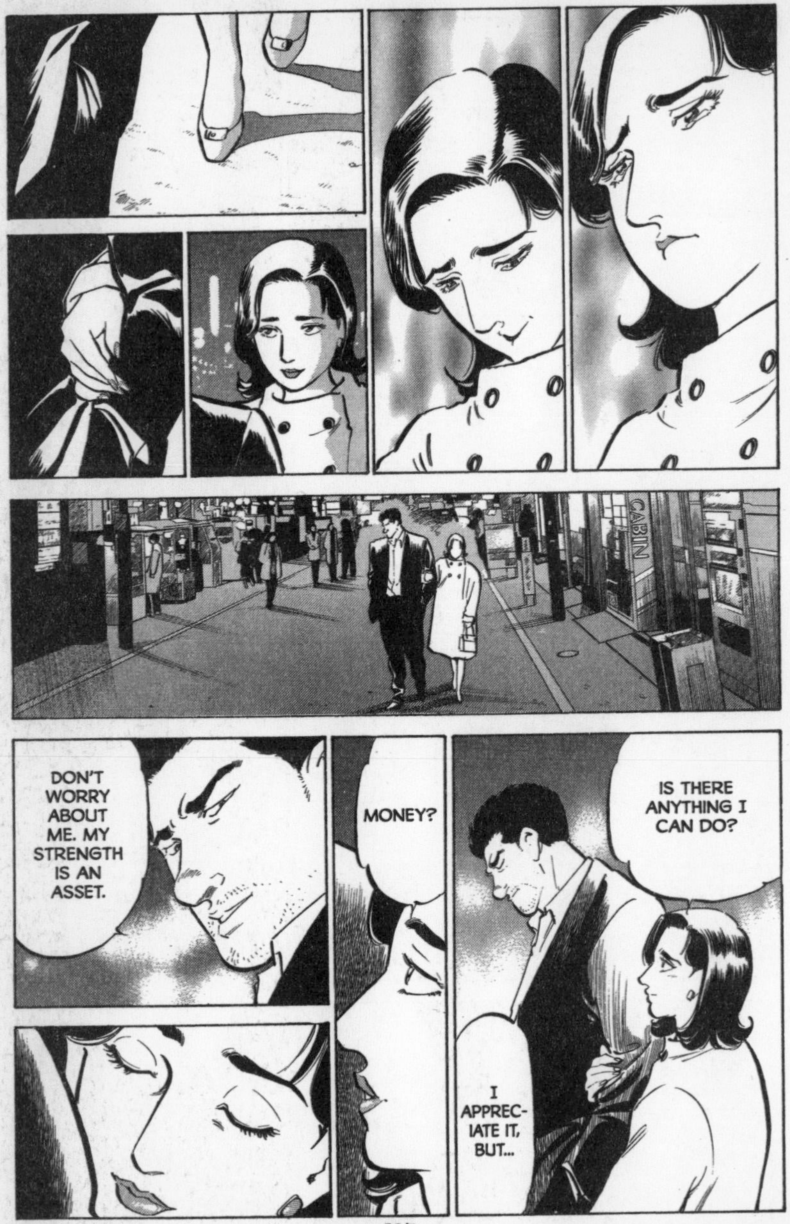
IS THERE ANYTHING I CAN DO?
I APPREC-IATE IT, BUT...
MONEY?
DON'T WORRY ABOUT ME. MY STRENGTH IS AN ASSET.

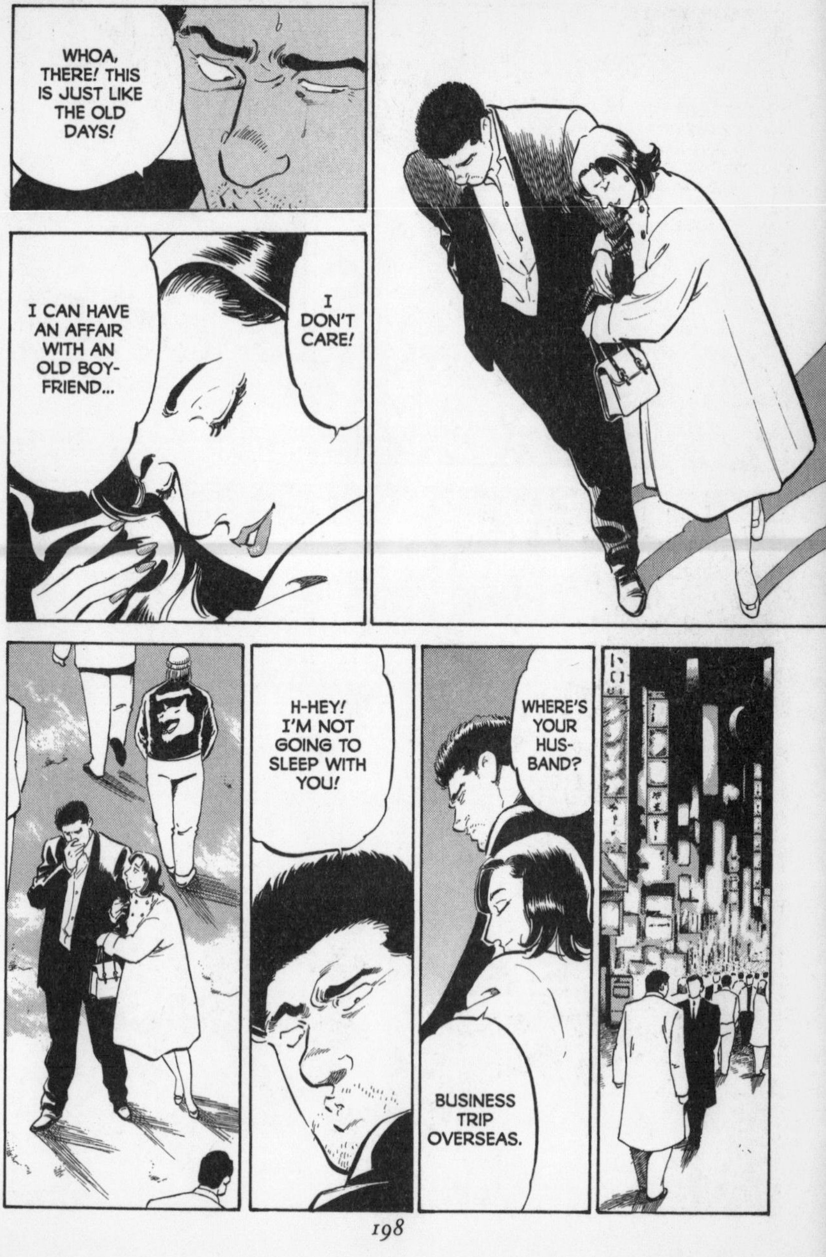
WHOA, THERE! THIS IS JUST LIKE THE OLD DAYS!
I DON'T CARE!
I CAN HAVE AN AFFAIR WITH AN OLD BOY-FRIEND...
WHERE'S YOUR HUS-BAND?
BUSINESS TRIP OVERSEAS.
H-HEY! I'M NOT GOING TO SLEEP WITH YOU!

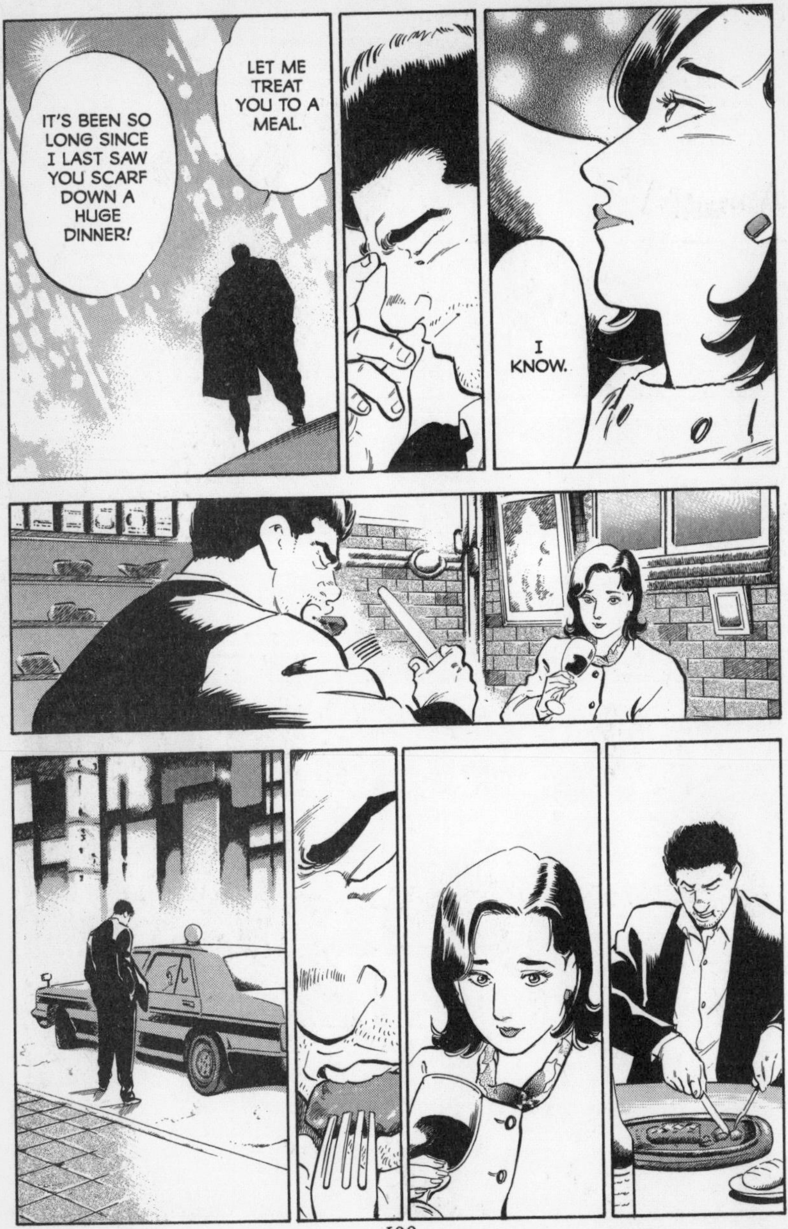
I KNOW.
LET ME TREAT YOU TO A MEAL.
IT'S BEEN SO LONG SINCE I LAST SAW YOU SCARF DOWN A HUGE DINNER!

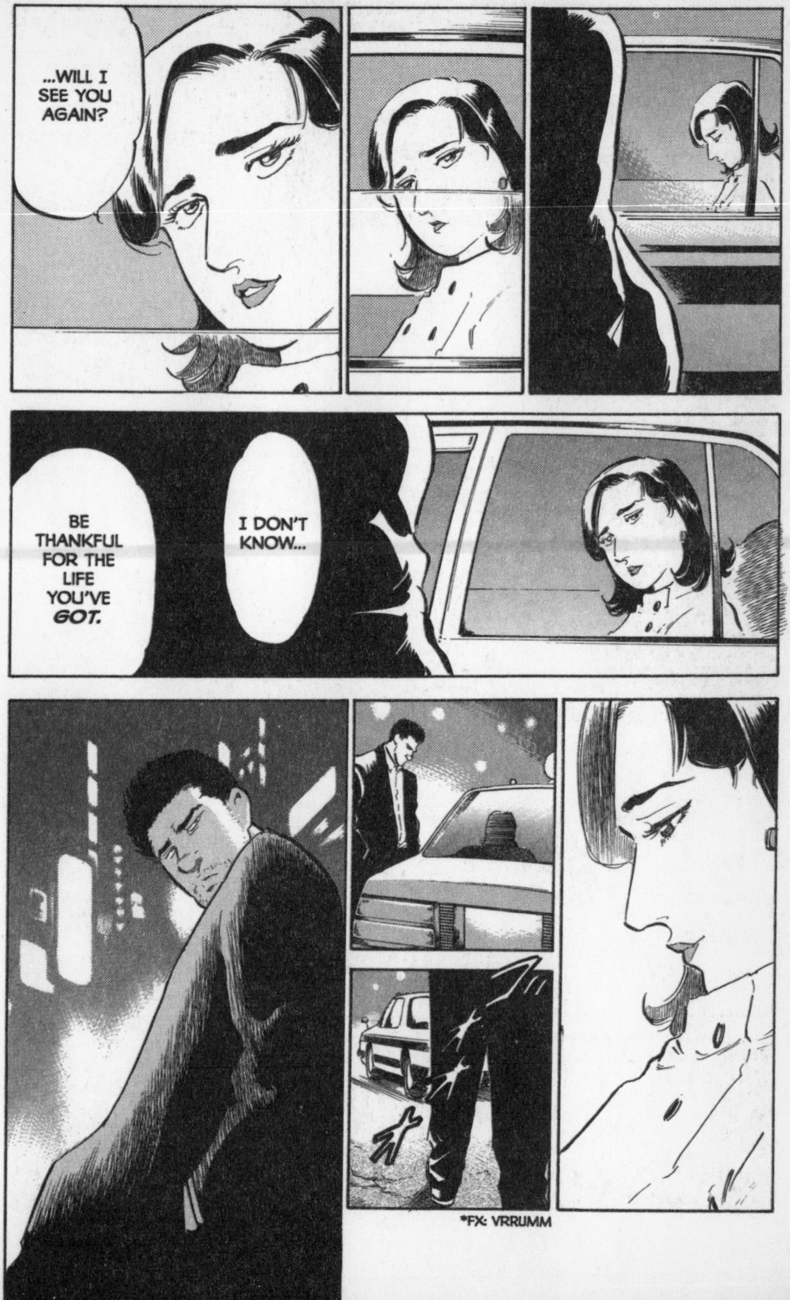
...WILL I SEE YOU AGAIN?
I DON'T KNOW...
BE THANKFUL FOR THE LIFE YOU'VE *GOT.*

*FX: VRRUMM

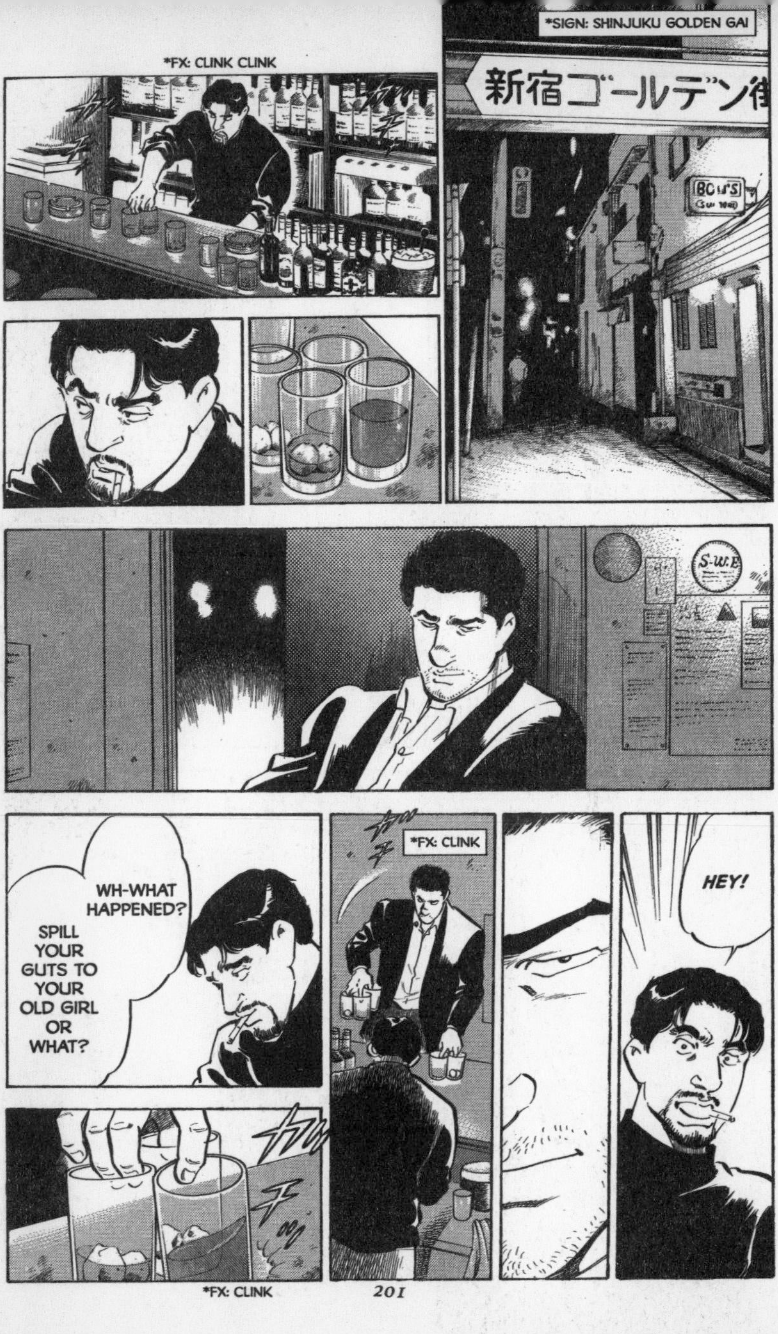
*SIGN: SHINJUKU GOLDEN GAI
新宿ゴールデン街
*FX: CLINK CLINK
HEY!
*FX: CLINK
WH-WHAT HAPPENED?
SPILL YOUR GUTS TO YOUR OLD GIRL OR WHAT?
*FX: CLINK

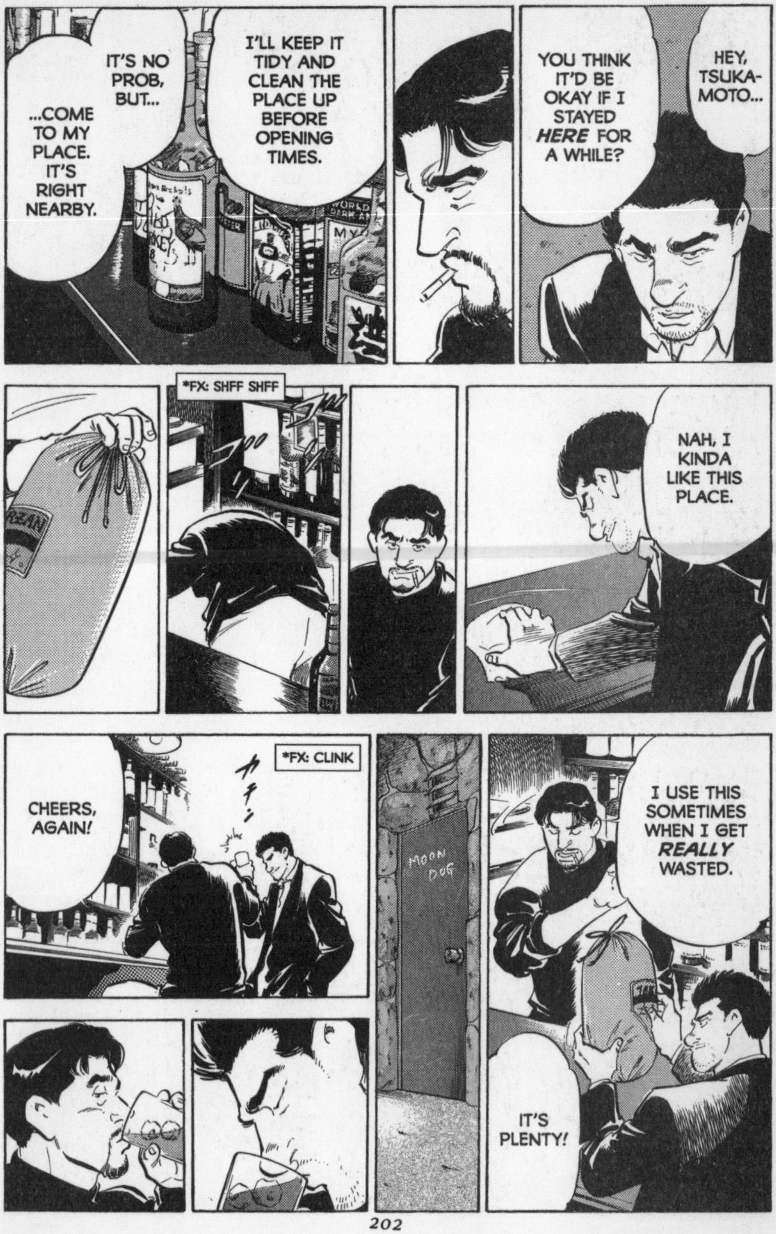
HEY, TSUKA-MOTO...
YOU THINK IT'D BE OKAY IF I STAYED *HERE* FOR A WHILE?
I'LL KEEP IT TIDY AND CLEAN THE PLACE UP BEFORE OPENING TIMES.
IT'S NO PROB, BUT...
...COME TO MY PLACE. IT'S RIGHT NEARBY.
NAH, I KINDA LIKE THIS PLACE.
*FX: SHFF SHFF
I USE THIS SOMETIMES WHEN I GET *REALLY* WASTED.
IT'S PLENTY!
MOON DOG
*FX: CLINK
CHEERS, AGAIN!

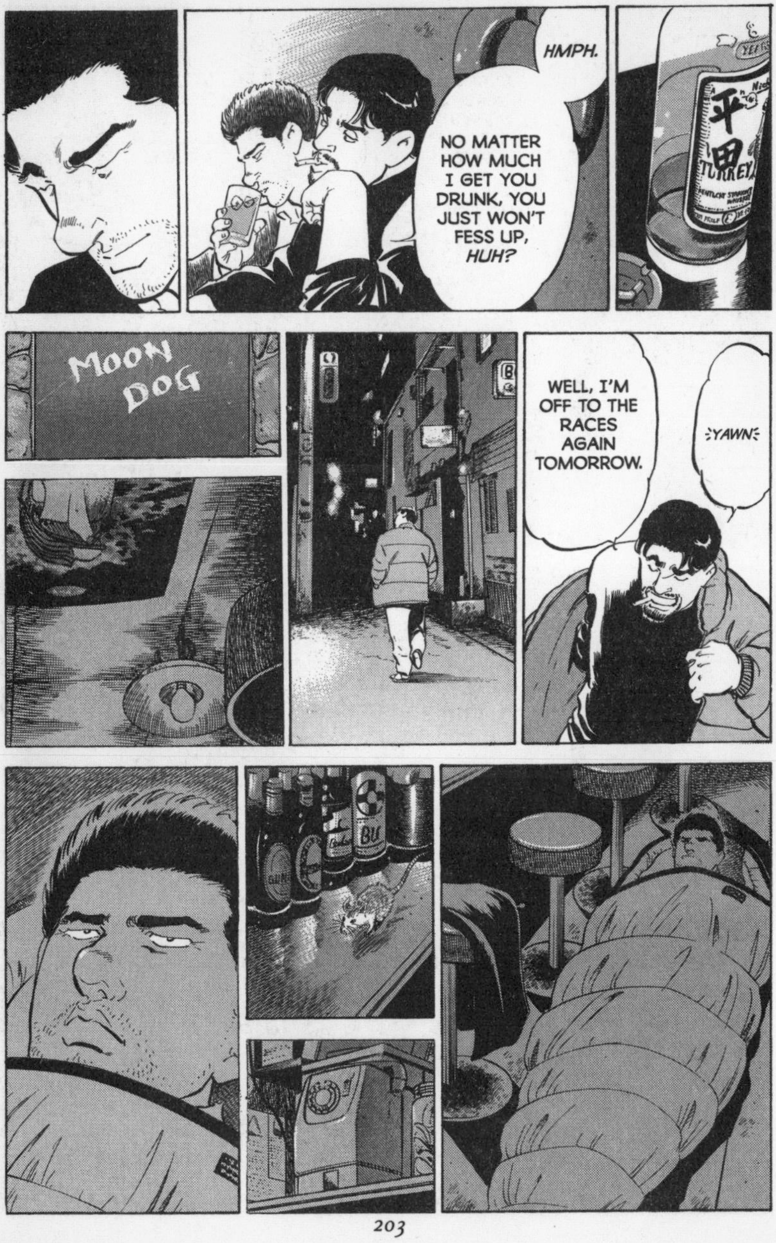
HMPH.
NO MATTER HOW MUCH I GET YOU DRUNK, YOU JUST WON'T FESS UP, *HUH?*
YAWN
WELL, I'M OFF TO THE RACES AGAIN TOMORROW.
MOON DOG

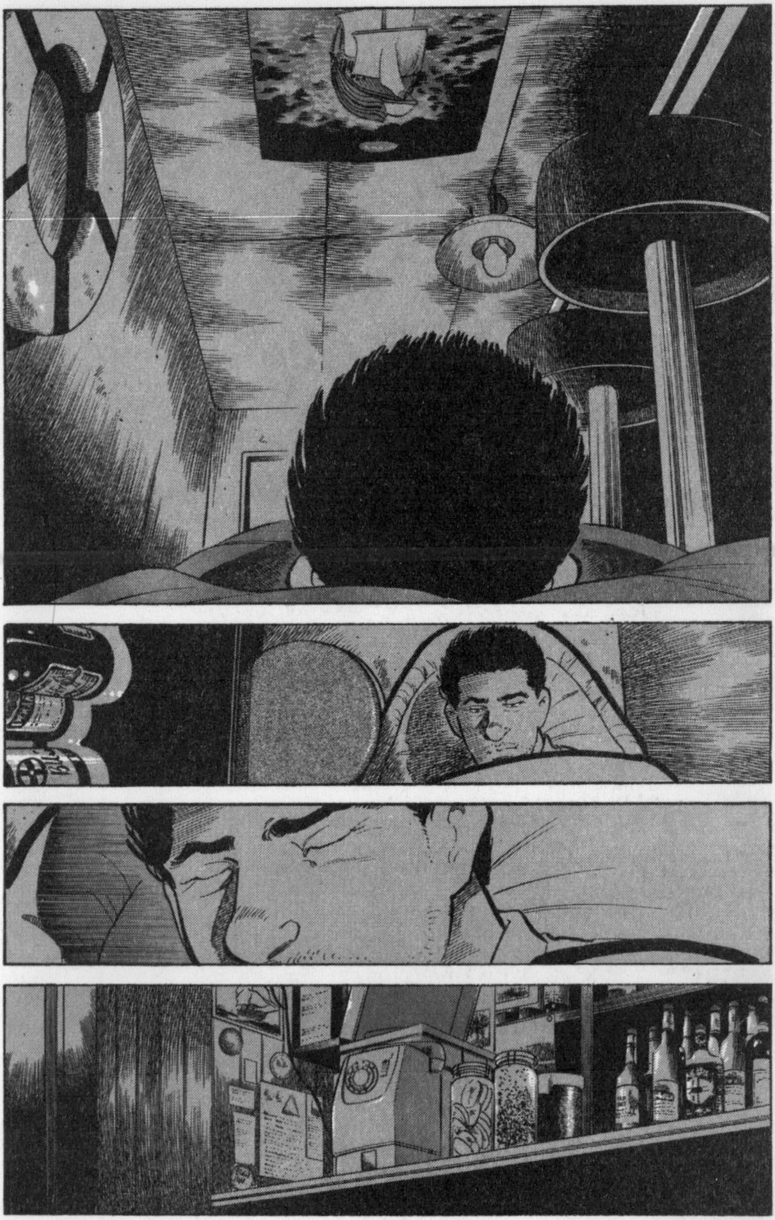

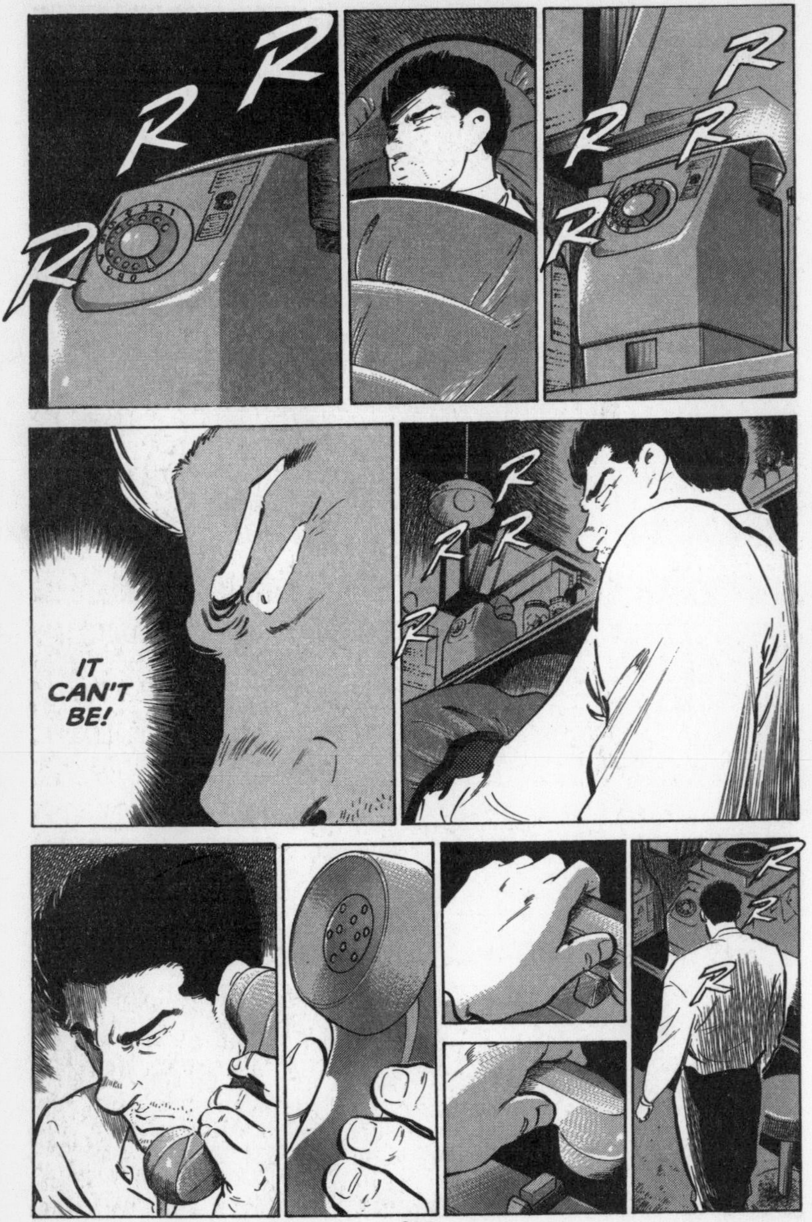
RRRRR
RRRR
RRRR
IT CAN'T BE!
RRR

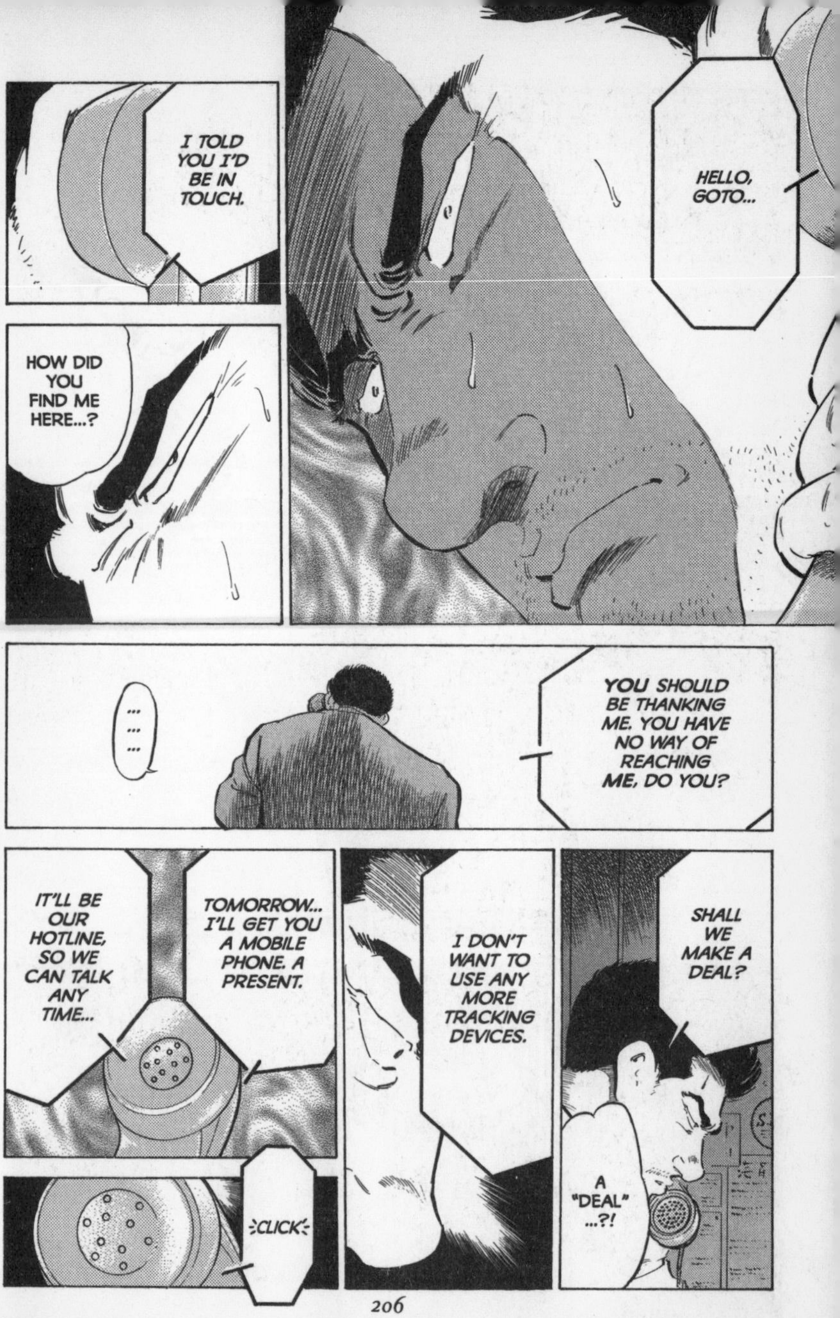
HELLO, GOTO...
I TOLD YOU I'D BE IN TOUCH.
HOW DID YOU FIND ME HERE...?
YOU SHOULD BE THANKING ME. YOU HAVE NO WAY OF REACHING ME, DO YOU?
... ...
SHALL WE MAKE A DEAL?
A "DEAL" ...?!
I DON'T WANT TO USE ANY MORE TRACKING DEVICES.
TOMORROW... I'LL GET YOU A MOBILE PHONE. A PRESENT.
IT'LL BE OUR HOTLINE, SO WE CAN TALK ANY TIME...
CLICK

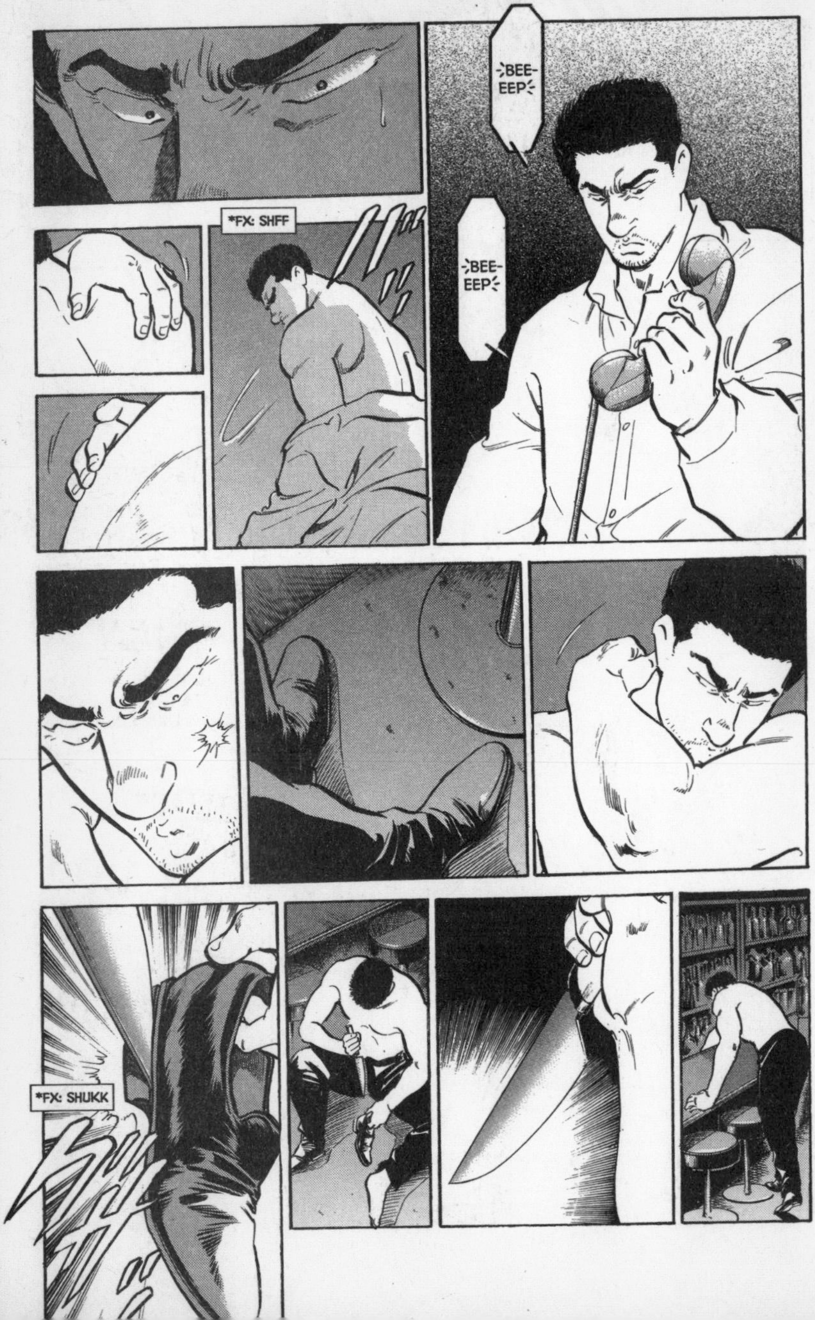
BEE-EEP
BEE-EEP
*FX: SHFF
*FX: SHUKK

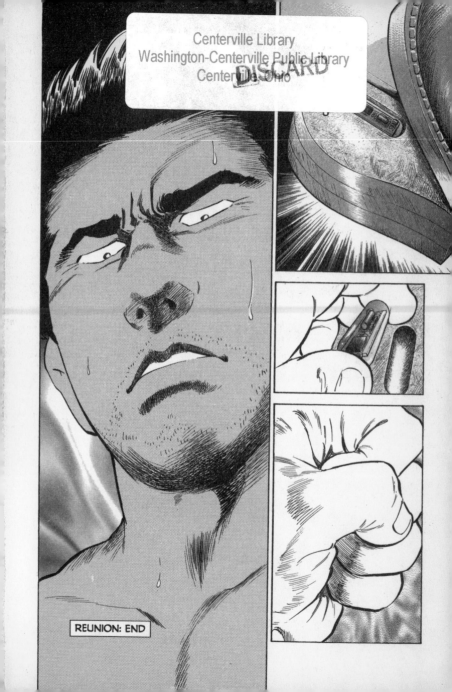

REUNION: END